AF685469

SOCIAL LEGISLATION IN THE CONTEMPORARY MIDDLE EAST

Sponsored by

The Subcommittee on Law and Social Structure
of the Joint Committee on the Near and Middle East
of the American Council of Learned Societies
and the Social Science Research Council

RESEARCH SERIES/NUMBER 64

Social Legislation in the Contemporary Middle East

LAURENCE O. MICHALAK &
JESWALD W. SALACUSE, Editors

iiS

INSTITUTE
OF INTERNATIONAL
STUDIES
University of California, Berkeley

NOTE ON TRANSLITERATION

We have not considered it necessary to impose a uniform system of transcribing words from Middle Eastern languages into the Latin alphabet. The transliterations and diacritical markings used in the various chapters of this volume have been determined by the individual authors.—*Eds.*

Library of Congress Cataloging-in-Publication Data

Social legislation in the contemporary Middle East.

(Research series, ISSN 0068-6093 ; no. 64)
Includes index.
1. Social legislation—Near East. I. Michalak, Laurence O. II. Salacuse, Jeswald W. III. Series: Research series (University of California, Berkeley. Institute of Internationl Studies) ; no. 64
LAW 344.56 86-18613
ISBN 0-87725-164-9 345.604

To

MALCOLM KERR

CONTENTS

Acknowledgments ix

Notes on Contributors xi

PART I: INTRODUCTION

1. Social Legislation in the Contemporary Middle East: Tools for Development, Tools for Domination
   Laurence O. Michalak and Jeswald W. Salacuse 3

PART II: IDEOLOGY, THE STATE AND LAW

2. Social Justice in the Ideology and Legislation of the Islamic Revolution of Iran
   Hamid Algar 17

3. Syria under the Ba'th: Social Ideology, Policy, and Practice
   Raymond A. Hinnebusch 61

PART III: DOMESTIC ECONOMIC AND SOCIAL IMPLICATIONS OF LEGAL POLICY

4. The State Apparatus and Social Legislation in the Maghreb
   Jean-Claude Vatin 113

5. Pendulum Swings in Land Laws and Rural Development Policies in Tunisia: History and Consequences
   Mira Zussman 161

6. Ruling Elites and the Young: A Comparison of Iraq and Lebanon
   Suad Joseph 191

PART IV: INTERNATIONAL ECONOMIC FACTORS AND LAW

A. Capital

7. Foreign Investment and Legislative Exemptions in Egypt: Needed Stimulus or New Capitulations?
Jeswald W. Salacuse 241

8. Technology Transfer and Social Structure in the Arab World
Ali E. Hillal Dessouki 263

B. Labor

9. International Labor Migration in the Middle East and North Africa: Current and Prospective Dimensions, 1975-85
James Socknat, Stace Birks, and Ismail Serageldin 277

10. Turkish Migration to Europe and the Middle East: Its Impact on Social Structure and Social Legislation
Nermin Abadan-Unat 325

Index 371

ACKNOWLEDGMENTS

The support of a number of organizations and individuals made this volume possible. The Social Science Research Council (SSRC) and the American Council of Learned Societies (ACLS) sponsored the Project on Law and Social Structure and the conference in Rabat of which this volume is the outgrowth. USAID provided the funding so that the project could be undertaken on an international scale.

Colleagues on the Subcommittee on Law and Social Structure of the Joint Committee on the Near and Middle East—Hossam Issa, Robert Lapham, Ann Elizabeth Mayer, Laura Nader, and Amal Rassam—collaborated with the subcommittee chair and coeditor of this volume in devising the conceptual focus of the conference. Robert Gates organized the logistics of the conference in Rabat, Morocco; other SSRC staff members—notably Rowland Mitchell and Nikiforos Dimandouros—also facilitated the completion of the project.

The meeting in Rabat was the second of a series of related conferences on law and social organization in the Middle East sponsored by the SSRC and the ACLS. The proceedings of the first conference—held in Bellagio, Italy, in 1980—have recently been published as *Property, Social Structure and Law in the Modern Middle East,* ed. Ann Elizabeth Mayer (Albany: State University of New York Press, 1985). Dr. Mayer and Dr. Laura Nader, who wrote the introduction to the Bellagio volume, provided helpful advice for this second volume too. In many ways the two volumes complement each other, and we recommend the Bellagio volume to those interested in law, the Middle East, or both.

A conference is more than the sum of its articles, and a number of participants in the Rabat conference who are not represented here contributed much through their perceptive discussion to shape this volume. In addition to those already mentioned, they include John J. Bentley, Mohamed Guessous, L. Michael Hager, Abdellah Hammoudi, Elbaki Hermassi, Hatem el-Karanshawy, Fuad Khuri, Samir Radwan, and John Waterbury. Malcolm Kerr, to whom this volume is dedicated, was the final speaker at Rabat, identifying and summarizing the main themes of the conference. Ever the practical scholar, his suggestions have been of considerable benefit to us in preparing this volume. His tragic death is a loss to both the West and the Middle East, depriving us of a respected scholar and a dedicated humanitarian.

In editing this volume, we could not claim expertise across the wide topical and geographical expanse represented in the several essays. We therefore sought advice from a number of specialists: Daniel Bates, Moustapha Ben Chenane, Ellis Goldberg, Robert Fernea, Frederick Huxley, Ira Lapidus, Ibrahim Muhawi, Ayad al-Qazzaz, Kevin Reinhart, Allan Samson, Dan Slobin, Shibley Telhami, and Ilter Turan.

The Institute of International Studies of the University of California, Berkeley supported the preparation of this volume with a quality and degree of assistance that has become all too rare in academic publishing today. Carl Rosberg and Paul Gilchrist of the Institute gave useful advice, Bojana Ristich made numerous editorial improvements, and Keith Weissman prepared the detailed index.

Finally, the contributors were patient and conscientious in putting their papers through two rounds of thoroughgoing revisions.

Our thanks to all.

LAURENCE O. MICHALAK
JESWALD W. SALACUSE

May 1986

NOTES ON CONTRIBUTORS

LAURENCE O. MICHALAK is Coordinator and Vice-Chair of the Center for Middle Eastern Studies at the University of California, Berkeley. He was rapporteur for the Rabat conference.

JESWALD W. SALACUSE is Dean and Professor of International Law at the Fletcher School of Law and Diplomacy, Tufts University, Medford, Massachusetts. He was chair of the Subcommittee on Law and Social Structure of the Joint Committee on the Near and Middle East of the ACLS and the SSRC.

NERMIN ABADAN-UNAT is Professor of Political Science at Ankara University, Turkey.

HAMID ALGAR is Professor of Near Eastern Studies at the University of California, Berkeley.

ALI E. HILLAL DESSOUKI is Professor of Political Science at Cairo University, Egypt.

RAYMOND A. HINNEBUSCH is Associate Professor of Political Science at the College of St. Catherine, St. Paul, Minnesota.

SUAD JOSEPH is Associate Professor of Anthropology at the University of California, Davis.

JAMES SOCKNAT is Senior Manpower Specialist in the Education and Manpower Development Division of the Europe, Middle East, and North Africa Region of the World Bank, Washington, D.C.

JEAN-CLAUDE VATIN is Directeur de Recherche at the Centre National de la Recherche Scientifique (CNRS), Paris, currently director of the Centre d'Etudes et de Documentation Economique, Juridique et Sociale (CEDEJ), Cairo, Egypt.

MIRA ZUSSMAN is Lecturer in Anthropology at San Jose State University, San Jose, California, and Postdoctoral Research Associate of the Center for Middle Eastern Studies at the University of California, Berkeley.

Part I

INTRODUCTION

Chapter 1

SOCIAL LEGISLATION IN THE CONTEMPORARY MIDDLE EAST: TOOLS FOR DEVELOPMENT, TOOLS FOR DOMINATION

Laurence O. Michalak and Jeswald W. Salacuse

The Code of Hammurabi and fragments of even more ancient legislation attest that for at least four millennia the peoples of the Middle East have had a special preoccupation with law. The relations within and among the region's diverse groups have found expression in equally diverse laws which were committed to writing earlier and more diligently than in other parts of the world. Rulers and regimes have embraced law as the ultimate cachet of legitimacy; revolutionaries and revisionists have invoked it in the name of reform; the intelligentsia has been shaped by or trained in the law; and the law in turn has been the model for most other disciplines in the Middle East. With colonialism and then independence, tensions between Western and indigenous cultures have been mirrored in competition among elements in the legal systems of the area.

Yet despite its importance to the region, law's relationship to Middle Eastern society is not well understood. We know little about how law affects the processes of social and economic change in the area, nor do we understand precisely the relationship between law and social structure. Recognizing these lacunae, the Social Science Research Council and the American Council of Learned Societies, through their Joint Committee on the Near and Middle East, established a Subcommittee on Law and Social Structure with a mandate to formulate a plan of action that would foster new insights into how law relates to the processes of social differentiation, change, modernization, and development in the Middle East. This volume has emerged from the work of the Subcommittee on Law and Social Structure.

Believing that law and the social sciences had been studied primarily by two distinct groups of experts—lawyers and legal historians on the one hand and social scientists on the other—the subcommittee sought to develop an approach which would integrate the expertise of these two disciplinary groups. To encourage interdisciplinary inquiry, the subcommittee organized a series of conferences and workshops on various topics, including property, personal status, social legislation, taxation, and dispute settlement. Seven of the contributions in this volume were presented at a conference on "Social Legislation and Social Structure in the Contemporary Near and Middle East" held in Rabat, Morocco, 26-29 September 1981. The essays by Ali Dessouki and Mira Zussman, presented at other meetings sponsored by the subcommittee, were added to the volume to render it more geographically and thematically comprehensive.

The purpose of this introduction is to provide a context for the nine essays in this volume and to delineate and interrelate their basic themes. Together, the essays offer a geographically broad perspective on the Middle East, from Morocco to Iran, and they present case material from about half the states of the area, including two non-Arab countries, Iran and Turkey. Two of the essays focus on the Maghreb, an area that scholars sometimes arbitrarily exclude in definitions of the Middle East, even though it constitutes the analytically inseparable western third of the Arab world. In addition to broad geographic coverage, the authors demonstrate a diversity of approaches. Our contributors come from the United States, Europe, and the Middle East, as well as from a variety of disciplines, including sociology, political science, religious studies, anthropology, economics, and law.

APPROACHES TO SOCIAL LEGISLATION AND LAW

As understood in the contemporary Western world, the concept of legislation rests on a number of assumptions. For many, legislation implies a legislature which produces, modifies, and reproduces a body of written law applicable to a nation-state, subject to review and interpretation through a system of courts, and enforced by an executive. Clearly such assumptions are far from universal in their validity. For example, under such a definition one could question whether social legislation exists in much of the Middle East at all. In varying degrees in different Middle Eastern countries the control of the country by the central government is still uneven, the polity is not yet fully a nation-state, and law is often executive fiat, little encumbered by legislatures and judiciaries. Furthermore, legislation in the Middle East has often been inspired—and sometimes imposed—from outside the region. Finally, individual countries sometimes possess several legal systems—customary, religious, and national—among which parties to a dispute can maneuver.

In addition to the assumptions attached to the concept of legislation, the term *social legislation* covers a vast and amorphous field without recognized boundaries. For some, it is synonymous with labor law; for others it includes laws governing health care, family assistance, housing, and social insurance. One scholar has suggested that social legislation defines "how the individual should be treated in society"; another proposes that it include all laws designed to achieve social justice. While a single, uniform definition for the concept of social legislation does not emerge in this volume, it is nevertheless evident that legal relationships affecting work and the relationships of people to production are generally central to our contributions. The quest for or failure of justice through social legislation is also an important theme. The essays show how various regimes have sought (at least ostensibly) to achieve social justice through their legal systems, with varying degrees of success. They also show that regimes can be discredited and new regimes and systems of legislation can be brought into being when there is a popular perception that social justice has not been served. Generally the contributors have approached the relationship of legislation to social structure by examining production and productivity, the distribution of wealth, and relationships of power within Middle Eastern societies.

AREAS OF DEBATE

The essays presented here reveal fundamental debates about the role of social legislation in the Middle East. The first and most important divergence of views concerns the nature and function of legislation itself. One group tends to view law as a positive force, while another views it as a force that defends narrower, more selfish interests. This dichotomy raises a number of related questions. Is social legislation in Middle Eastern societies a tool for public good and national development? Or is it a means by which elites can consolidate social control and undermine their competitors—in short, a tool for domination? If one can point to examples of both, which countries tend toward which alternatives? And if we accept that one country can exhibit elements of both, what conditions determine the mix?

The second disagreement concerns the effectiveness of law. Some see law as a potentially powerful instrument capable of bringing about the transformation of society, while others consider it weak and ineffective. Throughout the volume contributors weigh whether economic development and social justice can be attained through laws judiciously framed and enforced, or whether law, even at its best, is only an inadequate tool against the forces of international dependency which have prevailed, despite the nominal independence of the countries of the Middle East.

Characterizations along these two main axes of divergence, even corrected to continua rather than strictly opposed categories, necessarily oversimplify a complex subject. One might argue that executive power and social benefit are not incompatible—that the consolidation of power through legislative and other means can be a precondition to advancement of the common good. One might also specify that law is more effective for the modification of the internal rather than the international circumstances of a country. Differing assessments of the effectiveness of law may reflect contrasting social models within which law plays different roles. For some social scientists, law is a cause, a part of the infrastructure; for others, it is an outcome, a part of the superstructure.

A familiar example of the debate on the extent to which law can affect society is whether Ataturk's reforms of the 1920s produced fundamental changes in Turkey. The difficulty here is ascribing causes and effects. One may grant that women's status changed dramatically in Turkey, as indicated by the impressive percentage of women entering high administrative posts and the professional work force. But was this phenomenon due to changes in the law or instead to other causes, such as Turkey's loss of manpower in World War I or the process of industrialization? Alternatively it might be argued that law under Ataturk made a difference, but that Turkish society has not necessarily been changed in the ways that Ataturk envisaged. Ultimately the question of exactly how much of which social changes can be attributed to the effect of which law is unanswerable and not particularly useful. Social legislation does not operate as an isolated variable—a discrete cause of discrete effects—but rather as an instrument among an array of instruments for policy, a tool among tools.

AREAS OF AGREEMENT

Despite the diversity of approaches just described, a number of important areas of agreement emerge among our contributors. First is the central metaphor of our volume: law as a tool—benevolent or sinister, for the many or for the few, but a tool nevertheless. All of the authors take an activist approach to law, viewing it as a potential instrument for the attainment of particular ends. This contrasts with passivist approaches which emphasize law as custom and constraint, arising out of traditional social structure and practice. Indeed in the contemporary Middle East, legislation often conflicts with traditional practice.

Our authors' consensus on law as a tool is a departure from the mainstream of legal anthropology, which generally has regarded law as the codification of custom—in itself neither a cause nor an effect. In contrast, the authors in this volume usually view law as *both* effect and cause, arising out of specific social contexts and having specific consequences. In suggesting an instrumental approach to law, our purpose is not to reify law or to imply that it operates in a purely mechanical and unidirectional fashion. Legislation is a social process which involves feedback during both the framing and the application of law. Law produced by a society changes the society, and the changed society in turn changes law, so that the full effects of a particular law are not always foreseeable.

A second point of agreement among the scholars represented here is a commitment to an empirical rather than a theoretical approach to studying law. They do not begin with European and/or Middle Eastern theories of law and then attempt to apply them to Middle Eastern reality. The authors arrive at theory, but they start from contemporary practice. Case materials, instead of legal philosophy or the technicalities of legislation and regulation, have directed their inquiries. Indeed the doctrinal and statutory analyses so common to legal treatises are almost totally absent in this volume.

Indicative of this empiricism is a third common point in these essays—an attention to outcomes. It is a commonplace that "law in the books" often differs from "law in action." However, there has been little research on this gap between intent and outcome—probably because it is easier to analyze the texts of laws framed in the capital than to examine whether and how they are implemented in the countryside. If a law is to have any real effect, the state must put resources behind it—and not merely coercive resources, but material and symbolic ones as well. The authors here have done thorough fieldwork and can therefore juxtapose laws with outcomes.

It is not surprising that a concern with ideology is a fourth characteristic of the essays in this volume. An instrumental approach to law implies ends and therefore ideologies. It suggests that the holders of power have—or claim to have—a vision of the good society and that social legislation is a means to achieve that vision. However, "ideology" means different things to different authors—differences which correspond to their interpretations of law as a positive or negative force. Those who emphasize the positive aspects of law are concerned with the deep-seated beliefs and convictions that affect public policy. For those who accept that lawmakers work from a view of the good society, law is a kind of normative discourse of the society about itself—about what the society is and what it seeks to become. Conversely, those who emphasize the negative aspects of law tend to view ideology as a mask for the public rationalization of legislation for private gain.

Just as an instrumental approach to law implies ideology, so also ideology implies a process of development, of moving a society from where it is to where it should be. Especially as viewed from a Third World perspective, one of the most important aspects of social legislation is its relation to economic development, and this is a fifth concern voiced by our contributors. In particular, several of the essays examine the role of legislation in promoting the accumulation of development capital. Essentially two strategies for development can be (and usually are) combined. One is internal surplus extraction for state-directed capital accumulation and investment. It usually requires unpopular austerity programs, relatively low salaries, and the deferral of consumption. The Soviet Union under Stalin is an extreme example of this approach. The second is external—drawing capital from abroad through loans (which must be repaid), aid (which usually has strings attached), or foreign investors (who require both control of and returns on their investments). This strategy is exemplified by the "open door" legislation enacted under Anwar Sadat in Egypt. The result is a difficult double bind for development planning and legislation. The oil-producing countries seem at first glance to have escaped this dilemma. They already have capital; their problem is not its production but its reproduction—the translation of a finite natural resource with a fluctuating price into a stable development base. The following essays explore social legislation, including its development aspect, in both resource-rich and resource-poor settings.

Sixth, the role of individual leaders in the Middle East in shaping the law is of concern to several contributors. The political systems of this world area exhibit broad structural diversity—from monarchy to marxism—but some would argue that a tendency prevails in the Middle East toward government by a single leader, often accompanied by cults of the individual and larger-than-life pictures of the head of state in public places. In such settings legislation can to a large extent be characterized as the personal policy of the leader. Such a situation places a great burden on the leader; rather than drawing his legitimacy from the system, he must instead consistently legitimize himself through achievement, or at least through the rhetoric of achievement. The logic of legitimation in such a situation is that since development is the gift of the leader rather than the outcome of positive law, the proper response to the absence of progress is to change the leader rather than the law.

However, the view of the Middle East as rich in short-lived, charismatic leaders and poor in political institutions is less tenable today than two or three decades ago. The current heads of Middle Eastern states have been enjoying considerable longevity in office. Moreover, there has been an important degree of institution-building. One can point, for example, to long-standing political parties such as the Ba'th, the Destour Socialist Party, and others. With gradual changes in Middle Eastern leadership, charisma seems to be in ever shorter supply—from Ataturk to Evren, from Nasser to Mubarak, from Ben Gurion to Peres, from Mohamed V to Hassan II. Enduring older leaders such as Bourguiba often have lost their luster. The political situation in the Middle East today is better characterized in terms of personalistic rule than of Weberian charismatic leadership. The increased stability of regimes is perhaps due less to charisma than to increasingly powerful instruments of modern state control, inherited at independence from colonial powers and increasingly mastered by Middle Eastern heads of state. As state control increases and stronger institutions emerge, for better or worse, legislation has greater impact and therefore assumes greater importance.

INDIVIDUAL ESSAYS

The first two essays in this volume address the implications for social legislation of two distinctly different ideologies in two very different political contexts. *Hamid Algar* outlines Shi'i Islamic thought about social justice in Iran with emphasis on the contemporary period since the Iranian revolution. His article is informed by travel to Iran in 1983, when he was able to add case material on the process of Islamic legislation. Algar demonstrates an evolution in Shi'i thought from the theme of justice deferred and the separation of religion from government to the demand for justice in the here-and-now and the direct participation of the ulama in government. The essay chronicles the development and legislative implementation of an ideology, particularly with regard to land reform and labor laws, in the still unfolding Iranian revolution.

Raymond Hinnebusch examines the evolving relationship between ideology and practice in Syria under the Ba'th Party. Whereas Iran offers the case of an emergent regime, Syria offers an example of a long established ideology which has acceded to power after passing through many stages of practice and has become, in Hinnebusch's terms, "ritualized," "consecrated," and "routinized." The Ba'th has transposed ideological promise into legislative program, but there remains the problem of carrying out that program effectively. Hinnebusch shows the degrees to which legislative outcomes have or have not met expectations. Like Algar, he provides case materials on the development of agrarian legislation and labor law. In both areas he shows us the gaps between theory and practice and analyzes the complex factors which have thwarted implementation of the laws and the culmination of the Ba'th revolution.

Jean-Claude Vatin's is the first of three essays that emphasize the domestic economic and social implications of legal policy. Vatin does not share the optimism of Algar and Hinnebusch that social legislation can foster the good society. Of the authors presented here, he most emphasizes the dark side of legislation. With the Maghrebi states as examples, he shows that through the creation of monopolies in key economic and social domains, law can be a powerful vehicle for state control. Drawing on case material from labor legislation in Libya and Algeria, Vatin questions whether the state can indeed do all that it has taken upon itself. He argues that the citizens of the Maghrebi countries are coming to expect less of the state and that a "third economy"—neither socialist nor large-scale capitalist—is developing as people sidestep the inefficient official national market to develop private small businesses and limited enterprises. To Vatin law seems a weak tool for the common good but a powerful tool for private gain of the state elites.

Mira Zussman's study on land tenure laws in Tunisia complements Algar's and Hinnebusch's material on land reform and illustrates Vatin's judgment that the state is overextended—promising and controlling much, but delivering little. To the view from the capital city, Zussman counterposes the viewpoint of the rural farmer, who adopts changing strategies in response to the changing land tenure laws and agricultural development policies emanating from Tunis. The inconsistency of Tunisian land laws results in uncertainty and insecurity regarding title to the land, in turn rendering long-term agricultural investment an undesirable strategy for farmers. Zussman shows the effects of instability in law on a rural society whose advancement lawmakers ostensibly seek. She concludes that the only real winners in the land reform programs in Tunisia over thirty years of independence have been the large-scale landowners who were able to purchase colonial farms.

Suad Joseph examines education and employment legislation for their effects on youth. She contrasts the case of Iraq, where there is a high degree of central planning and promotion of youth activities, with that of Lebanon, where the state plays a relatively ephemeral role. Joseph emphasizes other loyalties that compete with or cut across citizenship in the Middle East, and she approaches the modern state in that region as part of the colonial legacy. Her essay suggests that law in etatist Iraq has been a powerful instrument for development, while in laissez-faire Lebanon it has been a weak instrument for domination.

Both law and social structure in the Middle East are influenced by external as well as internal factors. The last group of essays in the volume focuses on some of the most powerful of these external forces—foreign capital, foreign technology, and international labor migration. *Jeswald Salacuse* discusses the attempt in Egypt under former President Anwar Sadat to attract capital by granting foreign investors broad exemptions from Egyptian laws. Such an approach to foreign investment promotion, common to much of the Third World, causes many problems and has a significant effect not only on the investor, but on national and social institutions as well. For example, it promotes the creation of privileged social groups who enjoy many of the benefits granted to foreign investors with whom they are associated. Salacuse compares strategies such as Egypt's open door policy to the Capitulations—the concessions granted under the Ottoman Empire to European countries and European-protected minorities in the early period of European imperialism in the Middle East. In analyzing Egypt's open door policy, Salacuse demonstrates the impact of investment laws on the social structure of a host country.

Ali Hillal Dessouki analyzes technology transfer to the Arab world. He considers technology a form of property monopolized by the industrialized West, and he shows that choices among alternative technologies have important social effects. For example, he points out that some technologies are more labor-intensive and others more capital-intensive and that different technologies favor the development of products suited to the needs of different income groups in the society. Expressing a strong conviction for the relevance of law to social change, Dessouki argues for appropriate laws and policies to stimulate the adoption of appropriate technologies. As Joseph argues that the Lebanese state has abdicated its responsibility regarding the education and employment of youth, so Dessouki implies that the Arab countries may be neglecting their responsibilities to promote the adoption of appropriate technologies. Here it is not so much a question of the powerlessness of the Arab countries to shape their destinies as it is their failure to act in an area that clearly has powerful effects on social structure—a failure due not so much to dependency as to lack of will.

James Socknat, Stace Birks, and *Ismail Serageldin* report current labor migration patterns and project likely developments into the 1980s. They conducted a comprehensive study on labor migration in the Middle East, and this essay summarizes their findings. The topic of labor migration cuts across disciplinary as well as geographical boundaries, linking countries not only within the Middle East, but also between the Middle East and the West, and it is directly relevant to the problem of whether appropriate legislation can promote development. Statistics on labor migration are notoriously unreliable since much labor migration is undocumented and in fact illegal, rendering the topic a sensitive one. The authors have enhanced the reliability of their study, conducted under the auspices of the Technical Assistance and Special Studies Division of the World Bank, by cross-checking statistics and estimates from multiple sources.

Nermin Abadan-Unat's study of Turkish migration complements the general overview by Socknat, Birks, and Serageldin. Turkey is a particularly instructive case because Turkish migration is relatively better controlled by the government, so that its statistics are more reliable, and legislation through bilateral agreements plays a greater role than for most other Middle Eastern countries. Also,

Turkish workers migrate both to Europe (especially to West Germany) and other countries of the Middle East (especially Libya), thus providing useful comparisons and contrasts. Abadan-Unat distinguishes five major phases in the history of Turkish labor migration, from the mid-1950s into the 1980s. Her essay offers material on such topics as the impact of returning migrants on villages, social mobility, changes in family roles, and the use of remittances, and she describes the efforts of both the host and home countries to manipulate social legislation so as to increase the benefits and reduce the detrimental effects of international labor migration on their societies. On the whole, she seems pessimistic about the power of law. Even in Turkey, where the will to harness migration to development is strong and where innovative programs to attract migrant investment capital have been launched, legislation and bilateral agreements appear to have had relatively little success.

CONCLUSION

This collection makes no pretense to a unified theory of law and society, nor has our introduction attempted the magician's trick of conjuring one. Rather, one strength of the volume lies in the diversity of the authors' viewpoints, presented through case material from different Middle East settings. Underlying these contrasting analyses we have identified two fundamental issues—first, the nature of law (Is it a tool for development or for domination?) and, second, the effectiveness of law (What is its potential, and what are its limitations as an instrument for social transformation?). The divergences of view on these two questions show up all the more clearly in that the authors have given special emphasis to social legislation with regard to labor and land. A second strength of the essays is that from this diversity of approaches, there nevertheless emerges a remarkable degree of conceptual and methodological consensus. We have identified the elements of this consensus as an instrumental approach to law, an emphasis on empiricism, an attention to outcomes, and concerns with ideology, development, and the roles of leaders and institutions in the legislative process. These are the common points in a set of essays which we believe offers a fresh approach to understanding social legislation—especially in the Middle East but elsewhere as well.

Part II

IDEOLOGY, THE STATE, AND LAW

Chapter 2

SOCIAL JUSTICE IN THE IDEOLOGY AND LEGISLATION OF THE ISLAMIC REVOLUTION OF IRAN

Hamid Algar

> The history of the search for justice is not a series of disconnected events but a continuous process; it is like a river flowing down the bed of time. It is Abraham and Moses, Jesus and Muhammad; it is Hasan and Husayn. It is all those who shall continue this struggle down to its universal triumph at the end of time.
>
> 'Ali Shari'ati (*Intizar*: 47)*

The antecedents of the Islamic Revolution of Iran include not only decades of political struggle, but also ideological developments of great historic as well as intrinsic interest. Perennial themes of Shi'i Islamic belief and religiosity crystallized over many years into an ideological consensus that has been integral to the revolution. Numerous voices contributed to the formation of this consensus, and important points of difference still persist within it. What cannot be overlooked, however, is that a new mode of religious discourse has emerged in Iran which is virtually unique in the contemporary Islamic world. The revolution can be described in part as a revolution within Islam, and it is primarily this, rather than the Shi'i loyalties of the Iranian people, that makes of contemporary Iranian Islam such a distinct and vibrant phenomenon.†

*All translations are mine.

†It is true of course that this "revolution within Islam" has taken place in part through the activation or transformation of distinctly Shi'i themes, but this

Among the most important hallmarks of the new religious discourse is an emphasis on the political and socioeconomic dimensions of Islam, and the conviction that it is the mission of the revolution to act as a harbinger of universal liberation and justice. The understanding of "justice" has been transformed; from being an abstract value associated with the frustrated claims of the Twelve Imams to political authority, it has become the central aim of a revolutionary ideology.* This ideology stands, however, under the patronage of the Imams, permitting revolution to enjoy both the sanctity and the sanction of tradition.

Contemporary Iran is also of compelling interest in that it furnishes the first—and at present only—instance of the exercise of political power by an Islamic movement. The experiences of the first six years of the Islamic Republic are full of significance, therefore, not only for the general problem of transposing ideological promise into legislative program, but also for the particular one of implementing Islamic law in a society and economy long removed from the scope of its operation. After considering the emergence of social justice as a prominent theme in the ideology of the revolution, we will examine laws on land and labor drafted in the Islamic Republic that illustrate both of these problems.

SHI'ISM AND THE CONCEPT OF JUSTICE

The theme of justice is repeatedly invoked, of course, in the Qur'an; the insistence of the Divine Legislator on justice among men is the ultimate source of all viably Islamic contemporary concern for the establishment of justice. Justice is enjoined, explicitly or otherwise, in more than fifteen verses, some of which require interpretation in a socioeconomic rather than a judicial sense. Furthermore, the Qur'an condemns, for social as well as spiritual reasons, the accumulation of wealth, and prescribes measures that discourage the concentration of wealth in the hands of individuals and groups and ensures what has been called "social equilibrium" by a recent theorist (as-Sadr

is a different matter from equating Shi'ism as such with a superior degree of religious vitality.

*It is a distinctive article of Shi'i belief that the Prophet appointed as his successor 'Ali b. Abi Talib; he was the first in a line of twelve, known collectively as the Twelve Imams.

1972:638-42). Virtually all writing done in contemporary Iran on the theme of social justice takes the relevant Qur'anic verses as its point of departure.

The traditions of the Prophet Muhammad abound in exhortations to justice, as well as examples of its practice, and the Shi'i Muslims of Iran, no less than their Sunni brethren elsewhere, see in the Islamic state he founded at Madina the supreme and unequaled example of a just social order. (For example, see Shari'ati, *Az Hijrat.*)

Almost from the outset, however, there has been a distinctive Shi'i emphasis on the concept of justice and a peculiarly Shi'i understanding of it, one connected indissolubly with the persons and pronouncements of the Twelve Imams. The Imams were held to be the sole legitimate rulers not only because of divine appointment, accomplished through the intermediary of the Prophet, but also because they alone were able to enact justice among men.

While the supreme archetype of justice after the Prophet himself is 'Umar for Sunni Muslims, it is 'Ali for Shi'i Muslims—'Ali who is regarded as an unparalleled exemplar of all virtues. Upon assuming the caliphate, he is reported to have said the following:

> I swear by God that were it not for . . . the pledge that God has taken from the scholars of Islam not to remain silent in the face of the gluttony and plundering of the oppressors on the one hand, and the harrowing hunger and deprivation of the oppressed on the other hand . . . I would abandon the reins of government and in no way seek it ('Ali b. Abi Talib 1967:50).

'Ali's emphasis on justice as the essence of correct rule is also documented, in the view of Shi'i Muslims, by the celebrated instructions he gave to Malik ibn Ashtar, whom he appointed to the governorship of Egypt ('Ali b. Abi Talib 1967:426-45). With the martyrdom of 'Ali, the dual cause of Imamate (=legitimate rule) and justice received its first tragic blow and became indelibly tinged with suffering.*

*From a certain point of view, this "tinge of suffering" is not the result of historical contingencies. It is an inescapable consequence of the Imams being heirs to the prophets: part of what they inherit is the vexations suffered by all the bearers of God's word. For a poetic expression of the theme, see the celebrated poem of Muhtasham Kashani, the first two lines of which read, "When they summoned mankind to the table of sorrow, they first issued the summons to the hierarchy of prophets./ When it came to the turn of the *awliya* [=Imams], Heaven trembled at the blow they smote on the head of the Lion of God ['Ali b. Abi Talib]" (text and translation in Browne 1928:173-77).

There thus came into being a threefold association in the Shi'i consciousness among Imamate, justice, and suffering, an association that was powerfully reinforced by the death in battle of Imam Husayn at Karbala in 680. Husayn is seen as having risen in revolt against the Umayyads (usurpers of the caliphate) not to enforce a personal claim to rulership but to ensure justice among men. This view is derived from utterances such as the following, reportedly made on the eve of the fatal confrontation at Karbala:

> O God! You know that everything we did was not prompted by rivalry for political power, nor by a search for wealth and abundance; rather it was done in order to demonstrate to men the shining principles and values of Your religion, to reform the affairs of Your land, to protect and secure the indisputable rights of Your oppressed servants, and to act in accordance with the duties You have established and the norms, laws and ordinances You have decreed (quoted by Khomeini 1971:148).

When Husayn was martyred, it was not merely an injustice committed against his person, but also a violation of men's right to be ruled with justice. Hence the sufferings of men come to parallel and complement those of the Imam. The Imams and their followers were, moreover, repeatedly persecuted during the Umayyad and 'Abbasid periods, so that the Shi'i community as a whole came to be defined by the intensely felt experience of oppression. This experience gave rise to the saying, "Misfortune [*bala'*] accompanies loyalty to the Imam [*vala'*] as glitter accompanies gold" (quoted in Kashifi 1955:10).

The joint experience of oppression and calamity has also been reflected in the Shi'i exegesis of Qur'an, 28:4: "We desired to be gracious to those that were abased in the land, and to make of them leaders and the inheritors." This is a key verse for understanding the Shi'i view of justice, suffering, and history, and is now cited constantly in Iran in explanation of the Islamic Revolution. In its original context, the verse refers clearly to the delivery of the Children of Israel from the bondage of the pharaohs. Shi'i commentators have seen in it additionally a reference both to the Imams and to their followers. "Those that were abased in the land" are simultaneously the Imams, deprived of their right to rule, and their loyal followers, deprived of all justice. (See at-Tabataba'i 1973, 16:14-15.)

Shi'i awareness of the tragedy at Karbala and its lasting implications has not depended exclusively on written tradition and sectarian exegesis. Since at least the mid-eighteenth century, the Shi'is of Iran and elsewhere have commemorated the martyrdom of Husayn with dramatic performances known as *ta'ziya*.* In technique and composition, these performances have little in common with most formal drama. Their purpose is not the creation of materially plausible images of real or imaginary happenings, but the vivid evocation of highly emotive archetypes of suffering and power, justice and injustice. In the *ta'ziya*, what we may call "the universal Husayn" and his adversaries at Karbala step forth as transhistorical personages, with a living presence in contemporary society; the performance becomes a mirror in which the audience finds its own predicament reflected. In the perceptive words of 'Ali Shari'ati, "Everyone laments his own tragedy in the horrendous human tragedy of Karbala . . . and annually it is from this tragedy that he aspires to regain the rights he has lost" (*Husayn*:1).

The archetypal value acquired by the events at Karbala, suggesting they are capable of infinite replication, has meant an extension of their significance and encouraged the making of new and concretely political deductions. The murderer of Husayn comes to stand not only for the Sunni rulers who persecuted the Imams and their loyal followers, but also for unjust rulers who are Shi'i in a formal sense but are perceived as being the heirs of Yazid (the Umayyad foe of Husayn) in spirit. As early as the 1840s the Qajar rulers of Iran (1785-1924) were pejoratively associated with the Umayyads (Sepsis 1844: 106), and thereafter the use of Karbala as an image for the continuing predicament of the oppressed became increasingly frequent. (For examples see Algar 1972:233.) In revolutionary Iran it is now a standard part both of official discourse and of popular feeling.†

'Ali and Husayn are exemplars of justice belonging to the historical past, despite the reverberations of their presence in the Shi'i consciousness. The Twelfth, Occulted Imam of the Shi'a associates the theme of justice with the future course of history. Upon his birth

*For a discussion of most aspects of the ta'ziya apart from its political dimensions in modern Iran, see Chelkowski, ed. 1979.

†A recent and very striking example was provided by the death of seventy-two people in the bombing of the Tehran headquarters of the Islamic Republic Party on 28 June 1981. The number of the victims coincided with that of Husayn's companions at Karbala, and it was said that "the seventy-two companions of Imam Khomeini have gone from the Karbala of Tehran to join the seventy-two companions of Imam Husayn." (See *Soroush* [English-language edition], nos. 4/5 [June-July 1981]:88.)

he is said to have recited the Qur'anic verse discussed above, thereby suggesting a connection between his reemergence at the End of Time and the raising up of the abased and oppressed (Safi 1957:61). Other traditions confirm the messianic role of the Twelfth Imam as the bringer of justice. The Prophet is reported to have said concerning him that "he will fill the earth with justice as it has been filled with oppression, so that people are restored to their primordial state: the sleeping will be left undisturbed, and no blood will be shed." And in commenting on Qur'an, 57:17 ("Know that God will revive the earth after its death"), Imam Muhammad al-Baqir is recorded as saying, "God will revive it by means of him who shall rise (*al-qa'im*—an epithet of the Twelfth Imam), for he will revive the earth by means of justice after its death by means of oppression." (See al-Gulpayagani, *Muntakhab*:478 and Sachedina 1981:62-63.)

The occultation of the Imam meant that the cause of justice, inseparable from that of the Imamate, not only had been subjected to repeated defeat, but also had left the plane of history and become unattainable for an indefinite period. As a consequence, despite its inherently oppositional stance and insistence on justice, Shi'i Islam remained normatively quietist for many centuries.* That this quietism has now been so thoroughly replaced by revolutionary activism without in any way sacrificing awareness of the Occulted Imam is perhaps the most striking feature of contemporary Iranian Islam.

HISTORICAL ANTECEDENTS OF THE ISLAMIC REVOLUTION

The historical antecedents of the Islamic Revolution can be traced to the Qajar period, when the *'ulama* (religious authorities) first confronted the monarchy in a series of unconnected but increasingly frequent incidents and then involved themselves in the call for a constitution that would abolish the excesses of absolutism. A broad concept of justice, involving significant socioeconomic change, does not appear to have been prominent among their goals. During the nineteenth century 'ulama had occasionally assumed the leadership of bread riots and, more frequently, acted as the spokesmen for mercantile and artisan interests. (For examples see Algar 1969:108, 175-76, 205-16.) Their chief concern throughout the period seems,

*It is significant that even the establishment of the Shi'ism as majority persuasion in Iran was the work of heterodox Shi'is who had little in common doctrinally with the learned tradition of Twelver Shi'ism.

however, to have been the limitation of arbitrary rule and resistance to the foreign penetration of Iran that royal absolutism facilitated.

With the onset of the Constitutional Revolution (1905-11), justice began to be articulated as a political and legal concept, understood as the opposite of arbitrary rule. The constitutionalist 'ulama demanded the establishment of a "house of justice" (*'adalatkhana*), a term that appears to have meant an elected body of popular representatives (Kasravi 1961:67). The cause of justice had begun to return to the historical plane, but the meaning given it was as yet exclusively political, and influenced to some degree by the distinctly Iranian concept of justice—inherited from pre-Islamic times—as a commodity to be dispensed by a conscientious sovereign. The constitutional laws of 1906 and 1907 preserved the institution of monarchy and were silent on socioeconomic matters.

The reign of Riza Shah (the first Pahlavi autocrat), lasting from 1925 to 1941, was marked by extreme intellectual barrenness as well as political repression. Although 'ulama-led uprisings took place in Isfahan, Tabriz, Qum, and Mashhad, no attempts were made to formulate the political or socioeconomic precepts of Islam with a view to practical implementation. Justice appeared to have returned to total occulation.

After the deposition of Riza Shah and the installation of his son, political and intellectual activity resumed in Iran under conditions of relative liberty. The major goals pursued in the period beginning in 1941 and ending with the CIA-royalist coup of 1953 were the nationalization of the Iranian oil industry and the curbing of royal tendencies to absolutism. Politically active Islamic elements concurred in the granting of priority to these aims. Matters of socioeconomic reform did, however, begin to receive attention, and the expression "social justice" made its first appearance in Islamic usage. This newfound interest in socioeconomic matters was prompted by several factors: the deplorable state of hunger and deprivation in which the Iranian masses found themselves at the end of World War II; contemporaneous developments elsewhere in the Islamic world, notably Egypt, where the Muslim Brothers had formulated a complete socioeconomic program; and—most important—the necessity of competing with powerful leftist currents for the allegiance of the masses.

The speeches of Ayatullah Abu'l-Qasim Kashani, the main activist *'alim** of the period, display a concern primarily for nationalist

*Singular of 'ulama.

and constitutionalist objectives. Kashani is also on record, however, as having demanded the enactment of social justice and a drastic redistribution of wealth, both in order to fulfill the clear requirements of the *shari'a* (religious law) and in order to curb the spread of communism (Faghfoory 1978:146, 156, 161).

Allied with Kashani for much of his postwar career were the Fida'iyan-i Islam, an organization founded by Navvab Safavi (d. 1956) which was the first political grouping in twentieth-century Iran to conceive of the goal of an Islamic state and to work actively toward attaining it. Chiefly remembered for a series of important assassinations, the Fida'iyan also produced a detailed and pioneering blueprint for an Islamic state, society, and economy which in many ways foreshadowed the program of the Islamic Revolution almost four decades later. In this program the Fida'iyan gave the concept of justice a clear social and economic content for the first time.

The Fida'iyan identified "universal unemployment and poverty" as eleventh in a list of "roots of destructive corruption" that were destroying Iranian society and declared that "the legitimate rights of the poor must be given to them, in accordance with the criteria of Islam" (Fida'iyan 1950:13).* Among the measures the group proposed were the establishment of interest-free banking, the provision of free health care, and the construction of low-cost housing for the urban poor (pp. 31, 33, 40).

Of particular interest are the views of the Fida'iyan on the agrarian question. Taking as their point of departure the well-established principle that "the use of uncultivated (*ba'ir*) lands is the indubitable right of all Muslims," they argued that cultivation alone can confer ownership of land. The occupation of uncultivated land, the claim to own it without cultivation, and the sale of it without improvements to a new claimant to ownership are all illegal and unjust procedures. Equally, if one acquires ownership of a piece of land by means of cultivation but then ceases cultivation, the land is not saleable; it simply reverts to communal availability. The cultivation that results in ownership must be, moreover, personal and direct; it cannot be accomplished at a distance through interposing hired labor between oneself and the land (Fida'iyan 1950:25-26). In the light of these criteria, much of the land tenure system stood condemned.

*The program of the Fida'iyan was issued without any indication of authorship, but it was probably Safavi himself who wrote it.

The Fida'iyan put forth their socioeconomic proposals, unprecedentedly radical for the time, in a harsh and uncompromising language that threatened "the thieves, usurpers and bayonet-wielders with the fangs of popular vengeance" (Fida'iyan 1950:13). The program had little immediate political effect, but it inaugurated a new development in Iranian Islam: a concern with the solution of specific socioeconomic problems as an Islamic duty dictated by the idea of justice.

For all their novelty, the proposals of the Fida'iyan were points in a manifesto; they did not represent the application of an ideology. However, an ideological approach to the problems of religion and society, making possible the elaboration of a theory of social justice, did begin to evolve at about the same time that the organization of the Fida'iyan-i Islam was established. In 1942 Mehdi Bazargan, then professor of thermodynamics at Tehran University, presided over the founding of the Islamic Students' Association, which was soon followed by the emergence of other Islamic professional organizations. The prime concern of these associations, which held lectures and published books, was to vindicate the rationality of Islam and prove the compatibility of its doctrines with the findings of empirical science. Political and socioeconomic matters were present but not uppermost in the minds of their members. Thus Bazargan gave a series of lectures on the topic of "Labor in Islam," but his concern was less with the problems of industrial organization and worker-management relations than with work as an ethical concept. He stressed the high value given to labor by the Qur'an but drew no economic conclusions from his argument. Instead, accepting the European stereotype of the Islamic East as a realm of self-indulgent laziness, he called for the revival of endeavor and diligence in Iran (1965:75ff.). The exhortation was purely moral. In a later series of lectures Bazargan (1968) did indeed attempt to delineate a total ideological scheme of Islam, but his treatment of the subject was weak and superficial. His intellectual contribution, lasting for more than three decades, was nonetheless important. Together with his associates, he stimulated new ways of thought on social and religious questions, particularly among the secularly educated intelligentsia, and succeeded in presenting Islam as a "school of thought" (*maktab;* loan translation of *école*) with coherent teachings on all subjects of human concern.

Ayatullah Mahmud Talaqani (d. 1979) was an associate of Bazargan for many years, and participated with him in the development of a modernist Islamic literature. He was more closely interested in matters of a socioeconomic nature than Bazargan, and to him is owed the first detailed consideration in Persian of Islamic economics as the mechanism whereby the aspiration for justice is to be fulfilled. In *Kar va Malikiyat dar Islam* (Labor and ownership in Islam), Talaqani (1965:170ff.) draws together the injunctions of Islam concerning commerce, finance, industry, wealth, and ownership to construct a theoretical model of the Islamic economy. He regards this economy as having fourteen essential characteristics, of which four are the most significant. First comes the limitation of private ownership with respect to the categories of wealth that may be owned, the means by which they may be acquired, and the purposes on which they may be expended. Second is the linking of all socioeconomic activities and relations to the moral instincts and spiritual beliefs of man. Then comes the freedom to choose any legitimate form of economic activity and last, the equitable distribution of wealth among all members of society. Like many other discussions of Islamic economics, Talaqani's book includes a critique of both Marxist and capitalist economics; this is circumstantial evidence for the degree to which competition with alien ideologies spurred the elaboration of an Islamic alternative. Talaqani gives greater attention to the refutation of capitalism because in his opinion it was in the direction of capitalism rather than socialism that Muslim society had deviated (p. 275).

Talaqani's book first appeared four years after the death of Ayatullah Husayn Burujirdi, who had been the supreme religious authority (*marja'-i taqlid*) since 1945. Burujirdi had consistently failed to give effective guidance on political and social matters, and his death became the occasion for a reevaluation of the place of religion in Iranian society and the role of the religious leadership. As a result, the 1960s were a decade that witnessed not only the emergence of Imam Khomeini as a leading figure on the national scene, but also a reinforcement and expansion of modernist thought and expression. The chief result of both phenomena was the same: the transformation of religion into an ideology of revolutionary change. As a part of this process, the concept of justice, while still linked to the Imams, became fully articulated in a context of social concern, economic theory, and political action.

The increase in ideological activity found expression at first in a number of periodicals of which the most important were the yearbook *Maktab-i Tashayyu'* (The school of Shi'ism) and the monthly

Guftar-i Mah (Words for the month). Among the articles printed in the former was an early piece by Ayatullah Muhammad Husayn Bihishti, later to attain fame as the organizational genius of the Islamic Revolution, on the principles of Islamic banking. This article was later published in expanded form as a book and served as the theoretical basis for a prerevolutionary experiment in interest-free banking. (See Bihishti 1982:60.) *Guftar-i Mah* was published by the Anjuman-i Mahana-yi Dini (Monthly Religious Society), an organization established in 1960 under the leadership of Ayatullah Murtaza Mutahhari, a student and close follower of Imam Khomeini who was in addition a professor at the Faculty of Theology of Tehran University. During its three years of publication, *Guftar-i Mah* printed numerous articles on socioeconomic topics, including a preliminary draft of key sections of Talaqani's book on labor and ownership. (Concerning *Guftar-i Mah*, see Akhavi 1980: 118.)

Guftar-i Mah was obliged to cease publication in 1963, but later the same year there was established in Tehran the Husayniya-yi Irshad (Center for Religious Guidance), an institution destined to be far more influential than the Anjuman-i Mahana-yi Dini. Lectures given on Islamic ideology at the Husayniya attracted mass audiences, drawn from the same secularized milieu to which Bazargan and his associates had addressed themselves two decades earlier. The most important lecturer at the Husayniya was without doubt 'Ali Shari'ati, whose influence, particularly among the young, exceeded that of all the figures discussed so far. The determination and ability to construct an Islamic ideology were also clearer and stronger in him than in his predecessors, and an emphasis on social justice as the product and even purpose of all true religion is unmistakable throughout his work. The details of his biography need not concern us here; it is sufficient to note that he combined an early religious training at the hands of his father in Mashhad with an extensive acquaintance with European history and thought, acquired while studying sociology in Paris. (For a brief sketch of Shari'ati's life, see Tavassuli 1979:11-38.) This combination enabled him to take the decisive step to producing a new form of religious discourse, based partly on the discovery of new concepts and terms and partly on supplying existing concepts and terms with a new and extended content. Against the recognition of this achievement must be set the observation that the two elements of his intellectual background—Islamic and Western—were not fully integrated, so that for some his formulations and theories remained suspect.* However, his work affected even those who had misgivings concerning it.

For Shari'ati the concept of Islam as ideology was crucial. Highly critical of what he regarded as static traditionalism, he made an explicit distinction between Islam as culture and Islam as ideology. He denounced the former as devoid of social value, moral commitment, and revolutionary potential, identifying the philosopher Avicenna as its historic archetype (1979:68). The latter is dynamic, revolutionary, restless, insistent on change, refusing compromise, imbued with the spirit of self-sacrifice; its prime exemplar is Abu Dharr, the companion of the Prophet who spent years in exile (*Mazhab 'alayhi mazhab*:21).† What is needed is therefore clear: "I seek a return to Islam as ideology; what exists now (among the masses and the religious scholars) is Islam as culture" (*Islamshinasi*:97).

In the view of Shari'ati, the entirety of human history is a struggle between the forces of justice and oppression, a permanent dialectic between righteousness and tyranny. A remarkable if questionable feat of exegesis enabled him to see in the Qur'anic narrative of fratricidal strife between Cain and Abel both the beginning and the archetype of this transhistorical struggle. At the dawn of humanity, a "pole of Cain" and a "pole of Abel" came into being (1979: 97-111). The role of religion in this polar contest is to lead the pole of Abel and to defy injustice; hence "All prophets of the Abrahamic line, from Abraham down to the Prophet of Islam, proclaimed their missions in the form of rebellion against the existing secular power" (1979:66).

Given this historical mission of religion at the very heart of human society, it follows that the principle of divine unity (*tauhid*) cannot be confined to the plane of metaphysics or theology:

*For a balanced assessment of the strengths and weaknesses of Shari'ati's work, see the pamphlet issued by the Sazman-i Mujahidin-i Inqilab-i Islami (Organization of Mujahidin of the Islamic Revolution) on the second anniversary of his death.

†The promotion of Abu Dharr to a position of prominence in modern Shi'i ideology is due in part to the influence of Sayyid Qutb's *al-'Adalat al-Ijtima'iyya fi 'l-Islam* (Social justice in Islam), which has been translated into Persian. Sayyid Qutb's praise of Abu Dharr as one who stood selflessly for social justice has been enthusiastically echoed in Iran, as has too his criticism of 'Uthman, the third caliph, viewed by Shi'is as an adversary of 'Ali. (See the Arabic original of Sayyid Qutb's work, 1949:231-34.)

> *Tauhid* may be said to descend from the heavens to the earth, and leaving circles of philosophical, theological and scientific discussion, interpretation and debate, it enters the affairs of society. It poses the various questions that are involved in social relationships—class relations, the orientation of individuals, relations between the individual and society, the various dimensions of the social structure, the social superstructure, social institutions, the family, politics, culture, economy, ownership, social ethics, the responsibilities of individuals and society. *Tauhid* thus provides the intellectual foundation for all the affairs of society (1979:32).

There is not only an affinity but a causative interrelation between the structure of a given society and the form of religious belief it professes: religion is the "intellectual infrastructure of society" (Shari'ati, *Islamshinasi*:176). The society based on tauhid (*jami'a-yi tauhidi*) will be characterized by harmony, unity, and justice; it will be a reflection in creation of the characteristics of the Creator. The society based on the opposing principle of *shirk* will be one disfigured by injustice, hostility, and strife; the pantheon of gods warring in the heavens has its terrestrial counterpart in the clash of competing social classes (*Islamshinasi*:176-80; 1979:117-18).*

In this lasting struggle between the pole of Abel and the pole of Cain, between the social manifestations of tauhid and shirk, two sets of forces are at war. The pole of Abel consists of God and man—on the one hand, the Creator, and on the other hand, the people (*an-nas*), equated by Shari'ati with the masses. In a statement fraught with all kinds of theological and exegetical difficulties but highly significant for his thought, Shari'ati suggested that "wherever in the Qur'an social matters are mentioned, *Allah* and *an-nas* are virtually synonymous" (1979:116). Divine sovereignty thus comes to mean popular sovereignty, and divine ownership of the sources of wealth, popular ownership.

The pole of Cain is trinitarian in its composition, consisting of the holders of coercive power, the usurpers of popular wealth, and the official clergy of false religion (=shirk). Alliteratively, Shari'ati called these three respectively the manifestations of *zur* (force), *zar* (gold), and *tazvir* (trickery) (*Islamshinasi*:87).

*It is worth noting that the call for a society based on tauhid was frequently raised during the revolution as a slogan during mass demonstrations. (See Kamali 1979:473.)

Against this background of a historical dialectic mirroring the opposing forces of tauhid and shirk, Shari'ati reinterpreted many of the key themes of Shi'ism. Possibly most significant was his new understanding and popularizing of the term *mustaz'af* (the passive participle of the verb we have translated as "abased" in Qur'an, 28:4). It is no exaggeration to say that Shari'ati's influence is responsible for the place of honor this word occupies in the vocabulary of the Islamic Revolution. For him the Qur'anic expression, "those that were abased in the land," is "the exact equivalent of Frantz Fanon's *Les Damnés de la terre*" (Shari'ati, *Intizar*:52)—that is, it has a universal and permanent significance and is not confined in any way to the sufferings of the Imams and their followers, or even of contemporary Shi'i Muslims. The complete verse in which the expression occurs comes therefore to mean "The rule of humanity will be placed in the hands of those who have been abased throughout history, and they will be made the heirs of history, i.e., heirs to all that has been held as a monopoly by usurpatory powers throughout history" (51). The verse reveals itself as unmistakably universal, and it is only against the background of this singular exegesis that the almost messianic self-view of the Islamic Revolution can be understood.*

Shari'ati also subjected to a universalizing reinterpretation the central Shi'i mythos of Karbala. Reflecting on its significance and registering his dissatisfaction with the traditional mourning ceremonies, Shari'ati wrote that in his mind's eye, "The plain of Karbala suddenly stretched out to embrace the whole world, and the ranks of the seventy-two men who stood at the side of Husayn on the banks of the Euphrates stretched out into the past and future to embrace the whole of history" (*Husayn*:16). The historical event was thus explicitly transfigured into a transhistorical myth, an ideal confrontation between justice and injustice. There was nothing inherently new in this, but Shari'ati went beyond tradition by enlarging the significance of Karbala to embrace the whole of human history. For him the designation of Husayn as an "heir" in certain traditional invocations meant that he was an heir not only to the prophets, but also to "the red banner that was handed down to him from Adam and that he in turn passes on to all the guides of people, to all the seekers of freedom and justice in human history" (17). In a

*For example, in a speech commemorating the second anniversary of the Islamic Revolution, Imam Khomeini offered his congratulations not only to the people of Iran but also to "*mustaz'afin* of the world." (Text in *Jumhuri-yi Islami*, 13 February 1981/Bahman 23, 1360.)

word, Husayn is "the heir to all the revolutions in human history" (20); even those that come after him bear his stamp.

Shari'ati's understanding of the occultation of the Twelfth Imam and the anticipation of his return likewise hinges on the concept of revolution. The delayed return of the Imam from occultation, far from being an excuse for apathy and quietism, is in fact "a factor of historical optimism"; it is an assurance that "the outcome of history will be in favor of justice" (Shari'ati, *Intizar*:55). Anticipating the Imam's reemergence means, therefore, actively rejecting injustice—"saying 'no' to the *status quo*"—and orienting oneself with confidence and courage to "the inevitable revolution of the future," "the final and decisive revolution of history" (*Intizar*:35, 45; *Islamshinasi*:85; 1979:109). This equation of the renewed manifestation of the Imam with universal revolution has little in common with the copious and detailed accounts of the event contained in the traditional literature. Shari'ati remains, however, inalienably Shi'i by insistently connecting the universal triumph of justice with the promised manifestation of the Imam.

Shari'ati died in 1977, before he could fully synthesize his numerous and sometimes fluctuating insights into a codified system, but he left behind the pervasive conviction that Islam—especially Shi'i Islam is indeed an ideology—one, moreover, that demands revolutionary action of its adherents. By presenting the issue of justice as central both to the essence of religion and to its historical and social role, he aroused in many a new sense of moral and social responsibility and contributed substantially to a revolution he did not live to see.

The influence of Shari'ati is clearly visible in the writings of a number of other theoreticians of the 1970s who, basing themselves on his categories and terminology, pay concentrated attention to social and economic problems. For example, Zahra Rahnavard's *Mauzi'giri-yi Tabaqat-i Ijtima'i dar Qur'an* (The attitudes of social classes in the Qur'an) is an attempt at the classification of all Qur'anic verses relevant to questions of class structure. The author traces all references to the mustaz'afin and their trinity of opponents and discerns in addition a group she calls "the intellectual theoreticians entrusted with the education of the people"—*rabbaniyun* in the terminology of the Qur'an (*Mauzi'giri-yi*:73).

Habibullah Payman (pseudonym:Paydar), in *Malikiyat, Kar va Sarmaya az Didgah-i Islam* (Ownership, labor and capital from the viewpoint of Islam), combines the terminology and ideological perspective of Shari'ati with an examination of key economic problems that is indebted both to the work of Talaqani and to the Persian translation of Sayyid Qutb (1949).* Fusing social ideology and economic theory, Payman asserts that the Islamic economy has as its fundamental purpose the liberation of man "from all that holds him back from advancing to absolute perfection." The demeaning obstacles that bar man's path include not only poverty, but also all unjust, dominating, and exploitative relationships. The Islamic criterion of social development and progress is not to be found in the volume or mode of production but in the prevalence of just socioeconomic relationships (Paydar 1977:85-87). Despite his concern to situate the concept of justice in a precise economic framework, Payman's work is marked by a bombastic abstractionism reminiscent of much Iranian leftist writing (reflecting, too, his own past involvement with Marxism). His book nonetheless acquired some fame and importance in Iran as the major doctrinal text for a political organization led by Payman during the first two years of the Islamic Republic, the Junbish-i Musalmanan-i Mubariz (Movement of Militant Muslims). This organization was particularly noted for its urgent promotion of a radical land redistribution program. (See numerous issues of its weekly organ, *Ummat.*)

The most substantial work of Abu 'l-Hasan Bani Sadr, *Iqtisad-i Tauhidi* (The economics of *Tauhid*), enshrines those claims to economic expertise which were a major factor in his election as first president of the Islamic Republic in the winter of 1980. It too stands clearly under the influence of Shari'ati. Shari'ati had spoken of the society based on tauhid; it was a natural extension of the idea to propose an economy based on tauhid. As for the actual contents of the tauhidi economy, these were derived by Bani Sadr from *Iqtisaduna* (Our economics), an important work of the Iraqi Shi'i 'alim, Ayatullah Muhammad Baqir as-Sadr (d. 1981).† Bani Sadr supplemented his borrowings from as-Sadr with an examination of the

*See especially the section on "social solidarity" (*takaful-i ijtima'i*); both the term and the concept are borrowed from Sayyid Qutb.

†*Iqtisaduna* must surely count as the most impressive attempt to date to sketch a general scheme of the Islamic economy. Judicious and detailed in its argumentation, it goes a long way to substantiating the claim that "Islamic social justice is not an abstract concept . . . but has been defined and crystallized by means of a specific social plan" (as-Sadr 1972:264-65). The book has been widely read in Iran, both in the Arabic original and in a Persian translation by Musavi (1971).

position of Iran in the world economy in terms of the theories elaborated by his Paris mentor, Paul Vieille. Despite the derivative nature of Bani Sadr's book, the turgid style in which it is written, and the fact that his role in Iranian affairs is now at an end, *Iqtisad-i Tauhidi* is of value as one more document testifying to the currency of socioeconomic concern, expressed in Islamic terms, as a key element in the revolution.*

Other writers flourished in the same ideological climate as Shari'ati without being directly indebted to him for concepts or terminology. For example, Jalal ad-Din Farsi (later a leading figure in the Islamic Republic Party during its early days) published two years before the revolution a voluminous interpretation of early Islamic history that laid emphasis on socioeconomic developments and made liberal use of radical terminology (Farsi 1977). He described the appearance of Islam as being in itself a revolution, with creedal, moral, political, social, economic, and military components. After the death of the Prophet, the Islamic community was afflicted with a "creeping reaction" that triumphed fully in the time of 'Uthman. The caliphate of 'Ali constituted a resumption of the revolution, but it was followed by the more severe and permanent form of reaction that set in with the Umayyads. This terminology may sound anachronistic, but the book is based on solid research in primary Arabic sources. If allowance is made for the sectarian preferences of the author, it is seen to be an impressive treatment of its subject. Like many writings of Shari'ati, Farsi's book shows how considerations of socioeconomic justice came to be regarded as central both to the function of religion and to the identity of Shi'ism within Islam.

A note of caution against the possibly materialist implications of this view was sounded by Ayatullah Mutahhari, who had, significantly, an infinitely better grounding in the traditional disciplines of Islam than all the figures examined so far. Early an associate of Shari'ati at the Husayniya-yi Irshad, Mutahhari parted company with him on some of his interpretations, which he courteously but

*Bani Sadr fled Iran in the company of Mas'ud Rajavi, leader of the Sazman-i Mujahidin-i Khalq (Organization of People's Mujahidin). The Mujahidin attempt to capture power in Iran has definitely failed, but at one point their theories counted for something in the development of Islamic ideology, and ideally some mention of their writings should have been included here. We foreswear the attempt because of the complexity of the ideological and organizational history of the Mujahidin. For a critical but well-documented study of the subject, see Haqqju (1979).

effectively criticized. In particular he rejected the notion of an absolute and dialectical polarity in society between the mustaz'af and the *mustakbir* (the negative counterpart of the mustaz'af), a polarity of which all opposing pairs in the Qur'an (believer and unbeliever, virtuous and wicked) were often made the mere derivative Mutahhari, *Muqaddima'i*, 5:35-40, 162-90). However, that Mutahhari participated in the elaboration of an ideological scheme, with justice forming an important part of the social purpose of religion, is attested by numerous of his writings.*

Among the writers and theoreticians of the immediate pre-revolutionary period mention may finally be made of 'Ali Gulzada Ghafuri, an 'alim who lectured at the Husayniya-yi Irshad and had a fairly wide following among university students. In *Khutut-i Asli dar Nizam-i Iqtisadi-yi Islam* (An outline of the economic system of Islam), Ghafuri avoids the use of a modernizing terminology and instead collates material from *fiqh* (Islamic jurisprudence) relating to economic matters under the conventional headings of modern economics. He designates justice as the underlying principle of the entire economic system of Islam, and asserts that "any law or regulation, at any time or under any circumstances whatsoever, that is opposed to this indubitable principle of Islam, is automatically invalid from the viewpoint of Islam" (*Khutut-i*:18). In another work, *Nizamat-i Ijtima'i-yi Islam* (The social institutions of Islam), Ghafuri similarly maintains that the establishment of justice is one of three major fundaments of the Islamic social system. This he derives from the celebrated response of a Muslim commander to the question why he had brought his armies to Iran: "In order to deliver men from worship of each other into the worship of God; in order to deliver them from narrowness of vision to breadth of vision; and in order to deliver them from the injustice of other religions to the justice of Islam" 1970:26).

THE ISLAMIC REVOLUTION: IDEOLOGICAL CONSENSUS UNDER IMAM KHOMEINI

There had thus emerged in Iran, by the time of the revolution, not a codified ideology with a set of quasi-canonical texts, but what can be called an ideological consensus: a conviction that Islam,

Mutahhari has, in fact, a whole book devoted to the subject of justice, both as a divine attribute and a criterion for social relations ('Adl-i Ilahi*).

properly studied, yields a coherent set of political, social, and economic systems which have the establishment of justice as their God-given aim. The distinctively Shi'i association of justice with the Imams was turned into a factor of immediacy instead of abstraction, of revolution instead of quietism.

However striking this development may have been and however much suited to the temper and traditions of Iranian society, it is improbable that the ideology should have found expression in a successful revolution without the leadership of Imam Khomeini. In this there is a certain paradox, for the Imam is not an ideologue in the common understanding of the term.* He is, on the contrary, profoundly rooted in traditional modes of thought and expression which he has put to revolutionary use. It is precisely this ability to elicit a revolutionary content from traditional materials that has enabled him to articulate justice—the central theme of the ideological consensus—with unparalleled authority and effectiveness. For the deprived masses of the Iranian people—the mustaz'afin—the cause of justice has had a personal embodiment in Imam Khomeini, just as it does in the Twelve Imams, in the imagination and historical memory of the Shi'i community.

Imam Khomeini's political career began in the 1930s with his lectures on ethics at the Fayziya *madrasa* (religious college) which dealt in part with political and social matters and were attended by members of the general public as well as of the religious institution (see Algar forthcoming). The exact content of these lectures has not been recorded. His first published political statements came in *Kashf al-Asrar*, a book that was mainly a response to an antireligious tract but in part also an attack on the iniquity of Pahlavi rule. He denounced the Pahlavi regime as illegitimate, arguing that "neither it nor any of the monarchies or governments we see in the world is based on justice or a correct foundation that is acceptable to reason" (Algar, trans. 1981:169; from Khomeini 1943:221). Legitimacy is dependent on justice, and justice depends in turn on the implementation of the shari'a; the only legitimate form of government is therefore an Islamic government that enforces the shari'a (Khomeini 1943:222; in Algar, trans. 1981:170).

*This should not be taken to mean that he does not have a consistent and distinctive mode of thought and expression; the term "line of the Imam" (*khatt-i imam*), which has become current in Iran, has far more than a political significance.

This theme of justice and its virtual synonymity with Islamic government occurs repeatedly in the speeches and declarations that Imam Khomeini has made from his first appearance on the national scene in 1963 to the present. Thus in April 1963 he defined "the great aim of Islam" to be "to prevent oppression, arbitrary rule and the violation of law; to preserve the rights of Islam and the nation; and to establish social justice" (Algar, trans. 1981:176; from Khomeini, *Khomeini*:2). The attainment of this aim necessitates the overthrow of "those who have filled foreign banks with the wealth produced by the toil of our poverty-stricken people" (Algar, trans. 1981:178; from Khomeini, *Khomeini*:6), enabling "those who have been oppressed to assume leadership and become heirs to their own destiny and resources" (declaration of 11 October 1978; in Algar, trans. 1981: 241).* In February 1978, as the events that culminated in the abolition of the Iranian monarchy were just beginning, Imam Khomeini evoked the miserable state of the slum dwellers of south Tehran and the impoverished people of Khuzistan (1978:38; in Algar, trans. 1981:223). As the Islamic Revolution progressed, he promised "a government of divine justice" (declaration of 6 September 1978; in Algar, trans. 1981:233), emphasizing that "Islam stands on the side of the weak, the peasants and the needy" (declaration of 23 November 1978; in Algar, trans. 1981:244). When the Islamic Republic was formally declared on 1 April 1979, he told the Iranian people that "the regime of arrogance" had been destroyed by "God's powerful hand, which has shown itself as the power of the oppressed" (1979: 135; in Algar, trans. 1981:265). In other words, the "government of divine justice" now established is not only meant to serve the oppressed; it is also the very creation of the oppressed, who had become a manifestation of divine power, or of "the pole of Abel," to use the terminology of Shari'ati.

The centrality of justice to Imam Khomeini's concept of Islamic government is connected to his insistence on the role to be played by the 'ulama in administering the government, or at least supervising its operations. In the celebrated lectures on Islamic government that he delivered in Najaf in 1970, he first demonstrated that justice is one of the principal reasons for the necessity of establishing an Islamic government (1971:42-45). He then argued that the religious scholars (*fuqaha*) are the heirs to the governmental authority and responsibility

*The last expression echoes unmistakably Qur'an, 28:4, that key verse of Shi'i revolutionism.

of the Imams (1971:62ff.). There is therefore the same indissoluble connection between justice and the political involvement of the fuqaha as there is between justice and the Imamate. We have already seen that there is in traditional Shi'i thought an inner linkage of sympathy and destiny between the Imams and the mustaz'afin conclusion that the political involvement of the fuqaha—*vilayat-i faqih* (the governance of the faqih)—is coterminous with the assumption of political authority by the mustaz'afin is therefore a natural and logical one.*

In the view of Imam Khomeini, furthermore, there exists a closeness between the religious scholars and the masses that is both spiritual and material. In a speech delivered in 1979 on the sixteenth anniversary of the uprising of 5 June 1963 (Khurdad 15 in the Iranian calendar), he stressed that both that uprising and the Islamic Revolution itself were the achievements primarily of "Muslims from the lower echelons of society" acting under the guidance of the religious leaders; the masses and the 'ulama had stood together against tyranny and injustice. In addition, "the committed religious scholars who live two or three to a room in the narrow cells of our *madrasas* have a standard of living similar to that of the slum-dwellers on the edges of our cities, who are crowded, seven or eight people together, into some hole in the ground" (Algar, trans. 1981:268-74; from Khomeini 1979:347-53). The 'ulama share with the masses, therefore, not only the aspiration for justice, but also the experience of material deprivation. This assertion of a closeness between the 'ulama and the masses is valid on the whole, and there can be no doubt in any event that there has been a constant and vital interchange of loyalty and affection between Imam Khomeini and the mustaz'afin. "Orientation to the people" has been correctly identified as one of the chief characteristics of "the line of the Imam" (see Sazman-i Mujahidin-i Inqilab-i Islami 1979:31-32).

The principle of social justice, together with certain aspects of its economic implementation, was included in the draft constitution of the Islamic Republic published in 1979, although the expression itself was not used. Social and economic principles were spelled out in much greater detail in the final text of the constitution that was approved in a referendum in December 1979. For example, Article 2 specifies that the Islamic Republic is a system of government which secures

*For a full exposition of the arguments leading to this conclusion, see Anon. 1979.

"equity and justice"; Article 3 calls for "the planning of a correct and just economic system, in accordance with Islamic criteria, in order to create prosperity, remove poverty, and abolish all forms of deprivation with respect to food, housing, work and health care, and the provision of universal insurance"; and Article 43 insists on "the provision of basic necessities to all citizens" (Algar, trans. 1980:27, 28, 43-44).

The major organized political force to emerge in Iran after the triumph of the Islamic Republic, the Islamic Republic Party (IRP), has also pledged itself to the achievement of social justice. In its founding manifesto, published in the spring of 1979, the party lists the following as its sixth aim:

> the uprooting of poverty and deprivation through emphasizing the value of labor, rejecting all forms of exploitation, and creating a new economic system in which no one will be obliged to sell his labor for less than its true value; peasants, workers and all other toilers will receive a full return for their labor; the human and spiritual personality of every individual will be strengthened; and a heartfelt desire will be created in him to raise the level of his productivity and expertise and aid society in attaining technical self-sufficiency (IRP 1979).

THE ISLAMIC REPUBLIC AND SOCIOECONOMIC JUSTICE

In the six years that have elapsed since the foundation of the Islamic Republic of Iran, the main concerns of the new order have been the establishment of new political institutions, the clarification of ideological direction, and self-defense against violent disruption at home and aggression from abroad. Nonetheless, important efforts have been made to change the socioeconomic structure of the country and to fulfill the promise of social justice held out by the revolution and its ideological consensus.

Although legislative change has been slow in coming, neither symbolic nor practical action has been wanting. The mustaz'afin have been constantly eulogized by the leading figures of the Islamic Republic as the true architects of the revolution and as those with the greatest claims upon it. Their status has even been formally consecrated by the designation of Sha'ban 15—the birthday of the Twelfth Imam—as the Day of the Mustaz'afin. The real incomes of workers in both the public and private sectors rose in the immediate post-revolutionary period. The gross disparities of income between specialized technicians or administrators on the one hand and workers on the other hand that existed in state-owned industries (especially the National Iranian Oil Company) before the revolution have been abolished. Frequent production and other bonuses have been paid, and in the regulated apportionment of essential foodstuffs, made necessary by the economic consequences of the Iraqi aggression, priority has been given to low-income areas.

More striking, perhaps, than these measures have been the achievements of a series of service organizations that came into being after the revolution with the aim of improving conditions of life for both the urban and the rural poor. The most successful of these organizations has been the Reconstruction Jihad (Jihad-i Sazandagi), which has operated primarily in the countryside. Early on, the Jihad was able to establish itself as one of the chief revolutionary organs throughout the country, although it was not until November 1982 that its status was formally clarified with the passage of a relevant law by the Majlis. On the eve of the fourth anniversary of the revolution in February 1983, the Jihad was able to point to a long list of achievements that included building more than 21,000 kilometers of rural roads; bringing electricity to 2,184 villages; supplying piped water to 3,754 villages; installing hundreds of schools, bathhouses, clinics, and mosques in different parts of the country; bringing 178,445 hectares of land under cultivation for the first time; distributing free of charge large quantities of agricultural machinery; and vaccinating more than 5.5 million people against diseases such as cholera and typhoid (*Jumhuri-yi Islami*, 3 February 1983/Bahman 4, 1361). All this activity has greatly enhanced the presence of the revolution in the countryside and helped to frustrate attempts by urban-based leftists at gaining a foothold among the peasantry.

In addition to the Reconstruction Jihad, mention may be made of the Mustaz'afan Foundation (Bunyad-i Mustaz'afan), which is charged with administering for the benefit of the poor properties confiscated from the former royal family and its close associates; the Martyrs' Foundation (Bunyad-i Shahid), which attends to the needs of those whose breadwinners have fallen in defense of the revolution; the University Jihad (Jihad-i Danishgahi), which has mobilized faculty and students for the service of the poor as part of the reorientation of higher education known as the Cultural Revolution; the Housing Foundation (Bunyad-i Maskan), which has constructed thousands of units of free housing, mostly in the countryside; and the Movement for Instruction in Literacy (Nihzat-i Savad Amuzi), which by the end of its second year had taught the fundamentals of literacy to 374,000 people and currently has more than a million people enrolled in its classes (*Jumhuri-yi Islami*, 25 November 1982/Azar 4, 1361).

Clearly, however, the establishment of social justice must ultimately be a legal and structural matter; wage increases and volunteer services are not enough. This holds true particularly in view of Imam Khomeini's insistence that Islamic government is essentially a government that enacts divine law. Speaking in 1970, he even implied that legislation, in the strict sense of the term, would be unnecessary after the establishment of an Islamic government:

> The entire system of government and administration, together with the necessary laws, lies ready for you. If the administration of the country calls for taxes, Islam has made the necessary provision; and if laws are needed, Islam has established them all. There is no need for you, after establishing a government, to sit down and draw up laws, or, like rulers who worship foreigners and are infatuated with the West, run after others to borrow their laws. Everything is ready and waiting. All that remains is to draw up ministerial programs, and that can be accomplished with the help and cooperation of consultants and advisers who are experts in different fields, gathered together in a consultative assembly (1971: 190-91).

The experience of the past six years has shown, however, that particularly in areas of social concern such as land distribution and labor relations, far more is needed than the drawing up of ministerial programs. What has transpired, first in the Revolutionary Council* and then in the Majlis, bears a fairly close resemblance to a legislative process, one in which delays, uncertainties, disagreements, and conflicting social interests have all played a part. It is true that the stated purpose has been at all times to provide for the implementation of the shari'a, so that the drafting of laws has not been a form of legislation *ex nihilo*. However, the debates and controversies that have occurred in Iran since the revolution suggest that the transition from shar'i precept to concretely applicable law is not always easy or straightforward.

*The Revolutionary Council, appointed by Imam Khomeini on 12 January 1979, functioned as interim legislature until the election of the first Majlis of the Islamic Republic in the spring of 1980.

AGRARIAN REFORMS

The first major social issue to call for legal regulation after the revolution was that of land ownership. There was extensive peasant participation in the revolution in numerous parts of the country, especially in the Qazvin, Rasht, Amul, Arak, Bihbahan, and Khurramabad areas. Peasants demonstrated in their villages in favor of the revolution, traveled to nearby towns to participate in mass marches, and in some cases overran gendarmerie posts (see Anon. 1982:4-12). But the most distinctive aspect of revolutionary peasant activity was the forcible confiscation of land from large owners (called "feudals" [*fi'udalha*] in the terminology of the revolution), who were viewed as a prop of the Shah's regime and the socioeconomic order with which it was associated. Particularly in eastern Azarbayjan, Fars, and Khuzistan, these confiscations were sustained or even initiated by local revolutionary committees, but elsewhere locally influential figures were sometimes able to prevent or even reverse confiscations of land. (For a case study of a village near Shiraz, see Hooglund 1980:7-12.) The provisional government of Bazargan, a body far from revolutionary in its outlook, was generally unsympathetic to the confiscations, in part no doubt because its minister of agriculture, 'Ali Izadi, was himself a major landowner in Fars. A further element of complexity was provided by leftist groups that attempted to exploit the land issue in their efforts to penetrate the countryside (see *Jihad* 2, 29 [17 March 1982/Isfand 26, 1360]: 60).

When the Revolutionary Council began to examine the issue in the summer of 1979, disagreement immediately surfaced. The members of the council appealed to the Imam to arbitrate their differences, so he nominated a committee to draw up a bill which would settle the matter. The committee, consisting of Ayatullahs Muntaziri, Bihishti, and Mishkini, presented a Law for the Reassignment and Revival of Land (Qanun-i Vaguzari va Ihya-yi Zamin) that was ratified by the Revolutionary Council, after lengthy discussions, on 15 April 1980. (For the text of the law, see Anon. 1981:7-15; for remarks, see Bihishti 1982:398.)

The law dealt with three categories of land: lands at the disposal of the government because they contain resources such as forest and pasture which count as the property of the Islamic state (*anfal*); lands confiscated by revolutionary courts from persons guilty of crimes in connection with the former regime; and large private holdings that were legal according to laws prevailing before the revolution. The provisions relating to this last category (known as *band-i jim,* category c) proved to be highly controversial. Uncultivated (ba'ir) private holdings were pronounced subject to immediate confiscation for distribution among qualified peasants and cultivators. As for cultivated (*da'ir*) lands, if an owner held an amount in excess of three times what was required for the support of a household according to local norms (*'urf-i mahall*), he could retain only what he needed to support himself and his family; the surplus would be distributed among needy cultivators in the locality. No provision was made for compensation.

Overall responsibility for the implementation of the law was vested in a five-man committee headquartered at the Ministry of Agriculture in Tehran and consisting of a representative from the Ministries of Agriculture and the Interior, the judiciary, and the Reconstruction Jihad, as well as a nominee of the *vali amr* (the legitimate holder of authority—i.e., Imam Khomeini). The local implementation of the law was entrusted to seven-man committees answerable to the supervisory committee in Tehran and consisting of two representatives of the Ministry of Agriculture, one representative of the Reconstruction Jihad, one representative of the vali amr, and two reliable persons of proven piety and commitment to the revolution chosen from among the local population. Among the tasks of these committees was to define the 'urf of each locality and to establish priorities in both the confiscation and the reassignment of land.

The activities of the seven-man committees that were established throughout the country swiftly became a matter of violent disagreement. In part this was because of the uneven operation of the law and its lack of precision on number of key points, even when supplemented by a fairly detailed implementing protocol. More significant, however, was the opposition that arose from some influential religious scholars, particularly to the principle of dispossessing landowners only because of the extent of their holdings. For example, Ayatullah Kazim Shari'atmadari, an 'alim who had a large following in Azarbayjan and was fundamentally hostile to the main thrusts of the revolution, protested, in a letter to the Imam, against the confiscation of private, cultivated land and insisted that at the very least compensation be paid (unpublished interview of Ma'sum 'Abidi with Ayatullah Shari'atmadari; Qum, 29 February 1982). Similar attitudes were voiced by Ayatullah Husayn Khadimi in Isfahan, who found fault with the distribution even of ba'ir lands (see remarks in *Kayhan*, 9 October 1980/Mihr 17, 1359).*

Two scholars went so far as to issue *fatvas* (opinions) in condemnation of the law. Ayatullah Baha ad-Din Mahallati, one of the leading 'ulama of Shiraz, declared that "the law for agrarian reform which has been called Islamic contains provisions which are in clear contradiction to the criteria of Islam, to Ja'fari *fiqh*, and to the consensus of *'ulama* of both early and late times. . . . I pronounce it forbidden to implement this bill." Ayatullah 'Abdullah Shirazi of Mashhad likewise claimed that "numerous provisions of the law are contrary to the essential bases of Islam, the Ja'fari school, the practice of the Prophet and the Twelve Imams, and the view of all the jurisprudents of Islam." Neither scholar made specific mention of band-i jim, but it was universally understood that their main objection was to the redistribution of da'ir lands. Their conservative social biases were apparent from the claim that implementation of the law would create "deep cleavages between different classes (*aqshar*) of the people"—i.e., between peasants and landowners. (For texts of the fatvas, see *Ummat*, 23 February 1981/Isfand 4, 1359.)

The three authors of the bill defended its provisions as uniformly consistent with Islamic law. Bihishti, for example, regretted that "the understanding of Islam held by certain well-known *fuqaha* does not sufficiently accord with the understanding of Islam that is the basis of our revolution." He stressed that underlying the law was the celebrated rule that "dead land belongs to whoever cultivates it"; this rule establishes a link between cultivation and ownership, or at the very least bestows on the cultivator a prior claim to ownership. Further, while Islamic law accepts that real or legal persons may own factors of production (*'avamil-i taulidi*), including land, their right to ownership is always subject to curtailment by the vali amr if he deems such curtailment necessary for "preserving the essential interests of the *umma*." The determination of such essential interests is the exclusive prerogative of the vali amr, although he may solicit the views of anyone he chooses, or even delegate to others the determination of essential interests. The appointment of the three-man committee that had drafted the bill was an example of such delegation, said Bihishti, with the clear implication that to accept the land

*In December 1979 Ayatullah Khadimi mockingly referred—in the presence of this writer—to a revolutionary prosecutor in Isfahan who was particularly given to the confiscation of land as *Hujjat al-Komunizm* (proof of communism) instead of Hujjat al-Islam.

bill was therefore a matter of religious and political duty (Bihishti 1982:395-97).

On 3 November 1980 Imam Khomeini issued a declaration that suspended the distribution of lands belonging to band-i jim. It has been authoritatively suggested that the chief reason for the Imam's action was the insufficiently detailed nature of the law and the resulting inconsistencies that had arisen in its implementation (author's interview with Hashimi Rafsanjani, speaker of the Majlis; Tehran, 11 September 1982). Probably he was also motivated by a number of other factors: his desire, wherever possible, to maintain consensus—or at least the appearance of it—in the religious establishment; his interest in strengthening the prerogatives of the Majlis, the body to which resolution of the issue was later assigned; and, above all, his acute sense of timing. The Iraqi attack that had begun one and a half months earlier, as well as the attempts of the United States and its allies to impose an economic blockade on Iran, was placing a great strain on the economy, including its rural sector. It was therefore inopportune that so critical and controversial an issue as land redistribution be forced.

Nonetheless, various groups continued to agitate on the issue of band-i jim. Peasants from villages around the country drew up petitions calling for an end to the suspension (see *Ummat*, 23 February 1981/Isfand 4, 1359; 16 March 1981/Isfand 25, 1359; and 31 March 1981/Farvardin 10, 1360, and Anon. 1982:29-31), and their demands were echoed by the Islamic Rural Councils that had sprung up after the revolution (*Jumhuri-yi Islami,* 21 December 1982/Azar 30, 1361). It appears too that members of the Reconstruction Jihad were disposed to continue the confiscation and reassignation of land, for Bihishti found it necessary to warn them that the Imam's decree halting such action had to be respected (see Bihishti 1982:471).

Large landowners welcomed the suspension of the distribution of their lands, and in areas such as Sistan, where their influence had traditionally been strong, the erosion of their position was to some degree halted (see *Jihad* 2, 29 [17 March 1982/Isfand 26, 1360]). But nowhere have the landowners been able to reassert their former dominance; the revolutionary organs have remained intact and supreme in the countryside. It is important to realize too that the seven-man committees have continued without interruption to distribute categories of land other than band-i jim. In Fars, for example, about 90,000 hectares of *mavat* (lands never cultivated or unequivocally abandoned after being cultivated) and state-owned lands were distributed between July 1980 and December 1982 (*Jumhuri-yi Islami,* 23 December 1982/Day 2, 1361).

On 10 December 1981 the Imam formally charged the Majlis with drawing up a new agrarian law to replace the one enacted by the Revolutionary Council. After extensive preliminary work by a committee of the Majlis that included Riza Salamati, Minister of Agriculture, a draft was placed on the Majlis agenda in the fall of 1982. After thorough debate and revision, the bill was passed by majority vote on 28 December 1982. (See *Jumhuri-yi Islami,* 29 December 1982/Day 8, 1361. The full text of the law was published in the following day's edition.)

Containing twenty articles organized in six chapters, the new law is infinitely clearer on matters of detail than its predecessor. It distinguishes five categories of land: mavat; lands belonging to the community by their very nature, such as pasture lands, forests, and reclaimed land (*milli*); lands belonging to the state by virtue of legitimate prior acquisition or confiscation by a competent Islamic court (*daulati*); lands claimed by private owners but left uncultivated (ba'ir); and lands owned by private individuals and kept under cultivation (da'ir). The law specifies that the first three categories are at the disposal of the state, which may either make use of them itself as it sees fit or distribute them among qualified persons.

As for ba'ir and da'ir lands, the permissibility of acquiring and reassigning them—the most controversial aspect of the law passed by the Revolutionary Council—has been preserved in the new law, although with significant modification. Article 5 specifies that if owners of ba'ir land have permanently ceased cultivating it, it counts automatically as state property. If, however, they have ceased cultivation temporarily, whatever the reason may be, they are awarded a respite of one year to bring their land under cultivation. If the amount that they then bring under cultivation exceeds three times "local usage" ('urf-i mahall), the excess will be acquired by the state and reassigned to those needing land and demonstrably able to cultivate it. In any event, compensation is made for all ba'ir land acquired by the state.

In the case of da'ir lands, a claimant to ownership directly engaged in cultivation (or at least in the direct supervision of cultivation) may retain an amount not in excess of three times local usage. Owners not so engaged may retain only an amount not exceeding twice local usage. In either case, the surplus will be purchased by the state for reassignment to suitable persons. Owners of da'ir lands that do not exceed four times local usage are exempt from the operation of the law, unless they allow the cultivation of their lands to lapse, in which case they become subject to compulsory purchase after a respite of one year. Also exempt are fully mechanized lands and holdings that it is not in the public interest to disperse; the use and disposition of such lands is to be regulated separately by the Ministry of Agriculture.

The enactment of the law is the responsibility of the Ministry of Agriculture, which is to establish a five-man supervisory committee in Tehran, akin to the committee created by the previous law. The composition of this committee is also to be the same as that of the earlier body, except that the expression "representative of the vali amr" has been replaced by the virtually synonymous *ruhani* (religious scholar or leader). The local seven-man committees are also to be retained, with the same composition as before, except that the two peasants are to be rotating members, while the remaining members are to be permanent. In addition, the approval of the ruhani sitting on the local committee will be essential for any act of compulsory purchase or reassignation to take effect.

The law establishes priorities of implementation, both for the categories of land to be distributed and for the classes of potential recipients. Mavat and daulati lands are to be distributed first, followed by ba'ir and then da'ir lands. Peasants holding little or no land have first claim, followed by *khushnishinha* (agricultural laborers possessing neither land nor a fixed share in the produce of the land they work on behalf of others). After their needs have been met, persons with no previous agricultural experience but a proven interest and competence (as, for example, graduates of agricultural colleges) may be considered.

Despite the detailed nature of the law, the careful and precise language in which it has been phrased, and the long debates and controversies that preceded its passage, it seems that the issue of land redistribution has still not been definitively solved. The Council of Guardians (Shaura-yi Nagahban), the body charged by Article 96 of the Constitution with reviewing all laws passed by the Majlis to ensure their conformity with Islamic jurisprudence, has not yet given the law its approval. It is plausibly rumored that the compulsory purchase of da'ir land on the basis of purely quantitative determinations is proving indigestible to certain members of the council. The speaker of the Majlis, Hashimi Rafsanjani, has suggested that the total amount of da'ir land subject to distribution under the terms of the new law is not of great practical significance since much larger tracts of mavat and ba'ir lands are available for distribution (author's interview with Rafsanjani; Tehran, 11 September 1982). This may be the case, but the way in which the question is ultimately settled will be important evidence for the social orientation of the Islamic Republic and the extent to which socially innovative measures can emerge from the implementation of Islamic law in Iran.

One element of change that has now become permanent in the Iranian countryside consists of the Islamic Rural Councils (Shauraha-yi Islami-yi Rusta'i), bodies which enable the peasants to participate in the administration of their affairs. Some of these councils arose spontaneously during the revolution and its immediate aftermath, with the aim of coordinating peasant participation in the revolution and promoting peasant interests. Others were organized at a slightly later date in conjunction with the activities of the Reconstruction Jihad. Members of the Jihad felt it desirable to have an elected body of peasants with whom they might coordinate their activities and who might advise them on the type and scope of aid needed in each locality. For long, the councils lacked any legal status, and their members complained at the refusal of many government officials to support them in their conflicts with tribal chieftains and landlords. The absence of a statute regulating the responsibilities and composition of the councils also enabled members of counterrevolutionary groups to infiltrate some of the councils (see *Jihad*, September-October 1982/Mihr 1361:78-79). In September 1982 a law was passed which formally incorporated the Rural Councils, assigning responsibility for their organization and supervision to the Reconstruction Jihad. Further, the participation of the councils in all regional agricultural planning was made mandatory (*Jumhuri-yi Islami*, 30 September 1982/Mihr 8, 1361). Two months later, some 400 delegates drawn from the approximately 20,000 councils that have been established so far attended a seminar in Tehran at which a thorough purge of the gendarmerie and swift ratification of the land redistribution bill were demanded (*ibid.*, 7 November 1982/Aban 16, 1361). From this and other evidence it is plain that the Islamic Rural Councils continue to view themselves as advocates of peasant interests, despite the supervisory role assigned to the Reconstruction Jihad (most members of which are in any event in fundamental agreement with the demand for land redistribution).

Finally with respect to the countryside, we may mention a pension scheme established during the premiership of the late

Muhammad 'Ali Raja'i which is currently providing aid in kind and cash to more than 300,000 aged peasants across the country. Plans are underway to expand the coverage of this scheme (*Jumhuri-yi Islami*, 20 October 1982/Mihr 28, 1361).

INDUSTRIAL REFORMS

The problems of the industrial sector have also demanded legislative attention since the earliest days of the Islamic Republic. The rejection of capitalism involved in the assertion that Islam has a distinctive economic system necessitated a redefinition of the public and private sectors, to the benefit of the former, as well as a reordering of worker-management relations in keeping with the promise of social justice. There was also the acute practical problem of restarting industrial production after the inevitable disruptions that had accompanied the revolution. Finally, industrial workers had played an important part in the success of the revolution by means of their strikes, particularly in the oil industry, and their expectations of change were high.

The enlargement of the public sector was swiftly and easily accomplished. On 9 June 1979 the entire banking system of the country was nationalized (*Ittila'at*, 9 June 1979/Khurdad 19, 1358). Two weeks later, all insurance firms were nationalized (*ibid.*, 25 June 1979/Tir 4, 1358). Finally, on 6 July 1979 several categories of industry also passed into the ownership of the state: all metallurgical installations, shipbuilding yards, aircraft and automobile assembly plants, factories owned by industrialists who had fled the country, factories heavily in debt to banks, and factories owned by persons who had significantly contributed to the strengthening of the Shah's regime (*ibid.*, 7 July 1979/Tir 16, 1358).

No final legislative provision for the reordering of worker-management relations has yet been made. In advance of legislation, however, Workers' Islamic Councils have sprung up in the industrial zones of Tehran, Isfahan, Tabriz, and other cities. In many cases these councils grew out of the strike committees that were formed during the revolution, and in its immediate aftermath they came to assume managerial functions. They later shared these functions with the new state-appointed management in the nationalized industries, and are acknowledged to have played a highly positive and cooperative role in restarting industrial production in the face of difficulties such as the shortage of raw materials and spare parts and the uncertainty of the economic climate in the first year of the Islamic Republic. In recognition of this role, Ayatullah Bihishti told the coordinating body of the Islamic Workers' Councils of Tehran in the winter of 1980, "Today, all factories and workplaces belong in the first place to you" (1982:239-40).

The Revolutionary Council promulgated interim regulations for the functioning of the Islamic Workers' Councils, but it was not until three and a half years after the triumph of the revolution that a comprehensive labor law was finally drawn up. Some of its contents became known, in advance of publication, in the fall of 1982, and it was seen to be a remarkably illiberal and unimaginative measure. A storm of protest arose in the Islamic Workers' Councils. At a joint session of the Islamic Workers' Councils of Tehran, called on 11 November 1982 to discuss the draft law, a representative of the Ministry of Labor was given a frankly hostile reception. The complaint was made that workers' councils had not been consulted during the drafting of the law, and one of those present went so far as to say that "everyone in this country wishes to exploit us except the Imam" (*Jumhuri-yi Islami,* 11 November 1982/Aban 20, 1361). Four days later, the House of the Worker (Khana-yi Kargar), the central organization of the Islamic Workers' Councils, called on the Ministry of Labor to withdraw the law from public and official consideration (*ibid.,* 15 November 1982/Aban 24, 1361).

Undeterred by these protests, Ahmad Tavakkuli, the Minister of Labor, presented the complete draft, consisting of 113 articles, at a televised press conference on 21 December 1982 (report of Tavakkuli's press conference, together with complete text of the law, in *Jumhuri-yi Islami,* 22 December 1982/Day 1, 1361). The essence of the bill is contained in Chapters 2 (Articles 11-40), dealing with contractual arrangements between employee and employer, and 10 (Articles 90-99), concerning the solution of disputes. The former is probably the most important chapter of the whole bill in that virtually everything affecting the welfare of the worker—wages, hours, vacations, health insurance, retirement, pensions—has been made a matter of contractual agreement between employee and employer. No provision is made for a universally applicable minimum wage (or even for criteria whereby a minimum wage might be determined), a maximum working week, an annual vacation or even a weekly day of rest on Friday, an age of compulsory retirement, or a mandatory pension scheme. Articles 52 and 53, dealing with the employment of minors, do not establish a minimum age of employment or a maximum number of hours that may be worked and restrict themselves to assigning to a minor's guardian the competence to conclude a contract on his behalf, which the minor employee may cancel or renegotiate on attaining maturity, "except for reasons of overriding interest." As for the Islamic Workers' Councils, one of their fourteen functions is specified as "making all due effort to obtain in full the legitimate rights of employees"; however, although they may make suggestions "relating to the advancement of the workplace," they have no right to participate in its administration unless the contract between employee and employer provides for such participation (Articles 66 and 67). If disputes arise between employee and employer, the parties concerned—or their appointed representatives—must attempt to negotiate the matter. If they fail to reach agreement, the dispute is to be referred to an arbitration committee (*hay'at-i hall-i ikhtilaf*) consisting of the local prosecutor or his representative, a representative of the local office of the Ministry of Labor, a worker chosen by the Islamic Workers' Councils and approved by the Ministry of Labor, and an employer chosen by his colleagues and likewise approved by the Ministry of Labor. If the decision of the arbitration committee is unacceptable to one or both of the parties, the dispute must be referred to a competent court for a binding judgment (Articles 90-96).

Protests against the draft multiplied after publication of the full text. The Islamic Workers' Councils, meeting singly and in joint session in Tehran, unanimously denounced it as contrary to Islam, the Constitution of the Islamic Republic, and the legitimate interests of the workers (*Jumhuri-yi Islami*, 28 December 1982/Day 7, 1361). One of the most frequently voiced criticisms was that the draft law was based exclusively on a narrow and abstract reading of *bab al-ijara* (the provisions of Islamic law, elaborated in books of fiqh, concerning rental). All were in agreement that those provisions may legitimately be consulted in drafting the labor law, since the term *ijara* relates to persons as well as real property, "as when a free person rents out his labor making another the owner of his labor in exchange for a fixed wage" (Khomeini 1970:570). However, to consider labor relations only in terms of the categories provided in bab al-ijara is to overlook the actual state of a society in which unjust relations have long prevailed. For example, if the conditions of work are to be made the subject of discretionary agreement between employee and employer, this is obviously to the benefit of the employer, given the advantageous situation he enjoys as a result of widespread unemployment.

The law has also been denounced as unreasonably abstract in that it fails to serve, or be correlated with, one of the social purposes of the revolution: the redistribution of wealth. If that purpose falls short of complete fulfillment, one of the Islamic Worker's Councils has warned, "the door will be opened to counterrevolutionary agitation in the factories" (*Jumhuri-yi Islami,* 26 December 1982/Day 5, 1361).

Early in January 1983, a three-day seminar was held in Tehran to debate the draft labor law, with the participation of representatives of the Islamic Workers' Councils and members of the government. Minister of Labor Tavakkuli attempted to defend the draft, but he was opposed by Minister of Justice Asghari and Chief Justice Ayatullah Musavi Ardabili. The former denounced the draft as shameful in that it provided Iranian workers with fewer rights than comparable legislation in many other countries, and insisted that the law be revised to provide for mandatory unemployment and sickness insurance, a minimum wage, a weekly day of rest, and an annual vacation. Ardabili made a frank admission that none of the main problems confronting Iranian workers–housing, wages, working conditions, health care–had yet been fully resolved. He suggested plausibly that those responsible for drafting the law had no immediate acquaintance with the problems of workers, and called for a rewriting of the law in the light of those problems (*Jumhuri-yi Islami,* 6 January 1983/Day 16, 1361, and 8 January 1983/Day 18, 1361).

After the seminar, the commission formed by the Majlis to revise the draft law announced its intention of touring factories and workplaces throughout the country, and its chairman expressed the opinion that the law must provide for (among other things) a minimum wage, extra pay for overtime, and regular leave (*Jumhuri-yi Islami,* 11 January 1983/Day 21, 1361). This was a further indication of how unlikely it was that the labor law would be ratified without very substantial revision.

A debate of particular interest on the draft labor law has been taking place in the columns of *Jumhuri-yi Islami*, the daily organ of the Islamic Republic Party. A lengthy unsigned article condemning the draft and the way in which it had been prepared appeared on 31 December 1982. The authors of the draft were criticized for basing themselves narrowly on the bab al-ijara and reducing relations between employee and employer to a simple contractual matter. It should be the legal responsibility of the employer, the article stated, to provide his employees with all necessary forms of insurance in exchange for the permission to operate granted him by the Islamic state and for the share of public services—water, energy, transportation, communications, etc.—that he consumes in his enterprise. The Ministry of Labor responded five days later with the argument that "social rights" such as health and unemployment insurance ought not to be enmeshed with labor relations since no connection between the two categories of concern is to be found in the books of fiqh. The ministry's response also implied that the draft labor law had the approval of the Council of Guardians, although it had not yet been formally presented to them, so that those opposing the draft were in effect challenging the authority of Islamic jurisprudence itself (*Jumhuri-yi Islami,* 4 January 1983/Day 14, 1361).

Quite unabashed, the anonymous columnist returned to the attack and raised important points relevant not only to the draft labor law but to the whole task of drawing up an Islamic legal code:

> It is of course true that people have been working on Islamic jurisprudence for thirteen hundred years, and the 'ulama have clarified numerous details . . . . But when we speak of writing laws on the basis of fiqh, it is not a question simply of transcribing or translating books of fiqh. Naturally there are matters in fiqh which must be incorporated in the law, but quite apart from this those who write our laws must pay attention to those areas of concern which the shari'a has left to the discretion of the Islamic state. It is important that this be understood if we are to clarify what is meant by the expression "on the basis of fiqh." There are many laws we shall soon have to draft. In order to be successful in drawing them up, we must be aware that basing the law on fiqh does not mean translating or transcribing books of fiqh. In addition to according official status to the shari'a (a principle enshrined already in the Council of Guardians), we must pay attention to areas of concern where the Islamic state is empowered to decide. This is, in fact, the fundamental task facing those who are to draft our laws (*Jumhuri-yi Islami,* 5 January 1983/Day 15, 1361).

It is apparent from this exchange that the controversy over the draft labor law has involved two contradictory understandings of what is meant by the enactment of Islamic law. One understanding sees fiqh, in its traditional content and arrangement, as all-inclusive, so that the task before the Islamic state is simply the codification of its provisions, in abstract or even mechanical fashion, without detailed crossreference to the observable state of society. The other regards the received body of fiqhi provisions as constituting a necessary framework or point of departure; the established categories of concern of fiqh are, however, subject to revision, and its content may legitimately be expanded or supplemented in accordance with the public welfare as perceived by the Islamic state.* The difference between the static and the activist views of the law is obviously of great importance, both intrinsically and for the future of the Islamic order in Iran.

CONCLUSION

The process of drawing up and enacting social legislation, as measured by the two examples of land and labor, has been slow and hitherto inconclusive. Part of the explanation lies no doubt in the contingencies of the revolutionary situation. It was necessary first to draw up and ratify a constitution and then to construct a new set of political institutions on its basis before the task of drafting legislation could effectively proceed. Moreover, when the new institutions—the presidency, the Majlis, the Council of Guardians—were in place, they did not always function harmoniously. In particular, the deadlock between Bani Sadr and the majority in the Majlis (broken by the dismissal of the former in June 1981) caused a prolonged near-paralysis of both the executive and legislative branches. Orderly progress toward the reshaping of Iranian society has been hindered also by the twin depredations of the Iraqi invasion and the terroristic rebellion of the mujahidin. Possibly most damaging of all, however, has been the loss of leaders who possessed great intellectual qualities as well as moral and political authority—men such as Mutahhari, Talaqani, and Bihishti, whose continued presence on the scene might have resulted in a swifter and more radical solution of many problems. The absence of Bihishti, who headed the commission charged with revision of the whole legal system, has been felt with particular acuteness, and it is

*Chief Justice Ardabili seems to hold to this second view. He told me in an interview in Tehran on 5 September 1982 that with respect to laws touching on industry and agriculture, "Islam has established certain general principles; in implementing them, existing social realities must be taken into consideration. Laws are to be drawn up by jurists [*huquqdanan*] in accordance with the present state of thought and the aims that have been determined for those laws, and then forwarded to the *maraji‘* [highest authorities in fiqh] for revision and approval."

no accident that the demand is frequently made for legislation to be based on his views. (See, for example, the report on a meeting of the Islamic Workers' Councils of Tehran in *Jumhuri-yi Islami,* 11 November 1982/Aban 20, 1361. For a convenient summary of Bihishti's views on economic matters, see "Mas'ala-yi Malikiyat" [The question of ownership] in Bihishti 1981:53-134.)

At the same time, it cannot be denied that the Iranian experience has been beset by problems of a more fundamental nature. The ideological theme of social justice was articulated powerfully and convincingly enough to act as an important incitement to revolution, and it has provided a general direction to the social policies of the Islamic Republic. But despite the labors of various theoreticians, it has not been embedded in specific economic concepts and plans firmly enough to suggest a unanimously acceptable legislative program. It may well be in the nature of ideology to be more effective as moral impetus than as legislative instrument, and in any event it is fiqh rather than ideology that is destined to serve as the source of law in the Islamic context. However, not only social justice, but also the enactment of Islamic law has meant different things to different people. For some, proposals to redistribute privately owned land have been too radical; for others, the draft labor law has been too conservative. There are clear differences of opinion within the cabinet, within the Majlis, and within the Islamic Republic Party.* There are also differences among the 'ulama, which may be explained in part by social orientation and in part by the traditional autonomy of the *mujtahid* (scholar qualified to engage in original reasoning) in matters of legal judgment. But whatever particular explanation be adduced for each divergent opinion, the fact of divergence seems to indicate that fiqh, in its present state of elaboration, does not yield a set of ready-made, universally agreeable, and easily applicable laws for regulating the problems of land and labor.

None of this should be taken to mean that the endeavor of the Islamic Republic to recast the laws of Iran in an Islamic mold is ill-considered or destined to fail. It should be realized that the slowness

*Attempts are sometimes made in the foreign press to discern the existence of two hostile factions within the Islamic Republic Party, known as the Maktabis and the Hujjatis, attributing radical views to the former and conservative views to the latter (see, for example, Rouleau 1983). Such attempts are misleading, partly because there is no substantial Hujjati element in the party, and partly because differences of view on various issues result more from personal than collective decision.

and deliberation with which the process is moving forward has important compensatory aspects. It both reflects and reinforces the consultative nature of the new order in Iran, something obstinately overlooked by foreign analysts whose attention is often myopically fixed on the preeminence of Imam Khomeini in the republic. Hypothetically it would have been possible for the Imam and his close associates to impose their own opinions and preferences in all matters, somewhat in the manner of the "Islamization" programs that have become fashionable in certain countries. Instead a process of debate and consultation, both formal and informal, has been allowed, with the likelihood that the resulting statutes will have greater social relevance and acceptability than a set of measures dictated *ex auctoritate*.

Furthermore, it should be pointed out that a certain imbalance is discernible in the historical evolution of fiqh. Some areas of concern—the details of ritual worship, family affairs, penal provisions—have received massive attention, while others remain comparatively underdeveloped.* Social and economic problems, particularly in the contemporary forms they have assumed, certainly comprise one such neglected area, and it stands to reason that to repair the neglect is a task that cannot be swiftly accomplished in instant unanimity. Further, it is a task that cannot be fulfilled in a purely abstract and theoretical manner; it must necessarily be joined to the day-to-day governance of society and the state, ensuring an interplay of precedent and innovation, of general precept and specific implementation. After all, a roughly comparable process accompanied the crystallization of the traditional fiqh in its various schools. If the Islamic Republic of Iran ultimately succeeds in accomplishing a revision and extension of fiqh commensurate to the needs of contemporary Muslim society, its achievement will indeed be as great as that of the classical jurists. There can be little doubt concerning the depth of the aspiration to attain such a result, and the resources available for the task, in the wake of the Islamic Revolution, are considerable.

*It is symptomatic of this imbalance that it has been possible to draft laws of a strictly judicial nature with greater speed and confidence than those touching on social matters. By September 1982, roughly 2,480 judicial laws—civil and penal—had been drafted (author's interview with Ayatullah Ardabili; Tehran, 5 September 1982).

Postscript

Since the completion of this chapter a number of developments have occurred that may usefully be summarized as follows:

The Reconstruction Jihad

On 28 November 1983 a bill was passed establishing the Ministry of the Reconstruction Jihad, thereby integrating into the governmental structure one of the most effective and important organs to have emerged from the revolution. The tendency to bring all such organs under the direct control of the state has been criticized by Hujjat al-Islam Karrubi, head of the Martyrs' Foundation, as liable to infect them with all the ills of bureaucracy (see his remarks in *Ittila'at,* 21 February 1984/Bahman 1, 1362).

Agrarian Reform

The law passed by the Majlis on 28 December 1982 has been formally rejected by the Council of Guardians as incompatible with Islamic law. Speaking on behalf of the Council, Ayatullah Mahdavi Kani proclaimed the imposition of limits on legitimately acquired da'ir land to be improper. A committee of the Majlis is now engaged in drafting a new law.

Labor Relations

Ahmad Tavakkuli resigned as Minister of Labor in the summer of 1983, largely because of the tempestuously hostile reception given to the draft labor bill published at the end of 1982. A new draft has now been prepared in which important aspects of labor welfare have been made a matter for government regulation rather than contractual agreement between employee and employer. Minimum wages, maximum working hours, fixed annual leaves, pensions, overtime, and health insurance—matters which were completely ignored in the first draft—are now specified in some detail. According to Muhammad Salamati, parliamentary assistant to the Minister of Labor, the authors of the new draft recognize that fiqh provides no basis of precedent for such specification. They have argued instead that the Islamic state is free to impose conditions on the use of public resources such as water, fuel, electricity, roads, and foreign exchange; there is no right of unfettered access to those resources, especially for large-scale users such as industrialists, who consume a far greater share of public resources than ordinary individuals. The Islamic state therefore imposes on these large-scale consumers of public resources the condition that they grant to the workers they employ all the rights and benefits set out in the draft labor law. Each employer is to sign a contract with the state recognizing this obligation before he will be allowed access to the public resources essential to him for his business. If he violates his contract, he will be subject to a series of sanctions culminating in the sequestration of his enterprise by a revolutionary court.

Like its predecessor, the new draft also devotes some attention to the Islamic Workers' Councils. Here there is little improvement to be noted; the councils are to have primarily "ideological, cultural and political functions" and—according to Salamati—to fill the gap left by the nonexistence of labor unions, with which Iranian workers allegedly became disenchanted in the time of the Shah. It is clearly not intended that the Islamic Workers' Councils should represent the material interests of their members or have a say in the administration of the workplace. (See interview with Salamati in *Kayhan*, 17 January 1984/Day 27, 1362.)

The new draft was discussed in a seminar at the House of the Worker in Tehran attended by some five hundred people from the Islamic Workers' Councils of the capital. At a press conference on 24 February 1984, the summary of their deliberations was presented by Husayn Kamali, a member of the Majlis. In general, it was apparent that the new draft had been far better received than its predecessor, although the vague and awkward wording of some of its provisions was criticized and thirty-two specific suggestions for change and improvement were made. Moreover, the complaint was again made that the workers had not been adequately consulted in the preparation of the draft and that enough time had not been given them for reviewing its provisions. Strong exception was also taken to the very limited role given to the Islamic Workers' Councils, and it was even said that "labor unions under the Shah had more power than what is now to be assigned to the Islamic Workers' Councils." The demand was made for elected councils that would be authorized to engage in collective bargaining and to collect funds for use on behalf of their members (see *Jumhuri-yi Islami,* 25 February 1984/Isfand 6, 1362).

REFERENCES

Akhavi, Shahrough. 1980. *Religion and Politics in Contemporary Iran.* New York: State University of New York Press.

Algar, Hamid. 1969. *Religion and State in Iran, 1785-1906: The Role of the 'Ulama in the Qajar Period.* Berkeley and Los Angeles: University of California Press.

__________. 1972. "The Oppositional Role of the 'Ulama in Twentieth Century Iran." In *Scholars, Saints and Sufis,* ed. N. R. Keddie. Berkeley and Los Angeles: University of California Press.

__________. Forthcoming. "Imam Khomeini, 1902-1962: The Prerevolutionary Years." In *Islamic Political Movements,* ed. Ira Lapidus and Edmund Burke.

__________, trans. 1980. *Constitution of the Islamic Republic of Iran.* Berkeley: Mizan Press.

__________, trans. 1981. *Islam and Revolution.* Berkeley: Mizan Press.

'Ali b. Abi Talib. 1967 (1397). *Nahj al-Balagha,* ed. Subhi as-Salih. Beirut.

Anon. 1979 (1358 Sh.). *Vilayat-i Faqih ya ba Imamat Rasandan-i Mustaz'afin.* Tehran.

Anon. 1981 (1360 Sh.). *Nigarishi bar Layiha-yi Vaguzari va Ihya-yi Zamin.* Berkeley.

Anon. 1982 (1361 Sh.). *Dihqanan va Inqilab.* Tehran.

Bani Sadr, Abu 'l-Hasan. 1977. *Iqtisad-i Tauhidi.* Paris.

Bazargan, Mehdi. 1965 (1344 Sh.). *Kar dar Islam.* Tehran.

__________. 1968 (1347 Sh.). *Bi'sat va Idi'uluji.* Tabriz.

Bihishti, Ayatullah Muhammad Husayn. 1981 (1360 Sh.). *Se maqala.* Tehran.

__________. 1982 (1361 Sh.). *U ba tanha'i yek ummat bud.* Posthumously published collection of Bihishti's speeches and addresses. Tehran.

Browne, E. G. 1928. *A Literary History of Persia,* vol. 4. Cambridge: Cambridge University Press.

Chelkowski, Peter J., ed. 1979. *Ta'ziyeh: Ritual and Drama in Iran.* New York: New York University Press.

Faghfoory, Mohammad Hassan. 1978. "The Role of the Ulama in Twentieth Century Iran with Particular Reference to Ayatullah Haj Sayyid Abdul-Qasim Kashani." Ph.D. dissertation, University of Wisconsin.

Farsi, Jalal al-Din. 1977 (2537). *Inqilab-i Takamuli-yi Islam.* Tehran.

Fida'iyan-i Islam. 1950 (1329 Sh.). *I'lamiya-yi Fida'iyan-i Islam ya Rahnuma-yi Haqa'iq*. Tehran.

Ghafuri, 'Ali Gulzada. 1970 (1349 Sh.). *Nizamat-i Ijtima'i-yi Islam*. Tehran.

__________. *Khutut-i Asli dar Nizam-i Iqtisadi-yi Islam*. Tehran.

al-Gulpayagani, Lutfullah as-Safi. *Muntakhab al-Athar fi 'l-Imam ath-Thani-'ashar*. Qum.

Haqqju, 'A. 1979 (1357 Sh.). *Tahlili bar Sazman-i Mujahidin-i Khalq-i Iran*. Tehran.

Hooglund, Mary. 1980. "One Village in the Revolution." *MERIP Reports*, no. 87 (May).

Islamic Republic Party (IRP). 1979 (1357 Sh.). *Tarh-i Asasnama va Maramnama-yi Hizb-i Jumhuri-yi Islami*. Tehran.

Jihad. (Tehran). Organ of the Reconstruction Jihad. Various issues.

Jumhuri-yi Islami (Tehran). Daily organ of the Islamic Republic Party. Various issues.

Kamali, 'Ali. 1979 (1358 Sh.). *Inqilab*. Tehran.

Kashifi, Mulla Husayn. 1955 (1334 Sh.). *Rauzat ash-Shuhada*. Tehran.

Kasravi, Ahmad. 1961 (1340 Sh.). *Tarikh-i Mashruta-yi Iran*, 5th ed. Tehran.

Khomeini, Imam Ayatullah Ruhullah. 1943. *Kashf al-Asrar*. English translation in Algar, trans. 1981.

__________. 1970 (1390). *Tahrir al Wasila*, vol. 1. Najaf.

__________. 1971 (1391). *Hukumat-i Islami*, 3d ed. Najaf.

__________. 1978 (1398). *Sukhanrani-yi Imam Khomeini*. Tehran.

__________. 1979 (1358 Sh.). *Majmu'a-yi Kamil-i Payamha-yi Imam Khomeini*, ed. Sayyid 'Abd ar-Rasul Hijazi. Tehran.

__________. *Khomeini va Junbish*.

Musavi, Muhammad Kazim, trans. 1971 (1350 Sh.). *Iqtisad-i Ma*, by Baqir as-Sadr. Tehran.

Mutahhari, Murtaza. *'Adl-i Ilahi*. Qum.

__________. *Muqaddima'i bar Jahanbini-yi Islam*. Qum.

Paydar, Habibullah (pseudonym for Payman). 1977 (2536). *Malikiyat, Kar va Sarmaya az Didgah-i Islam*. Tehran.

Qutb, Sayyid. 1949. *al-'Adalat al-Ijtima'iyya fi 'l-Islam*. Cairo.

Rahnavard, Zahra. *Mauzi'giri-yi Tabaqat-i Ijtima'i dar Qur'an*. Tehran.

Rouleau, Eric. 1983. "De la terreur à Thermidor." *Le Monde*, 6-7 February.

Sachedina, Abdulaziz Abdulhussein. 1981. *Islamic Messianism*. New York: State University of New York Press.

as-Sadr, Muhammad Baqir. 1972 (1398). *Iqtisaduna*, new ed. Beirut.

Safi, Fakr ad-Din 'Ali. 1957 (1336 Sh.). *Lata'if at-Tava'if*, ed. Ahmad Gulchin-i Ma'ani. Tehran.

Sazman-i Mujahidin-i Inqilab-i Islami. 1979 (1358 Sh.). *Chand Musahaba-yi Matbu'ati ba Sazman-i Mujahidin-i Inqilab-i Islami.* Tehran.

Sepsis, A. 1844. "Quelques mots sur l'état religieux actuel de la Perse." *Revue de l'Orient* 3.

Shari'ati, 'Ali. 1979. *On the Sociology of Islam*, trans. Hamid Algar. Berkeley: Mizan Press.

__________. *Az Hijrat ta Vafat.* Tehran.

__________. *Husayn, Varis-i Adam.* Tehran.

__________. *Intizar, Mazhab-i I'tiraz.* Tehran.

__________. *Islamshinasi.* Tehran.

__________. *Mazhab 'alayhi mazhab.* Tehran.

at-Tabataba'i, Muhammad Husayn. 1973 (1393). *al-Mizan fi Tafsir al-Qur'an*, 2nd ed. Beirut.

Talaqani, Mahmud. 1965 (1344 Sh.). *Kar va Malikiyat dar Islam.* Tehran. Translation of extracts from this work in *Society and Economics in Islam*, trans. R. Campbell, pp. 24-72. Berkeley: Mizan Press.

Tavassuli, Ghulam 'Abbas. 1979. "A Biographical Sketch." In Sharia'ti 1979.

Chapter 3

SYRIA UNDER THE BA'TH: SOCIAL IDEOLOGY, POLICY, AND PRACTICE

Raymond A. Hinnebusch

The roots and consequences of the nationalist and populist "ideological revolution" which swept the Arab world in the 1950s and 1960s remain matters of considerable controversy. Some have argued that this ideology, never much more than a "cover" for the power hunger of handfuls of "military desperados," had the shallowest of social roots, or that it was "expressive" rather than "programmatic" and neither intended nor able to serve as an instrument of social transformation (Moore 1974). For others, the 1967 defeat by Israel, the de-Nasserization of Egypt, the rise of conservative petropower, and the resurgence of political Islam made it self-evident that the "Arab revolution" had failed (see Ajami 1981: esp. 24-50).

Close analysis shows such claims to be too sweeping, partial, and imprecise to capture more than one side of the very complex relation between ideology and practice in the "progressive" Arab states. The establishment of these regimes did frequently follow from a military coup, but the struggles at the top did not take place in a social vacuum; they rose out of societal crises, ideological ferment, and the emergence and politicization of new social forces.* The new leaders did not forge dynamic revolutionary states, but they did establish distinctive new authoritarian military-party regimes which have proven remarkably stable and adaptable in the face of exceptional environmental challenges. They did not carry out radical social transformations, but they did reduce social inequality, develop statist economic institutions, and establish relatively durable populist public policies. Thus the ideological movements did leave a

*The social background of these movements was demonstrated in a number of definitive works during the 1960s, including Binder (1964) and Halpern (1963).

recognizable, if distorted and often unintended imprint on their societies; their record is a complex mixture of success and failure. An adequate understanding of this complex relation between ideology and practice requires a careful specification of the social origins of ideology, of the outcome of efforts to put it into practice, and of the multiple variables which account for the typically mixed results. This chapter will attempt to do this in an examination of the relation between Ba'thist ideology and society in Syria.

IDEOLOGICAL "MOVEMENT REGIMES" AND THE BA'TH CASE: SOME CONCEPTS

There is no lack of literature on the linkages between ideological "movement regimes" and their societies.* It is widely agreed that the rise of a transforming ideology is typically a function of a societal crisis, without which radical ideologies remain confined to the political periphery. It is also accepted that an ideology must be understood as an expression of the particular aspirations, grievances, and social position of the social forces which propose and embrace it. A radical ideology typically expresses the interests of rising social forces challenging a dominant order; its function is to offer a critique of a flawed status quo and blueprints for change with which to mobilize a movement against incumbent elites.† The Ba'th, it will be argued, is a classical case of a lower-middle-class movement, born of the crisis of decolonization, rebelling against a traditional order.

Once a movement regime takes power, ideology becomes a legitimizing instrument for the regime, frequently a weapon in intra-elite conflicts, and sometimes a program of action. For the Ba'th, in the years after the power seizure, it served all these purposes. Whether ideology becomes a program effectively implemented depends on many factors. The ideology must not be purely expressive; it must offer a plausible analysis of the status quo and a blueprint for change. The revolutionary leadership must be strongly committed to it, must be able to forge instruments of implementation—notably a revolutionary party and a rationalized bureaucracy—and must win sufficient legitimacy and public compliance to support radical

*An ideological movement regime is taken here to mean a regime which rose out of a radical ideological movement.

†These propositions on the origins and functions of ideology are largely taken from the Marxist and Weberian traditions.

change.* In the case of the Ba'th a reasonably programmatic ideology emerged, but elite commitment to it proved lukewarm; instruments of change were created but were flawed, and legitimacy remained precarious. The environment in which a revolution must operate is bound to offer resistance to radical change. The struggle against enemies can be a powerful generator of revolutionary solidarity, but the power balance must not be too unfavorable or society too intractable. The Ba'th clearly never enjoyed a favorable environment.

The outcome of an effort to reshape society according to an ideological design may fail completely, bringing on counterrevolution. On the other hand, ideology may be successfully "routinized" in dynamic new institutions—typically a single-party state and a socialist or populist economy—constituting a more modernized and egalitarian social order. But perhaps most often the outcome is likely to fall somewhere between these poles. In one typical outcome, ideology exhausts itself without being sufficiently routinized in a new order, but not before a new elite and a new state are entrenched or before power and wealth are redistributed. In this case ideology is soon ritualized in a new conservatism, the state in time acquires patrimonial qualities, and resurgent market forces start to colonize the regime, giving birth to new inequalities.† Apter's (1965) model of the emergence of a "neo-mercantilist" regime from an exhausted "mobilization system" captures this outcome very well. The Syrian outcome seems to approximate it.

In the following section the Ba'th ideological tradition and the conditions which gave rise to and shaped it are examined; then the Ba'th's effort to translate ideology into practice is traced; finally the outcome of these efforts, as they have affected two key social sectors, peasants and workers, is analyzed.

SOCIAL ROOTS AND IMPLICATIONS OF BA'TH IDELOGY

THE FIRST GENERATION: AFLAQ AND THE PARTY CONSTITUTION

The Ba'th rose out of the twin national and social crises brought on by an uneven process of modernization and decolonization in

*The best analyses of efforts to build new political orders are probably found in Samuel P. Huntington's work (1968 and 1970).

†Huntington (1970) conceptualized the successfully institutionalized revolutionary party-state. The notion of routinization is of course Weber's.

postwar Syria. It was, on the one hand, a product of the struggle for independence and a reaction against the post-independence fragmentation and Western domination of the Arab world and the creation of Israel. It also expressed a revolt against traditional social and political structures inside Syria: the inegalitarian concentration of wealth, particularly land, in the hands of a small upper class; a backward economy unable to absorb emerging modern social forces and dependent on the West; and a weak state dominated by a traditional oligarchy. The Ba'th world view was the product of a stratum of middle-class intellectuals who, sensitive to the weakness of their country in the face of imperialism and frustrated by the little outlet allowed to their ambitions and aspirations by the traditional order, challenged the *ancien régime*; they did so in the name of a national renaissance *(Ba'th)*, social transformation, and political unification of the Arab world. Michel Aflaq, the philosopher-founder of the Ba'th party, crystallized the sentiments of this generation of middle class nationalists in an ideological world view which, more comprehensive and compelling than its competitors, would leave a powerful mark on the political attitudes of his followers and indeed on the whole Arab East.

Aflaq's thought centered around the struggle to forge a secular Arab national community which would embrace all Arabs regardless of sectarian, local, or social differences.* His self-assumed mission was to awaken in the Arabs national consciousness, self-respect, and identity, to effect an essentially attitudinal regeneration through education and propaganda. The concrete arrangements of social power in the projected new Arab community were of secondary concern to him, and his poetic, romantic method, aimed at inspiration, was incompatible with close social analysis. Hence Aflaq's thought contains only the vaguest of social blueprints. Nevertheless, his view of community did have social implications and, if it was to be realized, requisites which imparted a particular bias to Ba'th social doctrine.

There is an unmistakable collectivist strain in Aflaq's thought. In his exaltation of the nation and of public service over "petty material" and private interests; in his insistence that the realization of the individual must come through participation in the community,

*This analysis of Aflaq's thought rests on both primary and secondary sources, including the following: The primary text is Aflaq (1959); Khalidi (1966); Kannan (1960); Torrey (1969); Abu Jaber (1966:97-138); S. al-Jundi (1969); Allush (1962); Jabbūr (n.d.); Binder (1964); and Kerr (1963).

not against it—indeed through harmonization with the general will; and in his demand that all divisions in the community be submerged in a common brotherhood of "love," Aflaq was perhaps essentially reacting against a fragmented society; but he also contributed to a political tradition unfriendly to pluralism. His belief in the need for a socialist economic order in which the urge to community service replaced the selfish search for private gain as the motive force of the economy manifests a strong utopian suspicion of capitalism.

Aflaq's views were also strongly populist. The social injustice and exploitation in Arab society were, he believed, principal aspects of a decadence which had to be overcome. No authentic community could be created between exploiter and exploited, nor could the citizenry be nationally mobilized, until the oppressed masses were given a stake in the nation. The realization of national community required a "socialist" socioeconomic order able to ensure justice, equality, and a life of dignity free of deprivation for all citizens. Indeed the very success of the Ba'th movement depended on a populist alliance between nationalists and the "working masses," whom Aflaq saw as least corrupted by the selfish interests and foreign influence which stood in the way of national regeneration.

Aflaq was careful to distinguish his nativist "Arab socialism" from Marxist communism, however. Influenced by Western perceptions of Stalinism and repulsed by the sectarian composition, deference to Soviet interests, and disloyalty to Arabism of the Arab Communist parties—as well as his own party's rivalry with them for the loyalties of the lower classes—Aflaq strongly rejected communism. Its internationalism, he argued, was incompatible with Arabism; its restrictions on individual liberty were oppressive and excessive; its materialistic philosophy was antithetical to the spiritual community he wished to regenerate. Moreover, Aflaq believed that freedom and initiative required the preservation of small private property and the fusion of socialism with parliamentary democracy. And while he sought a populist political alliance against imperialism and exploitation, he rejected violent class struggle as antithetical to national solidarity; the principal political cleavage, in his view, was between nationalists and those who served the foreigner, not between classes. While Aflaq may have moved left over time, as Jabbūr (n.d.: 424) argues—i.e., from fearing that social struggle could split the nation to the belief that winning the masses for the nation required such struggle—he never accepted revolutionary violence or class hatred as a method or even showed much practical interest in mass social agitation. On the whole, Aflaq's world view can best be characterized as an egalitarian Jacobin variant of nationalism. His major ideological contribution was to fuse a progressive social content to Arab nationalism.

This social content of Ba'thism was given a much more explicit and programmatic form in the party constitution which emerged from the Ba'th's 1947 Founding Congress. In spite of the party's preoccupation with nationalist objectives and the presence in the party at that time of liberals and traditional Islamic elements suspicious of socialism, the congress produced a document which was remarkably radical for its time. To be sure, the community was defined in national, not class terms, and only those collaborating with imperialism were considered to be outside the pale. Western-style parliamentary democracy was taken as the most suitable political system. However, Syria's highly unequal distribution of wealth was denounced as unjust, and the great class gaps resulting from it had, it was argued, to be overcome. "Socialism," the party declared, was the social order best able to accomplish this and most appropriate to the creation of a national community. Socialism meant several things. A major role was prescribed for the state in society. It must plan development and pursue industrialization. A public sector would control public utilities, extensive natural resources, big industry, and transport; a national bank would dispense credit and abolish usury; and trade would be state-regulated in the interests of the nation and social equity. Private property and inheritance were guaranteed, but the state would ensure that private interests were pursued within the national interest and that property was not used for exploitation. The state would fix a fair wage, ensure work for all, and promulgate a labor code defining working conditions. Labor unions would be established to protect workers, workers would share in the management and profits of firms, and labor disputes would be settled by tribunals in which the state would arbitrate between representatives of employers and workers. The state would provide essential social services for all, including free medical treatment, social security, and old-age support. Finally, in what was for an agrarian society undoubtedly the most radical provision of the program, the Ba'th called for a land reform which would limit agrarian property to a size "in proportion to the means of the proprietor to exploit . . . without exploitation of the efforts of others" (Arab Ba'th Socialist Party 1962:238; for an account of the congress see as-Sayyid 1973:41-55).

This program was, to say the least, very ambitious. Yet no strategy or method was laid down for achieving it; indeed it appears to contain contradictions between means and goals. Allush (1962: 163) is probably correct in viewing the party's adoption of a liberal political regime as incompatible with the realization of such a radical social transformation or the operation of a state-dominated economy. In Jabbūr's (n.d.: 428) view, nationalism was the governing preoccupation of the early Ba'th, but to give the national design a content which seemed to include the best from both East and West—socialism and liberal political freedoms respectively—the party simply juxtaposed without synthesizing these various ideals. In this sense, Ba'th ideology was initially idealistic, contenting itself with the elucidation of an ideal social order without much concern for the realistic mechanics of implementation.

Nevertheless, three main themes of great potential practical import stand out clearly in early Ba'th social thought. First, there was a strong etatist disposition toward state-directed development and regulation of social and economic life. Second, there was a strong tendency toward an egalitarian redistribution of wealth. Third, there was a continued legitimation of small- and medium-sized private property, limiting the first two orientations. These orientations would leave a powerful mark on the attitudes of a generation of politically active Syrians.

This ideological thrust, far from being mere disembodied or imported theorizing, was an outgrowth of or response to concrete Syrian conditions and authentically reflected the ideals and interests of strategic segments of Syrian society. Whatever its shortcomings, it represented a plausible response to Syria's post-independence national and social crisis. In a society dominated by a traditional landed-commercial elite dependent on the West and with the barest interest in fundamental social change, it was perfectly convincing to argue that state leadership was required to bring about economic development free of foreign domination and to effect a more equitable distribution of wealth—changes without which there could be no real national independence and no national mobilization of the masses. Moreover, the Ba'th formula was an authentic reflection of the social interests of the petit bourgeois intellectuals who formulated it and compatible with those of the minority communities, the peasantry, and the working class from which some of them came and to whom they were addressing their appeal. In a society with limited opportunities for those who have modern educations but lack sizable landed or commercial property, the salaried middle class is likely to view a large role for the state as modernizing entrepreneur and employer and measures against large concentrations of wealth as essential to open up opportunities for itself. The appeal of land reform to a land-hungry peasantry and labor law and social security to workers is obvious. For Syria's minority groups, often deprived rurals traditionally considered less than equal by the Sunni urban establishment, a populist and secular nationalism which would incorporate them into the political community on an equal basis and benefit them economically was bound to have a powerful appeal. But both the petite bourgeoisie and the peasantry either have or aspire to own small private property. Hence they have no interest in the total abolition of private property advocated by communism, and it is scarcely surprising that Ba'thism stops well short of this. Finally, it is clear that although the Ba'th social program drew on Western political thought, its social prescriptions were far from alien to aspects of indigenous tradition. Islam's recognition of private property (but as a trust from the community), its egalitarian hostility to great wealth or corporate classes, and its stress on the role of the state in ensuring the welfare of the *umma* (community) were supportive elements in the formulation of and public receptivity to Ba'thism which have been obscured by the overt conflict between Ba'th secularism and political Islam.

Precisely because of its firm grounding in Syrian realities, the Ba'th credo proved a potent instrument of political mobilization. The Ba'th built a significant middle class-peasant political base which, although drawn disproportionately from people of rural and minority backgrounds, cut across urban-rural and sectarian lines as no other party did. It also recruited a major following among the significant rural, minority, and petit bourgeois elements of the officer corps. With fair amounts of brains, numbers, and guns at its disposal, the Ba'th rapidly emerged as a major contender in the Syrian political arena.*

THE SECOND GENERATION: IDEOLOGICAL RADICALIZATION

Subsequent to the Ba'th seizure of power in 1963, party doctrine underwent a significant radicalization in which the older

*For analyses of the social crises and circumstances which produced Ba'thism, see the following: Torrey (1969 and 1964); Abu Jaber (1966); S. al-Jundi (1969);

concerns with Arab nationalism though not abandoned were joined to concepts drawn from Marxism-Leninism. Several dovetailing developments account for this alteration. At the deepest level, the ideological mutation was set off by the rise to power inside the party of more youthful leaders from lower social strata than the party founders—chiefly junior officers and intellectuals of rural origin, many from peasant families. Their modest origins and closeness to peasant grievances made them much more antagonistic to the traditional urban establishment and more receptive to a radical revolution against it than the urban middle-class leaders. Shifts in global forces affected attitudes too: many of the new leaders had been politically socialized in the late 1950s, when Marxism-Leninism was acquiring a powerful new appeal to nationalists. The rise of national communism and non-Soviet Marxism, effacing the perceived contradiction between nationalism and Marxism; the increasing willingness of the Soviets to support "national roads to socialism"; the fall of Stalinism and the rising world prestige of the Soviet model—all contributed to a new receptivity to Marxism-Leninism in Ba'th ranks. The receptivity of younger Ba'thists to Marxism was also much facilitated by the apparent failure of the classical Arab unity preached by Aflaq after the collapse of the United Arab Republic (UAR) and the need for an ideological formulation less centered on unionism.

Once the party seized power, further impetus was given to ideological revisionism in its ranks. A ruling party intent on carrying out a revolution had to more clearly specify its goals and methods. In particular, there was a need to resolve the contradiction between the party's radical social goals and its commitment to constitutionalism. Younger radical Ba'thists had already discarded liberalism in principle. Once in power, they were determined to stay there and impose their revolution from above; in the face of strong resistance only an authoritarian model would serve their needs. Moreover, as their conflict with Nasser and his supporters widened, they needed a program distinguishable from and more "radical" and "scientific" than Nasserism which could justify their rejection of union on his terms—in other words, a doctrine of "revolution in one country." A radical redefinition of Ba'thism would represent a viable alternative to Nasserism, local communism, and even "Aflaqiyya" which the

as-Sayyid (1973); Salamah (1969); al-Qiyad al-Qaumiyya (1972); Dauk, ed. (1964-72); Allush (1962); Van Dusen (1975); Petran (1972:61-105); Warriner (1948); Hilan (1969:161-250); Lerner (1958:264-302); and Seale (1965).

new leaders hoped would justify their claims of power against these other contenders. Finally, embodying a corpus of experience in mass organization and statist development, Marxism-Leninism seemed an ideal source of guidance for the revolutionary project they wished to carry out. (For analyses of ideological change inside the Ba'th, see Rodinson [1968:155-58, 167-71]; Lencowski [1966]; and Rabinovich [1972].)

The social dimension of the doctrinal changes, expressed in two major Ba'th documents, the ideological report of the Sixth National Congress, *Some Theoretical Points of Departure* (Arab Ba'th Socialist Party 1973), and the Phased Program issued in July 1965 (Arab Ba'th Socialist Party 1965), took three major directions. First, while Arab unity was retained as a goal in the new creed, it was no longer viewed (as Aflaq is held to have done) as a nearly automatic solution to the Arabs' problems unless it emerged from a popular revolution and had a revolutionary socialist content. In effect, the Ba'th regime would concentrate first on the revolutionary transformation of Syria.

Second, liberal parliamentarianism was rejected as the proper political system in the projected new Ba'th order. Liberal regimes in countries like Syria were held to reflect the status quo distribution of social power and the feudal, tribal, and communal struggle while keeping the masses backward and passive; they were hence an unfit instrument for carrying out radical change. Instead the party now considered the ideal political model to be a Leninist-style "popular democracy" with a single "vanguard" party run on democratic-centralist lines and linked to mass popular organizations. The single party in this system would express the "general will" and act as the motor of change in its name; mass organizations and popular councils would keep the party in touch with mass sentiment, provide a means for the masses to control the bureaucratic apparatus without which the socialist experiment would degenerate into mere "state capitalism" and the rule of a new class, and allow the party to mobilize the masses against the "reactionary classes." These organizations would defend the particular interests of their members, but (unlike in liberal democracies) would do so in harmony with, not against, the higher interest of the whole community. This system would in principle provide the necessary balance of strong central leadership to direct radical change and mass participation to carry it out. It was held to be democratic because the single party represented and was supported by the masses and because it enjoyed internal democracy.

Third, the documents presented an analysis of the social situation in the Arab world and delineated a course of revolutionary change meant to transform it. The conception of social change held by the older Ba'thist leaders was analyzed and criticized. They were accused of having allowed their dispute with local communism and their petit bourgeois background to give an unscientific character to their socialism: their denial of the need for class struggle to reach socialism was utopian; their acceptance of an inherent right to private property was a petit bourgeois bias which ignored the principle that labor is the sole source of value and hence private ownership of the means of production, however constrained, necessarily exploitative. In consequence, the party had diluted its mass base with petit bourgeois and even bourgeois elements and had attempted to seek its goals through parliamentary reform. Then an analysis of the current socioeconomic situation in Syria was presented, the chief conclusion of which was that the bourgeoisie was no longer capable of economic leadership or capitalism of developing Syria. In developing countries, it was argued, capitalisms are inevitably foreign-dependent "comprador" enterprises. What capital they do not channel abroad is squandered on luxury consumption or invested in speculative real estate, commercial and usurious ventures, or—at best—light consumption industries. They cannot mobilize and invest capital in authentic productive development or break their links with neo-imperialism.

Given this analysis, the new credo held that the Ba'th must abandon its earlier idealistic social reformism for a rigorous scientific-socialist course. The party's social base must be rooted in the workers, peasants, revolutionary intellectuals, and soldiers, and although small tradesmen would be kept within the fold, bourgeois elements had to be excluded. The party would carry out a "socialist transformation," nationalizing the major sectors of the economy—industry, transport, finance, foreign trade—and replace private entrepreneurship with state planning and public investment as the motor of development. Such public control of the economy, it was argued, would snap ties of economic interest and dependency with the West which diluted nationalist commitments, and would permit the economic surplus to be invested in development rather than squandered, eliminate the exploitation of labor for the benefit of private owners, allow rewards to be linked to productivity, permit a more equitable distribution of resources, and replace private profit with the "real needs" of society as the criterion of economic decision-making. The state would direct resources into the "productive" industrial and agricultural sectors on which sound development depended. Industrialization was the top priority, but an agricultural revolution was also needed to provide markets and a surplus for industrialization and to raise rural living standards. In agriculture, socialism would aim to transfer the "land to him who works it," beginning with agrarian reform and service cooperatives and evolving toward the state farms and production cooperatives which could most effectively mobilize resources, modernize technique, induce cooperation, and blunt the rise of rural capitalism; the state, through large-scale investment in irrigation, land reclamation, and technical innovation, would stimulate agricultural transformation. While socialization of the entire economy was seen as the ultimate goal, in the interim a role for private enterprise in internal trade, construction, tourism, and small industry would be preserved; the petite bourgeoisie would be socialized only gradually and by persuasion. Finally, the state would provide public services, redirecting them toward the poor and rural parts of the population.

This ideological redefinition pushed the Ba'th palpably leftward, away from social-democratic toward East European models, and in some ways more clearly defined its course. It legitimized a more substantial attack on private property, a bigger state sector, and less scope for pluralism than the Aflaqist tradition; in the adoption of Leninist political organization, it "solved" the previous contradiction between radical social ends and a liberal political system. But in some ways the new credo was also idealistic: its radical attack on the principle of private property (however small) and its vision of an ultimately fully collectivized society were at odds with the interests and outlook of much of the Ba'th's constituency, and as such were to leave little real impact on social policy. The new program was, aside from these defects, a coherent prescription for radical change which to be successful depended not only on state power but on a high level of ideological commitment to it in the party. There is little doubt that some Ba'thists believed strongly in it, and they constituted the driving force behind the structural changes which would in fact be carried out in the face of great resistance after 1963. But some Ba'thists rejected it as a deviation from the authentic Ba'th tradition and dropped out or were pushed out of the party, sometimes to go into opposition. Some cared little about ideology and used or discarded it as it suited their personal ambitions. The majority accepted and were willing to follow the new program, excepting its most extreme provisions. However, as the effort to implement the program encountered obstacles and incurred costs, they proved ready to accept basic compromises in it and to acquiesce in its gradual abandonment as a guide to public policy. In short, it appears that there was enough ideological commitment to carry the party partly down the revolutionary path, but not enough to overcome the major obstacles and challenges which stood between it and the ultimate success of its program. In the next section, these challenges and the Ba'th's efforts to overcome them will be examined.

IDEOLOGY AND PRACTICE: A MACRO VIEW OF CHANGE AND RESISTANCE

THE ROAD TO POWER: MAKING REVOLUTION IN A HOSTILE ENVIRONMENT

The circumstances in which the Ba'th party seized power—and in consequence the method used—could hardly have been less auspicious for a revolutionary project. During the 1950s, the Ba'th had indeed forged a significant political base, but by the early 1960s factional rivalries, quarrels with Nasser, the hero of Arab nationalism, and the suppression of the party under the UAR had caused the virtual dissolution of the party organization, cost it a big part of its nationalist constituency (especially among urban Sunnis), and scattered and demobilized its remaining partisans. Yet at this juncture, when the party was reduced to a small elite and at odds with mass Nasserism, it seized state power in the only way it could: a military coup carried out by Ba'th army officers. While this should not disguise that the coup was in a sense the delayed outcome of the political mobilization of the 1950s and represented wider social forces than the handful of officers who carried it out, the circumstances of the party's power seizure had profoundly negative consequences for its revolutionary project. At odds with a wide spectrum of the politically active public, from Nasserites to the traditional establishment, its hold on power rested almost entirely on army backing. Inevitably the party would be dominated by the officer-politicians who had brought it to power and kept it there. Its hope of forging a new political and social order and winning mass support for it was prejudiced from the start, but whether from idealism, ambition, or resentment, the new leaders seemed determined to turn a coup into a revolution. An analysis of their effort is indispensable to any explanation of the fit and gap between ideology and practice in Syria. (On the post-coup dilemmas, see Rabinovich 1972; on the conflict with Nasser, see Kerr 1971.)

Center-Building: The Obstacles to Institutionalized Authority. A first necessary priority on the Ba'th's political agenda was the creation of a cohesive center of institutionalized authority able to give unified sustained direction to the revolutionary course. The elite did build a new set of party-state institutions which have survived to this day, but the effort to make them a source of unified stable authority ran up against enduring obstacles.

First, the new elite was fragmented by a multitude of cleavages reflecting the heterogeneity of its social origins. Generational, urban-rural, and civil-military conflicts marked the early days of the regime. Personal rivalries among prominent party officers—e.g., Amin Hafiz, Muhammad Umran, Salah Jedid, Hafiz Asad—have never ceased to plague it. Sectarian conflicts have been particularly enduring. From the outset the elite has been a multi-sectarian alliance, but minority groups, especially Alouites, have been significantly overrepresented in strategic positions.* Although almost every major intra-elite conflict has pitted cross-sectarian coalitions against each other, sectarian rivalry has made for inter-elite distrust, which, exploited in power struggles, again and again shattered elite cohesion. Moreover, as Alouite over-representation has increased over time, so also have sectarian mistrust and Alouite particularism.

What made intra-elite social cleavages all the more damaging was the fact that the elite could not arrive at a strong ideological consensus to contain them. Rather, conflict between proponents of more moderate and radical variants of the Ba'th tradition, often reinforced by and reinforcing social cleavages, only further divided the elite; at the same time, the ideological commitment of significant segments of it to either doctrinal variant remained lukewarm. In consequence, much elite political energy was exhausted in intra-elite conflicts at the expense of a unified sustained effort to put the

*The Alouites are a heterodox Islamic minority concentrated in Latakia and Tartous and representing about 12 percent of the population. Due to their special attraction to the army and Ba'th party and efforts of Alouite leaders after the Ba'th power seizure to put kinsmen in trusted positions of power, they constitute a disproportionate portion of the top power elite. This has been profoundly resented by parts of the Sunni Muslim majority.

party's program into practice. Moreover, as the more ideologically committed elements gradually lost out in power struggles—the Aflaq faction in 1966, the Jedid radicals in 1970—leaving the field to the pragmatists of the Asad era, what initial unifying vision the Ba'th had was eroded.*

A second obstacle to center-building was a persistent military praetorianism originating in the party's rise to power on the back of the army and sustained by the continuing role of military politicians in the leadership. Formal party institutions did help to contain praetorianism but could never exclude the use or threat of force as the ultimate resort in intra-elite conflicts. All power contenders had to seek support in the military and exclude rivals from it; hence the politics of purge, appointment, and transfer in the army ran parallel with that of debate and votes in party assemblies, and in the end every major turnover in the elite has come by military coup. This has gravely endangered regime cohesion and made it impossible to create an institutionalized system of leadership recruitment and accountability. Although the elite remains a civil-military coalition, not a classical military dictatorship, the continuing use of coercion in the decision-making process inevitably permitted military domination of the party, alienated many partisans who did not possess coercive resources, and depressed intra-party political participation and in consequence the very vitality of the party as a political force.

Third, there has been a steady erosion in the ideological-political energy of the elite center over time. This is due in part to praetorianism and to the decimation of ideologues in intra-elite conflict, especially the fall of the radical faction in 1970. It is also due to the high costs of strong resistance to the regime by powerful interests. But the gradual "embourgeoisement" of the elite, through corruption and semi-licit business activities, played a growing and decisive role in ideological decline, which in the Asad years has become unmistakable.

As ideology has receded, two other orientations have emerged: a technocratic or military professionalism, which places economic growth and military security above social equality and national revolution, and a growing reversion to the traditional use of political

*On elite composition, see Van Dusen (1975: esp. 139-41); Van Dam (1979: esp. 98-103 and appendix tables); Macintyre (1969); and Ben Tsur (1968). On intra-elite conflicts and cleavages, see Van Dusen (1972); Rabinovich (1972); Petran (1972):167-258); Seymour (1970); Kerr (1975); and Razzaz (1967).

power for private—personal or sectarian—gain. One aspect of this is that Alouites, through sectarian solidarity and favoritism toward their own, were transformed from a deprived radical group into a privileged segment in the Ba'th state; although this gives them a big stake in the regime and imparts a tenaciousness to the elite in the face of opposition, it feeds intra-elite distrust and diverts it from public to private goals. It must finally be noted that although the elite has changed from a petite bourgeoisie into a new "state bourgeoisie," it has yet to fully amalgamate with the old private bourgeoisie to produce a new unified conservative upper class; until such an amalgamation takes place, the elite is unlikely to wholly abandon Ba'thism.

By the 1970s the effort to build a revolutionary party-state center had thus largely failed. Instead a more traditional form of center emerged in which the personalized authoritarian presidency of Hafiz Asad was raised above collective party leadership institutions and rested as much on a personal clientage network of sectarian partisans dominating strategic levels of the security apparatus as on the party. Asad's rule has combined presidential (legal) legitimacy, sectarian clientalism, and continued decision-making in consultation with party and state elites to produce a more stable, albeit no more institutionalized center of authority than heretofore.*

Elite-Mass Linkage: Flawed Instruments of Mobilization. As the Ba'thists themselves realized, their revolutionary project could not dispense with an ideologically disciplined revolutionary party. It was needed to mobilize popular support for the regime against the inevitable opposition to radical change and as a motor of development to replace the landlords and merchants whom the regime was removing from the strategic levers of the economy.

A great deal of energy was indeed invested in the forging of such a party, and one bearing some resemblance to the Leninist model did in fact emerge. A party apparatus, possessing more than 150,000 members and linked to a set of auxiliary organizations embracing wider circles of the population, now links the Ba'th center to society. But the ideological discipline of this political machine has rapidly dissipated. A system of selection and socialization structures was developed to maximize the ideological commitment of recruits,

*The best works on the Asad regime to date are Maoz (1975 and 1978), and Dawisha (1978).

but it was too often bypassed. The need to rapidly expand the party subsequent to the power seizure; intra-elite conflicts which impelled rival leaders to bring a maximum following into the party bases (often as much on the basis of friendship, kinship, and sectarian ties as ideological commitment); the constant attrition during intra-elite conflict of old members who had served the party prior to its power seizure and their replacement by newcomers frequently drawn by the advantages of membership in a ruling party; and the unconcern of the "pragmatic" leadership after 1970 to attract troublesome ideologues to the party—all diluted ideological with careerist, personalistic, and primordial recruitment motivations. As a result, while some party members were true militants and most were generally loyal and infused with a vague nationalist-populist orientation, too many (according to the regime's own internal documents) exhibited traits detrimental to a revolutionary party: a "personal" rather than a team style of work; negligence; "feverish craving after benefits and posts"; bureaucratic attitudes toward the masses; "revolutionary chattering"—i.e., idle talk of revolution without concern for the concrete methods of carrying it out; and "sick" (tribal or sectarian) relations.

The party has in consequence fallen far short in the performance of its functions. In the countryside it has penetrated and established Ba'th nucleii made up of educated youth and small or middle peasants in hundreds of villages. But it has little mobilized these peasants for the revolutionary transformation of the countryside, and in most villages a part of the population remains inert or under the influence of *zaim* or landlord. In the cities the party has formally organized about half of the working class, but it has largely been unable to penetrate the great traditional urban quarters where the masses remained attached to the Ba'th's rivals, the *ulema,* merchants and notables. The party has had little obvious success in imparting ideological drive and discipline to the state apparatus or the public sector; indeed partisans serving in public institutions are at least as guilty as others of the corruption and negligence which has enervated state institutions. Thus the party has not effectively served as the dynamic, unifying force needed to overcome bureaucratic inertia and fragmentation. By the late 1970s it seemed to resemble less and less a "vanguard"-type party and more a "patronage" party in which personal and sectarian-based relations were at least as important as ideological and organizational bonds.

As an instrument of regime consolidation, however, the party has proven invaluable. It constitutes a network of linked strongpoints cutting across sectarian and regional cleavages which limits opposition access to the masses and helps hold a fragmented society together. It links a significant mass base to the regime, without which it could probably neither have survived nor given roots to the new social order it set out to build (Hinnebusch 1980 and 1976).

Forging a New Socioeconomic Order: The Limits of Coherence. Ba'th ideology called for the creation of a new "socialist" order. In practice this meant the formation of a large public sector designed to replace private entrepreneurship as the cutting edge of development, a redistribution of resources and opportunity, and administrative efforts to control and narrow the scope of the market. Accordingly a series of nationalizations brought the heights of the modern Syrian economy—finance, large and medium industry, foreign and parts of internal trade—under state control and with them a good portion of the economic surplus. A middle-sized private capitalist sector was allowed to persist in internal trade, housing, small industry, construction, and agriculture. It was in principle rigorously regulated, and the regime initially intended that its scope be gradually narrowed. In agriculture, land reform broke up the great *latifundia* and, together with a cooperatization effort and the implacement of a state-run credit, supply, and marketing system, produced a significant smallholding sector linked to the state. A wave of populist legislation slashed government salary differentials, subsidized or applied price controls to basic consumption goods and production requisites used by the poor, broadened public employment, enhanced labor security, and introduced progressive taxation. Subsequent to Asad's seizure of power in 1970, several alterations were made in this model. A gradual economic liberalization revitalized the middle-sized private sector, reopened access to foreign trade channels for it, and opened Syria to an influx of Arab oil capital, Western contractors, salesmen, and consumption goods. But the public sector remained the main channel of development investment, and the agrarian reforms were left intact.

The effort to make and keep this new order both efficient and equitable has run up against a number of apparently intractable obstacles. Many seem reducible to a technical failure of the regime to adequately develop the necessary instruments to manage the new economy. First, the planning apparatus remains rudimentary, confined to little more than the projection of budgets, unable to hold state agencies to plan objectives or to efficiently allocate resources and overcome bottlenecks. The state lacks the macroeconomic fiscal and monetary tools and the effective regulatory mechanisms needed to control the market. The public sector has failed to develop effective management and incentive systems and hence to extract and efficiently use a sufficient surplus for continued self-sustained growth, and the overstaffing dictated by both employment-maximization policy and political patronage has dissipated a portion of the potential surplus. A significant private capitalist sector has persisted, but the regime has failed to effectively tax it, control its prices, or steer its activities into productive channels. Under the radical Ba'thists, private business, alienated and depressed, siphoned its surplus abroad and put much of its efforts into black marketeering; in the post-liberalization period, although private business has revived, much "entrepreneurship" is channeled into luxury importing, housing and land speculation, black marketeering, and the exploitation of the public sector by suppliers and contractors in league with an increasingly corrupt officialdom. In short, the state has taken over the heights of the economy, and intervened in and tried to reshape the market, but it has failed to adequately develop the instruments of a command economy to do the job properly.

The regime's inability to develop effective instruments of economic control can be partly explained by the lack of a clear design for doing so. The regime's socialist ideological prescriptions were drawn at a high level of abstraction; in the effort to implement them, the Ba'thists had to draw on external experience and expertise—from the Eastern bloc, Egypt, the UN—but they appear never to have synthesized these disparate elements into a coherent indigenous strategy or tradition of operationalization. Moreover, the regime has failed to develop the incentives and personnel practices needed to recruit, train, and motivate the skilled manpower to run an effective economic apparatus. The modesty of public salaries—particularly in the post-1973 inflation—and the ability of nearby states to offer much higher remuneration, the political alienation of bourgeois professionals, and their frequent replacement by incompetent politicos have translated into a damaging brain drain from public service. The continuing lack of an effective personnel policy which could put "the right man in the right place" and the all too frequent allocation of appointments and rewards on the basis of political loyalties or personal and sectarian (i.e., Alouite) connections, rather than skills and performance have undermined motivation among those who remained. Ultimately, however, behind these factors seems to stand a failure of leadership: too fragmented or engrossed in the struggle for power and too little committed to their socialist project, the Ba'th elite has failed to provide the direction from the top to put in place the practices which might have made for a dynamic new economic order.

A second major vulnerability in the Ba'th economic model is what might be called an apparently built-in tendency to "resource overcommitment." For ideological reasons and in order to build and maintain a populist coalition, the regime simultaneously committed itself to an ambitious development effort, a welfare state, and a nationalist foreign policy. The consequent resource crunch after the 1967 war helped produce an economic liberalization which was in part an effort to relieve this crunch and in part a concession to the opposition meant to broaden the regime's base. But liberalization led to an explosion in luxury consumption by both the bourgeoisie and the political elite. Thus the regime has attempted to have, at once, high rates of investment and high rates of public and private consumption, the resource gap being "covered" by deficit financing and subsidies from the Arab oil states.

In a sense, this "overcommitment syndrome" may be inherent in the authoritarian-populist state. Lacking much traditional or legal legitimacy, such a state depends almost exclusively on performance for acceptance—i.e., the satisfaction of public demands. Driven to expand its always precarious legitimacy, it seeks to maximize its support coalition. Initially it seeks to mobilize the quiescent masses on its side, thereby raising their aspirations and in consequence the commitments of the state to them. Later it tries to buy off the opposition of older privileged groups and satisfy the expectations of the emergent newly privileged in its own ranks. The more it seeks public support, the more demands it must satisfy and the less its capacity to curb consumption in the interest of investment. In spite of the authoritarian concentration of power, therefore, the state proves in many ways to be "soft," unwilling or unable to make the hard, often unpopular decisions on which development may depend.*

*A revealing analysis of the planning process and of the problems of the public sector is contained in Hilan (1973). On the socialist measures, see SAR (1965a); Ducret (1969); and Keilany (1973). Among the better studies on the structure and performance of the economy are Hansen (1969); Hilan (1969);

What can be said about the overall performance of the Ba'th "model"? In spite of its flaws, the developmental and distributive performance of the regime has not been without some real achievements. The public sector has channeled substantial investment into an ambitious development effort which is laying the basis of a modern agroindustrial economy; this effort—notably in industrial diversification, the development of infrastructure, a petroleum and power sector, and the development of the Euphrates Basin—has given Syria an economic "great leap forward" and sustained a very respectable rate of growth. Moreover, it was accompanied, at least initially, by substantial redistributive measures. Without the socialist model, simultaneous increases in growth and equality would probably have been incompatible, since in a privately dominated economy redistributive measures, if they can be legislated in the face of powerful interests, typically depress investment. However, the resource crunch—resulting not only from the overcommitment of resources, but also from inefficiencies in their mobilization and use—has had growing social costs which increasingly threaten Syria's advances on both the developmental and distributive fronts. One cost has been an increasing vulnerability to decisions taken in other Arab capitals, with consequent loss in political independence. Another cost has been an inflationary spiral. Another is the emergence of new inequalities: inflation erodes the income of workers and public sector employees, while in the absence of effective price controls and progressive taxation new fortunes are being made in the private business sector. Perhaps ultimately most serious, the licit or illicit participation of much of the Ba'thist elite in this enterprise has steadily eroded its commitment to an egalitarian society.

The Domestic Political Arena: A Bifurcated Polity. The success of a revolution depends on public support and compliance; coercion, while necessary, is never enough. At the outset, the Ba'th controlled the instruments of coercion, but quarrels with Nasserism, its insistence on ruling alone, and its threat to powerful established interests alienated wide segments of the political arena and virtually isolated it. Subsequently, through social reform, political organization,

and Arudki (1972). My analysis also relies on the various reports of the World Bank, the UN Development Program (UNDP) office in Damascus, the many publications of the Office Arabe de Presse et de Documentation (Damascus), and those of the Syrian Central Bureau of Statistics, especially the *Statistical Abstract*.

nationalist militancy, and the growing dependence of large segments of the population on the state, the regime built a constituency from elements of the salaried middle class, the minority communities, and the workers and peasants. In particular, by mobilizing significant segments of the rural periphery, it created a wider political arena in which the balance of power was much more to its favor than before.

However, the Ba'th regime has never been able to win widespread public support or achieve more than a fragile legitimacy. For one thing, its base, probably encompassing about a third of the population, was never mobilized intensely enough to overwhelm the hostile or capture the loyalties of the undecided; and owing to the limited extent to which an authoritarian regime can satisfy the participatory demands of even its own supporters, to its mixed record in fulfilling its ideological promises, and to its apparent loss of commitment to them in the 1970s, this base has periodically suffered erosion and fragmentation. For another thing, the regime has failed to either eradicate or accommodate powerful centers of urban opposition; from 1963 to 1980 the opposition has been able to mount no less than seven major uprisings against Ba'th rule. In the 1960s Nasserism set the loyalties of large segments of the urban middle and lower classes against the Ba'th. Liberal elements of the professional middle class have never accommodated themselves to authoritarian rule or state controls over society. Political Islam represents the most powerful and durable wing of the opposition. Its opposition to the Ba'th stems chiefly from resentment of the secular, minoritarian caste of the party elite and the damage done to traditional interests by state intervention in the market and village, hitherto dominated by the traditional urban establishment. The fusion of a conservative brand of Islam with the age-old commercial tradition of the Syrian city has produced a powerful and deep-rooted urban "counterculture" which has proven impervious to Ba'thism.

Because the regime has opened few institutionalized channels of access to decision-makers for opposition elements, their political activity takes covert or anomic anti-regime forms, which, though risky and costly, have not been ineffective in wringing concessions from the regime. Disinvestment, the brain drain, street disturbances, and the economic guerrilla warfare of the *suk* (traditional marketplace) against the government in the 1960s played a role in derailing the radical Ba'th leadership and bringing to power a new conciliatory leadership which muted the secularism and radicalism of its predecessors and pursued economic liberalization and political relaxation.

In the late 1970s, however, renewed massive urban opposition showed that the city had yet to accommodate itself to Ba'th rule. In short, the regime has alienated a multitude of political rivals but has proven unable to either eradicate or submerge them in a total mass mobilization. Hence it has had to constantly alternate between repression and concession. In consequence, the regime has been overly engrossed in coping with political threats at the expense of sustained attention to the implementation of its social program. It has been deprived of the broad legitimacy needed to mobilize society for social transformation and of the compliance of large sectors of the public necessary for the institutionalization of a new social order. (On the Ba'th's rural base, see Hinnebusch 1982a; on urban opposition, see Hinnebusch 1982b).

The External Environment: A Revolutionary Island in a Hostile Sea. The Ba'th inherited an external environment dominated by Western and Israeli power; the Ba'th movement represented a revolt against and threat to the status quo regional order over which they presided. Pan-Arabist in orientation, the Ba'th aspired to export its revolution to the whole Arab world in a challenge to Western interests and the Western bridgehead in the area, Israel. The Ba'thists felt deeply about the Palestinian cause, knew that the legitimacy of their rule rested to no small extent on acting in its name, and believed that the struggle against Israel could serve as a mobilizational catalyst for their revolution. But they failed to make a realistic assessment of the balance of power in the region and brought on themselves the disastrous 1967 war; in no respect were the Ba'thists more idealistic or out of touch with reality than in their policy toward Israel, and no flaw in their ideology was to cost them more.

The 1967 defeat was a decisive factor in the failure of the Ba'th to carry through its social revolution. It demoralized the whole Ba'thist movement and in time shifted the balance of public sentiment in Syria and elsewhere against radical nationalism and populism as a credible response to the crises of Arab society. It decisively weakened the radical wing of the party, which was most committed to the revolutionary design, and led to its overthrow by a "pragmatic" wing which wanted to suspend the socialist revolution in the interest of the national defense against Israel. The national unity needed in this struggle required concessions to the bourgeoisie; the Arab money needed to rebuild the army, concessions to the conservative oil states. The Fifth (1971) and Sixth (1975) Regional

Congresses of the party formally approved this major ideological revision; they held that the "contradiction of the stage" was the national one between Israel and the Arabs; the main priority for which "all resources must be mobilized" was the recovery of the occupied territories, and hence all lesser social contradictions had to be subordinated to this national aim (Arab Ba'th Socialist Party 1971 and 1975). From these decisions flowed economic liberalization, the revitalization of the capitalist impulse, growing dependency on Arab money, and, in good part, the corruption and ideological exhaustion of the Ba'th political elite. Fifteen years after Asad's rise to power, the struggle with Israel continues, engrossing the elite in matters of national security before all else, and diverting a massive portion of the state's resources—which might otherwise go for socioeconomic development—into support of a huge military establishment which dominates and drains Syrian society as never before. And of course the social revolution remains suspended—indefinitely. The current external environment, marked by Israeli military dominance, growing Western influence, and conservative Arab petropower, could not be less favorable to a radical national and socialist experiment.

SOCIAL POLICY AND THE BA'TH'S PEASANT AND WORKER CONSTITUENCIES: TWO MICRO STUDIES

This section will attempt to examine in greater depth the effect of ideology on social policy, legislation, and practice. It will try to test the extent to which the Ba'th's ideologically inspired social policies have been able to more widely distribute welfare and social power to its ostensible populist constituencies—i.e., peasants and the urban working class.

PARTY AND PEASANT: AGRARIAN POLICY

The Ba'th's rural policy has taken two basic thrusts: one, redistributive, includes land reform and agrarian relations legislation; the other is an effort to forge new rural institutions in place of the old: a peasant syndicate, a state agricultural apparatus, and cooperatives. This policy has aimed to weaken the power of the party's rivals (particularly landlords), build a base of peasant support, and shape a new, more equitable and productive rural social order.

Redistributive Policy. Land reform legislation reduced the ceiling on ownership to an average of about 40 ha of irrigated land and 100 ha of dry land (SAR 1965a:143-59). It, along with the complementary distribution of state-owned land (hitherto largely controlled by big landowners) resulted in a transfer of about 18-20 percent of the cultivated surface to small peasants representing about 20 percent of the rural population in agriculture.* Drawing on scattered and not always readily comparable evidence, Table 1 presents a very tentative estimate of the effect of land distribution (and the sale of holdings induced by policies unfavorable to absentee owners).†

Table 1

SYRIA: DISTRIBUTION OF LANDHOLDING, 1950 AND 1970

	1950		1970	
Type of Landholder	Percent of Population	Percent of Land	Percent of Population	Percent of Land
Large (100 ha +)	1%	50%	.5%	13%
Medium (10-100 ha)	7	35	12.0	52
Small (1-10 ha)	22	15	47.5	35
Landless	70	0	40.0	0

Sources: 1950: Computed from IBRD 1955 and Hilan 1969; 1970: Estimated from SAR, CBS 1977b.

NOTE: I believe the CBS data are accurate enough to support the rough orders of magnitude indicated in the table.

The very large estates, which averaged 700 ha and sometimes ran to thousands, have disappeared. The landless stratum has contracted, and a significant portion of it has been raised to the status of small holders; 76 percent of the land surface is now held

*According to government sources, which seem plausible, 102,238 families received land out of an estimated 500,000 families in agriculture (UN 1971:37).

†It may be noted that while about 10 percent of the cultivated surface in Syria is irrigated, about 13 percent of the surface distributed in the land reform was irrigated (SAR, CBS 1977a:218, 225).

in small parcels not exceeding 16 ha of irrigated and 60 ha of dry land (interview, Deputy Minister of Agriculture and Agrarian Reform; Damascus, 1974). Fragmentary evidence suggests palpable increases in the income of beneficiaries: one scholar (Shakra 1966: 181-98) estimated a 43 percent increase in the income of peasants on dry land and an 18 percent increase on irrigated holdings.

Syria's agrarian relations legislation was designed to protect the 40 percent of cultivators who did not own land after the reform (about half of whom worked as sharecroppers or tenants and half of whom were wage laborers), as well as small holders who must deal with investors owning machines or irrigation pumps. It regulates the conditions of labor, fixes minimum wages, and sets returns to the various factors of production contributed by landowners, investors, and cultivators. The law requires written contracts and forbids personal servitude or life-long contracts. It also forbids owners to terminate a contract with a tenant except through the agrarian courts and on condition that the owners work the land themselves or by hired labor and pay an indemnity to the tenants. This has much reduced the previous practice of expelling tenants; except for the termination of contracts for the nonpayment of rent or shares, tenants seem to have gained quasi-permanent tenure under the law. In addition, the law limits payment for the provision of land to 20 percent of the crop, as compared to the previous 50 percent; payments for tractor and irrigation services were also cut. It is estimated that the law has thus increased tenant income 30 percent on dry land and 20 percent on irrigated land. The law also sets minimum wages and working conditions for agricultural laborers; however, while permanent skilled workers (such as tractor drivers) gained income and tenure from the law, unskilled seasonal and day laborers have no employment security and their minimum wages are no improvement over free market rates. The regime has made no effort to unionize such laborers (and indeed in the late 1970s the private sector was paying higher wages than the state or cooperative sectors). With the spread of the peasant union in the countryside (see below), the agrarian relations law seems to be reasonably but not wholly enforced (SAR, Ministry of Labor and Social Affairs 1970; interviews, Ministry of Labor and Social Affairs; Damascus, 1974; ministerial documents in author's possession defining returns to various factors of production).*

*On the proportion of the agricultural population with land, sharecropping tenures, or working as agrarian laborers, see SAR, CBS 1977b and 1976.

Political Organization. The regime has tried to organize the countryside politically through the General Federation of Peasant Syndicates. In principle, the federation was to serve as an elite-mass linkage, permitting the regime to mobilize the peasants for rural transformation and to turn a dispersed, passive peasantry into an organized political power. The party built the organization virtually from scratch, recruiting and training small and middle peasants and returning them to their villages to organize. These cadres—in principle committed to regime goals through political indoctrination and organizational control from above, enjoying access to party and government officials, yet remaining in the village working their land and kept accountable by periodic local elections—would, it was thought, be in a promising position to link the Ba'th state center to the peasant masses. By the 1970s perhaps 30 percent of the peasantry had indeed been organized in some 3,000 village unions federated in an organizational pyramid reaching to the national level.

As an instrument of elite-mass linkage, the organization deviates considerably from the ideal. In its voluntaristic recruitment from a local base and its provision of channels for the flow of political communication and mobility upward from this base, the union is more than a mere new bureaucracy, but it has been affected by many negative bureaucratic traits: higher level leaders spend too much time in their offices and too little in the field, and too few local cadres have proved to be dynamic, innovative leaders in the village. In its relatively modern structure and task orientation, and in the lack of great asymmetries in the personal resources of leaders and the rank and file, the organization is more than a traditional clientage network, but it is riddled with traditionalistic traits. It has been unable to exclude the local, kinship, and sectarian rivalries which divide Syrian society, to prevent local notables from sometimes infiltrating and derailing its work, or to keep cadres from building personal clientage networks or favoring their own kin. It has proven difficult to get cadres to follow systematic methods of planning and work.

The "mobilizational" record of the union is, not surprisingly, mixed. It has enabled the regime to penetrate the formerly "encapsulated" village, bypassing traditional "gatekeepers," and thus to build a constituency in the village; however, a part of the village remains under the sway of traditional opponents. The organization has proved useful in securing cooperation of the peasantry with the regime's rural policy, such as cooperatization, and enforcement of the agrarian relations law, of state marketing, and of the state agricultural production plan. Where full-fledged cooperatives did not exist, the union helped in the distribution of credit and production supplies. It has helped to impart a development consciousness to village leaders, played a modest role in local self-help projects, and, in some villages, served as an arena of conflict-resolution. But the union can hardly be said to have mobilized the peasants for rural transformation. Especially since 1974 the union has had primary responsibility for the cooperatives. But it has failed to generalize or vitalize them by overcoming the traditional cleavages which fragment or paralyze them or by getting peasants to increase savings and investment. It has not become a vehicle of either cultural or economic revolution in the village. As an interest group in the political system, the union carries modest weight, being too dependent on the party to wield much clout in the decision-making process. But it does have institutionalized access to the various state committees which take decisions affecting peasant interests and to the bureaucratic apparatus which services the agrarian sector, and its congress resolutions, which seem to authentically express peasant interests, represent a channel of communication with the political elite (see Hinnebusch 1979:43-47 and 1976).

Socioeconomic Development. The regime has tried to reorganize agricultural production, replacing the old landlord/merchant-dominated system with a new state/cooperative-centered one. An expanding state apparatus, charged with planning and stimulating production, delivering agricultural services to producers, and marketing a part of the crop, has gradually penetrated the countryside. The effort to plan has not been very successful. Planning has generally relied on prices and investments determined at the center, but the price mechanism has been too rigid to be very effective. More recent experiments with compulsory comprehensive planning from the village level up have been limited by the inadequacies of planning and control instruments (interviews, Agricultural Section of State Planning Commission; Damascus, 1979). The Agricultural and Cooperative Bank is charged with the main supply of credit and production requisites to peasants; it labors under bureaucratic bottlenecks and insufficient credit resources. Dealing mostly in short-term loans, it has not much stimulated long-term investment; however, it has provided low-cost credit and inputs to thousands of peasants, relieving them of dependency on merchants and landlords and of the old threat of expropriation for unpaid debts. The state controls the marketing of three major crops—cotton, sugarbeets, and wheat; state prices have sometimes been below international ones, and to the extent that state marketing has thus been used as a means of rural taxation, it has conflicted with the other regime goals of stimulating production and raising peasant incomes (Kholy n.d.; SAR, Ministry of Agriculture and Agrarian Reform 1977:260-61, and CBS 1977a:838). The state is charged with research and the diffusion of technical services and innovation through extension services or the cooperatives, but with the exception of cotton improvement and the introduction of a productive new wheat strain, its performance has been severely constrained by shortages of funds and technical personnel (Dessouki n.d.). The state has channeled substantial investment into irrigation and reclamation; despite some advances, too much of this has been so long-gestating or devoted to stemming the long neglected tide of salinity to have made a major difference. In general, the organizational and technical capacity of the state apparatus has been too mediocre and its resources too slim to allow it to play the leading part in stimulating the agricultural revolution foreseen by the Ba'th.

The cooperatives, another pillar of the regime's rural infrastructure, are ideally to provide a framework for common developmental action by peasants and a channel of innovation and assistance from the center. Almost all the cooperatives are of the "service" variety, although there have been experiments with a handful of production co-ops. Village cooperatives, the basic units of the system, are composed of a general assembly, in which all members have one vote, and a management board, through which peasant leaders run cooperative affairs. A cooperative supervisor gives technical advice and exercises administrative and financial inspection but has no formal power to veto board decisions. Peasants largely work their (privately owned) land individually, but credit and supplies are channeled through the cooperative; moreover, there is some tendency toward observation of a common rotation, and some cooperatives collectively own tractors, irrigation pumps, storage, and pasturage. At the provincial and central levels, a cooperative superstructure (since 1974 run by the peasant union) is charged with diffusing cooperative education and providing services; it has a modest storage capacity, a tractor and harvester fleet, and has tried (with indifferent success) to undertake cooperative marketing of onions, potatoes, grapes, and peanuts

(Jum'a 1971; General Federation of Agricultural Cooperatives 1969; al-Imam 1972).

The performance of the cooperative system has been mixed. Productivity is no lower but no better than in the private sector.* It does its part in the distribution of supplies and credit received from the state and is usually able to repay the cost of such loans. Cooperative marketing is very modest, so private middlemen continue to operate between peasant and consumer. The cooperatives are supposed to encourage savings and investment, but their resources and investments remain quite modest. Ten percent of profits, subscribed share capital, one quarter of the price of agrarian reform land received by peasants, and the rent of common pasture is supposed to go to cooperative coffers, but often does not. The second five-year plan (1966-70) foresaw allocation of only 2.5 percent of peasant income to cooperative investment, though assessment of beneficiaries for the costs of state development projects and individual investment inside the cooperatives must be added to this. The result is that the cooperatives are undercapitalized. There is an average of only one tractor for each three cooperatives, excluding tractors owned individually by members. One reason for low investment is the tendency of poor peasants to consume increments in income. Another is the low confidence of many peasants in the cooperatives due to the failure to keep cooperative accounts up to date, considerable corrupt practices, and a collective responsibility for debts which has allowed shirkers to burden other members with their personal debts. These problems of confidence, in turn, are partly due to inadequate leadership and control by supervisors and accountants, who are undereducated, undermotivated, and overworked; in 1970 one supervisor was available for every three cooperatives. The persistence of clan and family conflicts among peasants has also hampered development of cooperative consciousness. Finally, the cooperative movement has so far been extended to only about a third of the peasantry. The slowness of cooperatization seems to reflect the individualistic cautiousness of the Syrian peasant toward collective organization, the organizational limitations of the regime, and its unwillingness to risk rural alienation through forced cooperatization. The cooperative movement has helped to

*The internal statistical reports of the Ministry of Agriculture and Agrarian Reform show that the output of cooperatives in various crops is roughly proportional to the surface organized in cooperatives.

buttress the security and income of a portion of the small peasantry and has given some the opportunity to improve their positions, but it has not so far contributed much to the hoped-for agricultural revolution (Jum'a 1971:20-29; internal statistical report of the Ministry of Agriculture and Agrarian Reform; interviews with Director of Cooperatives, Ministry of Agriculture and Agrarian Reform, and Agricultural Section of State Planning Commission; Damascus, 1974).

The aggregate impact of these policy initiatives has substantially altered the agrarian structure. The old system, marked by great latifundia, subsistence cultivation, and the beginnings of capitalist commercial agriculture, has given way to one mixing state, cooperative, private small-holding, and medium-sized capitalist farms. The land reform has certainly produced a much more egalitarian rural structure and reduced the vast asymmetries in resources between landlord and peasant which formerly obtained. However, the Ba'th slogan, "The land to him who works it," is far from realized. Landlords still control large portions of the best land and work it by hired labor. Moreover, both urban absentees and rich peasants work their land with wage labor or let it to tenants; 17 percent of small and middle holdings are not personally cultivated (SAR, CBS 1977b). Even the cooperatives hire wage labor for certain tasks. On the other hand, the small and middle peasantry, hitherto of modest social weight in the rural social structure, now expanded and buttressed by land reform, protective legislation, and state aid, has become an important social force. But the landless workers, the bottom rural stratum, have been neglected, are poorly paid, and are exploited not only by private employers, but also by the cooperatives and the state.

These structural changes have had a mixed effect on production and distribution. Agriculture was stagnant in the 1960s in part due to agrarian instability; stabilization in the 1970s led to a modest expansion in output. (For the value of agricultural output and gross output figures, see SAR, CBS 1977a:213-15.) But since population growth and the demand for food and agricultural raw materials for industry and export did not cease to grow, the modest performance of the agricultural sector has made it a drag on the development effort.

The income distribution effects of agrarian changes appear overall to have been equally undramatic. Undoubtedly much agrarian revenue, formerly siphoned off by landlords and merchants, now stays in the village; though there is evidence of a decline in the terms of trade for the rural sector in the late 1970s, there is currently little evidence that the state extracts much surplus from the village. The social structure is now more open, and rural opportunities for upward mobility through education and nonagricultural employment have expanded. Rural per capita income and consumption have steadily albeit modestly grown in spite of high population growth. However, urban income growth has been more rapid; as a result, contrary to the Ba'th's proclaimed intentions, urban-rural income disparities may have actually widened (see SAR, CBS 1977a:905, and compare CBS 1961-62 and 1971-72). This is due less to urban exploitation of the village as heretofore than to the pattern of state development investment, which has concentrated on industry and long-gestating agricultural projects such as the Euphrates project, to the neglect of the traditional agricultural sector.

Thus in practice, Syria under the Ba'th has followed a "third" way in its agricultural policies, neither truly capitalist nor Stalinist. This has probably spared Syria's peasants much misery, since these two roads have typically made the peasant bear the heaviest burdens of modernization. However, in the absence of the ruthless but successful methods of capital accumulation and social reorganization pioneered by these systems, Syria's rate of development has perhaps been more modest. It may also be fair to suggest that on the whole the Syrian peasant has done less well under the Ba'th than might be expected from a rural-based populist regime.

THE BA'TH AND THE WORKING CLASS

Although the Syrian workforce continues to be dominated by self-employed peasants, traders, and artisans, the working class has become an important sociopolitical force; in the 1970s, workers made up one fourth of the labor force (SAR, CBS 1977a:139). The Ba'th has long considered the working class a major constituency. It has sought to organize it in syndicates under party leadership, involve it in the management of the public sector, and elicit its support through populist social benefits. Ba'th ideology commits the party in principle to increased social equality in the interest of workers.

Political Organization. When the Ba'th came to power, only a small part of the working class was unionized. Although as a result of a history of political work in the unions the Ba'th enjoyed some labor support, its rivals—particularly Communists and Nasserites—also commanded the allegiance of parts of the working class. Thus labor constituted an independent sociopolitical force ambivalent toward the regime. Ba'th policy was to bring the existent labor movement under its tutelage, expand it, and mobilize workers against the party's urban rivals and in support of its socialist policies. The effort to do this took the form of legislation from above and organization from below. Law 31 of 1964 laid down the organizational pyramid of the General Federation of Workers' Syndicates. It also empowered the government to appoint and remove leaderships of the federation's constituent unions at the governorate level, thus allowing it to engineer the election of a friendly federation leadership. And it provided for the reconstitution of factory committees (abolished under the previous conservative government) which the new regime hoped to make an organized Ba'th presence in the factories. Such administrative measures would not in themselves have been sufficient to secure the Ba'th's position, and two other factors also played a role in the growth of Ba'th influence over the movement. Most important, the 1965 nationalizations were very well received by workers, enabling the Ba'th to broaden its support among them and winning it the cooperation of many Communist and Nasserite syndicalists.* Then, evidently more confident of its position, the regime was able to respond to worker dissatisfaction with appointed leaderships; a new syndical law was issued in 1968 (SAR 1968) providing for the election of all leadership bodies. However, covert intervention by the regime in these elections has been common. In all elections the Ba'th has consistently obtained a majority in the central leadership organs of the General Federation. Greater representation of Nasserite and Communist unionists has been tolerated in intermediate and lower level leadership bodies; however, the 1968 law significantly strengthened the powers of the Ba'th-controlled central organs over these bodies. In the late 1960s close collaboration developed between radical Ba'th syndicalists and their Communist counterparts, while in the early 1970s, as a result of a national-level accord between the Ba'th, Nasserites, and Communists to form a national front, the Ba'th's former progressive

*According to the findings of a former factory owner who surveyed worker opinion in several factories, workers supported the nationalizations, having assimilated the labor theory of value. (See Kassm 1968:124-25; see also Petran 1972:178-79.)

rivals were given a share of the seats in the General Federation's central leadership (Petran 1972:230-31). Under this formula, in the labor movement as elsewhere, the Ba'th retained a majority. Thus in 1974, the central syndicate leadership committee was made up of five Ba'this, three Nasserites, and one Communist. It is essentially through Ba'th trade unionists (subject to party discipline and expected to enforce the party line in the syndicates) that the regime now controls the labor movement.

Structurally the union resembles a pyramid: several specialized unions are headed by leaderships elected from factory committees and federated at the province level, where congresses elect a national-level general congress; this, in turn, elects a twenty-one-member council and a nine-member executive bureau which presides over the specialized departments of the union apparatus and is headed by a president. The executive bureau is responsible before the general congress (in principle, the supreme authority in the union), but the Ba'th majority in this body is simultaneously subordinated to party discipline and supervised by the party Maktab Ummāl (Workers' Bureau). The union president is automatically a member of the Ba'th Party Syrian Congress (Mu'tamar Qutrī), and other syndicalist partisans are sometimes so by election. Indicative perhaps of the actual power of the union in the Ba'th political system is the fact that its president has usually been considered to have party status equivalent to that of a provincial-level branch secretary *(amin fara')*, thus subordinate to the party's top leadership (i.e., the joint Regional and National Commands), although occasionally (as recently) the president has achieved membership in this leadership. Representatives of the union are also accorded seats in the various labor committees and public-sector governing boards which take decisions affecting the immediate interests of workers, as well as in the national parliament (SAR 1968; interviews, members of leadership of General Federation of Workers' Syndicates; Damascus, 1974 and 1979). Thus the Ba'th has successfully incorporated the trade union movement as one of the "mass organizations" making up its party-led "popular democracy."

This *gleichschaltung* has not necessarily rendered the union movement impotent or diminished it as a force for workers' interests. Indeed prior to Ba'th rule, just a small proportion of the labor force was unionized and it was fragmented, precluding the development of much union power; strikes were rare and more rarely successful (Allouni 1958:75). Particularly in the early years of Ba'th rule, the syndicate became a center of radical worker activism in support of the socialist transformation and against the propertied classes. Radical Ba'th syndicalists, considering themselves Marxists—such as the longshoreman leader of the union in the 1960s, Khalid al-Jundi—worked to forge working-class consciousness and to make the union a base of power (see K. al-Jundi n.d.). Of course the union never was able to compete with the party, army, or government as a power center. Syndicalist opposition to the 1970 seizure of power by the party's right wing under Asad was conspicuously ineffectual, and by the 1970s radical activists had been pushed out of the union leadership in favor of more compliant moderates; but the union still occasionally showed signs of political independence—e.g., in 1973, when the entire leadership threatened to resign unless permitted to condemn the massacre of fellow syndicalists in the Sudan. Also, at least two top members of the party leadership in the 1970s, Abdullah al-Ahmar (party assistant secretary-general) and Muhammad Hadid (a member of the Regional Command), made political careers in syndicalist work.

The union has genuinely tried to promote worker interests in the councils of the Ba'th state. It has proposed legislation favorable to workers. For example, it has submitted a proposed new labor code to replace that of 1959. It has pushed for the rationalization of job classification to ensure equal pay for equal work and compulsory hiring through government labor exchanges on a first-come basis to curb favoritism and nepotism. Its role in the enforcement of social legislation already on the books is not without significance: it has not been uncommon for legislation to remain wholly or partially unenforced for failure of the government to assign sufficient resources or to develop the policy instruments to enforce it; the union has tried to overcome such inertia, pushing for the full implementation and extension of favorable legislation—e.g., in its efforts to cut red tape in the dispensing of social security, to have social security extended in the private sector, and to achieve full representation in all management bodies. And of course the union is an advocate of wage increases.

However, it is clear that the union is expected to limit its pursuit of workers' interests by deference to the general good the party claims to represent. And it has had to forego the use of labor's main instruments of leverage, particularly the strike. Syndicalist leaders must try to make a case by persuasion in government councils, appealing to the party's socialist ideology or its desire to keep the workers' support and exclude the influence of rivals from their ranks; if the regime is not responsive, there are no institutionalized mechanisms through which union demands can be further pressed. Indicative perhaps of the union's strengths and limitations is the fact that it was given the major responsibility in drafting the new labor code, but that certain government and public-sector managerial interests have stalled acceptance of the version that it has promoted. Moreover, in the late 1970s, as many of the gains of the working class were eroded by inflation, the regime tried to use the union as an instrument of control to absorb and contain rather than advance working-class demands. Recent government intervention against radical candidates in trade union elections suggests that covert hostility between the regime and elements of the union movement persist and may indeed be increasing.*

The actual degree of working-class support for the regime is hard to assess, but on the whole it seems lukewarm at best. In the beginning many union activists were committed to rival political forces. The socialist transformation won over many worker activists, and on several critical occasions in the 1960s they were able to mobilize much of the syndical movement against challenges by the propertied classes and the Muslim Brotherhood to the Ba'th's radical course. But in the post-nationalization period, many workers remained discontented with salaries, disciplinary procedures, and the quality of management, which, as Petran (1972:230-31) writes, appeared to many of them to be as unproductive and authoritarian as the old private owners. The persistence of active opposition was indicated by incidents of sabotage in the factories. Personal, political, and sectarian favoritism in personnel practices has caused resentments, while a recent erosion of earning power through inflation—at a time when regime elites seemed to be enriching themselves—cannot fail to have disillusioned many workers with the regime. Still, for most workers there must seem little viable alternative to the Ba'th, for the largely bourgeois opposition would probably be less responsive to their interests.

Whether as an instrument of control or representation, the scope of the syndicalist organization has steadily expanded (at a rate three times that of the pre-Ba'th period) from 60,000 in 1963 to

*This analysis is based largely on interviews with leaders of the General Federation of Workers' Syndicates and several of the reports of the leadership to the union's general congresses; also see *Le Monde* 1978.

289,000 in 1977. About 50-60 percent of the labor force is now organized. The union has developed a corps of full-time syndicalist cadres which run and expand the organization and operate vocational and training institutes. However, while virtually the whole public sector is organized, significant portions of the private sector, where unionization is perhaps more important, are not. Smaller firms tend to be outside the scope of the movement, and in the lucrative building industry only about one fourth of the labor force is unionized (Ittihād al-'Am l-naqābāt al-ummāl n.d.).

Finally, it is worth noting that the party has tried to organize self-employed artisans in a separate syndicate. The ostensible aim has been to provide cooperative supply and marketing services and to free artisans of dependence on the merchants who traditionally took much of the value of artisanal products (interview, head of Popular Organizations Bureau of Damascus City Party branch, 1974). It is clearly also aimed at diluting the political influence of urban notables and Islamic opposition forces over this traditionally conservative segment of the working force. The intensity of the rebellion mounted against the regime from traditional urban quarters in the late 1970s suggests this effort has had little success.

Public Sector Management and the Worker. According to Ba'th ideology, it is worker participation in the management and profits of production which distinguishes socialism from state capitalism, and, formally at least, Ba'th legislation provides for such participation. Under the self-management decree of 1964 (SAR 1965b) the workers were supposed to replace proprietors in directing their firms, albeit under the "supervision of the state," and, through sharing of profits, were to be brought to identify with the firm as their own. The decree provided for an elected workers' council in the factory and the election by the union committee of five workers to a seven-man management board. The manager was appointed by the government to run the factory, but policy—particularly matters of personnel and working conditions—was the prerogative of the board as a whole, and all "transactions" of the manager had to be countersigned by a worker representative. The manager could appeal to the government to override decisions of the management board (SAR 1965b:31-33). The effect of this system was to disperse authority among the central government, the manager, and the workers—evidently at the expense of efficiency. Accordingly, in 1967 under Law 21 the system was altered. "Democratic management" replaced "worker self-management" as the official slogan, and effective worker representation on management boards was reduced to three on five to nine man bodies, which were evidently located at company administrative headquarters rather than in a factory itself. In practice, the power of the manager over labor appears thus to have been restored. Workers do retain a voice in decision-making—most likely to be heard in matters of personnel and labor discipline—but their capacity to play a wider role in enterprise affairs is enfeebled by their normally minority status on the boards and the authority of expertise enjoyed by the other members of the board (interviews, General Federation of Workers' Syndicates; Damascus, 1974).

Profit-sharing has in practice been similarly diluted. It was originally seen not only as a matter of justice, but also as an incentive system to boost production; 25 percent of the profits of a firm would accrue to the workers who produced it—10 percent as a direct bonus and 15 percent in the form of social services and housing (SAR 1965b). Evidently the system failed to sufficiently link personal effort and reward when applied to the whole enterprise, and in firms enjoying few or no profits the system was probably counterproductive. The introduction of an Economic Penal Code in 1966 providing punishments for labor negligence indicates the regime believed that labor discipline would require negative as well as positive sanctions. In the 1970s profit-sharing was replaced by a new system: each worker would receive a family allowance of 15 Syrian pounds per month per dependent—a provision which substantially increased worker income (Petran 1972:232). Experiments were also made with a more refined incentive system: a 1970 law provides for bonuses allocated according to the productivity of workers, but its implementation would have required indicators of productivity not readily available; in any case, the bonuses provided were probably too modest to act as incentives (Arudki 1972, 1:430-32). Experiments with incentive plans have succeeded in selected factories, but an effective industry-wide incentive system still appears to be lacking (interview with factory manager, Damascus, 1974; also report of UNDP on the Management and Productivity Center, Damascus, 1967).* The union has experimented with moral incentives, and the portraits of "heroes of production" can be seen in city squares. On the whole, labor discipline seems to be lax and problems with

*The UNDP report claims that productivity increased 40 percent in a textile factory where UN experts helped introduce an incentive system.

negligence in the use and maintenance of machinery, endemic. Hiring is not infrequently "by card"–i.e., party membership–and the dismissal of workers is very difficult. In general the Ba'th management system, which replicates neither capitalist nor socialist systems but mixes elements of both without a coherent synthesis, appears less effective than either in motivating and disciplining the labor force.

Labor and Welfare Policies. The Ba'th regime has introduced or further developed a series of populist policies meant to reflect its egalitarian commitments and win support from workers.

The current labor code, which originated in 1959 and has been substantially amended since, supposedly helps shape the labor market in a way more favorable to workers. Under it, labor disputes must be settled by state arbitration rather than strikes or dismissals. Labor inspectors are empowered to arbitrate, and if this fails, conflicts are settled by arbitration committees made up of representatives of the two sides and the Ministry of Labor and Social Affairs. Workers may be fired only with committee approval and on payment of an indemnity (Arudki 1972, 1:400-12). Of the 3,000-6,000 cases before the system each year, half are settled by inspectors; of the half brought before the committees, an average of only 5-10 percent result in discharge of the worker (SAR, Ministry of Labor and Social Affairs 1977:80). The law also provides for the fixing of minimum wages semi-annually by similar three-party provincial-level committees. The minimum wage is supposed to guarantee the workers' "essential needs" and thus take into consideration the cost of living; however, evidence suggests the committees merely reconcile the demands of the employer and union representatives and that, except in the case of large firms judged to have the ability to pay more, they closely follow the market rate (Atasi 1968). In at least one case where a committee decreed large wage increases, those exceeding 10 percent were disallowed by the government (document of SAR, Ministry of Labor and Social Affairs on definition of minimum wages, in the author's possession). The labor code also sanctions the closed shop and collective contracts, forbids union-busting tactics, regulates hours, and provides for holidays and sick pay. The law is evidently evaded–especially in the small informal sector, where child labor is employed–but the expansion of unionization in the last decades has increased its effective enforcement.

Social security legislation is on the books, but, typically, it remains only half implemented almost two decades after promulgation. To be sure, coverage has steadily expanded, and by 1977 a bit less than half of wage-earners were included; most of those in big industry and government enjoy protection, while those in small industry and agriculture are mostly excluded (Arudki 1972, 1:414-19; SAR, Ministry of Labor and Social Affairs 1977:95). Except for the payment of an indemnity to discharged workers, there is no system of unemployment compensation currently operative.

For both ideological and political reasons the Ba'th is committed to maximizing employment opportunity. Indeed new employment expanded at a rate of 4-4.5 percent per year from 1960 to 1975, exceeding population growth; open unemployment has declined (from 8 percent in 1960 to 4.5 percent in the 1970s). While the development effort has accounted in part for this, much investment (e.g., in the petroleum sector) has been too capital-intensive to absorb significant new quantities of labor; the proportion of the labor force in industry and construction has only slightly increased over the last two decades (SAR, CBS 1977a:142-43, 173, 179, 300-302). Much potential unemployment has thus had to be absorbed by the government sector; public employment has expanded from 22,000 in the late 1950s to 250,000 in the 1970s when one in seven persons was so employed. Public policy has helped to reduce the "reserve army of unemployed" to the benefit of labor, but at the expense of public salary levels and savings.

Finally, the regime has developed policies of intervention in the commodity market meant in principle to ensure the basic needs of its lower and lower-middle-class constituency and to prevent exploitation by the private commercial sector. A wide variety of products are subject to price controls, although enforcement is evidently of limited effectiveness. In addition, certain commodities produced for popular consumption by the public sector have been marketed at low prices, at least until the mid-1970s, when many were allowed to rise considerably. The state also subsidizes, at significant cost to the treasury, a group of essential commodities—flour, vegetable oil, rice, sugar, cement, and fertilizer—most of which are rationed. While the subsidy provides a crucial social support for low income families, its egalitarian thrust is blunted by the availability of ration cards to higher income families and black marketeering in which subsidized commodities are sold at market prices in Syria or smuggled outside the country (Arudki 1972, 2: 199-268; Hilan 1973:248-300).

Income Equality. The Ba'th is ostensibly committed to greater equality of income and to raising the income levels of the working class, but its record is mixed. The regime originally pursued equality with some vigor. Its strategy was to reduce higher incomes, stabilize prices, and raise wages, but only very slowly. For the first decade of Ba'th rule this policy seemed to succeed, to the benefit of most workers. The high incomes of top bureaucrats and managers were slashed; in government the range between salary levels was narrowed to a very modest 5:1 ratio. Nationalizations, land reform, and a progressive income tax probably reduced the share of national income going to property owners. Prices were fairly stable, and real wages for workers rose gradually but steadily. In the 1970s, however, this policy fell apart. The cumulative impact of development and military spending, combined with the economic liberalization which relaxed controls over private business, resulted in an inflationary spiral which eroded the real income of those on fixed wages. The government responded by raising public-sector salaries (60 percent between 1970 and 1975 and more thereafter), but this fell short of rises in the cost of living and was of little consolation to private-sector workers. At the same time, the incomes of merchants, contractors, land speculators—and corrupt members of the political elite—kept pace with or exceeded inflation levels. Not only was the taxation of high incomes inefficient, but tax laws were altered to favor entrepreneurs on the pretext of stimulating investment. By the late 1970s the regime seemed to be losing the political will or capacity to protect the incomes of its working-class constituents or to prevent the reemergence of new inequalities eroding the redistributive effect of earlier reforms.

CONCLUSION

The crucible of the Ba'th movement was Syria's postwar national and social crises. Ba'thism represented a set of proposed solutions to these crises, expressing the interests and world view of rising strategic social forces in revolt against the old agrarian-mercantile order: the emerging salaried middle class, the new officer corps, the mobilizing minorities, the awakening peasantry, the new working class. Possessed of a fairly coherent ideology and sufficient guns, brains, and numbers, the Ba'th was able to topple the old order and consolidate a monopoly of state power. In the hands of the new elite, ideology was a program to be carried out, a tool in the power struggle, and an instrument of regime legitimation.

The Ba'th set out to reshape society according to an ideological design imposed from above. The major steps along this road—nationalizations, land reform, the creation of a new party-state—were completed with relative success; but as the regime sought to institutionalize these changes in a detailed new social practice penetrating village, factory, and neighborhood, it encountered mounting resistance, experienced a "loss of detail," exhausted its ideological energies, and in the end left a big gap between theory and reality.

No single factor can account for this outcome; rather the cumulative, mutually reinforcing impact of several "variables" pushed the Ba'th off its intended course. One decisive variable was the relative failure of the Ba'thists to forge a powerful institutionalized center of revolutionary authority. Most immediately this failure resulted from the social fragmentation and military praetorianism which plagued the elite. These phenomena grew out of the Ba'th's development as a socially heterogeneous, civil-military coalition; they persisted because the party could not generate the powerful, intense ideological consensus needed to tame the power struggle at the center and unite the elite behind its revolutionary project. These failures of leadership translated in turn into flaws in the instruments the Ba'th created to carry out its revolution. The inability of a disunited leadership to impose appropriate party recruitment practices and state personnel policies resulted in a party insufficiently ideologically committed and a state apparatus insufficiently qualified or rationalized to carry out a social transformation.

The resistance and reaction of the Ba'th's environment to the party's efforts to reshape it also played a decisive role in the outcome. Powerful domestic opposition, deeply rooted in a segment of society little represented in the Ba'th's coalition and possessing a counterculture little receptive to Ba'th ideology, continued to dominate the private market and the traditional urban quarter. Lacking the ability to penetrate and mobilize the traditional urban milieu against its rivals, the Ba'th could not deprive the opposition of its political base; lacking the will to wholly eradicate the private sector, efficient instruments to control it, or the dynamic public sector needed to relegate it to the economic peripheries, it could not deprive the opposition of its socioeconomic bases. The persistence of strong domestic opposition deprived the Ba'th of the political legitimacy and public compliance crucial to its effort to socially transform Syria. When external reaction—principally the 1967 defeat by Israel and the growing influence of conservative petropower—was added to domestic discontent, the "negative feedback" from the Ba'th's environment began to divert it from its course.

The post-defeat demoralization of the Ba'th and the fall of its left wing greatly weakened the ideological impulse from the center. Massive military needs and the inability of the state to extract a large surplus from the economy created a growing resource gap; accepting aid from the oil-rich states presented an apparently painless way out of the dilemma, and the new pragmatic leadership was happy to take it. Together these factors produced the major post-1970 alteration in the Ba'th's socioeconomic course. This policy shift, in turn, not only significantly slowed the effort to implement the Ba'th's social program, but it also began to erode part of what had already been achieved. A revived capitalist sector became an engine of new inequalities working against the redistributive reforms of the regime, while the growing links between this sector and segments of the elite, as well as the influx of petrodollars and foreign contractors, greatly accelerated tendencies already at work toward the embourgeoisement, corruption, and ideological exhaustion of the elite. In short, the Ba'th was diverted from its course by a convergence of two basic factors: its own ideological and organizational vulnerabilities, and the resistance and reaction of the powerful external and internal interests threatened by its course.

Although the ideological tide receded, it nevertheless left behind a deposit: new structures, vested interests, rights, and practices. While greatly distorted, the imprint of ideology is recognizable in three major durable consequences of the Ba'th's work: a new state, a restructured economy, and a modest redistribution of social power.

First, a formidable, remarkably stable party-state has been consolidated. However, as much Bonapartist as Leninist, it is profoundly ambivalent in character. A large, well-organized party apparatus dominates significant sectors of state and society, but is itself subordinated to an authoritarian presidency resting on and accountable to the army as much or more than the party. The party has incorporated a significantly wider constituency into the state than any previous Syrian regime, but its ability to mobilize these followers is in decline, and large segments of society remain impervious to it. It remains partially committed to populist-etatist policies, but its universalistic outlook is increasingly diverted by sectarian particularism and the embourgeoisement of its leadership. By the mid-1970s it had become more an instrument of patronage and control than mobilization and transformation. Yet it is still chiefly the party which gives the regime the measure of legitimacy it enjoys: without it the survival of the regime in the face of intense internal and external pressures for more than two decades is hard to imagine.

This party-state presides over a dual socioeconomic order no less ambivalent in character. The economy is dominated by a large state sector which continues to serve etatist and populist purposes. The state sector remains the engine of an ambitious development effort, the main channel of agro-industrial investment, and hence of productive dynamism in the economy; it is also a source of populist benefits—cheap food, employment, and aid and protection for small peasants. Yet, lacking effective instruments of a planned command economy to direct it or a dynamic ideological party to drive and control it, it falls far short of socialist practice. In the populist requirements and patronage practices to which it is subjected, it even lacks much of the economic rationality of an efficient state capitalism. In its diversion of resources to the support of oversized civil and military bureaucracies, whatever their contributions to defense and welfare, it drains and burdens the modest resource base of a poor society.

Below the state sector is a middle-sized private sector, commercial and speculative in character, which provides some services and supports a significant sector of the population but which contributes little to production, corrupts public life, fuels a costly wave of luxury consumption, and is the engine of new inequalities. In the countryside land reform and the state-cooperative infrastructure remain obstacles to the growth of a large agrarian capitalism but have not themselves produced much agrarian dynamism; the door is thus open to the emergence of a middle-sized agrarian capitalism. Finally, in its dependence on subsidies from the petropowers and its growing business relations with capitalist countries, Syria's economy is being reintegrated, after a brief attempt at withdrawal, into the world capitalist market.

These developments have shifted the bases of social power in Syria. The Ba'th's initial social thrust was largely at the expense of the traditional agro-commercial establishment; it resulted in a bigger, stronger state and widened lower middle strata—the salaried middle class, public-sector workers, small and middle peasants—which are dependent on and possess a stake in an etatist-populist orientation. But the revitalization of capitalism, fueled by petrodollars and protected by its links to the political elite, is likely to continue, again shifting power and wealth toward the old and new bourgeoisies and away from the public, labor, and peasant sectors. Yet the interests and survival of the regime are too dependent on its statist-populist base for it to permit their destruction; hence the persistence of a dual economy, the ambivalence of public policy and elite orientation, and the rise of conservatism, but the persistence of populism, are likely for the foreseeable future. That an ideology which seeks a compromise between capitalism and communism and is based on social forces located between the rich and the poor and bridging the public and private sectors should have resulted in such ambivalence is perhaps scarcely surprising.

In sum, the outcome of the Ba'th enterprise is an authoritarian state resting on a dependent lower-cum-middle-class social base and a dual economy; in orientation it is caught between the persistence of statist and populist interests and the growth of traditional particularism, elite embourgeoisement, and private power. Ba'th ideology was routinized enough to give durability to the main structures and interests the regime created, but not enough to produce the dynamic new social order it envisioned. Hence authoritarian populism, as it loses its mobilizational qualities, is well on its way to turning into some form of post-revolutionary neomercantilism. Such a development appears by no means untypical of authoritarian-reformist experiments in the Third World.*

REFERENCES

Abu Jaber, Kemal S. 1966. *The Arab Ba'th Socialist Party.* Syracuse: Syracuse University Press.

Aflaq, Michel. 1959. *Fi Sabīl al-Ba'th.* Beirut: Dār al-Talī'a.

Ajami, Fouad. 1981. *The Arab Predicament: Arab Political Thought and Practice since 1967.* Cambridge: Cambridge University Press.

Allouni, A. Aziz. 1958. "The Labor Movement in Syria." *Middle East Journal* (Summer).

*In addition to the sources cited, my analysis is generally based on several research projects conducted in Syria: on the party and agrarian organization, 1973-74, and on the political economy of development in the summers of 1977 and 1979.

Allush, Naji. 1962. *al-Thawra wa al-Jamāhir.* Beirut: Dār al-Talī'a.

Apter, David. 1965. *The Politics of Modernization.* Chicago: University of Chicago Press.

Arab Ba'th Socialist Party. 1962. "Constitution." In *Arab Nationalism: An Anthology,* ed. Sylvia Haim. Berkeley: University of California Press.

__________. 1964. "Resolutions of the 6th National Congress of the Arab Ba'th Socialist Party." *Arab Political Documents, 1963,* pp. 439-42. Beirut.

__________. 1965. *al-Manhaj al-Marhalī* (The phased program). Damascus.

__________. 1971. *Resolutions of the Fifth Regional Congress.* Damascus.

__________. 1975. *Resolutions of the Sixth Regional Congress.* Damascus.

__________, National Command. 1973. *Some Theoretical Points of Departure.* Damascus.

__________, al-Qiyad al-Qaumiyya. 1972. *Dirāsa tarikhīyya tahlīlīyya lil-Nidāl Hizb al-Ba'th al-Arabī al-Ishtirākīyya.* Damascus.

Arudki, Yehia. 1972. *al-Iktisād al-Surī al-Hadīth,* 2 vols. Damascus: Ministry of Culture.

Atasi, Nadr. 1968. "Wage Fixing and Wage Structure in Syria." *International Labor Review* 98, 4.

Ben Tsur, Avraham. 1968. "The Neo-Ba'th Party of Syria." *Journal of Contemporary History* 18: 165-78.

Binder, Leonard. 1964. *The Ideological Revolution in the Middle East.* New York: Wiley.

Dauk, Bashir, ed. 1964-72. *Nidāl al-Ba'th,* 10 vols. Beirut: Dār al-Talī'a.

Dawisha, Adib. 1978. "Syria under Asad, 1970-78: The Centres of Power." *Government and Opposition* 13, 3 (Summer).

Dessouki, S.M. n.d. "Report." Damascus: FAO.

Ducret, Jean. 1969. "Secteur public et planification en République Arabe Syrienne." *Proche Orient études économiques* (January-June).

General Federation of Agricultural Cooperatives. 1969. "Report and Resolutions of the First Congress of the General Federation of Agricultural Cooperatives." Damascus.

Halpern, Manfred. 1963. *The Politics of Social Change in the Middle East and North Africa.* Princeton: Princeton University Press.

Hansen, Bent. 1969. *Economic Development in Syria.* Santa Monica: Rand Corporation.

Hilan, Rizkallah. 1969. *Culture et développement en Syrie et dans les pays retardés.* Paris: Editions Anthropos.

__________. 1973. *Sūriya bayna al-takhallaf wa al-Tanmīyya.* Damascus: Mitba'a Ta'āwuniya (Cooperative Press).

Hinnebusch, Raymond A. 1976. "Local Politics in Syria: Organization and Mobilization in Four Village Cases." *Middle East Journal* 30, 1.

__________. 1979. *Party and Peasant in Syria.* Cairo Papers in Social Science 3, 1 (November). Cairo.

__________. 1980. "Political Recruitment and Socialization in Syria: The Case of the Revolutionary Youth Federation." *International Journal of Middle East Studies* 11: 143-74.

__________. 1982a. "Rural Politics in Ba'thist Syria." *Review of Politics* 44, 1.

__________. 1982b. "The Islamic Movement in Syria: Sectarian Conflict and Urban Rebellion in an Authoritarian-Populist Regime." In *Islamic Resurgence in the Arab World*, ed. Ali E. Hilal Dessouki. New York: Praeger.

Huntington, Samuel P. 1968. *Political Order in Changing Societies.* New Haven: Yale University Press.

__________. 1970. "Social and Institutional Dynamics of One-Party Systems." In *Authoritarian Politics in Modern Society: The Dynamics of Established One-Party Systems,* ed. S.P. Huntington and Clement Henry Moore, pp. 3-47. New York: Basic Books.

al-Imam. Ahmad Zaki. 1972. "The Co-operative Movement in Syria." Damascus: ILO.

International Bank for Reconstruction and Development (IBRD). 1955. *The Economic Development of Syria.* Baltimore: Johns Hopkins.

Ittihād al-'Am l-naqābāt al-Ummāl. n.d. *Dalīl al-Naqābī.* Damascus.

Jabbūr, George. n.d. "al-Fikr al-Siyāsī wa 'ilāqatuhu bil siyāsa wal tanmīya wa-musādaruhu fī al-qutr al-'Arabī as-Sūrī." Unpublished Ph.D. dissertation, Cairo University.

Jum'a, Naim. 1971. "Organizations Serving in the Rural Areas." Damascus.

al-Jundi, Khalid. n.d. "La Structure de la gauche arabe." Damascus.

al-Jundi, Sami. 1969. *al-Ba'th.* Beirut: Dār al-Nahār.

Kannan, Taher. 1960. "Introduction to the Ba'th." *New Outlook* (July-August).

Kassm, Muhammed Rafik. 1968. "Nationalization of the Syrian Textile Industry with Special Reference to Labor Behavior." Ph.D. dissertation, University of Pennsylvania.

Keilany, Ziad. 1973. "Socialism and Economic Change in Syria." *Middle East Studies* 9, 1 (January).

Kerr, Malcolm. 1963. "Arab Radical Notions of Democracy." *St. Anthony's Papers* 16: 9-40.

__________. 1971. *The Arab Cold War.* London: Oxford University Press.

__________. 1975. "Hafiz Asad and the Changing Patterns of Syrian Politics." *International Journal* 28, 4: 289-306.

Kholy, Hussein. n.d. "Report." Damascus: FAO.

Khalidi, Tarif. 1966. "A Critical Study of the Ideas of Michel Aflaq." *Middle East Forum* 42, 2.

Lencowski, George. 1966. "Radical Regimes in Egypt, Syria, and Iraq." *Journal of Politics* 28, 1 (February).

Lerner, Daniel. 1958. *The Passing of Traditional Society*. Glencoe, Ill.: Free Press.

Macintyre, Ronald Robert. 1969. "The Arab Ba'th Socialist Party: Ideology, Politics, Sociology and Organization." Ph.D. dissertation, Australian National University.

Maoz, Moshe. 1975. "Syria under Hafiz al-Asad: New Domestic and Foreign Policies." *Jerusalem Papers on Peace Problems:* 5-29.

__________. 1978. "Hafiz al-Asad: A Political Profile." *Jerusalem Quarterly* 8 (Summer): 16-31.

Le Monde. 1978. "Le Régime fait face a un large mouvement de mécontentement." 21-27 December.

Moore, Clement Henry. 1974. "On Theory and Practice among the Arabs." *World Politics* 24 (October): 106-26.

Petran, Tabitha. 1972. *Syria.* New York: Praeger.

Rabinovich, Itimar. 1972. *Syria under the Ba'th, 1963-66.* New York: Halstead Press.

Razzaz, Munif. 1967. *al-Tajriba al-Murra.* Beirut: Dār al-Ghandur.

Rodinson, Maxime. 1968. *Israel and the Arabs.* Middlesex: Penguin.

Salamah, Ibrahim. 1969. *al-Ba'th min al-mudāris ila al-thakanāt.* Beirut.

al-Sayyid. Jallal. 1973. *Hizb al-Ba'th al-Arabī.* Beirut: Dār al-Nahār.

Seale, Patrick. 1965. *The Struggle for Syria.* London: Oxford University Press.

Seymour, Martin. 1970. "The Dynamics of Power in Syria since the Break with Egypt." *Middle Eastern Studies* 6.

Shakra, Akram S. 1966. "Land Reform in Syria." Ph.D. dissertation, University of Oklahoma.

Syrian Arab Republic (SAR). 1965a. *Documents sur la transformation socialiste.* Damascus.

__________. 1965b. "Legislative Decree No. 55 Providing for the Implementation of Self-Management." In SAR 1965a, pp. 31-33. Damascus.

__________. 1968. "Law for the Organization of Unions." Damascus.

__________, Central Bureau of Statistics (CBS). 1961-62. *Household Income and Expenditure Survey.* Damascus.

__________, __________. 1971-72. *Household Income and Expenditure Survey.* Damascus.

__________, __________. 1976. *Population Census in Syrian Arab Republic 1970.* Damascus.

__________, __________. 1977a. *1976 Statistical Abstract.* Damascus.

__________, __________. 1977b. *1970 Agricultural Census Data.* Damascus.

__________, Ministry of Agriculture and Agrarian Reform. 1977. *The Annual Agricultural Statistical Abstract.* Damascus.

__________, Ministry of Labor and Social Affairs. 1970. *Kanūn lil-Tanthīm 'Alaqat al-Zirā'ī.* Damascus.

__________, __________. 1977. *The Annual Statistical Bulletin of the Ministry of Labor and Social Affairs.* Damascus.

Torrey, Gordon. 1964. *Syrian Politics and the Military.* Columbus: Ohio State University Press.

__________. 1969. "The Ba'th: Ideology and Practice." *Middle East Journal* 23, 4.

United Nations. 1971. "Development Planning and Social Objectives in Syria." *Studies on Selected Development Problems in Various Countries in the Middle East, 1971.* New York.

Van Dam, Nikolas. 1979. *The Struggle for Power in Syria.* New York: St. Martin's Press.

Van Dusen, Michael H. 1972. "Political Integration and Regionalism in Syria." *Middle East Journal* 26, 1.

__________, 1975, "Syria: Downfall of a Traditional Elite." In *Political Elites and Political Development in the Middle East,* ed. Frank Tachau. New York: Halsted Press.

Warriner, Doreen. 1948. *Land and Poverty in the Middle East.* London: Royal Institute of International Affairs.

Part III

DOMESTIC ECONOMIC AND SOCIAL IMPLICATIONS OF LEGAL POLICY

Chapter 4

THE STATE APPARATUS AND SOCIAL LEGISLATION IN THE MAGHREB

Jean-Claude Vatin

Traditionally social legislation has been presented as a means both to improve the situation of a people and compensate for "natural" or given inequalities. However, because it is produced by governments, social legislation is also a weapon used by the political class to penetrate civil society and reinforce its own capacity of mobilization, as well as its monopoly over social activities.* For the Maghreb (Morocco, Algeria, Tunisia, and Libya), we will argue that social justice and political necessities clash in a specific way, and that laws regarding social welfare have to do not only with social justice, but also with social order (B. Moore 1978; von Hayek 1976; Segalman 1977; Brooke 1979). We will also suggest that the political process by which elites extract support from the masses through social legislation has certain inherent tensions. In order to demonstrate these points, we will examine two different fields of social policy: (a) Social law in general, where certain labor rights and guarantees (hiring and dismissal, working hours and conditions, pay, pensions, and other benefits) are limited by the nature of labor jurisprudence; and (b) Education and vocational training, where legislation, although drafted by the elites, is not really adapted to their own declared development plans.

*Regarding the political class, we shall differentiate between its bases of *legitimacy* and *efficacy*. It is the latter which helps determine the value of a country's national capabilities, as Organski's works have clearly demonstrated (see Organski and Kugler 1980; see also Farnetti 1971).

I would like to thank Amal Rassam for her thoughtful comments on an earlier draft of this paper, as well as the following for their useful remarks: John Bentley, Michael Hager, Abdallah Hammoudi, Elbaki Hermassi, Raymond Hinnebusch, Hatem el-Karanshawy, Malcolm Kerr, Ann Mayer, Laurence Michalak, James Socknat, and John Waterbury.

RELATIONSHIP AMONG STATE, LAWS, AND SOCIETY: THREE INTERPRETATIONS

Insofar as social legislation is concerned, the intricate relationship among state, laws, and a society can be analyzed in terms of three different approaches. First, for those who think that the world of the present is the best of all possible worlds and that the future tends toward progress, social legislation is the instrument given to a central authority to help transform the society which has selected it. Laws have thus been enacted to provide a national community with almost mechanical remedies to social problems. However, the "price" of modernization, which has led to ruptures within a social body in a stable though fragile balance, has been so high recently that the state has had to construct special counterweights. Ethnic groups, social classes, those threatened by the impact of development–i.e., economic and cultural victims of transformation–should be morally protected by the state. The duty of new states in particular is to compensate for the internal disruptions caused by the movement from tradition to modernity, from local economy to the world market, from agriculture to industry. Thus the myth of benevolent care by the state, of civil society progressing through the efforts of its own representatives, has been revived. This does not imply, however, that legislation always achieves its social goals; shifts orchestrated by planners do not always produce the expected results. But the general view is that good must ultimately prevail over evil in politics and that governments are constituted to meet the social requirements of their citizens.

The second approach is antithetical to the first. It suggests that politics tends naturally toward evil, and that governments are inclined to use their power to manipulate societies. The state tends to increase the scope and degree of its intervention and social control under the pretext of purported threats and difficulties. As the only group capable of satisfying the desires which its own intervention helped create, the political class reinforces its position at the top of the system. Moreover, it is able to manipulate society for its own benefit. Hence (for example) the recent tendency to intervene in dislocated, bifurcated, or fragile Muslim communities in the name of Islamization; hence the government appeals to religious ideology to escape political criticism and avoid attacks on economic grounds. Hence ideological answers to concrete problems.

Between these two approaches a third might prove more accurate as it includes elements of the other two. Domestic policies, as elaborated through social legislation, have a logical basis—i.e., a rationale. However, the rationale is not free from affectation or disguise. Leaders do not do what they pretend, and they do not do it for the reasons they put forward. Obviously distinctions must be made among three types of rationality:

a) That of the political system as a whole (which depends not only on its historical and social foundations, but also on its efforts to become increasingly autonomous);
b) That of the body in control of the system (which tends to reinforce its own base and legitimacy through its policies and the actions of its legal apparatus and bureaucracy);
c) Those of the social groups within the political community (each of them with interests diverging from those of the center).

It is thus possible to see social legislation as a provisional and ambiguous compromise produced by interests which are not necessarily complementary. According to this approach, government policies in general and social legislation in particular are not "manufactured articles" produced by a single social "factory" (either the political system or civil society). They are neither the results of unified social demands nor the one-sided decisions of political leaders. Rather they contrive to answer the various needs and demands of both state and society at the same time.

In this context the relationship between social legislation on the one hand and political and economic power on the other cannot be analyzed in neutral terms. For example, when a law is passed, the specific legal text is not accepted out of unselfish motives. Rather it passes for two reasons: (a) A faction of the community which would profit from the law puts pressure on the state to pass it; and (b) The state not only responds to a specific group's request, but also profits from it to reinforce the social integration and political support of that group without weakening the allegiance of other groups. In other words, the moving mechanism of actions and demands in any independent political system varies according to both the autonomous capacity and power of the superstructure which controls society and the way socioeconomic forces are integrated in the system and related to one another.

The interrelationships among the political players are not as simple as they may appear. For one thing, pressure groups might express wishes which do not correspond to the expectations of their own bases. For another, the state might misjudge a popular motive or select an unsatisfactory legal solution. Furthermore, the delay between the expression of a demand and the implementation of legislation might be so long that the politcal response will seem inadequate because the demand has changed in the meantime. Finally, the administrative agents who are in charge of keeping watch on the population and translating its requirements into policies—i.e., the politicians who are responsible for making laws and the bureaucrats who are in charge of implementing them—may pervert the effect of the legislation at any point in the process.

SOCIAL LEGISLATION AND ITS SOURCES IN THE MAGHREB

If social legislation includes all law governing the relationship of the individual to work experience in the broadest sense—including social protection, education and vocational training, minimum wages and work conditions, and equal access to food and culture—then we must deal with a large amount of juridical output in the Maghreb since independence (charters, codes, laws, decrees, decisions, orders, administrative memoranda, etc.). Also, a wide sample of economic, social, and political activities must be taken into account.

With regard to employment, it is necessary to look at the economic conditions of the labor market in each of the four Maghrebi countries, as well as the interdependence of employment, seasonal employment, underemployment, and unemployment. Ideally, a detailed analysis of job and vocational training should rely on well-established data giving exact figures and allowing any social scientist to compare the figures for technical training, on the one hand, and those for the general system of education, on the other. In practice, however, such data are difficult to obtain and compare. Here the Algerian case is striking because the technological institutes are directly under ministries and state industrial bureaucracies, while universities and engineering schools belong to the Ministry of Higher Education and Research. Moreover, the methods and degrees of specialization in each economic sector are not easy to pinpoint.

Working conditions and wage policies vary according to the economic sectors of production, but the impact of any change in one area is usually observed only much later in other areas. Thus in the high plains of the Constantine region, east of Algiers, it took planners a long time to discover that mechanics in agricultural cooperatives were leaving the farms for the new factories which had just opened in the small towns nearby. The wages—which were higher in industry than in agriculture—were partly responsible, but the working conditions and the lure of the cities also played a part. When the government decided recently that the basic pay in the rural areas (which had not been increased for several years) would be the same as that in industry, the cost of agricultural produce rose accordingly.

Workers' protection is another useful field of investigation, with its judicial, social, financial, and political aspects. In Algeria the texts for the socialist management of business—the *Charte* and *Code de la gestion socialiste des entreprises (GSE)* of 1971 and the *Statut général du travailleur* of 4 July 1978—seemed to indicate that the country had broken new ground in this area and was ahead of the other Maghrebi countries.* But legislation is not necessarily the same as practice. It was admitted that practice differed from the rules even in heavy industry factories such as those of Annaba and Arzew. When we attempted to investigate the private sector, it was impossible to learn exactly how social security, insurance, and various types of reimbursement functioned. It was possible to ascertain that in the state-run domain of economic production an increasing proportion of strikes had taken place (despite their having been declared illegal), and they had been acknowledged by both the Union Générale des Travailleurs Algériens (UGTA)—Algeria's national labor organization—and the Ministry of Labor.† Establishing a comprehensive list of strikes in all economic branches was impossible, but one could read the texts of the work laws regarding safety devices laid down for the workers' benefits, employment organization, income assistance, etc.

In regard to worker participation, we endeavored to learn how a worker could (a) Benefit from a profit-sharing program; (b) Partake in the management, decisions, and control of a farm, business concern, firm, or factory through specific institutions as set out in the *GSE*; and (c) Upgrade his qualifications through vocational training. Here again the picture was vague and varied according to the sectors of production, as well as to the type of ownership (e.g., the state sector covered by the *GSE*; the collective sector—*autogestion*; or the

*The *Charte* and *GSE* involved one hundred firms and half a million workers. (Both 1971 and 1978 legislation data are in Algeria, *JORADP*, 8 August 1978.)

†In 1979 alone the following public sector workers went on strike: dockers (twice), postmen (for the first time since independence), air controllers, and bus drivers in Algiers.

private sector).* It is even more complicated when we estimate the impact of two important factors. First, in the Maghrebi countries employment has been the exception or at least the privilege of a minority, while unemployment has been widespread. Second, much of the working class, mainly composed of formerly rural people, has had to migrate to Europe to find jobs. Thus an important part of the Maghrebi proletariat has been living under the rules of a capitalist economy within industrially developed countries.† The very perception of the workers' world in the Maghreb has been modified as a result of these two factors, which constantly interfere with the study of the working situation.

THE STRUCTURE OF EMPLOYMENT

The transformation of the systems of production has been remarkable in all of the Maghreb in recent years—i.e., 1968-80 (see Edwards, ed. 1974). From the Egyptian-Libyan border to the Atlantic Ocean, not one of the economic systems is comparable to its colonial predecessor. The transformation has caused a redistribution of the wage-earning population. In Algeria industrialization has led to the creation of numerous jobs, as have food, agricultural products, and synthetic textiles in Morocco, and the tourist trade and manufacturing activities in Tunisia. In addition, a large number of public offices have been established in the three countries since they became independent. Furthermore, the rate of growth of the labor force—which depended on the rate of growth of the population—has been successfully matched by a regular annual increase of employment. In the early 1960s labor forces in North Africa grew at approximately 1.1 percent each year—similar to the rate of the developed countries at that time. Between 1965 and 1980 this growth rate reached 2.5 percent (while it dropped to 1.0 percent in the West). The challenge

*For instance, in 1979—eight years after the promulgation of the *GSE*—only 57 firms representing a total of 832 units and 263,318 workers came under its auspices. This leaves out a large portion of the public sector, especially hydrocarbon production, banking, information and culture, and health services. (See "Rapport de la CNO" 1981.)

†This has had an important financial impact. For instance, Moroccan migrant workers in Europe sent home the equivalent of over 3 billion Moroccan dirhams (MD) in 1978. That is more than tourism (MD 1.6 billion) or even phosphates (MD 2.1 billion) brought into the Moroccan treasury.

of creating new jobs at such a pace was formidable; it has been met remarkably well on the whole (Turnham 1980; cited in Edwards, ed. 1974:12).

The "economic revolution" has not benefited all social categories, however. For instance, the wage-earning classes appear to be on the increase if we consider figures for the whole Maghreb. But if we compare the number of people with a regular salary to the total population, we see that the former has not grown significantly during the last decade. Furthermore, the "modern" sector of the economy is of importance for a small part of the population only; capitalist activities in Morocco and Tunisia, which are obviously linked with the Western market, do not yet concern the majority of the working population. In Algeria industrial labor, which appears considerable when viewed from the outside, seems to be more marginal within the country itself. This does not mean that the "Singapore syndrome" described by Clifford Geertz (1977) applies to the Maghreb—i.e., a situation in which a part of a country's economic production has developed through close links with the world market while the rest continues along the lines of the traditional economy (local markets and small production). Not one of the Maghrebi states corresponds to the Singapore model today. Nor have Maghrebi workers ever been the homologues of workers in industrialized countries. That neither model applies illustrates that most of our tools for studying labor, workers, and social legislation in North Africa do not fit stereotyped explanations and theories.

Concepts themselves are only partly useful. For example, what do the words *labor, employment,* and *unemployment* mean? As early as 1963 Pierre Bourdieu demonstrated that the words were understood differently from one individual to the next (see Bourdieu et al. 1968).* A manual worker who does not get a regular salary cannot consider himself employed, while the man who is busy with small jobs of different kinds considers himself a worker. What then do the concepts of *manpower, labor market, qualifications,* or *specialization* mean? What about *investment, market value, marketing,* or *interest*—

*Edwards, ed. (1974:10-11) provides us with a typology of unemployment: (a) Open unemployment; (b) Underemployment; (c) The visibly active but underutilized; (d) Hidden unemployment; and (e) Prematurely retired. This might help the sociologist introduce more adequate categories, but it does not provide us with a satisfactory means of investigation.

among others? What do planners put under the heading of "active population"?* Apparently experts on individual countries change their minds from one period to another, while the interpretations of specialists from different countries diverge. Thus in Algeria the 1977 census considered the active population to be individuals between 18 and 59 years of age, while the 1966 census mentioned people between 15 and 54. Moreover, in 1977 only employed women (*occupées*) were taken into account, while women had been totally excluded in the 1966 figures.† Similarly, the official Tunisian data of 1975 referred to the same age classes as the Algerian data of 1977; however, Morocco still based its figures on the 15-65-year-old stratum of "employed" and "unemployed." As with age classifications, the concept of "merchant" differs according to government categories in Rabat, Algiers, Tunis, and Tripoli.

From another point of view, how can formal national accounts assess the sector of small businesses, tradesmen, and noncommercial labor? It is difficult to measure statistically because its members do not file the reports on which planners and economic advisers base their calculations. Civil servants report official figures. But in societies where so many people perform services without asking for money; where bartering still flourishes; where small trades and unknown "professions" help an important part of the population survive in a disrupted economy or in a state of crisis; and where many forms of exchange cannot be calculated, many of the modern instruments of economic estimation are inadequate, if not superfluous. Various attempts to study the labor market in terms of segmentation (i.e., through systematic analyses of distinct markets which can be differentiated from the national one) represent a first step toward a more efficient approach to the structure of employment. But nothing is certain regarding the adequacy of the techniques used by Edwards, ed. (1974), Piore (1972, 1978), and others when applied to the labor

*See the different meanings various authors and statistical documents attach to *active, working, employed,* or *part-time employed.* The basic active population can include employed individuals, the unemployed who have previously worked, the unemployed who have not yet worked, and women in part-time employment.

†Out of 17.3 million in 1977 the "theoretical" working population of Algeria would have been 7 million, including women. However, official data refer to a "practical" working sample (including only women having a permanent job—i.e., 2.7 percent of the female population).

markets of Maghrebi economies (see also Ryan 1980; Sengenberger 1979).*

Finally, are the figures comparable among agencies and among countries? Can we base our analysis on statistics which might not be reliable or accurate—that is, when they are available? To take but one example, most of the data produced by the ministries of labor, industry, education, and agriculture—each of which has a bureau of statistics—as well as by offices for planning and accounting all have confronted observers and analysts with the difficult task of comparing various data before they could draw any conclusions. Even if bureaucracies in the four Maghrebi countries provide experts with an impressive collection of annual data, we encounter some difficulty in making the right estimates.†

POLITICAL ACTORS AND JURIDICAL DOCUMENTS

The successive stages of legislation might be described as follows: (1) Perception of a cause (popular demand, state manipulation); (2) Production of a law (technical elaboration after discussion, bargaining, and compromise); (3) Enforcement (technical and practical aspects); (4) Application and control through intermediaries (police, justice); (5) Backlash (consequential effects on the population as well as on the political system). These stages are both very clear and highly artificial. They do not help us to answer practical questions such as (for example) who would be responsible for the drafting of a law on the technical training of adolescents in Tunisia. President Habib Bourguiba is the obvious source, as his signature appears at the bottom of the text when the law is promulgated. The prime minister and the minister of education might have initialed the document as well; the ministers of youth and sports and of social affairs might have been concerned too. Perhaps the deputy minister in charge of planning collaborated at some stage. But the whole text might also have been prepared by the secretary of state in charge of social affairs and vocational training and then modified by the Council of Ministers. We

*In the Maghreb we will suggest that if there is a segmentation of the labor market, it is not twofold but threefold because there is a third sector corresponding to the "third economy" (see below).

†Even such careful works as Palloix (1980) or the various North African yearbooks do not allay reservations about the reliability of statistics on the Maghreb.

might be able to trace the origins of the law while finding some motion voted on by the Destour Socialist Party or the national trade union organization. The fifth five-year plan for economic and social development (1977-81) might also give some clues owing to special paragraphs on "the future prospects for employment" (600,000 persons will be looking for jobs during the 1980s, and 525,000 could find one if the plan works well). Likewise, the local press could have mentioned the problem of young people finishing school without any special training.

Our major concern remains, however: What influence was exerted upon those who chose to deal with the issue of vocational training for youth? What range of possibilities did the legislators have? What were the interrelationships between the elaboration of the vocational training legislation, on the one hand, and overall national education policy, on the other? Were economic provisions and orientations taken into consideration? Which personalities, committees, and pressure groups intervened, at what stage, and with what effect? Other questions come to mind. For example, as far as access to knowledge is concerned, does the law reflect a vision of social equality and justice borrowed from Tunisian tradition? If so, is it Islamic-oriented? Which Islam was mentioned—the customary, the reformist, the neo-secularist? Or was it Western-oriented, clearly stamped, for instance, by the French Jacobin legacy?*

SOCIAL LEGISLATION AS AN INSTRUMENT OF STATE CONTROL

Recalling the approaches described at the beginning of this essay, we could tentatively adopt the position that legislation in the Maghreb has been to a significant degree more a means used by the states to penetrate society than a direct answer to popular demands. All indications are that the story of the countries of North Africa has been the story of the extension of state power. Through bureaucracy,

*With reference to the impact of legislation on the population, we could ask the following: How do young people feel about a particular law, and what are their parents' reactions? How do the beneficiaries of social legislation manifest their support for the government? What do people who cannot benefit from some legislation say about it? If there are opponents, on what grounds do they criticize the provisions or clauses of any proposed law? On this issue see von Sivers (1981), a highly suggestive article on the differences in work ethics in the industrial and the bazaar sectors of Algeria.

the control of the political structure, institutionalized intermediaries (political parties, trade unions, professional associations, and the like), and the drafting of legal codes, governments have acquired a powerful set of tools for extending their domination over the population. Almost all political sectors have been monopolized by the state apparatus, and in this context social legislation is a means to an end.

Let us take Libya's labor law of 1 April 1970 as one case in point. It is evident that everything concerning employment offices, the recruitment of foreigners, vocational training, and contracts of employment, as well as working hours, the well-being of employees, and trade union and labor disputes, has been determined by the Revolutionary Council. The Ministry of Labor and Social Affairs issued a memo in which the basic principles of the law were explained:

> The September First Revolution announced . . . that its objective [was] the establishment of social justice in order to realize sufficiency of production and equity of distribution. The prerequisites of this justice start from ensuring the individual in a manner which liberates him from fear and need, secures an honorable life for him, and grants him the right to work under equal opportunities, thus enabling us to build the edifice of the Libyan Arab Republic on a strong and solid foundation as far as social, economic, and political aspects are concerned.
>
> Such being the case, it was imperative that the State should reconsider all social and economic legislation. . . . It became necessary that special attention be paid to labor legislation inasmuch as work in the Libyan Arab Republic is a right, duty, and honor for every capable citizen. The stepping up of production and success of overall national planning depend principally on work. Labor relations are by nature many sided. Besides the employees, there are employers, as well as the capital invested in industrial and commercial enterprises. On this combination of elements production depends, and the creation of a fair equilibrium between them results in the stability of economic life (Libya, Ministry of Labor and Social Affairs 1970; see also Libya, Revolutionary Command Council 1970:58).

In Libya there was no opposition to such solid principles. They accorded with official statements which provided for "regulation of the relationship between laborers and their employers, participation of laborers on the boards of directors, entitlement to 25 percent of the net profits of their companies, and the prohibition of arbitrary dismissal of workers" (Libya, Revolutionary Command Council n.d.). Provisions for regulating the employment of juveniles and women, protecting employees from work hazards, determining salaries geared toward a certain standard of living, and establishing that a minimum number of Libyans be employed in foreign firms—all these were recorded in the new law to indicate that things had changed in Libya and that the revolutionary state was also a welfare state which had been created for both the benefit and the defense of the people.

There was an obverse side to the law, however. For instance, in Chapter 2, Part 1, dealing with employment offices, the most important provision was that "the employment of individuals should be accomplished through [official government] offices or [employment should be given] to those who hold certificates of registration from any of these offices" (Libya, Revolutionary Command Council 1970:89). In the same spirit, all the articles referring to trade unions in Part 4 indicated that from the moment the law was passed, it would not "permit the formation of more than one trade union for the laborers and employees of one industrial vocation" (p. 101).* Moreover, most of the provisions in the document were aimed at strengthening the control of the Ministry of Labor and Social Affairs over the working community. There was even a list of prohibitions regarding trade union activities, among which the most important was "the establishment of direct or indirect relations between a trade union and any foreign trade union" (p. 103).

This specific example is a perfect illustration of the twofold nature of state intervention—i.e., protection and control. A single measure may even meet both requirements, however contradictory they may appear. Thus in Chapter 3, Part 1, of the Libyan law, the provisions pertaining to the employment of foreigners in the country have been laid down "to protect Libyan manpower in the face of foreign competition" by fixing the minimum percentage of Libyan employees which must be hired in particular industries and establishments (Libya, Revolutionary Command Council 1970:90). The express purpose was not only to protect Libyan workers, but also "to exercise full supervision over the employment of foreigners in

*Because of the way in which all workers' unions had been unified by President Moamar Qaddafi for some time, the Congress of Arab Unions did not accept the membership of Libyan unions.

the country" (*ibid.*), while at the same time keeping a close eye on Libyans employed by foreign firms.*

It could be argued that the ideology of Libya today gives such a labor law new meaning because labor questions are dealt with on a more egalitarian basis. For instance, we know that President Qaddafi laid down more explicit and drastic principles in his *Green Book,* the third volume of which was published in 1979. His political "neo-Maoism," a mixture of a Marxist approach and a return to the Quran and Shari'a law, causes him to advocate the elimination of anything leading to social classes, economic exploitation, and injustice in general. According to him, justice should be restored through a socialization of the means of production—i.e., through the elimination of both private property and wage labor. Thus he has attempted to limit individuals to the ownership and profit of one house or flat only. However, the new system to reward labor has not satisfied all workers, and wage labor in banking and oil has not been abolished. It appears that Qaddafi has instituted a new definition of the concepts of natural law and direct democracy.

The Libyan law on social security of 14 April 1980 (Libya, *El Jarida Er-Rasmiya* 1980:514-51)—which includes the zakat system and other institutions of Islamic solidarity in its article 2—could be considered from the viewpoint of the twofold nature of state intervention. It provides for social security according to the Qaddafiyan philosophy—i.e., through "popular committees." A pyramidal system of representation is indicated, with a general committee at the top and popular committees at the local level (art. 4); the latter have financial autonomy (art. 6). On the surface the law appears to be a generous text filled with revolutionary spirit. The beneficiaries of social security are called "associates," and the popular committees represent them. However, the document makes no mention of how such committees are to be elected. From what we know of recent popular committees in Libya, there is no proof of any elections whatsoever. Leaders select the members from among those who have openly supported the regime's policies. Hence popular committees appear to be a medium of the political center in the field of social legislation (see al-Assiouty 1981; Cooley 1982:chs. 9 and 12; Wright 1982; Ansell and al-Arif 1972; and Mayer 1977).

*A propaganda booklet makes the two aims of the legislation perfectly clear when it states the following: "The state has paid due attention to labor education to make workers aware of their rights and duties and to help them carry out their role in building the democratic socialist society effectively" (Libya n.d.:231).

Another case in which a set of social issues has been taken over by the state to reinforce its grip over society can be seen in Algeria. The statute of workers of 1978, although different from the Libyan in many respects, provides us with some analogies (Algeria, *JORADP* 1978; on social legislation see Algeria, Ministry of Work and Social Affairs 1976).

If we look at the general framework of what should be the work laws in Algeria for the future, we find an extensive chapter on salaries: 85 of the 216 articles of the work statute (title 4) are devoted to them. Salaries had been a crucial subject for years because of wide discrepancies both between private and public sectors and within the public sector alone. For example, the salary for an employee with particular qualifications can vary by a factor of three, depending upon the employer—a ministry, national firm, semi-official institution, etc.

There was a certain moral argument which allowed the state, through the work statute of 1978, to become the only institution to decide and regulate salaries. After 1978 employers were no longer free to determine wages. Furthermore, articles 131 and 132 mentioned that disparities between rural and industrial salaries would be eliminated after a period of transition. The measure to equalize rural and urban wages had been laid down so that the statutory minimum guaranteed wage would be the same for all branches of economic activity—a move intended to stop peasants from migrating from the country to the towns.* All the regulations regarding earnings tended to make the system of remuneration the same throughout the country. Wage earners (and wage costs) were defined according to a fairer scale. All adjustments of wages were strictly prescribed. In the interest of equality, there was but one wage table which was itself aligned to an index.

It was impossible to eliminate all discrepancies in wage rates—especially among manual, clerical, and professional (or "mental") categories of work, or between fixed salaries and piece wages, not to mention categories for extra pay, bonuses, and allowances. Moreover, workers did not necessarily consider bureaucrats to be qualified to assess the relative difficulty of a given job and the remuneration it should be accorded. On the whole, however, people saw a great

*In 1977 the agricultural sector, comprising 41.3 percent of the population, received 15.3 percent of the national income, while the nonagricultural sector, with 58.7 percent of the population, received 84.7 percent of the income.

improvement with government intervention (see Algeria, *JORADP* 1978:art. 211 on the National Committee on Salaries). A greater number of salary earners felt increasingly secure, especially because along with the benefits discussed, other social measures on paid leaves, sickness and disability benefits, pensions, insurance, and unemployment plans had been extended through the work statute of 1978 to accommodate broader categories of beneficiaries.*

It may be argued that the standardization of wages of the working community was not merely for egalitarian reasons, but for political reasons as well. The work statute aimed first to satisfy the workers of the socialist sector, which most supports the economy of the country. The charter of socialist management presented the workers as producer-managers (*producteurs-gestionnaires*). The producer-managers, who were also salaried workers, ran the socialist sector on behalf of the Algerian people, the legal (although symbolic) owners. For them to run the sector effectively, the work statute had to meet a second requirement: organization of the socialist enterprises. In consequence, labor legislation as framed in capitalist countries—where it was made for the protection of labor against the owners of the means of production—could not be the same in a country where workers were not considered to be "exploited" since in some sense they were co-owners. Thus labor grievances, where they existed, did not entail the same sort of mediation or arbitration as they would have in a Western context.

Because of the different relationship between employees and employers in the Algerian context (the parties engaged in negotiations could not be considered social enemies), organization, union policy, and union regulations had to be put in different terms.† Settling labor claims and wage disputes had a diffferent meaning from the capitalist context. Moreover, strikes would become contradictory. As article 61 of the 1976 Constitution had made clear, and as article 21 of the work statute repeated, the right to strike was the privilege of the private sector, where it was often the only way to make labor claims heard or to protect workers from exploitation. Whether partial or total, sit-down or slow-down, spontaneous or

*See articles 9-18 of the work statute, dealing with the protection of the worker and his/her family.

†The employee-employer relationship has been replaced by that of worker-employment organization. On the state-run sector, see Belloula (1977); Boutefnouchet (1978); and Ghezali (1980).

prearranged, no strike has been allowed within the public sector. Thus the workers' protective legislation is also a form of anti-strike legislation.

The right of association exists of course. Freedom of participation in a professional association has been made explicit in the work statute (art. 24). However, organized labor must express itself through the only authorized union (UGTA).

It is apparent that in addition to the desire of legislators to reorganize the working community—the stated objective—there was another aim: to further political command of the whole society.* By entering the intricate world of wage rates and imposing its own system, the state apparatus had further extended its sphere of influence. By asking workers to fulfill certain moral and practical obligations, as defined by chapter 2, title 1, and especially by articles 27, 28, and 35 of the work statute (which seem to be logical counterparts to the social guarantees), those in power have strengthened their capacity to intervene in the labor force. As there is no wage policy without wage control, there is no labor legislation without labor regulation. (Commentaries on the Algerian work statute can be found in Korichi 1980: 21-34; Igl 1981:315-38; and *El Moudjahid* 1978 [various issues].)

THE STATE-SOCIETY COUPLE

State penetration of society in the Maghreb has deepened since the 1960s. It did not come about only through the influence of the political class at the top of the nation-states. It received substantial support from the population. People have not stopped petitioning the state for assistance. Social demands have been a constant in Maghrebi politics as they have been elsewhere around the world. Popular expectations have tended to transform the center's apparatus into a slot machine which distributes social security, health services, financial assistance, and insurance, as well as jobs and education.

Not so long ago, students brought up in the middle class had one ideal: to enter the civil service, earn a high salary, and then be recruited by a ministry prestigious enough to afford them a certain amount of influence. In Algeria after the economic boom of the 1970s, the ideal for any student with a university degree was to

*It was only after the control of the workers had been achieved that the government prepared for the drafting of the National Charter of 1976.

become a salaried member of one of the national firms, such as SONATRACH (the oil and natural gas company), which was then considered the top and had become the symbol of modern management and industrial technology—and a generous distributor of wages. The dream was for a job with some responsibility and autonomy, but also with an office, a car, and a flat (all paid for by the employer) in the capital city, as well as the possibility of upward mobility and an increasing income. Tunisian and Moroccan students had similar hopes, although the business professions held more allure than the state service.

All this was still true some years ago. Now, however, it is questionable whether the state has maintained its positive aura and legitimacy. For instance, suspicion was aroused when peasants found that the so-called Ben Salah experience in Tunisia and the "agrarian revolution" in Algeria had not only failed to increase their incomes, but had also multiplied bureaucratic controls on production. The urban population expressed dissatisfaction when it realized that it might not be worth earning 10 percent more each year if inflation cancelled out the increase. In Algeria the prestige of being a civil servant or employee in a national company diminished once heavy industrialization had become the focus of criticism and the powerful ministry headed by Belaid Abdesselam had been dismantled. Gradually various groups in the Maghrebi population began to feel the state's growing incapacity to meet social needs.

There is a good deal of evidence pointing to popular changes in attitude. For example, although the economic and social problems are greater, the ordinary citizen has lower expectations regarding the state's intervention. "Depolitization" is the word used by analysts to account for this modified behavior, although the term is not entirely appropriate considering a continuing popular interest in political and national questions. It is likely that Maghrebis have become more realistic in recent years—even fearing the intervention of their government—for the more expensive and detailed is legislation, the less autonomy is left to either the people in general or to economic entrepreneurs. Excepting the "new bourgeoisie" (the trade and bureaucratic ranks of the bourgeoisie), a trend is evident across the entire Maghreb to return to traditional practices, to collective or individual actions, and it is especially strong among the lower middle class (see CRESM 1980; Peneff 1981).

Economic activity gives a good idea of the changing attitudes. Small is not that beautiful; nevertheless, small companies and limited partnerships need few workers and can thus flout labor and trade regulations. A company may recruit women and children who work at home, or it can use seasonal, part-time, unskilled workers. Ignoring the legislation on the recruitment and dismissal of employees is much easier in these contexts. In addition, a family firm can avoid paying both taxes and wages and can evade union and government control.

A feature common to the economy of almost every nation in the world, whether capitalist or socialist, industrialized or developing, has given rise to many terms—"third economy," "parallel economy," "underground economy," "informal economy."* State-run or liberal economies leave the door open for small investment, allowing those with almost no access to capital to do business. In countries with capital-intensive projects (such as Algeria), employment cannot be offered on a large scale, so private enterprise becomes a vital necessity.

The fact that a third economy exists is less compelling than the question of how it emerged and continues to function. The third economy developed while state penetration itself was growing (which is logical), but the traditional sector (sometimes the subsistence sector in various branches of production) also remained. This nonstructured part of the economy—which is out of the control of government—has made noticeable progress in the Maghreb in recent years. The success of the small-scale entrepreneurs and of small-scale commercial activities in urban areas is patent. Domestic workshops, home work, and outwork have been constants in the Maghreb, providing indirect wages and bolstering the barter economy. It is striking that, far from diminishing, they have increased, becoming more evident features of the economic landscape.

At the lower economic level it is apparent that odd jobs have multiplied in relation to the development of cities. Families are increasingly dependent on multiple sources of income for survival. Either one person has more than one job, or various members of a family hold down undeclared jobs. The number of those engaged in curious and arcane functions in cities has been growing rapidly. There is a sizable list of apparently useless tasks, of "nonexploitative" activities, of marginal jobs—all of them bringing small sources of income to a great number of people who appear on no official record whatsoever. Retail dealers with small-scale shops can at least be

*In the United States this economy might amount to $20 billion a year. In Italy it is said to account for one third of national economic activity.

spotted, and it is likely that they pay state and city taxes. But how can researchers estimate the number of self-employed persons who serve as low-price retailers, peddlers, hawkers, pushcart vendors, and middlemen in the streets and who go unreported? Zakiya Daoud (1983) and Chantal Bernard (1983a) have attempted to study such occupations in Morocco without being able to give a thorough account of odd jobs. Their findings may help us understand why what planners call absolute poverty (in the shantytowns of Casablanca or Rabat, for example) does not lead to starvation and total economic deprivation.*

At the upper level of economic activity, those from the new bourgeoisie who have a university degree or a good socioeconomic background (or come from a wealthy ethnic group such as the Soussi and Fassi of Morocco, the Kharedjite communities of the Mzab in Algeria, or the island of Djerba in Tunisia) have a better chance of making money outside the public sector than in it. In fact, since the state sector, which is supposed to cover an extensive portion of the market, has proven unable to do so, they are taking advantage of every opportunity to play an intermediary role between the national and world markets. Their income has not much to do with the ownership of the means of production, but rather with a monopoly of the trade of some specific goods, with the export-import business, or with licenses to import particular products. Some profit from the fact that the state in the Maghreb (with the possible exception of Libya) demonstrates liberal views, favors free enterprise, or (in the case of Algeria) considers that "nonexploitative" undertakings should be supported.† Others have become experts—consultants, lawyers, and the like.

In sum, there has been a change in social relationships which is linked with the transformation of the economy, on the one hand, and with the perceptions of the state and its inability to govern the whole economy, on the other. Such a change might have two political implications: Either social tensions will rise, leading to political criticism from the exposed part of the population—a situation which

*Daoud and Bernard have established lists of third economy occupations. For other Maghrebi countries see Bernard (1980b) and IEDES (1979).

†In Algeria repeated references have been made to "nonexploitative," "nonparasitic" capital since the National Charter. In December 1981 the Central Committee of the Front National de Libération (FLN) drew a more explicit line between "good" and "bad" private enterprises, gauging them according to their contribution to national development.

might end in a reinforcement of militant Islamic movements (in Tunisia and Algeria especially), as well as in a strengthening of left-wing groups (in Morocco). Or there will be some accommodations as some individuals find ways to evade regulations while others turn to the third economy to provide them with the minimum for survival. It may be important for governments to be able to use elements from the religious code in order to justify their ways and means, as well as the origins and impacts of social legislation. But the Tunisian and Moroccan examples—which have given rise to divergent laws by citing the same Quranic verses or by referring to contradictory *hadith* (sayings attributed to the Prophet Mohammed) to support similar decisions—have demonstrated that the Muslim vocabulary cannot be randomly manipulated without risk.

EDUCATION, VOCATIONAL TRAINING, AND EMPLOYMENT OBJECTIVES

Throughout the Maghreb the respective systems of education have been improving since independence. An increasing number of children are going to school (from the high of 72 percent in Algeria to the low of 56 percent in Morocco, according to estimates my associates and I collected in 1976); in addition, more students are going to universities and graduating; in Morocco the number doubled between 1976-77 and 1980-81. (Table 1 presents figures from 1960 and the late 1970s.) These improvements in education have had an effect on the traditional equilibrium within each society. Social redistribution has followed compulsory schooling. The welcome impacts of such a cultural change have been felt everywhere, especially in cities, the job market, and economic production. Increasingly qualified young people have emerged. Now the North African economies have better trained personnel at their disposal.

In spite of the positive aspects, there are negative aspects as well. On the one hand, there are still more highly sophisticated and specialized jobs than qualified applicants. On the other hand, the economy cannot absorb all the candidates looking for jobs.* The gap between skilled workers in industry and the sub-proletariat or the

*An Algerian government decision to open new universities (for a total of twenty-one in the coming years) has many ramifications. For one thing, how will all the graduates be absorbed by the market when full employment in several branches of the economy is not yet close to being attained?

Table 1

EDUCATION IN THE MAGHREB, 1960 AND LATE 1970s

Country	Number Enrolled in Primary School as Percentage of Age Group: Total		Male		Female		Number Enrolled in Secondary School as Percentage of Age Group		Number Enrolled in Higher Education as Percentage of Population Aged 20-24		Adult Literacy Rate (*Percent*)	
	1960	1979	1960	1979	1960	1979	1960	1979	1960	1978	1960	1977
Tunisia	66%	102%[a]	88%	119%	43%	85%	12%	25%	1%	5%	16%	62%
Libya	59	123	92	128	24	119	9	67	1	6	22	
Morocco	47	75	67	93	27	56	5	22	1	4	14	28
Algeria	46	98	55	113	37	83	8	31	[illegible]	4	10	35

Source: World Bank 1982:149-57.

[a]For countries with universal primary education, the figures may exceed 100 percent because some pupils may be below or above the official primary school age.

partially employed has widened. There are evident contradictions between the system of education and the needs of economic development.* Adolescents who did not finish school are looking for jobs and having no success because they never acquired a professional skill. Government discourses have praised technical and scientific development to the hilt and have transformed it into a myth, hence depreciating agricultural work; at the same time governments have been unable to build up strong technical and professional systems of education.† Students with degrees have difficulty adapting to the requirements of their first jobs because they are not prepared for the transition from a theoretical to a more practical world. Before we present a comparative picture of training policies in the Maghreb, let us first consider policy in Algeria to illustrate some of the general contradictions we have noted.

According to the 1977 Algerian census, the population jumped from 11.8 million in 1966 to 17.3 million—an annual increase of 3.2 percent. During the same period the urban population rose from 33 to 41 percent. Thus the urban population was increasing twice as fast as population in general. In the year 2000 the population will have reached between 34 and 40 million; more than half of that number will be in cities, with perhaps one quarter concentrated in the four provinces which include the most important metropolises (Algeria, Bureau of the Census, 1978, 1979, 1981; see also Sutton 1980).** (For urbanization data on the Maghreb, see Table 2.) According to official data, employment figures have not kept pace with the rapid population increases. While 430,000 nonagricultural workers who entered the labor market between 1966 and 1973 were offered

*Analysts will agree that such contradictions are hardly the Maghreb's monopoly. Henry J. Burton (1973) notes the following: "In few countries has education policy been related very closely to employment. The result has been not only the appearance of educated unemployed, but also bottleneck shortages in various parts of the economy." Edwards and Todaro acknowledge that "Clearly, some education is demanded for its own sake as a consumption good," but argue that "The investment demand for education can be seen as a demand 'derived' from high-income opportunities in the modern sector" (1974:316).

†In Algeria technical and professional education has been suppressed at the elementary and middle levels. (The new polytechnic colleges are not technical schools strictly speaking.) In Morocco there is no technical and professional education. In Libya a recent effort has been made to develop this domain, according to the information that we have gathered. However, technical education still lags far behind the country's needs (see Libya 1971).

**The four provinces are Algiers, Annaba, Constantine, and Oran.

Table 2

URBANIZATION IN THE MAGHREB, 1960-80

	Urban Population				Percentage of Urban Population			
	As Percentage of Total Population		Average Annual Growth Rate *(Percent)*		In Largest City		In Cities of over 500,000	
Country	1960	1980	1960-70	1970-80	1960	1980	1960	1980
Tunisia	36%	52%	90%	30%	40%	30%	40% (1)[a]	30% (1)
Libya	23	52	80	83	57	64	0 (0)	64 (1)
Morocco	29	41	42	46	16	26	16 (1)	50 (4)
Algeria	30	44	35	57	27	12	27 (1)	12 (1)

Source: Adapted from World Bank 1982:149-57.

[a]Figures in parentheses indicate number of cities of over 500,000 persons.

480,000 jobs, these figures are totally misleading because 120,000 workers left agriculture to find jobs elsewhere during that period. The fact that unemployment in the nonagricultural sector dropped from 28 to 15 percent between 1966 and 1979 must be weighed against the fact that there was 40 percent unemployment in the agricultural sector, where only 90,000 new jobs had been created. The five-year plan for 1980-84 and expert projections estimate that slightly less than three million jobs should be created by 1990: half a million in industry and administration (health services, education, and the like), 700,000 in building and public works, and over one million in services, transport, and trade. Cadre personnel should triple (from 100,000 to 300,000), and supervisory staff and technicians should reach a total of 900,000 (from a base figure of 360,000). Meanwhile, the number of workers (half a million) will have increased fourfold.

These are the broad figures. They suggest the need for an enormous financial investment in vocational training, advanced education for adults, and expansion of educational facilities. Such an investment might exceed Algeria's capacities in the near future, especially if we consider related factors: (a) The high inflation rate (17 percent in 1978); (b) The annual cost increase of agricultural products (19 percent) and the increasing cost of the external servicing of the debt (which can be viewed as either 10 percent of the GNP or 25 percent of the exports of goods and services in 1980) and which, when taken together with food imports, consume half of the annual hydrocarbon income; and (c) The disequilibrium between regions in which most of the industrial development is concentrated and the rest of the country.*

In more detailed analysis some of Algeria's employment problems become clear. First, if we look at official data from the Secretary of State for Planning (later Ministry), we notice that agricultural employment did not improve during the period 1973-77. At the same time, nonagricultural employment grew as approximately 100,000 jobs were created each year (see [among others] Murgue 1977; Sari 1975; Ali-Toudert 1979).† (Employment statistics are presented in Table 3.)

Second, if we consider urban and rural employment for the decade 1966-77 (including full- and part-time workers), it is apparent that the urban population profited from economic development while the rural population's employment was at a standstill. Moreover, the percentage of unemployed is much higher among the rural population. Table 4 presents employment figures by major economic services or activities, and Tables 5 and 6 provide additional breakdowns;** Table 7 provides comparison figures for the Maghrebi countries. (More detailed information can be found in ILO 1981.)

Third, the number of workers employed in most branches of manufacturing increased, but production did not grow accordingly. Production per employee has been maintained in some branches and improved in others. However, the general trend since 1978 has been a decline in both the public and private sectors (see Table 8).

*Forty-five percent of nonagricultural employment (building and public works excepted) is concentrated in the four provinces noted above.

†The massive growth of employment—especially in the wage-earning categories—has had some influence in reducing political conflicts since the death of President Houari Boumediene. There have been strikes (as noted earlier) but no open political protests. (On the issue of employment and political conflict, see Bernard 1980a.)

**The figures in Tables 4-6 correspond to the following population:

		Active	Activity Rate
Total population:	15,645,491	3,371,023	21.5
Male:	7,773,060	3,070,706	39.5
Female:	7,872,431	300,317	3.8

Table 3

ALGERIA: EMPLOYMENT STATISTICS, 1966-77
(Thousands)

Population Factor[a]	1966	1969	1976	1977
Total population	11,820	13,200	16,700	17,200
Working population	2,565	2,912	3,590	3,740
Urban working population	1,017	1,212	2,055	2,195
Employed	682	853	1,840	2,020
Unemployed	335	361	215	175
Percent of urban working population	33%	30%	10%	8%
Rural working population	1,548	1,698	1,535	1,545
Employed[b]	1,037	849	721	726
Percent estimated underemployed[c]	43%	50%	63%	63%

Source: Algeria, Secretary of State for Planning 1966 and 1977.

[a]Algerian residents abroad not included.

[b]Part-time employment included.

[c]The underemployed are defined as working less than 180 days per year.

Table 4

ALGERIA: WORKING POPULATION BY MAJOR ECONOMIC SERVICES OR ACTIVITIES, 1966 AND 1977

	1966		1977		
Economic Service or Activity	Number	Percent	Number	Percent	Index (1966 = 100)
Agriculture	852,300	49.4%	692,160	29.6%	82.3
Manufacturing	172,400	10	401,462	17.2	232
Construction and public works	90,900	5.4	345,816	14.8	380
Commerce and banking	140,100	8.1	183,580	7.9	131
Transport, storage, and communication	75,500	4.4	132,420	5.6	175
Administration	336,800	19.5	397,019	16.9	117
Other services or activities	56,900	3.2	127,615	7.8	324
Total	1,724,900	100	2,336,972	100	135

Table 5

ALGERIA: WORKING POPULATION BY DIVISIONS OF ECONOMIC ACTIVITY, 1977

Major Division of Economic Activity	Working Population				Employers and Self-Employed			Employees		
	Number	Percent	Males	Females	Number	Males	Females	Number	Males	Females
Agriculture, hunting, forestry, & fishing	682,700	20.3%	676,186	6,514	330,003	327,973	2,030	302,067	298,135	3,932
Mining & quarrying	69,172	2.0	67,130	2,042	448	448		68,495	66,473	2,022
Manufacturing	261,705	7.8	243,508	18,197	32,727	31,425	1,302	220,566	204,087	16,479
Electricity, gas, & water	30,276	0.9	28,531	1,745	232	232		29,922	28,193	1,729
Construction	345,318	10.2	342,480	2,838	23,141	23,112	29	319,414	316,615	2,799
Wholesale/retail trade, restaurants, & hotels	214,028	6.4	208,290	5,738	122,553	121,764	789	85,791	80,979	4,812
Transport, storage, & communication	132,351	3.9	127,843	4,508	26,428	26,423	5	105,399	100,906	4,493
Financing, insurance, real estate, & business services	17,767	0.5	14,858	2,909	810	803	7	16,846	13,944	2,902
Community, social, & personal services	431,480	12.8	347,947	83,533	3,531	3,405	126	422,314	339,233	83,081
Not adequately defined	1,186,226	35.2	1,013,933	172,293	21,131	20,176	955	25,878	21,741	4,137
Total	3,371,023	100.0	3,070,706	300,317	561,004	555,761	5,243	1,596,692	1,470,306	126,386

Table 6

ALGERIA: WORKING POPULATION BY MAJOR OCCUPATIONAL GROUP, 1977

Occupational Group	Number	Percent	Employers and Self-Employed	Employees
Professional, technical, & related	217,391	6.4%	5,049	212,101
Administrative & managerial	18,319	0.6	1,138	17,119
Clerical & related	324,617	9.6	1,290	323,234
Sales	190,494	5.7	149,362	36,658
Services	249,143	7.4	12,407	235,450
Agriculture, animal husbandry, forestry, fishermen, & hunters	654,558	19.4	331,243	269,671
Production & related, transport equipment operators, & laborers	1,046,942	31.0	115,005	923,350
Workers not classifiable by occupation	324,492	9.7	2,435	14,548
Persons seeking their first job	345,067	10.2		
Total	3,371,023	100.0	617,929	2,032,131

Table 7

THE MAGHREB: LABOR FORCE BY ECONOMIC SECTOR AND GROWTH RATE, 1960-2000
(Percent)

	Population of Working Age (15-64 Years)		Labor Force in: Agriculture		Labor Force in: Industry		Labor Force in: Services		Average Annual Growth of Labor Force		
Country	1960	1980	1960	1980	1960	1980	1960	1980	1960-70	1970-80	1980-2000
Tunisia	53%	55%	56%	34%	18%	33%	26%	33%	0.7%	2.9%	2.6%
Libya	53	51	53	19	17	28	30	53	3.6	3.5	3.0
Morocco	53	51	62	52	14	21	24	27	1.6	2.9	3.3
Algeria	52	49	67	25	12	25	21	50	1.0	3.5	3.5

Source: Adapted from World Bank 1982:149-57.

Table 8

ALGERIA: PRODUCTION AND EMPLOYMENT IN MANUFACTURING BY BRANCH AND SECTOR, 1974-78

Branch	Public Sector				Private Sector			
	1974		1978		1974		1978	
	Production *(Million AD)*[a]	Number Employed	Production *(Million AD)*	Number Employed	Production *(Million AD)*	Number Employed	Production *(Million AD)*	Number Employed
Steel, metal production and transformation, electrical and engineering industries	791.4	46,356	1,684.2	69,102	274.2	10,192	184.7	16,346
Building materials	278.5	13,984	796.7	21,879	60.0	1,958	67.2	2,175
Chemicals and rubber production	341.6	2,943	488.3	13,584	189.7	5,619	169.5	6,250
Food processing	1,219.3	19,492	1,315.2	35,720	339.5	13,113	482.0	10,278
Textiles and clothing	183.1	14,556	475.2	19,932	697.4	14,907	798	15,529
Leather and shoe industries	97.7	4,363	182.3	6,270	170.5	1,930	135.7	1,991
Wood processing and paper producing	237.4	9,934	299.6	18,037	275.0	6,469	194.2	8,409
Other	13.3	168	39.2	620	20.4	5,066	34.1	5,497
	3,162.3	111,796	5,280.7	185,144	2,026.5	59,254	2,065.4	61,475

[a] AD = Algerian dinars.

Fourth, while statistics on wages have been disputed by experts, it is generally agreed that wage increases for the average income have amounted to 5-10 percent per year in the nonagricultural sector (industry, trade, transportation, construction and public works, cottage industry, civil service, and other services (see *Révolution africaine* 1977; Algeria, Secretary of State for Planning 1977; Benachenhou 1975). Once again this is a much better figure than that for rural areas—even if we take into consideration that the cost-of-living index doubled between 1969 and 1978, with corresponding annual inflation of between 8 and 12 percent. (For two different sets of statistics, see Table 9.)

Table 9

ALGERIA: MONTHLY INDUSTRIAL INCOME, 1968-76

SOURCE 1[a]

Category of Worker	1968 *(AD)*	1976 *(AD)*	Growth, 1968-76 *(Percent)*	Annual Growth *(Percent)*
Managerial staff	1,700	2,400	41.18	4.40%
Trained personnel	1,200	1,700	41.67	4.45
Specialized workers, qualified	870	1,200	43.68	4.63
Laborers	450	670	48.89	5.10
Weighted average per worker	750	1,066	42.13	4.49

SOURCE 2[b]

Category of Worker	1968 *(AD)*	1976 *(AD)*	Growth, 1968-76 *(Percent)*
Managerial staff	1,700	2,851	67.71%
Trained personnel	1,200	2,112	76.0
Specialized workers, qualified	870	1,182	35.86
Laborers	450	915	103.33
Weighted average per worker	750	1,148	53.07

[a] *Source:* Algeria, Secretary of State for Planning; cited in Palloix 1980:560.

[b] *Source:* Ait-Hamou and Boukhobza 1979; cited in Palloix 1980:560.

Fifth, it is evident that the private sector grew less rapidly than the public sector (see Table 10). Even in branches like construction and public works (fields where private firms have traditionally been dominant), state workers outnumbered private workers. The public sector was and still is the driving force of the growth process. This means that the state is the most important owner, producer, and employer in the country.*

Not long ago (in 1970-75) analysts predicted that the private sector would increase more rapidly than the public sector; thus a political threat could come from a dynamic proletariat employed by private contractors–i.e., from a class more willing to fight social battles and to ask for better wages and better protection. Because the private sector was not limited by the charter of the *GSE,* strikes were allowed. Tensions between the personnel of privately owned factories and the unemployed would be acute. Moreover, workers who were less well paid, less qualified, and had much less job security than those in the public sector could become frantic in case of economic difficulties. The UGTA itself insisted at that time on the revolutionary potential of this faction of the working class, which could develop a class consciousness in conditions similar to those of a capitalist environment. In practice, owing to the increase of the public sector

Table 10

ALGERIA: WAGE EARNERS IN PRIVATE AND PUBLIC SECTORS, 1973 AND 1977

	1973		1977	
Sector	Number	Percent	Number	Percent
Private	266,520	44.3%	342,070	36%
Public[a]	335,000	55.7	613,025	64
Total	601,520	100	955,095	100

[a]Excluding civil servants.

*In 1981 it was estimated that among 150,000 private firms, only one out of 30 employed wage labor (and 34 percent of them had fewer than 5 workers). On the issue of private sector vs. public sector, see Elsenhans (1982:62-72).

and a widening gap between it and the private sector, most of the negative projections regarding the rise of a pugnacious proletariat have been dismissed (Palloix 1980).

A working class has been evolving since the birth of industrialization. It is largely composed of wage earners who are not very well paid but who enjoy far more professional stability than most of the peasantry. If this class is ready to ask for social rights, the protection of its privileges, and some participation in the management of factories and firms, it is not as ready to indulge in political conflict with the government. In consequence, as long as the state is able to offer enough jobs to those with degrees, as well as to those excluded from the system of education, the regime will not need to fear a political opposition which might endanger its base; rather it will need to neutralize social demands through specific solutions, as well as through control groups whose tendency might be to ask for more privileges. For this aim, social legislation is still the best weapon.

The present government bet in Algeria is that both public and private sectors will be able to sufficiently meet employment demands to keep the population pacified. A danger comes from the new "quality" of the unemployed. After independence the unemployed were for the most part from rural areas and illiterate. Their lack of skills was linked with their lack of education. They could aim only toward inferior jobs in the modern sector. If they could not get a job, they were condemned either to multiple odd jobs or to migration to Europe—or a return to the countryside. Today this lumpenproletariat of unskilled and uneducated people without any real political consciousness has become almost obsolete. Job-seekers now come from cities, and they have at least some education. However, they do not have access to any of the resources their predecessors had. Thus they might very well resent their deprived status and make political claims of an unexpected type.

TRAINING POLICIES

Usually there are two means of causing the systems of education and employment to conform: either by market structures or by planning. In the first case, demands emanate from economic needs. Education has then to be adapted to meet the market's requirements. Such is the means in Tunisia and Morocco, both of which have significant private education sectors. In the second case, the state controls all aspects of education and orients students according to the needs of planned development. Algeria serves as an example, as all private education has been nationalized since 1976. (Libya too might be considered in this regard.)

These two opposing categories of education, however, are not mutually exclusive. In Tunisia and Morocco liberalism does not prevent the state from making recommendations and from playing a role in the vocational orientation of youth. In Tunisia students with a baccalaureate are asked to specialize in particular fields in college. On the other hand, Algeria has not been able to produce all the skilled manpower that it needs, despite its total control over the schools and vocational training. Indeed there is substantial evidence of inadequate planning. For example, 30,000 Algerians were in the vocational training apparatus in 1981, while twice as many were needed. More than 60,000 children by the age of 12 had failed to enter the lycées that year, while apprenticeship programs recruit only adolescents over 15. Three percent of youth succeed in entering the university, but the university supplies more workers to the job market than do the vocational training programs (see Djaad and Akeb 1981; Zemouri 1981). Moreover, many students have received a specific type of training which should lead to a certain branch of economic activity, but they are recruited by another branch. Let us thus leave aside artificial differentiations and turn to recent trends regarding (1) The working population; (2) The various activities in which manpower is used; and (3) Labor recruitment.*

The Working Population. Across the entire Maghreb the labor force has increased in recent years (as we have seen). This fact requires examination for several reasons. First, according to statistics, the proportion of the labor force to the entire population has remained about the same—that is, roughly 1:4. This is because of a growth in the important segment of the population which is too young to work: around half of the Maghreb's inhabitants are under sixteen years old. This means that the proportion of individuals between fifteen and twenty-four has been constantly increasing (36 percent in Tunisia in 1979—12 percent more than thirteen years before). Second, the move toward urbanization has not stopped. And (as noted) urban employment has developed more rapidly than rural

*Much of the discussion here is from CRESM, *AAN 1980—La Politique de l'emploi—formation au Maghreb (1970-1980);* see also Bernard 1983a.

employment; what we have emphasized for Algeria is true for the Maghreb in general. The annual rate of increase of urban dwellers is over 5 percent. (The rural areas have less development; the extreme is Algeria, with only 2 percent increase.) Thus (leaving Libya aside) the Maghreb will soon be half urbanized. Furthermore, the role of the active population in the countryside will further diminish as new jobs are increasingly created in urban areas (see Hanane 1983; Amrani 1983; Daoud 1983).

The proportion of people with salaries has also increased in recent years (three fourths of the employed population in Algeria today). A majority, of course, live in cities, where future developments are not always predictable. The creation of new jobs might decrease despite the plans of ambitious technocrats. The "modern" sector might become saturated: industry needs a relatively limited number of skilled workers, and the state bureaucracy, which had systematically overrecruited recently, will not be able to maintain the same pace. Probably because of such uncertainties, all Maghrebi governments tend to favor the creation of small commercial and manufacturing enterprises and give some formal support to the landowners of small and middle-range parcels. Such uncertainties also explain the large number of self-employed workers (27 percent in Tunisia and 22.5 percent in Morocco). In order to compete with larger firms and to minimize their costs, private contractors recruit among the less skilled and less qualified workers, whom they can also pay less. Among small private firms, full-time employment is less the rule than in the "modern" sector. As a result, there are occasional workers (true for one third of the working population in Tunisia) and part-time workers (see Fetini 1981). In addition, apprentices and family aids are used more systematically. Moreover, the private sector employs a high proportion of women in Morocco and Tunisia (one fifth of the working population), and many employees in domestic workshops or home workers are women (and children) (see Amrani 1983; Talahite-Hakiki 1983).

In this context the main problem in all Maghrebi countries is not so much the quality of education and training. It is rather an incapacity to produce the required numbers of well-trained graduates in specific categories–engineering, administration, shop supervision, and highly skilled work. It looks as though vocational guidance, selecting students for a particular type of education, professional training, school careers, and programs of study in general have had only an indirect connection with economic activity.* On the one hand, education has improved in general. The number of children excluded from the channels of national acculturation through education has greatly decreased, and some parts of the labor force have received better training. On the other hand, the populations in general are not well prepared to work at productive tasks in the modern sector. Although leaders proclaim their nations' needs for technical expertise and professional ability, they still let some unwritten law of "natural selection" decide who will succeed in the archaic school system, and they leave the old system of "general education" in elementary schools, lycées, and universities intact. What few technical programs exist in the educational apparatus are oriented exclusively to modern branches of production, engineering, and technology, ignoring the craft and agricultural specializations which are in fact more needed.†

Manpower Distribution and Activities. The lack of adequate data prevents us from a detailed study of all aspects of manpower in the Maghreb. Nevertheless, we can offer some considerations which are relevant to North Africa in general. While the state bureaucracies still recruit personnel (around 15 percent of the active population is in the civil service), they are no longer a growing sector of employment. Moreover, the modern industrial sector does not absorb much of the surplus labor any more, with the possible exception of some manufacturing firms (such as those in Tunisia which account for 41 percent of the jobs created since 1977, one third of which are in textile industries). In Algeria the construction and public works sector (public

*Can the Maghrebi countries afford both a general system of education (which would profit the whole population) and specific programs for a highly trained elite of economists and engineers? Both rich Algeria and poor Tunisia, which have spent respectively one fourth and one third of their annual budgets on education, still lack the resources to pursue both aims simultaneously. In both countries recent education figures indicate that about three quarters of the children attend school (with different figures for boys and girls, as well as for urban and rural populations). However, to maintain these high attendance figures, both countries have adopted the practice of split sessions (pupils attending either mornings or afternoons).

†There are exceptions of course. Training in the agricultural sector has shown important progress; however, there are proportionally more engineers than skilled workers, although the latter are most needed. On Algeria, see Bedrani (1983) and Haddab (1983); on Tunisia, see Gachet (1983); on Morocco, see Pascon (1983). The Algerian government has decided to support the training of 40,000 apprentices (Law of 27 June 1981).

and private firms) offers better opportunities for employment than do public administration and industry.

In general, given the low absorptive capacity of modern production, near stagnation in agricultural employment, and low qualifications of labor, it is understandable that potential workers have a dual perception of the economy—i.e., the modernized and the less modernized domains of activity. The latter—small-scale transformation and equipment industries, small-scale production of salable goods—has created a parallel market. Machine and repair shops, assembly and fitting shops, weaving sheds, and cottage industries have appealed to young rural migrants, educated (though not graduated) urban dwellers, and women, all of whom are willing to accept both lower wages and the absence of protective legislation. As for the reserves of the regular army of laborers, they either compete for precarious employment at the margins of both the state-run and privately owned sectors, or they carry on small businesses, follow sedentary pursuits, or engage in duties of minor importance in various branches of production—all of which constitute a subsistence sector.*

Thus there is in effect a sectoral dualism between a predominantly modern, well-structured form of production and a more traditional and less structured one, between a rationalized field and a heterogenous one.† Algeria—where even processing industries use more modern technology than manpower and where small-scale trade production has developed at the same time—is certainly the country where contradictions in the development of both sectors are the most striking.

In theory, one might expect these dual sectors to be in conflict. In practice, however, in liberal, capitalist, dependent national systems

*The concept of dualism has been used in different contexts. For instance, with regard to the transfer of technology, Frances Stewart states that "The dualistic model rests on the assumption that the modern sector in developing countries uses only the most recent technology from developed countries, that the factor requirements of that technology are rigidly determined, and that no adaptation or innovation in the LDC takes place" (1974:94). John S. Furnivall (1945:167-71) uses it in a broader sense. Dualism is part of what Furnivall calls the "plural economy." See also Smith (1965). We are using it in a sense closer to that of certain economists—for instance, Berger and Piore (1980) and Azouvi (1981).

†Once again we suggest that Maghrebi markets (and economies more generally) are not based on a dyad but on a triad: a modern sector, a traditional one, and a third which corresponds to what has been described as a parallel or third economy.

(Tunisia and Morocco), the less structured sector has helped to maintain necessary links between the modern sector associated with the international market, on the one hand, and the more traditional one, on the other. In Algeria the creation of heavy industries (iron and steel, hydrocarbon transformation), as well as (later) of processing industries has been made easier (not to say possible) thanks to the private sector and perhaps the development of a third economy. Because of the complementary nature of the systems, unemployment has not reached more dramatic proportions since 1972. However, whether complementary or in conflict, both sectors are increasingly unable to offer jobs to the growing number of young people, especially those who are just entering the labor market. (In Morocco in 1976, 60 percent of the unemployed were under twenty-five years old, and 40 percent were looking for their first job.)

Labor Recruitment. Degrees and diplomas, which used to play a more important role than vocational training and professional experience in the process of labor recruitment, seem to have diminished in value. After independence, graduation from the school system was overrated because the colonially controlled education system had allowed very few native North African children to attend European institutions. For a while, after more democratic access to schools was established, successfully completing elementary or secondary school meant almost direct access to a job. When state and local bureaucracies, as well as services in the economy, started filling up, the *certificat d'études* (diploma for completing elementary school) and even the baccalaureate lost their prestige. They were no longer the keys to employment and social status. In Morocco and Tunisia (more than in Algeria, where the influence of general education and diplomas persisted until 1976 at least), access to the modern sector has required higher degrees of qualification. In the Maghreb, employment selection tends to be based on criteria other than education, such as technical qualifications and professional competence. In addition, ethnic, social, and family connections and patron-client relationships remain important.* In other words,

*For instance, young Soussi, Fassi, Mzabi, and Kabyles—sons of shopkeepers, merchants, and tradesmen—do not need a diploma to have access to jobs: their ethnic backgrounds and family ties provide them with training and employment. Similarly Maghrebi private entrepreneurs, who have accumulated enough capital during the period of industrialization, do not need a degree to invest in profitable activities.

if degrees and diplomas are still necessary, they are no longer sufficient.

This somewhat new situation does not mean that people who left school without finishing have a better chance of finding a job than ill-prepared graduates. Far from it. The former are increasingly deprived of access to the modern economic sectors and are forced to turn toward private enterprise, crafts, parallel branches of production, and less secure jobs in general (see Oufrima-Bouzina 1983; Bernard 1983b). University graduates tend to match their degrees with certain "respectable" jobs, which have more to do with planning, administration, responsibility, and control than with practical and technical tasks (see Glasman and Kremer 1978). In Algeria and Morocco more than half of the engineers in agriculture are working in urban offices. In Algeria local engineers control firms built by foreign companies, which have to import their own personnel to operate the firms. Both the vertical and horizontal structures of the economy play their part. All employees and staff, blue- and white-collar workers, adjust their views of what the best job is according to the prevailing benefits. For example, it is more profitable to be in tourism than in crafts in Tunisia, to be in phosphates than in the processing industries in Morocco, and to work in a hydrocarbon firm than in an iron and steel plant in Algeria.

From a practical point of view, the growing respectability of certain economic functions has led to a twofold perception of employment in the industrial sector: the highly qualified and highly paid personnel who are the beneficiaries of expansion (most of them living in cities), on the one hand, and the unskilled workers, on the other—too many of whom are forced to seek jobs with low wages, little stability, and few chances of promotion. As the economy was dividing into two domains, so was employment. It is in the processing industry that the gap between a high-salaried elite and a basic labor force can best be observed in the Maghreb.

The only economic branch which could bridge the gap might be crafts, with its system of patrons, journeymen, and apprentices. It is one of the few branches where at least a minimum of technological skill is transmitted (see Charmes 1983). Vocational guidance still exists, as production is highly differentiated according to basic goods (leather, cloth, wood, metal, etc.). Technical training—whatever the training level imparted by masters to apprentices directly—implies practical instruction. Ad hoc methods or techniques which are picked up by apprentices while looking at what the master is doing are a long-standing tradition, with periods of training and certification varying from one profession to another. In Tunisia and Morocco crafts corporations have played a greater role than modern economists had predicted.* Aspiring entrepreneurs, who have proven able to master not only the techniques of a profession, but also the methods of buying goods and selling finished products, might find some incentive to launch their own enterprises once their training period is completed.† This would facilitate a transition from apprenticeship to ownership of small-scale industries. Some scholars have suggested that this unstructured, nonmodern activity might be the "intermediary route" for the Maghrebi economies, which have a strong labor force but are not able to make the best use of it.

CONCLUSION

Social legislation figures in a complex political equation which includes the ambivalent relationships between state and society, social input and political gain, the contradictory needs of individual protection and collective organization, equality and freedom, equity and growth, social justice and economic planning, public monopoly and private action.** The Maghrebi systems have tried to square the circle with varying success (see Hutchinson 1975).

The states which initiated social legislation promised more than they could deliver, and they were thus unable to extend social coverage beyond a "small majority." Those which drafted the legislation did not do it out of pure idealism. They were answering popular demands for greater equity and state support. At the same time, by passing specific laws in the name of the common good, the elites aimed to satisfy their own interests and increase their influence. Even

*After Algeria's independence, handicrafts, which had become a vestigial activity, had a brief revival, but the process of systematic industrialization led again to their decline. Today the government seems ready to sponsor a redevelopment of this branch of production.

†When interviewed, an artisan in wood made the following observation: "Once the worker has learned a manual skill and is able to make certain objects, he leaves his master. He takes away with him his master's knowledge; he is ready to open a workshop and to set up his own business" (quoted in Charmes 1983: 393).

**All these formulas have been used by analysts. See, for example, Kolm (1972), Mehmet (1978), and Weeramantry (1976).

in countries which had never been etatist, such as Morocco (where the monarchy rested on political clientage), leaders aimed at extracting more from the people in order to reinforce the state's unity and the nation's capacities. (On political aspects, see [among others] C. H. Moore 1970; Hermassi 1972; Leca and Vatin 1975; and Waterbury 1970.) Penetration provoked resistance, as government assistance also meant government infringement of civil liberties, while tighter control over economic activity provoked both resentment and reaction.

The balance between what the state demands of its citizens and what it provides them in return has always been difficult to maintain. This is especially true in countries where the rulers tend to put authority before equality. Whether populist or conservative, the Maghrebi regimes have come to either domesticate their trade unions (Algeria, Libya) or clash openly with them (Tunisia, Morocco). Whatever their techniques and policies, states have been unable to develop the instruments of social management without tensions.*

Another problem arises from popular perceptions of social legislation. Such legislation means protection for those of the employed who can take advantage of it. For them it is a progressive instrument. However, for the unprivileged–i.e., those who cannot legitimately demand coverage–it remains a dream. For them it is but one more element of inequity. Insiders support a political system from which they expect some rewards in exchange for their support. Outsiders might lose confidence in the state's guarantees because they have few opportunities to become beneficiaries. The former feel more free because they are protected, while the latter resent their state of

*Industrial disputes provide us with accurate parameters of tension. They increased in all countries in the 1970s. In Tunisia, for example, they have been tabulated as follows:

	1971	1972	1973	1974	1975	1976	1977	1978	1979
Number of disputes	32	150	49	131	363	373	452	178	240
Workers involved *(Thousands)*	2,623	18,458	18,473	21,000	40,671	67,386	88,335	21,433	22,430
Working days lost *(Thousands)*	3,587	31,589	49,653	8,197	11,750	27,500	140,200	36,938	35,287

Source: ILO 1981.

exclusion.* Yet another group—small businessmen who want to escape regulation and taxation, owners of private firms, employers who have been eager to reduce their social expenses—perceives social legislation as a useless financial burden which it seeks to avoid.

In most Maghrebi countries remarkable efforts have been made in the educational system—in Algeria, Tunisia, and Libya more than in Morocco. Nevertheless, the system has been less efficient than expected: academic programs and development plans still fall short of stated economic and political goals. The percentage of children attending school has reached a plateau for the time being. Too many pupils leave school before the end of the regular program of instruction. Those who succeed in their baccalaureate examinations, see no better solution than to enter university in order to obtain a degree which appears more socially rewarding than technically efficient or economically productive for the collectivity. The service sector still polarizes the attention of all social classes, while it is middle-level professionals who are most needed. Individual promotions and success are still an ideal for the young generation, while economic activities tend increasingly to demand collective action.

Do so many inadequacies exist because societies are unable to adapt their projects to their means? Do they provide educational opportunities and social protection in the name of justice while they are at the same time compelled to ration jobs in the interest of economic realism? Have some development plans been drafted according to models which are not altogether appropriate? Do experts fail to arrive at the right suggestions because they are preoccupied with importing modern technology rather than developing domestic resources? Or are politicians often unable to effect the necessary changes due to either bureaucratic paralysis or the state's dearth of social resources and lack of political legitimacy? If economic provisions are inadequate, is it partly due to the formidable resistance of societies to new orders and rituals?

Scholars favor explanations according to their countries of origin and their disciplines.† But one fact remains salient: leaders have used

*The word "protection" has a twofold meaning. When it has to do with the state of being protected, it refers to defense, cover, or safety. When it is linked with the act of protecting, it often connotes patronage, influence, or the person or group which protects—all of which lead to various forms of dependency.

†Algeria has certainly been the most studied country of the Maghreb. While some French observers have seen state capitalism as responsible for most of its contradictions and inadequacies (such as Rouffinot and Jacquemot 1977),

social legislation for their own benefit. They have proclaimed their faith in modernization projects while maintaining the old system of social selection through a somewhat obsolete mode of education. Hence peasants, unskilled workers, and craftsmen are kept from the mainstream of social transformation and thus form political power. Social legislation in the Maghreb is apparently more concerned with the social reproduction of the labor force and the political reproduction of the elite than with a transformation of the social structure.*

Algerian economists have forwarded more sophisticated suggestions—among them Benissad (1979), Benhouria (1980), Benachenhou (1980), Sid Amer (1978), Ghezali (1980), Hersi (1981), and Metboul (1981). Among the literature in English, an interesting view has been given by John Nellis (1980).

*One of the favorite questions of political scientists is How long will people be tolerant of the gap between the haves and have-nots?

REFERENCES

AAN. Annuaire de l'Afrique du Nord. See Centre de Recherches et d'Etudes sur les Sociétés Méditerranéennes–CRESM.

Ait-Hamou, R., and Boukhobza, M. 1979. *Eléments sur l'emploi et les revenus dans les principales villes d'Algérie.* Algiers: AARDES-SEP.

Algeria. *Journal officiel de la République Algérienne (JORADP).* Algiers. See in particular 1978. "Law 78-12 of 5 August 1978." Vol. 32 (8 August).

__________. 1971. *Code de la gestion socialiste des entreprises (GSE).* Algiers.

__________, Bureau of the Census. (CNRES). Various years. *Tableaux et premières analyses globales.* Algiers.

__________, __________. 1978. *Deuxième recensement général de la population et de l'habitat du 12 février 1977. Résultats préliminaires par commune et dispersion.* Algiers.

__________, __________. 1979. *Tableaux récapitulatifs par wilaya.* Algiers.

__________, Ministry of Work and Social Affairs. 1976. *Recueil de législation du travail.* Algiers.

__________, Secretary of State for Planning. Various years. *Recensement.* Algiers.

Ali-Toudert, Abdallah. 1979. In *Intégration–2.*

Amrani, Fadila. 1983. "Mutations de la population active et limites du système éducatif. Le cas tunisien de 1970 à 1980." In *AAN 1980,* pp. 12-23.

Ansell, Meredith O., and al-Arif, Ibrahim M. 1972. *The Libyan Revolution: A Sourcebook of Legal and Historical Documents.* Stoughton, Wisc.: Oleander Press.

al-Assiouty, Sarwat Anis. 1981. "Qaddafi's Green Book and Social Legislation." Paper for the Social Science Research Council Conference on Social Legislation and Social Structure in the Middle East. Rabat, 26-29 September.

Azouvi, A. 1981. "Théorie et pseudo-théorie: Le dualisme du marché du travail." *Critiques de l'économie politique* 15 (April-June): 3-52.

Bedrani, Slimane. 1983. "Contenu du travail et formation de l'agriculture en Algérie. Essai de bilan." In *AAN 1980,* pp. 131-54.

Belloula, Taleb. 1977. *De l'organisation socialiste des entreprises.* Algiers: Editions ANEP.

Benachenhou, Abdellatif. 1975. "Réflexions sur la politique algérienne des revenus." *Revue algérienne des sciences juridiques, économiques et politiques.* March. Algiers.

__________. 1980. *Planification et développement en Algérie.* Algiers: OPUA.

Benhouria, Tara. 1980. *L'Economie de l'Algérie.* Paris: Maspero.

Benissad, Mohamed E. 1979. *Economie du développement en Algérie: Sous-développement et socialisme.* Algiers: OPUA.

Berger, S., and Piore, M.J. 1980. *Dualism and Discontinuity in Industrial Societies.* Cambridge: Cambridge University Press.

Bernard, Chantal. 1980a. "Occupation massive et sous-activité; la situation algérienne de l'emploi au terme du deuxième plan quadriennal (1974-1977)." In *AAN 1978,* pp. 295-313.

__________. 1980b. "La petite activité non exploiteuse en Algérie." In *Secteur informel et petite production marchande dans les villes du tiers monde,* ed. Philippe Hugon. *Revue tiers monde* 21, 2 (April-June).

__________. 1983a. "Conclusion." In *AAN 1980,* pp. 433-69.

__________. 1983b. "Les non-diplômés scolarisés au Maroc: Une ressource en main-d'oeuvre spécifique pour une retraditionalisation de l'économie urbaine." In *AAN 1980,* pp. 409-32.

Bourdieu, Pierre, et al. 1968. *Travail et travailleurs en Algérie.* The Hague: Mouton.

Boutefnouchet, M. 1978. *Le socialisme dans l'entreprise.* Algiers: Editions ANEP.

Brooke, Rosalind. 1979. *Law, Justice and Social Policy.* London: Croom Helm.

Burton, Henry J. 1973. "Economic Development and Labor Use: A Review." *World Development* (December).

Centre de Recherches et d'Etudes sur les Sociétés Méditerranéennes—CRESM (Aix-en-Provence). *Annuaire de l'Afrique du Nord (AAN).* Since 1962. Paris: Editions du CNRS. (See "Chroniques"; "Chronologie"; "Documents.")

__________. 1980. *Les classes moyennes au Maghreb.* Paris: Editions du CNRS.

Charmes, Jacques. 1983. "L'apprentissage sur le tas dans le secteur non structuré en Tunisie." In *AAN 1980,* pp. 351-95.

Cooley, John K. 1982. *Libyan Sandstorm: The Complete Account of Qaddafi's Revolution.* New York: Holt, Rinehart and Winston.

CRESM. *See* Centre de Recherches et d'Etudes sur les Sociétés Méditerranéennes—CRESM.

Daoud, Zakiya. 1983. "Emploi sans formation et formation sans emploi." In *AAN 1980,* pp. 71-85.

Djaad, A., and Akeb, F. 1981. "Les déshérités scolaires." *Algérie–Actualités,* 23 July.

Edwards, Edgar O., and Todaro, Michael P. 1974. "Education and Employment in Developing Countries." In Edwards, ed.

Edwards, Edgar O., ed. 1974. *Employment in Developing Nations.* Report on a Ford Foundation study. New York: Columbia University Press.

Elsenhans, Hartmut. 1982. "Contradictions in the Algerian Development Process: The Reform of the Public Sector and the New Approach to the Private Sector of Industry." *Maghreb Review* 7 (May-August): 62-72.

Farnetti, Paolo. 1971. *Sistema politico e societa civile di teoria e ricerca politica.* Torino: Giappichelli.

Fetini, H. 1981. "Recherches sur les deux modèles coopératifs et d'emploi-substitution, 1960-1970." Thesis in Economics, Faculty of Economic Studies, University of Aix-Marseilles II.

Furnivall, John S. 1945. "Some Problems of Tropical Economy." In *Fabian Colonial Essays,* ed. R. Hinden, pp. 167-71. London: Allen and Unwin.

Gachet, Jean-Paul. 1983. "Choix technologiques et formation dans l'agriculture." In *AAN 1980,* pp. 105-30.

Geertz, Clifford. 1977. "The Judging of Nations: Some Comments on the Assessment of Regimes in the New States." *Archives européennes de sociologie* 13, 2:245-61.

Gellner, Ernest, and Vatin, Jean-Claude, eds. 1981. *Islam et politique au Maghreb.* Paris: Editions du CNRS.

Ghezali, Mahfoud. 1980. *La participation des travailleurs à la gestion socialiste des entreprises.* Algiers: OPUA.

Glasman, Dominique, and Kremer, Jacques. 1978. *Essai sur l'université et les cadres en Algérie: Une technocratie sans technologie?* Paris: Editions du CNRS.

Haddab, Mustapha. 1983. "La formation scientifique et technique: La paysannerie et le développement en Algérie." In *AAN 1980,* pp. 155-72.

Hanane, Larbi. 1983. "Essai d'approche de l'emploi industriel au Maroc." In *AAN 1980,* pp. 221-49.

Hayek, Friedrich A. von. 1976. *The Mirage of Social Justice.* London: Routledge and Kegan Paul.

Hermassi, Elbaki. 1972. *Leadership and National Development in North Africa.* Berkeley: University of California Press.

Hersi, Abderrahmane. 1981. *Les mutations agraires en Algérie depuis 1962.* Algiers: OPUA.

Hutchinson, Jospeh D. 1975. *The Challenge of the Third World.* Cambridge: Cambridge University Press.

IEDES. 1979. Colloquium: "La petite production marchande en milieu africain." Paris, 8-9 March. To be published under the title of *Vivre et survivre dans les villes africaines*—forthcoming.

Igl, Gerhard. 1981. "Le statut général du travailleur en Algérie." In *AAN 1979* pp. 315-38. Also published as "Sozialpolitik, Soziale Sicherheit und Sozialrecht in Algerien." *Afrika Spectrum* 81, 1:37-56.

International Labour Office (ILO). 1981. *Yearbook of Labour Statistics 1981.* Geneva.

Kolm, Serge C. 1972. *Justice et équité.* Paris: Editions du CNRS.

Korichi, Abdelaziz. 1980. "Le statut général du travailleur en Algérie." *Intégration,* 14 December: 21-34.

Leca, Jean, and Vatin, Jean-Claude. 1975. *L'Algérie politique: Institutions et régime*. Paris: Presses de la Fondation Nationale des Sciences Politiques.

Libya. *El Jarida Er-Rasmiya*. Tripoli. Official government legislation publication. See in particular 1980. "Law 13 of 14 April 1980 on Social Security." Vol. 11 (8 June): 514-51.

__________. n.d. *The Human March in the Libyan Republic*. Tripoli.

__________, International Labor Office. 1971. *Libyan Arab Republic: Industrial Vocational Training Scheme*. Tripoli.

__________, Ministry of Labor and Social Affairs. 1970. "Explanatory Memo." Tripoli: Dar el-Fikr.

__________, Revolutionary Command Council. 1970. The New Labor Law. Tripoli: Dar el-Fikr.

__________, __________. n.d. *Comprehensive Social Planning for the Prosperity of Citizens*. Tripoli.

Mayer, Ann. 1977. *Islamic Law in Libya: Analyses of Selected Laws Enacted since the 1969 Revolution*. London: School of Oriental and African Studies.

Mehmet, Ozay. 1978. *Economic Planning and Social Justice in Developing Countries*. London: Croom Helm.

Metboul, A. 1981. *Evolution des structures de l'économie algérienne, 1967-1980*, 2 vols. Algiers: OPUA.

Moore, Barrington. 1978. *Injustice: The Social Bases of Obedience and Revolt*. White Plains, N.Y.: M. E. Sharpe.

Moore, Clement Henry. 1970. *Politics in North Africa: Algeria, Morocco and Tunisia*. Boston: Little, Brown.

El Moudjahid (Algeria). French edition. 1978. 6 July; 14-15, 18-20, 22-23, 25-26 August; 14-16 September.

Murgue, Bernard. 1977. In *Maghreb développement*—3.

Nellis, John. 1980. "Maladministration. Cause or Result of Underdevelopment: The Algerian Example." *Revue canadienne des études africaines* 13, 3:407-22.

Organski, A. F. Kenneth, and Kugler, Jacek. 1980. *The War Ledger*. Chicago: University of Chicago Press.

Oufrima-Bouzina, Fatima. 1983. "Déperditions scolaires et insertion des jeunes au marché de l'emploi en Algérie durant la dernière décennie." In *AAN 1980*, pp. 397-408.

Palloix, Christian. 1980. "Un essai sur la formation de la classe ouvrière algérienne entre 1963 et 1978." *Revue tiers monde* 21 (July-September): 557-74.

Pascon, Paul. 1983. "Le technicien entre les bavures et le bricolage." In *AAN 1980*, pp. 173-80.

Peneff, Jean. 1981. *Industriels algériens*. Paris: Editions du CNRS.

Piore, M. J. 1972. "Notes for a Theory of Labor Market Stratification." MIT working paper 95, October.

__________. 1978. "Dualism in the Labor Market. A Response to Uncertainty on Flux: The Case of France." *Revue économique* 10, 1 (January): 26-48.

"Rapport de la CNO sur l'état d'application de la GSE." 1981. *Révolution et travail* 420 (24 January).

Révolution africaine. 1977. 28-September-4 October.

Rouffinot, Marc, and Jacquemot, Pierre. 1977. *Le capitalisme d'état algérien.* Paris: Maspero.

Ryan, P. 1980. "The Empirical Analysis of Market Segmentation." Paper, Kings College, Cambridge University.

Sari, Djilali. 1975. In *Maghreb-Machrek*—summer issue.

Segalman, Ralph. 1977. *Conflicting Rights: Social Legislation and Policy,* 2 vols.; vol. 2: *The Deviant, the Society and the Law.* Washington, D.C.: University Press of America.

Sengenberger, W. 1979. "Sources of Labor Market Segmentation with Special Considerations of the Business Cycle." In *Low Pay and Market Segmentation,* vol. 2, pp. 331-64. Cambridge: IWPLMS conference; Cambridge University.

Sid Amer, Tayeb. 1978. *L'industrialisation de l'Algérie: L'entreprise algérienne dans le développement.* Paris: Anthropos.

Sivers, Peter von. 1981. "Work, Leisure and Religion: The Social Roots of the Revival of Fundamentalist Islam in North Africa." In Gellner and Vatin, eds., pp. 355-70.

Smith, M. G. 1965. *The Plural Society in the British West Indies.* Berkeley: University of California Press.

Stewart, Frances. 1974. "Technology and Development in LDCs." In Edwards, ed., p. 94.

Sutton, Keith. 1980. "Population Growth in Algeria, 1966-1977, with Some Comparisons from Tunisia." *Maghreb Review* 7 (May-August): 41-50.

Talahite-Hakiki, Fatiha. 1983. "Scolarisation et formation des filles en Algérie: Préparation au salariat ou production de ménagères modernes?" In *AAN 1980,* pp. 289-324.

Turnham, David (with assistance of I. Jaeger). 1970. *The Employment Problem in Less Developed Countries: A Review of the Evidence.* Paris: OECD Development Center, June.

Waterbury, John. 1970. *The Commander of the Faithful. The Moroccan Political Elite: A Study of Segmented Politics.* London: Weidenfeld and Nicolson.

Weeramantry, C. G. 1976. *Equality and Freedom: Some Third World Perspectives.* Colombo: Hansa Publishers.

World Bank. 1982. *World Development Report 1982.* New York: Oxford University Press.

Wright, John. 1982. *Libya: Modern History.* Baltimore: Johns Hopkins University Press.

Zemouri, K. 1981. "Formation professionnelle. Priorité à la demande." *Révolution africaine,* 2-8 October.

Chapter 5

PENDULUM SWINGS IN LAND LAWS AND RURAL DEVELOPMENT POLICIES IN TUNISIA: HISTORY AND CONSEQUENCES

Mira Zussman

The impermanence of institutions and the proliferation of supposedly enduring reforms have been and continue to be impediments to the agricultural development of Tunisia. Agricultural policies have reflected fluctuations of both the prevailing national political climate and international trends in development theory. As a result, the country has oscillated between two competing ideologies—centralization and decentralization—and has produced a succession of agrarian reforms and land tenure policies which have been both unevenly applied and unenthusiastically received by rural people.

Here I will outline the stages of Tunisian rural development planning from independence in 1956 to the end of the Fifth Plan period in 1981 and provide a case study of the land reform experience as seen by its beneficiaries—in this case, the rural people of Chouigui, a village in the lower Medjerda Valley (northern Tunisia).* The concluding remarks will focus on some of the consequences of frequent policy change. The sequence of the discussion in the sections below can be characterized as follows: (1) Preliminary steps in nation-building; (2) Debate; (3) Experimentation; (4) Failure and restoration; (5) Moratorium; and (6) Confrontation and the reactivation of tradition. This sequence follows a pattern which reflects the permissive, consultative atmosphere of Habib Bourguiba's

*Chouigui, within the delegation of Tebourba (which I was studying), is important because it was successful in every era. This led to complete dissatisfaction by the local people because success meant *no* redistribution of land parcels to local peasants (unlike the situation in all neighboring areas). A repeated theme in Tunisia was that success leads to failure.

presidency from independence to the present (see, e.g., Moore 1965). In the name of modernization and development, no stone has been left unturned: Tunisia has provided the testing ground for a good many theories, practices, and programs. This experimentation in development reforms may reflect strength and open-mindedness on the part of Bourguiba's presidency or its ambivalence and lack of commitment or direction, if not all of these traits. There is no doubt, however, that the succession of reforms has taken its toll on rural people.

THE "NON-PLAN" PERIOD: TUNISIFICATION (1956-61)

The complex sequence of post-independence reforms did not begin with the expropriation and nationalization of colonial estates. Instead the French Protectorate era (1881-1956) was followed by a transitional period—between 1956 and 1964—after which all remaining colonial farms were expropriated. This era was characterized by initial exaltation in the liberation (the "Non-Plan" Period) and subsequent caution and debate (the Pre-Plan Period—below). It has been argued forcefully that at the dawn of independence and for the first six to eight years of the new Tunisian republic, there was in fact no agrarian policy to speak of and indeed no economic planning at all (Poncet 1962; Zghall 1968; Makhlouf 1971). What is meant by this is the absence of a uniform and consistent theoretical outlook—neither a *politique agricole* nor a *politique économique*. That is not to say that this period was without reforms. On the contrary, it is noted for a number of unprecedented laws. These include the abolition of *habous* laws which nationalized public habous property (property belonging to the Islamic community and administered by religious functionaries) and forbid the establishment of new private habous foundations, and the agrarian reform laws of the lower Medjerda Valley, which required irrigation of all irrigable land, specified what to grow in which kind of soil, dictated the spacing of different crops and trees, and threatened expropriation for non-compliance. Moreover, Bourguiba encouraged people to work harder and to give up fasting during Ramadan in order to make the country more productive:

> "At the time when we are doing everything possible to increase our production, How" he asked, "can we resign ourselves to give up our efforts and permit the production level to descend to the

zero mark? . . . I do not believe that religion should be able to impose such a sacrifice. . . . This is an abusive interpretation of the religion. When fasting, man's physical forces are so depleted that he is obliged to cease all activity. No dogma is justification for such a rhythm. . . . All practices of this religion are issues of logical intentions. But when they become incompatible with the necessary struggles of this life, this religion must be amended" (Bourguiba speech, 2/5/60; cited in Moore 1965:56-57).

What has appeared to some as a "piecemeal" approach to economic and social planning in fact had an articulated philosophical basis. Bourguiba pinpointed this basis in a speech to fellahin in the lower Medjerda Valley:

> In this republic of 4 million people, how can we leave family units, which are states in miniature, ruled by autonomous chieftains, to fend for themselves? The state, which sees beyond the individual, must intervene for the sake of national solidarity (Bourguiba speech, 6/11/61).

Promoting both solidarity within the nation-state and the concept of the national good was the first priority of the new government and a theme which would pervade all subsequent economic and social planning. One manifestation of this theme took the form of land grants to heroes of the struggle for independence and the post-independence activists of the Neo-Destour, the New Constitution Party.* Selected properties of the nationalized habous land—totaling 120,000 hectares—were distributed as agrarian reform parcels, or "attributaries" *(lotissements)*. The new rural communities took the form of central villages surrounded by individual family parcels. They were designed such that the awardees in any given community were from as diverse backgrounds as possible, with members sharing only their dedication to the state. It was hoped that this cross-cutting of tribal and regional affiliations, as well as the awarding of some parcels to women who had been active in the Neo-Destour, would serve as an example to be followed by the surrounding population.†

*The sole political party in Tunisia. A Tunisian can either be a member or not.

†This hope was undermined by the fact that some of the awardees—including all of the female awardees—had little or no experience in agriculture, and many had no desire to learn. In addition, the awardees were given state and foreign aid as well as help in loan applications which further undermined their credibility as role models for fellahin with no such benefits.

The theme of providing models for the rural population was also to be repeated in every phase of the development process, although in each period the model to be emulated changed.

During this initial period the first agrarian reform communities were symbols of the new government's twofold commitment to the bulk of the population: to modernize the agricultural sector and to transform the "traditional mentality" of rural Tunisians. Throughout the ensuing years these goals too have remained.

Beginning in 1959 agrarian reform parcels were distributed throughout the lower Medjerda Valley, particularly to families of former colonial workers who eagerly had awaited the redistribution. The attributary parcels were within the irrigated perimeters of the state domain and therefore fell under the jurisdiction of the Office de la Mise en Valeur de la Vallée de la Medjerda (OMVVM)—the Medjerda Valley Land Improvement Agency. Its precursor under the French Protectorate had been the Commissariat de la MVVM (CMVVM), organized in 1953. The CMVVM had acted as a liaison between the government and agriculturalists in an effort to carry out development projects. These projects included the construction of dams, reservoirs, and irrigation canals; soil and water protection; rural evaluation studies; and agricultural extension services, including experiments in innovative agriculture (Chennoufi 1977).

After independence the "Tunisification" program—that is, the transfer of colonial landholdings to Tunisian nationals or into the state domain—affected well over 50 percent of the land in the lower Medjerda Valley. The Law of 9 July 1958 inaugurated the OMVVM and gave it jurisdiction over all the land recovered by the state within the boundaries of CMVVM projects. The OMVVM distributed land to rural Tunisians in accordance with the agrarian reform laws, but it retained (and continues to retain) authority over the land.

The OMVVM distributed two kinds of lots. The first—known as Promotion Paysanne—split up parcels into four to twelve hectares, allowing the recipients to attain the status of "petits proprietaires aisés [et] travaillant de leurs mains"* (*Revue Medjerda* 1960). While in some regions the redistribution program called for grouping the fellahin into newly constructed villages along the lines of the hero communities, most of the agriculturalists were dispersed throughout

*"Relatively well-off small landholders who [nevertheless must] work with their own hands." In Tunisia there is a major distinction between landowners who must touch the soil themselves and those who hire laborers.

the countryside, each family living on its own farm. The second type of lot—called Minimum Vital—gave each fellah two or three hectares, a house, and common pastureland. These fellahin were expected to work as seasonal laborers for their neighbors (Chennoufi 1977).

The law differentiated agrarian reform parcels from private land (i.e., titled land or land bought from Europeans before expropriation went into effect); until an agrarian reform parcel was paid for it was considered still within the state domain and under the jurisdiction of the OMVVM. The Agrarian Reform Law of 11 June 1958 spelled out the obligations of agrarian reform farmers with regard to their parcels. The main points were the following:

1. Land could not be fragmented or in any way divided smaller than four hectares, while the upper limit of land ownership was fifty hectares per agriculturalist (Articles 5 and 15).
2. Agriculturalists in the irrigated perimeters were obligated to irrigate at least two thirds of their land when appropriate and pay the OMVVM for the service of irrigation at rates established by the law (Article 2).
3. Improving the land was an obligation of the fellahin within the irrigated perimeters. The law included an annex listing the crops suitable for different soil types, and regulations were given regarding the spacing of fruit trees approved for a given area (Article 19).
4. The OMVVM could proceed against those who did not exploit their rural property rationally. The law specifically included proper distribution and use of irrigation water on the land (Article 15).
5. Landowners could be required to join and participate in production, marketing, and service, or agro-industrial cooperatives created by the OMVVM (Article 22).
6. Landowners not conforming to the law could be expropriated by the state and their land transferred to the OMVVM. The OMVVM, however, could renounce its rights to expropriate landowners who exceeded the allowable plot size (i.e., above fifty hectares) if the land was intensively cultivated and employed an adequate work force (Articles 7, 8, 12, and 14).

In brief, the agrarian reforms made the OMVVM much more

than a government commission dedicated to building dams and irrigation canals. The office defined and set standards of "rational" agriculture and could expropriate landowners who did not conform to the law—or ignore infractions so long as the land was rationally cultivated. It collected land taxes, payments, and rents; it had been created as a semi-autonomous office under the Ministry of Agriculture and was expected to support itself in part through the sale of irrigation water and supplies—a good incentive for promoting irrigated farming—as well as through taxes and other revenues. Fellahin on the agrarian reform parcels could not sell their land until it had been fully paid for, and agriculturalists who did not pay for their irrigation water could be sued by the OMVVM. Most important, the OMVVM had the power to transform land tenure patterns whenever it deemed necessary.

Laws during this period which affected a smaller but more affluent segment of the rural population included the encouragement of private entrepreneurs (mainly large-scale landowners) in the purchase of colonial estates. These land transfers involved much larger individual pieces of property than any of the agrarian reform parcels discussed above (i.e., twenty to fifty hectares instead of three to six hectares). Laws were passed to standardize a procedure for Franco-Tunisian landholding partnerships. A European landowner was allowed to remain on his estate only under joint title with a Tunisian counterpart who was to be trained in modern European agricultural techniques for the eventual proprietorship and management of the farm. For European landowners who refused to believe that decolonization was imminent (despite the new independent republic), this rather generous policy provided an impetus for a smooth land transfer at the same time that it allowed the colons continued profits and control over the fate of their farms. However, altruism was less the motivating force for this policy than prevention of land-quality deterioration (from colonial intensification in the later years of the Protectorate) and prevention of production losses during the transitional period.

THE PRE-PLAN PERIOD: CENTRALIZATION (1962-64)

In 1962 it became clear that the distribution of small-scale agrarian reform parcels was problematic. Full and just implementation of the program was costly and logistically complex (CREA 1974:

322). Furthermore, there was a growing concern over the production capacity of inexperienced ex-colonial workers and the fear that distribution of the best agricultural land in the country would be wasted in small-scale farming. Land that was depended upon to bring agricultural self-sufficiency to the new nation would have to be managed—or at least closely monitored—by experts. Centralization—that is, the state's consolidation of decision-making authority—was taken into consideration as an alternative to redistribution.

The 1960s in Tunisia were characterized by initial debate on and subsequent mobilization of centralization policies. The goal was to accelerate the nationalization and Tunisification of land, government, and industry; to increase production and modernize all sectors; and to integrate the individual into the state by involving him in the development process. Ahmed Ben Salah, minister of both planning and finance, fought a long uphill battle to promote socialism ("Neo-Destourian socialism") as the only viable route to development. With Bourguiba's eventual support, his efforts culminated in the 1962 drafting of the first cohesive, all-encompassing national plan—the Ten Year Perspectives on Social and Economic Development (1962-71)—which outlined the direction and procedures of the national socialist experiment. Colonial land was to be fully expropriated by 1964; the resulting state land was to be administered by the newly formed Office des Terres Domainales (OTD), or Office of the State Domain, and a cooperative system of agriculture was to be installed over the approximately 700,000 hectares of nationalized state land (CREA 1974:308).* Service and marketing cooperatives were to be established for private farmers outside the jurisdiction of state land. Prices were to be stabilized, unemployment was to be arrested, self-sufficiency was to be achieved, and sale of agricultural products was to be centralized through state agencies. The interim of preparation for the Ten Year Perspectives was called the First Plan, or more commonly the Pre-Plan Period (*ibid.*).

The cooperative movement would involve the individual in a system which required the weaning and eventual forfeiture of a certain amount of self-interest—the surrender of a degree of allegiance to the family in favor of fulfilling one's obligation as a

*Colonial landholdings reached 725,000 hectares in 1939 and may have risen to as much as 750,000 hectares by independence (see Poncet 1962:305). The nationalization of 700,000 hectares, which includes habous, reflects the fact that some colonial land had already been privately purchased by Tunisians or redistributed by the government by 1962.

citizen of the state. Rural people were expected to subordinate their desires for a family parcel of land (despite the previous redistribution plan and prototype attributary communities) in favor of participation in large-scale agricultural production cooperatives (Unités Coopératives de Production Agricole—UCPAs), managed by the OTD, and pre-cooperatives (P-Cs—see below), managed by the OMVVM.

The national ambivalence was displayed even by the plan's provisional terminology. The initial phase of the Ten Year Perspectives (i.e., 1962-64) was known as the *Pre*-Plan Period, and the cooperatives in the irrigated perimeters were called *pre*-cooperatives. Indeed the High Committee of the Plan assured nervous opponents of the cooperative movement that the agricultural production cooperatives "would be instituted on an experimental basis only" (Moore 1965:200) and later intimated that the UCPAs could possibly be redistributed to members after a twenty-year trial period. The entire development plan was conceived of as an *experiment* in socialism—not a commitment to socialism—and so the impermanence of the new rural institutions was presaged if not assured.

THE SECOND PLAN PERIOD: SOCIALISM (1965-68)

The experiment in socialism began with a collection of statistics on the nation's agriculture, industry, demography, and employment. The tabulations graphically illustrated the magnitude of the agrarian problem. Forty-three percent of Tunisian land was found to be agriculturally unproductive, and only five percent was found to be intensively worked. In 1964 the OMVVM and OTD began studies of their respective territories (irrigated and dry land respectively) and began mapping out the boundaries for the production cooperatives. (Thus the OMVVM exercised its right to cooperativize well before it had finished distributing the small-scale agrarian reform parcels.) Using maps of the colonial estates, the two agencies worked out not only boundaries but also potential carrying capacities (i.e., the number of families which could be supported on any given UCPA or P-C), the number of work days and income per cooperateur per year, and the number of seasonal workers to be employed. (Seasonal workers were to be from the families of resident cooperateurs and would thereby supplement family income.) Intended land improvements and production increases over the subsequent

Figure 1

PRE-COOPERATIVES IN THE DELEGATION OF TEBOURBA

(Valid 1969)

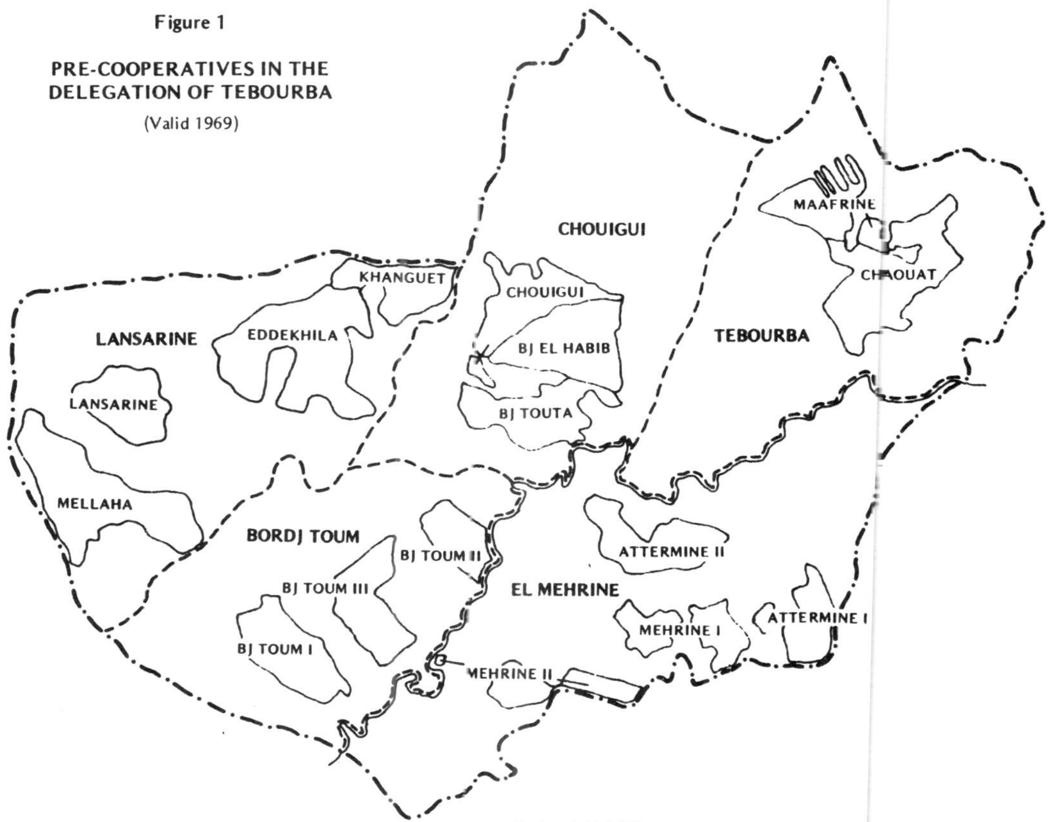

Scale—1:200,000

ten years were projected along with water requirements and revenue increases. These cooperative agricultural communities were laboriously planned; they were designed to speed up the development process and educate the rural population, not only in terms of production, but also in terms of household management and job counseling for the children of cooperateurs. The optimistic ten-year projection of growth and development was well publicized. The cooperatives looked good in print—but at the ground level the view was different.

The problems were manifold. The rural population, particularly the former colonial workers, had anticipated the attribution of family parcels and had been sorely disappointed. Furthermore, cooperativization had been imposed from above and had little popular backing. According to Moore and Lewis, Tunisia's cooperative law differed from most "as it left out the usual definition of a voluntary organization of people to obtain a certain goal" (1968:42). The cooperatives were more production-oriented than people-oriented. Members had no voice in decision-making, and yet there was a shortage of trained administrators on the farms; the cooperatives could provide neither an adequate number of jobs nor incentives, and production soon suffered from a lethal combination of drought and chaos (Ben Brahim 1975; Makhlouf 1968; Zamiti 1970). In 1968, at the close of the Second Plan Period, the question that the authors and authorities of the socialist experiment had to face was whether to halt the expansion of the cooperative sector, continue at the same pace, or expand the movement (CREA 1974:376). They chose expansion.

THE THIRD PLAN PERIOD: DECENTRALIZATION (1969-72)

Despite growing opposition to the movement, in January 1969 President Bourguiba gave the order for "cooperation in everything, except women" (Ben Brahim 1975:19). Six hundred new cooperatives, amounting to 500,000 hectares of *land outside the state domain*, were to be added in the north of the country alone. The evolution of the agricultural cooperatives between 1962 and 1968 had proceeded at a cautious pace and had been limited to former colonial and habous territory. The 1969 generalization of the movement and expansion onto the landholdings of large- and small-scale private farmers was both overzealous and insensitive. The increases in the cooperative movement (shown in Table 1) demonstrate the dramatic sequence.

Table 1

TUNISIA: ANNUAL INCREASES OF COOPERATIVIZATION, 1962-69

Date	Number of Cooperatives	Total Area (*Hectares*)
December 1962	15	10,211
December 1963	81	74,560
December 1964	65	159,430
December 1965	92	339,530
December 1966	121	557,550
December 1967	70	715,110
December 1968	116	1,078,730
August 1969	N.A.	4,667,000
December 1969	N.A.	1,172,000

Source: Adapted from Ben Brahim 1975:17.

In an attempt to draw support from the private sector, the government placed large-scale landowners—particularly from among local leading families—in administrative positions. Often they were appointed "president" of cooperatives composed of their own land and were thereby promised a degree of management control over their former properties. Given the numerous examples of already floundering cooperatives, however, large- and small-scale farmers felt that they could do better on their own. Dissatisfaction among cooperateurs now combined with the outrage of fellahin in the private sector, and the cooperative movement came to a halt. On 22 September 1969 President Bourguiba signed a law which would allow the return of private parcels and the dismantling of cooperatives created after December 1968.

The collapse of the cooperative movement meant the redistribution of agrarian reform parcels and the return of well-documented private parcels. Because of the rapid succession of tenure forms, agrarian reform farmers became confused with regard to their land payment obligations. Were they still expected to pay for the parcels, and if so, how much and to whom? Were their previous payments ever recorded, and did they count toward current landholdings? Many fellahin ignored land payments—some reasoning that the parcels were their due after the cooperative fiasco and others believing that the government would one day reconsider recooperativization when the administrators (*mas'oulin*) had worked out the details.*

The years 1969 to 1972 were used to assess the political and economic damage done by the experiment in socialism. A new *politique économique* had to be devised. In the meantime, the OMVVM and the OTD returned to their role of managing land within the state domain and were faced with the task of reorganizing the public sector. The new agrarian plan called for the coexistence of three sectors of Tunisian agriculture: the public domain (i.e., state land), the cooperative sector, and the private sector (Kassab 1979: 436). The state was loath to give up its fine landholdings. Within the public domain there would be three categories of farms:

1) *Agro-Combinats.* The agro-combinats were to be farms devoted to agro-industrial production, such as cattle-breeding and milk-processing. In 1970 these state farms encompassed 68,000 hectares of rich agricultural land in the north—some of which came from expropriated or purchased private Tunisian landholdings.
2) *Pilot Farms.* These consisted of large-scale demonstration parcels which would promote new techniques as an example to agriculturalists in the private sector. Private farmers (large- and small-scale) were encouraged to seek advice and technical assistance from the agronomy specialists (often foreign) on the pilot farms, while these specialists worked in conjunction with the National Agronomy Research Institute and the FAO to develop cereal hybrids particularly suited to different localities.
3) *Experimentation Farms and Agricultural Education Centers.* These farms were similar to the pilot farms but were devoted primarily to arboriculture, cattle-breeding, and pasturage. The agricultural education centers were for the training of young agriculturalists in modern methods, particularly mechanization.

All of the farms in these three categories would be directly managed by the OTD. However, the cooperative sector would be "semi-autonomous"—that is, overseen by an OTD-appointed director who

*One's "papers" for attributary parcels did not actually award title to the land but rather gave the right to an allotment of water for irrigating a particular land parcel.

would function as an advisor and state representative as well as have veto-power over any management decisions not in accordance with OTD goals. Farms within this sector were renamed agricultural production cooperatives (Unités Coopératives de Production—UCPs) to distinguish them from their predecessors (UCPAs and P-Cs).

After the Law of 19 May 1970, the OTD presided over 732,000 hectares—80,000 of which were to be sold at auction. The recomposed categories of the state domain are shown in Table 2. It should be noted from the table that in 1970 the OTD was responsible for 32,000 hectares over and above its original landholdings ten years earlier—despite decentralization.

Table 2

TUNISIA: FARMS OF THE STATE DOMAIN, 1970

Farm Type	Total Area (*Hectares*)
Agricultural production cooperatives	210,000
Service and amelioration cooperatives	200,000
Agro-combinats	68,000
Pilot farms and education centers	62,000
Parcels for young agriculturalists	112,000
Parcels to be sold at auction	80,000

Source: CREA 1974:394.

The UCPs were organized such that the cooperateurs would elect their own president and executive council. The president, rather than the OTD-appointed director, would manage the farm and represent the cooperateurs' interests in dealing with the central OTD administration. Cooperative members would have a general assembly in which to voice their opinions or objections to OTD or local UCP policy. They would also be able to vote on how best to utilize their shared profits. The general assembly of UCPs would allow cooperateurs a voice in farm management that the salaried workers of agro-combinats would not have. However, agro-combinat workers—as salaried workers of the state—would have guaranteed income and benefits, while cooperateurs would receive only weekly advances (not salaries but *shares*) based on annual UCP profits.

THE FOURTH PLAN PERIOD: ENTREPRENEURISM (1973-76)

While the OTD and OMVVM proceeded to reorganize their respective sectors, the Fourth National Plan took the spotlight off agrarian reform and placed it on encouraging entrepreneurs to invest in industry. Tax and customs exemptions were used to motivate foreign and local businessmen. Of the highest priority was the creation of jobs.

In agriculture the goal once more was to raise production. The method, however, involved no land reform measures. Instead it focused on three less controversial problem areas: (1) The lack of trained personnel; (2) The deterioration of equipment; and (3) Technical education of farmers—a modified and specialized version of the "transforming traditional mentality" goal.

The lack of trained personnel meant a dependence upon foreign advisors in the planning and execution of agricultural programs. In the identification of Ben Salah as the author of Neo-Destourian socialism, it is frequently forgotten that foreign agricultural advisors—namely a team mostly of Belgians—had been instrumental in designing the cooperative blueprint. These same advisors were later contracted to engineer the dismantling of the cooperatives, and, not surprisingly, they were now in charge of training Tunisian agricultural engineers and extension workers. (By the end of the Fifth Plan period, this Belgian team—having worked twenty years in Tunisian agricultural planning—would exit under the new policy of self-reliance.) Under the Fourth Plan agricultural education flourished and was established in rural primary schools as well as in specialized agricultural institutes throughout the country. Furthermore, an effort was made to upgrade the National Agronomy Institute and to encourage higher enrollment.

Equipment, the second area of concentration, had been left by the wayside throughout the preceding tumultuous era. Much of the equipment upon which depended the upgrading and mechanization of production methods was left over from the colonial period and in sore need of repair or replacement. In 1973 alone, 224 reaper-threshers and 1,799 tractors were imported and credit made available through the agriculturalists' union to encourage purchases by small- and mid-scale farmers (*Annuaire Agricole de la Tunisie* 1975). Irrigation projects were also expanded, and farmers were encouraged to utilize existing water channels and to use or purchase hydroelectric pumps in order to extend irrigated agriculture.

To upgrade the technical education of farmers (the third focus), under a program of agricultural extension farmers would be instructed in the use and utility of new equipment, high-yield strains, fertilizers and phosphates, soil preparation, and crop rotation. Especially emphasized were the advantages of converting dry land to irrigated culture wherever possible. Agricultural extension was particularly important in the lower Medjerda Valley, where the OMVVM, as long promised, had redistributed agrarian reform parcels. Through extension the OMVVM could monitor, influence, and coordinate all production and marketing of the thousands of families within the boundaries of the irrigated perimeters—and indeed this was the goal. Farmers were encouraged to be innovative (either through specialization or diversification) as long as they moved in the direction of meeting national needs—as defined by the OMVVM.

THE FIFTH PLAN PERIOD: BUREAUCRATIZATION (1977-81)

In keeping with Tunisia's post-cooperative decentralization policies, the OTD was—in theory—expected to disengage from its many landholdings. However, in 1978, when the tallies were made, it was found that the OTD was managing 220 UCPs—covering approximately 230,000 hectares—and 210,000 hectares of agro-combinat farms. This was an *increase* in both categories that was essentially incalculable since it entailed the regrouping of farms from other OTD categories. Furthermore, there was an increase in the number of accusations of mismanagement, corruption, and lack of democratic procedure on the cooperatives. The UCPs were to be owned and managed by the cooperateurs, but this was not the case. The problem was stated succinctly by the editors of the opposition newspaper, *Démocratie*:

> The authorities claim that [the UCPs] are at one and the same time the property of the State and of the people. In fact, the land of the UCPs remains the property of the State and the cooperateurs are proprietors only in the area of production and not at the property level (9 December 1978; my translation).

This same observation had been made by Zamiti (1970) and others at the demise of the cooperative movement seven years earlier. *Démocratie*'s (9 December 1978) solution was to make the UCPs wholly autonomous—with the exception of state technical advisors,

FIGURE 2. LAND TENURE IN THE DELEGATION OF TEBOURBA, 1979

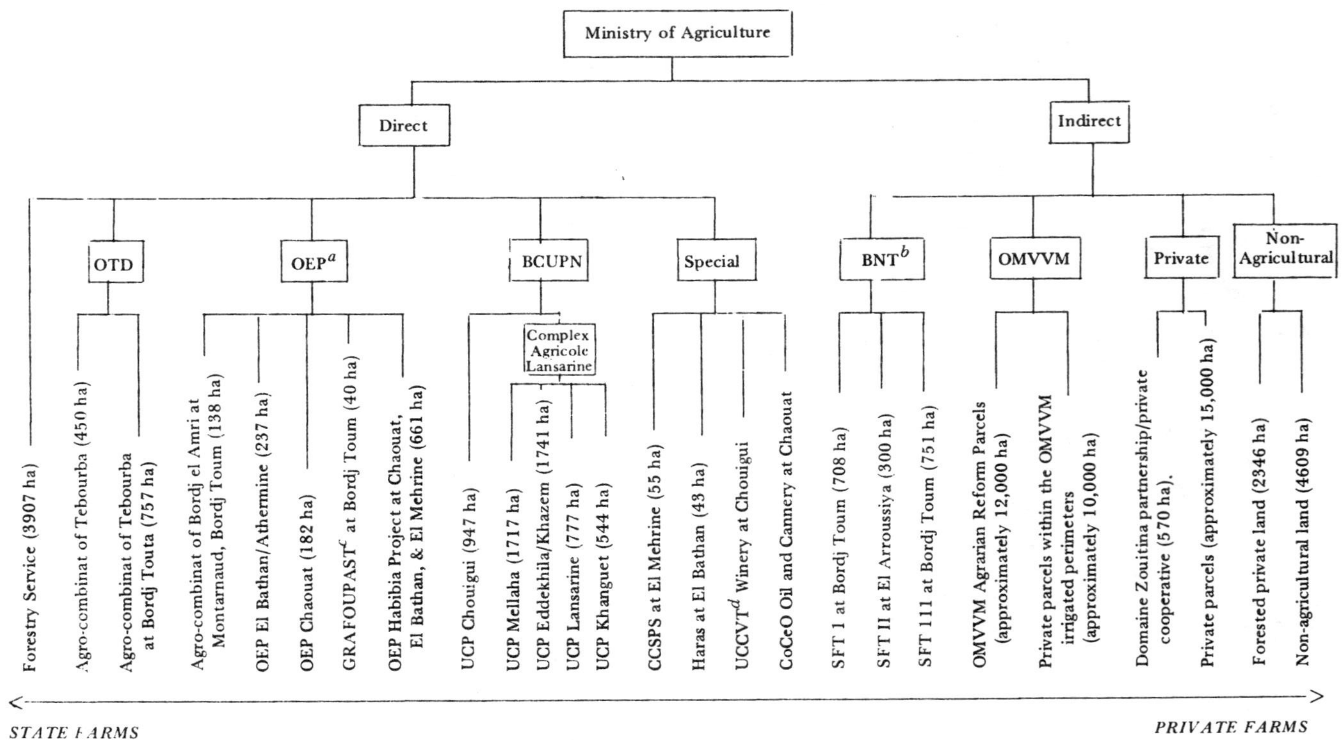

[a]Office d'Elevage et Pâturage.

[b]Banque Nationale de Tunisie.

[c]Graines, fourages, et pâturages.

[d]Union Coopérative de Cultivation Viticole Tunisienne.

who would "introduce a high level of technicity, create enthusiasm among the cooperateurs, and ensure democratic proceedings, as well as ensure that the profits go to those who work the land." The irony lies less in the fact that these goals were incompatible than in *Démocratie*'s advocating what in theory already was the status of the UCPs vis-à-vis the state.

The agro-combinats fared no better. Staff at *Démocratie* and at the Ministry of Agriculture agreed that the agro-combinats suffered from mismanagement, open conflict between workers and administration, and lower production than in the private sector, but they attributed these problems to different causes. *Démocratie* claimed that all production decisions were firmly in the hands of the bureaucracy ("*c'est le fonctionairisme*"), while the Ministry of Agriculture said that difficulties arose because of a "destructive mentality" on the part of some workers on agro-combinats to "abort production, to force the State to give up its lands, and to blame the whole thing on poor State management" (*Le Temps*, 9 November 1978). *Démocratie* concluded forcefully that it was regrettable that the best agricultural land in the country was proving to be more of a burden than a boon to the national economy.

In part as a result of the confrontation, the OTD was reorganized in 1979 and decided to disengage from a number of its landholdings. However, the office had considerable trouble choosing which farms to liquidate and finally solved the problem by simply transferring the headache of the UCPs into the jurisdiction of a new agency in the Ministry of Agriculture—the Bureau de Contrôle des U.C.P. du Nord (BCUPN). Decentralization to the OTD meant proliferating small, specialized agencies to manage the state domain. It did not mean privatization of farms.

This was a familiar tactic of the OTD. Since the early 1960s the number of specialized land management agencies had increased dramatically. One fellah described the state land management bureaucracy in this way: "The OMVVM is the mother, the OTD is the father, and all the others [agencies] are their sons." The smaller agencies and the state-managed farms have been shunted back and forth between these parent organizations with serious consequences in all quarters. In the delegation of Tebourba over half a dozen agencies now duplicate the land management and agricultural extension tasks once divided neatly between the OTD and OMVVM (see Figure 2). In addition, there are overlapping jurisdictions, as, for example, when the OMVVM takes on irrigation projects on OTD farms.

A CASE STUDY: CHOUIGUI (1881-1981)

The land history of Tunisia has deepened the cynicism and sense of futility of rural people. Many of the experiences they underwent during the colonial period appear to be repeated. Outsiders have come to expropriate, distribute, regroup, and redistribute land parcels. Land tenure is in constant flux. In the course of a lifetime, fellahin have been colonial workers, agrarian reform farmers, cooperateurs, state farm workers, and once again agrarian reform farmers. Many of their fathers had been simply nomads.

Decentralization has meant the proliferation of agencies managing or giving directives on the farms. It has not meant the dissolution of all state farms or rural autonomy. Disappointed cooperateurs, state farm workers, and fellahin are demoralized and unproductive. They see the problem as a matter both of too much change and none at all. The land history of Chouigui is in some respects typical of the Tunisian experience and in other ways unique, for Chouigui was a model of success both as an agricultural community and in its cooperative experience. In order to understand its success—and the ironies which emerged as a result of that success—it is instructive to begin with a brief colonial history of Chouigui.

When the French Protectorate was established in 1881, the ambiguous land tenure of areas like Chouigui caused difficulties for those who farmed or grazed their sheep in the area. They had neither legal claim to the land, nor was Chouigui habous property (i.e., exempt from sale, fragmentation, or expropriation by the French).* Within two years of the establishment of the Protectorate, Chouigui was settled by the French and became one of the earliest French agricultural communities in Tunisia. By 1885 the French Ministry of the Interior received hundreds of requests for land at Chouigui from landless French workers and farmers. By 1888 Chouigui was a thriving, well-established French village surrounded by 3,000 hectares of colonial vine, cereal, and fodder lands. Colonial inspectors considered the Domaine de Chouigui to be a "remarkable example of French agriculture utilizing the most modern agricultural methods known" (France, Ministry of Foreign Affairs 1888). The inspectors found French relations with the indigenous population to be satisfactory and declared that "the streets of the Arab quarter

*Habous land was later colonized through *enzel* transfers, or "long-term lease"—a loophole in the transfer of inalienable property.

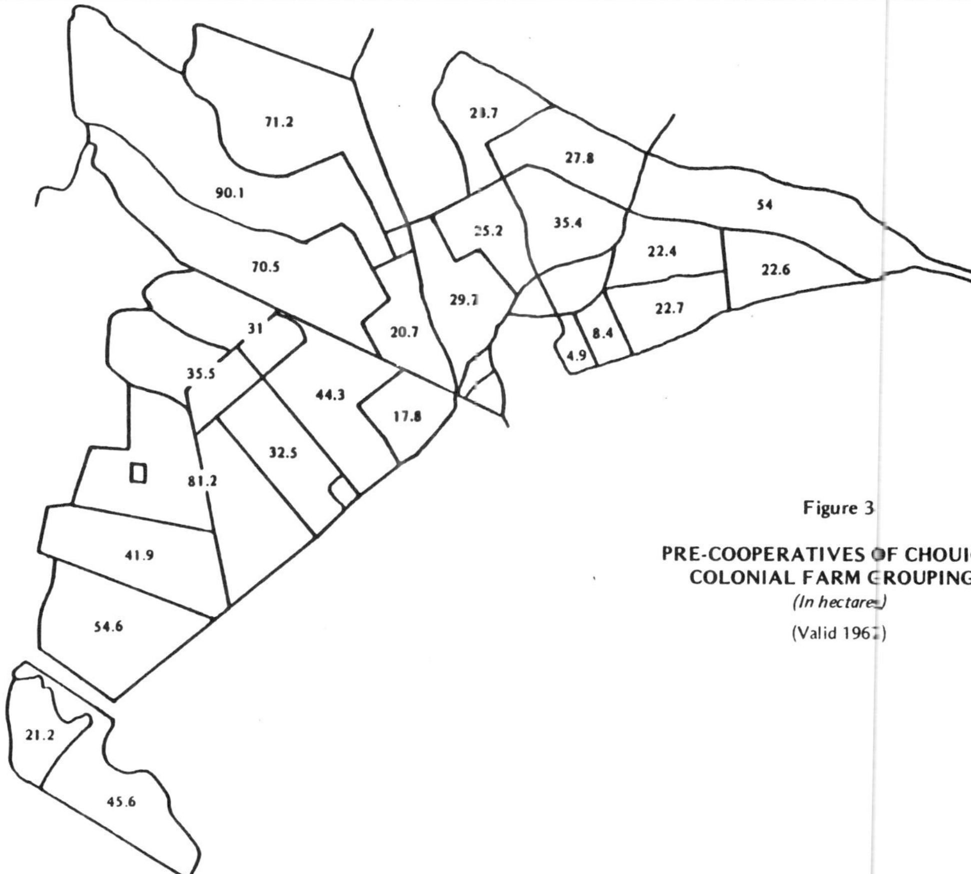

Figure 3

PRE-COOPERATIVES OF CHOUIGUI: COLONIAL FARM GROUPINGS

(In hectares)

(Valid 196[illegible])

are clean, and its inhabitants give us testimony of their gratitude for improvements which are to their advantage" *(ibid.)*. The French farmers responded to this positive evaluation by requesting expansion of colonial farming in the region from 3,000 to 30,000 hectares.

The *colonie française* at Chouigui was presided over by Commandant Gerodius, who "ruled his world with military precision and paternal benevolence" (France, Ministry of Foreign Affairs 1888: 146). Four hundred people lived in the village in houses grouped around the commandant's large villa. Gerodius, along with three other landowners of the area, formed an agricultural association, the Société Foncière et Agricole de Chouigui, which later grew to become the powerful French agriculturalists' union of Tunisia, the Société d'Agriculture de Tunisie. The commandant was elected its president unanimously. By 1920 the association opened a cooperative winery, Cave Viticole de Chouigui, and began producing its own label of wine. The combination of strong leadership and a unified organization helped Chouigui to prosper well after the demise of its founder, the commandant.

By the time the independent Republic of Tunisia was embarking upon the Ten Year Perspectives, Chouigui's ready-made agricultural association and cooperative winery provided a model from which to work. Parceling Chouigui into five-hectare family lots was unthinkable. The OMVVM took over the Domaine de Chouigui en masse and transformed half of it into the prototypical Pre-Cooperative of Chouigui (P-C Chouigui—see Figure 3). Likewise, the cooperative winery simply changed its name and became state-owned. P-C Chouigui included the farms of twenty colons who had belonged to the association and encompassed 935 hectares of unirrigated rolling hills, half of which was devoted to vines and the other half to olive orchards. Tunisians who had been workers on the colonial farms became cooperateurs on the same farms. They were joined by others recruited by the OMVVM in an effort to make Chouigui more labor-intensive. The goal was one hundred cooperative families. Not long after P-C Chouigui was established, the second half of Chouigui was cooperativized. P-C Bordj El Habib was installed on the landholdings of another twenty colons of Chouigui. A fellah of Chouigui and former P-C member recalls this period vividly:

> At the time of independence and after, I worked for the Neo-Destour. . . . In 1964 or so, the Destour sent me out to tell the colons that they had to leave their land. I even went to the farm at

Chouigui where I was born—and I told Monsieur Jean that he had to leave his farm.

Many families left the very next day. . . . They had known their days were numbered and had already made arrangements in France. Well, the next few months people were waiting around to see what would happen. The work had just about stopped and nobody knew what to do. For a few months it was pretty much *laissez-faire*. Whoever was there would take what he could or work whatever land he wanted. There was no bookkeeping. The sheep were allowed to roam all over the grape vines. There were lots of payoffs and graft. Everything had come to a halt.

Ben Salah came forward and had the idea of the pre-cooperatives and convinced Bourguiba that they were a good idea and he was the one who formed the pre-cooperatives. They put in charge of the P-Cs those people they thought would be responsible. They found unemployed civil servants and made them the *responsables*. I myself was given a job in charge of the warehouse on the P-C where my land is now [Bordj El Habib]. This was in 1968.

At the end of the year all the harvest was to go to Tunis from all the P-Cs and the profit was to be divided equally among all the members of all the P-Cs. Twenty million francs were spent putting it all together and at the end of the year we only got back ten million—not even enough to pay our creditors. The rich P-Cs were supposed to give to the poor ones and all the profits were supposed to be shared equally. But the P-C at Chouigui was the only rich P-C. To reimburse all those P-Cs that had lost money on their harvest, they took from the rich ones like Chouigui and called it a loan. It was a real *chakchouka* [vegetable stew]. Too many loans everywhere. People were stopping each other on the street saying, hey, where's my money?

A lot of us wanted our old jobs back, but the *m'atmed* [delegation governor] said no—instead what we'll do is make it your own land, your personal land. Ben Salah said okay, go ahead and make it the property of the poor, take the land of the P-Cs. So Ben Salah came to Tebourba and said that everyone should share and everybody applauded Ben Salah. He told the rich landowners to lend their tools and their tractors and their know-how to the poor ones. And he asked them if everyone agreed and everybody applauded and agreed. . . .

And the next day, poor fellahin came to ask to borrow a tractor and to borrow tools or whatever from the rich landowners but no one would lend us any machinery. The day before they had all applauded, but the next day nobody would give. The workers said, let's band together and go to the sheikh to apply the law. And we took the tractors in a group by force with sticks in our hands. The situation was awful and it went on two weeks like that.

Bourguiba's son went to Bourguiba and said to him, "Do you want a revolution in the streets? The people won't swallow the pre-cooperatives." And Bourguiba answered that Ben Salah told him that the P-Cs were rich and that he had shown him wells that they had dug for new water supplies. But the people knew that the wells were just shallow holes that they had made the day before and put the water into them and said that the cooperatives had dug the wells. And that Ben Salah had shown Bourguiba huge fields of watermelons that the P-Cs had grown and that showed that they were prosperous.

But we knew that the watermelons had been bought at the *souk* [market] and placed in the fields to make them look prosperous. And when Bourguiba came to inspect, everybody was clapping with the same rhythm and chanting *"Bour-gui-ba—dz-bi-sag-ik"* [Bourguiba, push with your foot!—meaning that if he would push with his foot, he would roll the watermelon away and see that it was not attached to the vine], but he didn't hear or didn't understand.

When Bourguiba found out from his son that he had been lied to, he called in Ben Salah and asked why he had lied. He put him in prison and also put the Minister of Agriculture in prison. We on the pre-cooperatives waited to see what would happen. . . . The m'atmed asked, well, what about splitting up the P-Cs and putting about thirty families on each one? So they decided on the lotissement into thirty parts. Lots were handed out and we didn't have to pay for them. But who knows? We have papers signed by the Ministry of Agriculture. It tells us what we can do and what we can't do with the land. If it says vegetables, then you can't plant grain or fruit trees—and the rich pre-cooperatives—the ones that did well and loaned all their money to the poor ones—they stayed cooperative. But the money they lent out was totally lost. The cooperateurs at Chougui never saw their profits to this day; perhaps the money never reached the other P-Cs in need. [At this point the fellah demonstrated by taking money out of his pants' pocket and moving it into his shirt pocket, indicating graft on the part of the director] (personal interview).

The agriculturalist quoted above had been sympathetic to the goals of the cooperative movement, saying "It's good for a poor man, but for the rich, they're better off when they run their own farms!"—but after his experiences during the cooperative period (and later with his agrarian reform parcel) he became cynical over the implementation of any government program.

When the cooperative movement collapsed in 1969, P-C Chouigui was the only OMVVM cooperative in the delegation of Tebourba to survive. In 1972 neighboring P-C Bordj El Habib was parceled out to its former cooperateurs. Forty-seven landless families received agrarian reform parcels ranging from ten to thirty hectares. The successful *pre*-cooperative of Chouigui became a *permanent* cooperative—the UCP of Chouigui. Management was transferred to the OTD and later to the BCUPN.

UCP Chouigui continues to be productive enough to award bonuses in some years to its cooperateurs. The state-appointed director also receives a bonus in a profitable year. Directors, however, come and go. Cooperateurs say that some directors receive production bonuses before they have been at Chouigui long enough to furnish the director's villa (Gerodius's old villa) or even to find their own way to the fields. In addition, the cooperateurs claim that the UCP is more successful than their own bonuses show. The director responds that profits are reinvested in the farm—providing new housing for forty farm families and replacing the old, poorly yielding colonial vines. Time and time again, one can see the cooperateurs cynically pantomime taking money out of their pants pocket and placing it in their shirt pocket. They say that a director sits in an office and profits from their labor, either through undeserved bonuses or "creative" bookkeeping. A director, say the cooperateurs, may be replaced if he is found to be dishonest, but his replacement—sent to Chouigui from Tunis—will be no different.

Chouigui's cooperateurs feel that they have been victimized long enough. They say that they have the least autonomy and the fewest benefits of any agriculturalists in Tunisia. They are not eligible for membership in the workers' union because they are not officially workers, nor are they eligible for membership in the agriculturalists' union because they are not private farmers. The cooperateurs' union was closed when the cooperative movement was dismantled. This lack of status is symbolized by the BCUPN's inability to decide whether to provide cooperateurs with the yearly gift of blue workers' overalls because such action would imply that they should receive other benefits as well, such as health and retirement benefits. To make matters worse, the incentive to work cooperatively—once valued with pride at Chouigui—has diminished as the cooperateurs watch the farms of their Bordj El Habib neighbors prosper. They want the cooperative disbanded and parceled out to them. They insist that the land would be more productive if each was given his own parcel. Hadj Mahmoud, an outspoken cooperateur of P-C Chouigui describes the current status at Chouigui as follows:

> We have our meetings and elections coming up in just two days and this is what I have to say: We get a director and he stays six months or a year—I don't even know his name. He does nothing, just sits in his office at Chouigui, sits at his desk or rides in a big car to Tunis. He rents a house in Chouigui for 55 dinars a month! Can you imagine anything in Chouigui renting for 55 dinars a month? That's more than double my monthly salary. And where does that 55 dinars come from? From *our* treasury of course—55 dinars of *our* money. . . . The old director who was here during the sixties took one thousand dinars of our money to give to UCP Mezez or one of the others. He wrote out a check, but for some reason, it never got there. To this day the money is unaccounted for—and where did it go?
>
> I was born in a ma'amera [hut] made of mud and straw right over there in the Lansarine. I've worked here my whole life. . . . Everything I have is right here. I don't want to live in one of those houses they built for us on the outskirts of Chouigui. . . . Here I have more space and a bit of garden and nobody keeps his eyes on what I do and what I have. I have my own animals: four sheep, three goats, two cows, and some chickens. Where would I put them in Chouigui? So I don't have electricity. They promise it to the cooperateurs who move to Chouigui, but it'll take a long time to put it in. Besides, the houses may be subsidized but you still have to pay for them! That's not where I want to put my profit shares. I have enough almond and olive trees for my family—and now that there's irrigation on the cooperative, I'm going to tap into it and use UCP water to grow my own vegetables. . . . But I work for wages and not for myself.

Let me explain how things work here. Say the UCP makes fifty million. Well, then, five million goes to the cooperateurs, five million goes to the machinery, ten million goes to the next year's crops, and thirty million goes to the state! The UCP is "buying" the land from the state and *we* are the landowners [*patrons*]! Don't I look like a *propriétaire*?" [he pointed to his worker clothes]. I work twenty days a month and get minimum wage, 1.332 TD per day, but they call it an "advance"—not "wages." We're going to vote for a higher daily advance. We want 1.800 TD and then we can live. They give us twelve sacks of wheat and a hundred liters of olive oil and if you have children in school they give you another ten dinars a year. But none of my children are in school. My son is only twenty-five. He married a Sidi Bechir girl two years ago and they're already having children. He's a temporary worker [*waqti*] waiting to take my place as a cooperateur but I am still strong—and besides, maybe they won't replace us. Look at Bordj Touta [nearby agro-combinat whose workers are being replaced by mechanized farming.]

At the meeting we're going to vote in some competent people. The cooperative used to be profitable, but now it's not. Men don't know how to work any more. They think that if they just stand there long enough that it's called work. . . . We work for nothing. If they parceled out the UCP today, I could take my wife to Mecca on the profits from next year's harvests. I went to Mecca four years ago and paid for it out of the year end's profit. I got over three hundred dinars that year. Now where are the profits? We've already borrowed more than we would get back at the end of the year after the harvest. They mostly reinvest into the cooperative—building those houses at Chouigui, fixing the winery, buying machinery, and a lot of things that we didn't vote for. We want to decide where the money goes and we want it to go to *us*. But they limit what we can vote on. We can elect a president and a council, but not much else. If we could, we would vote to split up the cooperative of Chouigui and divide it between us like they did with Bordj El Habib. They say that we're the *patrons*, the *propriétaires*, but we're not. We're nothing (personal interview).

The general assembly meetings and elections for the UCP Chouigui which Hadj Mahmoud anticipated with both eagerness and bitterness did not take place on schedule; instead they were postponed indefinitely—and were not held at all that year.

The cooperateurs are the last remnant of a movement officially declared a failure. Their experience and the land history of Chouigui has taught them that success is punished and failure rewarded. They are the landless, their neighbors the landed. They are left with a single outlet through which to vent anger and frustration: sabotage. Their goal is explicit and acknowledged by the central BCUPN office. That goal is to make Chouigui fail so that once and for all, the land they were born on can be parceled out to them and called their own.

CONCLUSIONS

A quarter of a century of post-independence agrarian reforms have left Tunisia with the mixed blessing of mixed farming. The fellahin do not object to the diversity of farm types per se; rather it is the lack of resolution of the ambiguities and contradictions in the reforms which leads to resentment and opposition. Thus while the implications of the term "centralization" have been unmistakable to farmers and policymakers alike, "decentralization" has been an ambiguous term which has generated a good deal of misunderstanding.

The agricultural production cooperatives remain the most problematic of farm types in Tunisia. Ben Salem reminds us that a major goal of the cooperative movement was "an almost utopian *decentralization* of decision-making," and yet, even at the height of the movement, decision-making was centralized under the supervisory control of emissaries from the Ministry of Agriculture (1976:279; my emphasis). The contradiction between cooperative theory and practice is still in evidence. Furthermore, the struggle between policies aimed at maintaining state control and those advocating greater farmer autonomy has persisted past the demise of the cooperative period. Even policies advocating small-scale family attributaries are not actually aiming for farmer autonomy, for they too are to be monitored and directed.

On the whole, farm boundaries and forms have fluctuated according to whether the current development plan called for capital-intensive large-scale farming or labor-intensive small-scale farming. The Sixth Plan, still being debated in the Tunisian General Assembly, calls for some compromise between the two (personal communication). This compromise may result in the reaffirmation of mixed farming or may introduce a new experiment in intermediate farming. Most recently, land tenure reforms have focused upon a hitherto untouched category of landholdings—fragmented private parcels. These are being regrouped and modified in both shape and size in order to conform to newly introduced irrigation techniques. Thus while cooperateurs look jealously at agrarian reform farmers, and the latter look longingly at private parcels, those on private landholdings are watching their own farms being regrouped and moved from spot to spot on a developer's map. Ralston, Anderson, and Colson summed up the problem of such instability:

> The poor in the non-Western world have much less reason than ourselves to regard organizational forms as sacrosanct. They are more accustomed to change than the citizens of the industrial nations of the West. They have seen international development programs of many kinds come and go in the course of a few years. Not only have their governments changed, frequently the institutions of government have been revolutionized during their lifetime, and not only once. Local institutions have had to adjust, often drastically, in response to external forces. Periodically they are under threat of reform from the center. Voluntary organizations in high favor in one year have fallen from favor the next and been banned or had their activities placed under close scrutiny. People are well aware that the institutions and personnel they now confront may be equally ephemeral. Since they are skeptical that any particular set of officials or agencies can make good on long-term promises, they have even less reason to be interested in cooperating in programs that do not provide immediate benefits (1981:35).

Families living on pilot farms and agro-combinats have worked on the same farms often for generations, irrespective of who owned the land. They preceded the current tenure form and hope to outlive it—expanding their households, grazing their sheep, and planting crops for home consumption. They were never under the illusion that the land belonged to them; as a consequence, they are not bitter about not owning it now. Their standard of living has improved as both their wages and benefits have increased.

The cooperatives which were "national successes"—as measured in "rational" terms—have been continued by the government, but the cooperateurs lead the most unsatisfactory and unsuccessful lives according to their expectations. In contrast, cooperatives which failed have been disbanded and their cooperateurs "rewarded" with individual agrarian reform parcels.

Those who were awarded agrarian reform parcels anticipate both future land reform and/or the day when they will be required to pay for their land—an event for which they are ill-equipped. In any case, they expect their "ownership" may be interrupted by what one fellah called "the politics of the future." Believing that the land and not their personal belongings will be regrouped has led them to reduce agricultural investment in favor of the accumulation of luxury items. The fellahin on these farms consider private ownership of one's own land the basis of a security which would allow them to make agricultural investments without fear.

Meanwhile, agrarian reform—which initially affected state land acquired from colonial expropriation—has come to encompass private landholdings as well (as noted). The OMVVM's plan to regroup private parcels places the same restrictions on private farms as exist on agrarian reform parcels. Thus in what must appear to be the ultimate irony, private farms—despite legal title to the land—may now face expropriation for noncompliance with OMVVM directives. Although this plan has not yet taken effect, private farmers are beginning to invest in nonagricultural endeavors and are opting out of agriculture altogether.

If we look at agrarian reform in Tunisia in terms of "winners" and "losers," clearly there are many losers. The state has not reached its goals of modernizing the rural sector, changing the traditional mentality of fellahin, or raising agricultural production enough to achieve self-sufficiency. Nor have poorer fellahin obtained their dream of private family parcels which they can work with a minimum of interference. The real "winners," if they may be called such, are large-scale landowners who purchased colonial farms through the partnership program. These individuals not only were able to maintain control of their land during the cooperative period and be handed back their property intact, but also were able to expand their acquisitions and enlarge their role as leaders in community affairs and national politics.

REFERENCES

Ben Brahim, A. 1975. "The Tunisian Cooperative Experience." Unpublished Master's thesis, University of Minnesota.

Ben Salem, L. 1976. "Decision-Making in an Experiment in Agricultural Cooperation." In *Popular Participation in Social Change*, ed. J. Nash et al. Chicago: Aldine Press.

Bourguiba, H. 1974. *Articles de presse*. Tunis: CDN.

Centre de Recherches et d'Etudes Administratives (CREA). 1974. *La Politique économique de Tunisie*. Tunis: Ecole Nationale d' Administration.

Chennoufi, S. 1977. *Mise en valeur et réforme agraire dans la basse vallée de la Medjerda*. Toulouse: Le Mirail.

Démocratie (Tunis). 1978-79. Various issues.

France, Ministry of Foreign Affairs. 1888-1950. Unpublished Tunisian archives. Paris.

Kassab, A. 1979. *L'Evolution de la vie rurale dans les régions de la Moyenne Medjerda et de Béja-Mateur*. Tunis: Tunis University.

Makhlouf. E. 1971. "Les Coopératives agricoles en Tunisie: Structures et difficultés." *Revue tunisienne de sciences sociales*, no. 26:74-114.

Moore, H. 1965. *Tunisia since Independence: The Dynamics of One-Party Government*. Berkeley: University of California Press.

Moore, M., and Lewis, M. 1968. "Agrarian Reform and the Development of Agricultural Cooperatives in Tunisia." In *Year Book of Agricultural Cooperation*, pp. 29-52.

Poncet, J. 1962. *Paysages et problèmes ruraux en Tunisie*. Paris: Presses Universitaires de France.

Ralston, L.; Anderson, J., and Colson, E. 1981. *Voluntary Efforts in Decentralized Management*. Berkeley: Institute of International Studies.

Le Temps (Tunis). 1978-79. Various issues.

Tunisia. 1958-78. *Agrarian Reform Laws of the OMVVM and OTD*.

__________. 1960. *Revue Medjerda*.

__________. 1975. *Annuaire agricole de la Tunisie: L'Agriculture en Tunisie*. Tunis: Agence Générale d'Edition et de Publicité.

Zamiti, K. 1970. "Les Obstacles materiels et idéologiques à l'évolution sociale des campagnes tunisiennes." *Revue tunisienne de sciences sociales*, no. 21 (May):9-55.

Zghall, A. 1968. "L'Elite administrative et la paysannerie en Tunisie." *Revue tunisienne de sciences sociales*, no. 16:41-52.

__________. 1974. "The Reactivation of Tradition in a Post-Traditional Society." In *Post-Traditional Societies*, ed. S. Eisenhardt, pp. 225-37. New York: Norton.

__________. 1977. "Pourquoi la reforme agraire ne mobilise-t-elle pas les paysans maghrebiens?" In *Problèmes agraires au Maghreb*, ed. B. Etienne et al., pp. 295-312. Paris: Centre National de la Recherche Scientifique.

Zussman, M. 1982. *The Fellahin of Tebourba: Rural Development and Farmer Strategies in Northern Tunisia*. Unpublished Ph.D. dissertation, University of California, Berkeley.

Chapter 6

RULING ELITES AND THE YOUNG: A COMPARISON OF IRAQ AND LEBANON

Suad Joseph

Control over the allegiance and behavior of the young tends to be contested in all societies. In state societies ruling elites are key contenders, and their strategies vis-à-vis the state significantly shape the nature of that control and the outcome of the contest. In this chapter I shall focus on the training of the young, particularly for labor-force participation, as an arena in which control over their allegiance and behavior is played out. I shall compare Iraq and Lebanon, two Middle Eastern countries whose ruling elites have very different strategies toward the state and thus very different forms of control over the young.*

*Iraqi data were gathered in 1974 in a trip sponsored by the General Union of Iraqi Students and in a fieldwork project carried out in the spring and summer of 1980 under a grant from the Iraqi Ministry of Culture and Information. Lebanese data were gathered from fieldwork carried out primarily in 1971-73. Part of the research was carried out under a predoctoral research grant from the National Institute of Mental Health (NIMH). Another part was carried out for a study sponsored by the UN Economic and Social Office in Beirut (UNESOB). That was later synthesized by the United Nations into a comparative world study, *Service by Youth* (New York: United Nations, 1975). Additional data were gathered in numerous trips from 1974 through 1980. I shall discuss the two countries primarily from the late 1960s up to the beginning of the wars in which they are currently engaged. Iraq has been embroiled in a war with Iran since 1980. The war in Lebanon, which has both domestic and international aspects, began in 1975.

I am grateful to Ellis Goldberg, Laurence Michalak, and Amal Rassam for their helpful comments on earlier versions of this chapter.

EMERGENCE OF THE IRAQI AND LEBANESE STATES

Like many developing countries, Iraq has not produced a sense of nationhood. The European powers established the Iraqi state after World War I by rather arbitrarily piecing together three vilayets, or provinces, from the Ottoman Empire (Baghdad, Basra, and Mosul). The population is thus composed of quite different ethnic, religious, and linguistic groups who historically have had no sense of belonging to a common independent state. However, since 1968 Iraq has been controlled by one political party, the Arab Ba'th Socialist Party, permitting a relative coherence between party and state programs. The Ba'th, which took over after a revolution in 1968, proclaims a systematic ideology organized around socialism and pan-Arab nationalism. Moreover, the top leadership of the state and party has been relatively homogeneous. The ruling elite has been largely of petty bourgeois origins, and many are closely related through personal ties. While members of this elite have not yet comprised a class, they have been attempting to construct the basis for their own class development. The primary instrument for this class construction has been the state. The elite has been aided in this project by the vast resources available to the state as a result of oil nationalization. The revenues from oil have been used to build national institutions—the military, industry, schools, youth groups, unions, women's organizations—which have been controlled by the Ba'th. The rapid growth of the country and dispersion of the national wealth and resources have gained popular legitimacy for the ruling elite among some sectors of the population. Since the ruling elite of the Ba'th and of the state are one and the same and since their ideology is nationalist, there has been some degree of identification between the legitimacy of the leaders and the state.

Lebanon, on the other hand, has been controlled by fluctuating alliances of leaders called *zu'amā'* (political patrons), who represent different ideological orientations and come from different class backgrounds, religious sects, and regions. Formally plural, the government has been organized to represent the legally recognized religious sects on a proportional basis in government agencies and programs so that the religious and ethnic heterogeneity in the population has been manifested in the state as well. Like Iraq, Lebanon was arbitrarily established by European powers from the Ottoman Empire and has lacked a sense of nationhood. The ruling elite also does not comprise a class. However, Lebanon's elite has been more heterogeneous than

Iraq's, consisting of feudal landlords, a financial bourgeoisie, compradores, and some petty bourgeois elements--from all the major sectarian groups. Their power has been based on sectarian, kin, and regional affiliations outside of the state. For the ruling elite the state has been primarily an avenue of resources to be redirected to their clientele outside the state. The elite have made little effort to build the state in Lebanon; rather they have tried to expand the private sectors. This is manifest in the relatively small revenues available to the state for national development. Lebanon has had far fewer resources than Iraq; the resources it has had have remained primarily in the private sector. Rather than within the state, the political process and the center of social action have been outside, where the ruling elite have exercised direct control over their individualized clientele. As access to resources and services has been seen to be achieved through personal association with zu'amā', popular legitimacy in Lebanon has been focused on the persons of the leaders, regardless of whether they are currently in the state. Their legitimacy has not translated to the state.

A NOTE ON DATA AND TERMINOLOGY

Developing countries are often criticized for their lack of planning and for contradictions in their development programs. However, it is important to note that planning at state levels for long-term development is relatively recent even in more advanced countries. It is with industrialization and more systematic state involvement in economic regulation that planning has evolved as an ongoing government enterprise. The advanced industrial states differ considerably in the degree and quality of state planning, and their planning is often unwieldy and contradictory.

In developing countries planning is a new phenomenon. It may be the responsibility of a ministry, dispersed throughout the government, or controlled by a small ruling elite. In addition, countries vary in the degree and manner in which plans move from paper into practice. The range and uneveness in this process, however, is by no means limited to developing countries and must be seen in light of the recency of planning and the recency of the developing states.

The problems in defining the "young" are complex, culturally and statistically. In Arabic the "young" are often referred to as "youth" (*shabb*—male youth; *shabba*—female youth), a term which describes a male or female who is usually unmarried and is not a child. Some young people may still be referred to as "youth" even if married, particularly if they are dependent on parents and do not yet have children. Shabb/shabba usually refers to individuals in their late teens and twenties. The members of youth groups in both Iraq and Lebanon are usually persons in this age group, although members can be older and the groups are run by men and women in their thirties and forties. Statistical problems result from the lack of reliable censuses in many developing countries. Government statistics are often confused and contradictory. Furthermore, there are no internationally agreed upon definitions which would facilitate data collection and cross-cultural comparisons.*

In this chapter I shall use the term "young" and use it to refer to those 0-24 years. I prefer this term because training of the young (including preparation for labor-force participation) begins in the very early years of life and continues, with variations, for many years. The "young" avoids the distinction between "children" and "youth" and also leaves open the issues of marital status and dependency, which are not immediately relevant to this discussion. Despite my attempts at clarification, however, there will be some inconsistencies owing to the variability of the data.

POPULATION, LABOR FORCE, AND ECONOMY IN IRAQ

POPULATION

In Arab terms Iraq has a large population—approximately 13 million in 1980—outstripped only by Egypt, Morocco, Algeria, and the Sudan. The population has been growing at the rapid rate of 3 percent annually, jumping from 8.1 million in 1965 to 12.2 million in 1977 at the last census (Iraq, Ministry of Planning 1978b). The census reports a crude birth rate of 42 births per 1,000 inhabitants.

Since Iraq was pieced together rather arbitrarily, the diverse ethnic, linguistic, and religious groups now comprising it cannot be

*For example, the United Nations sponsored a conference in 1970 on children and youth in national planning in the Arab states. The reports in the conference used the term "children" to mean those 0-14 years of age when differentiating "children" from the economically active population (15-64 years) and used it to mean those 0-24 years of age when discussing matters of dependency, training, and education (UNESOB 1970).

said to be a nation. The large majority of Iraqis are Muslim, probably evenly divided between Sunnis and Shī'ites. At least 25 percent of the population is non-Arab (Gotlieb 1981:155).* The largest non-Arab group is the Kurds, who are Sunni and have been estimated at 4 million (*ibid.*). Until the formation of Israel, the Jews were the second largest non-Arab minority, but now they number only a few hundred. A Turkic group, the Turcomans, comprises another large non-Arab minority. In addition to the groups mentioned, Iraq also has smaller groups of Armenians, Assyrians, and Indians. Among these groups the Shī'ites are the largest Arab group in Iraq. However, the Sunnis have been predominantly in control of the contemporary state and have used their position to control and suppress Shī'ites, Kurds, and other minorities (Batatu 1981; Gotlieb 1981).

In 1965, 51.1 percent of Iraq's population lived in cities. By 1977 the urban areas claimed 63.5 percent. Rural to urban migration accounted for a large proportion of the urban increase (Iraq, Ministry of Planning 1978a:11). Between 1965 and 1977 the cities grew an average of 5.3 percent yearly, while the rural areas grew only 0.9 percent. During that same period approximately 1.5 million persons migrated from the 1,400 villages to urban areas (Birks and Sinclair 1982:245). Most of these were young people—mainly male—seeking employment.

LABOR FORCE

The labor force has expanded with population growth. There was a 27 percent increase in those gainfully employed between 1968 and 1977, from 2.3 million to 3 million (Birks and Sinclair 1982: 247). By 1977 only 2.4 percent (75,000) of the economically active were unemployed (Iraq, Ministry of Planning 1978b:39). Iraq's development plan for 1976-80 anticipated a further expansion of job opportunities of 550,000—half of which were targeted for women (Iraq, GFIW 1978).

The expansion of the labor force was only in part the result of population growth, however. The Ba'th party's economic program, which focused on development of the services sector and industry,

*The Sunnis and Shī'ites are both divided between Arab and non-Arab groups. However, the numbers of the non-Arab Shī'ites (primarily Persians) have been diminished by a series of deportations—60,000 deported in 1974 and 35,000 in 1980 (Gotlieb 1981:154).

required both an increase in the labor force and an upgrading of its quality. The upgrading was achieved largely through massive educational and training programs (discussed below). The increase in the labor force over and above population increases resulted from both a campaign to mobilize Iraqi women and the importation of foreign workers. Iraqi women were attracted and pressured into the wage labor force through media campaigns and the institution of programs which facilitated their labor-force participation. The importation of non-nationals into the labor force was occurring in large numbers prior to the 1980 Iran-Iraq war. Batatu (1981:518) quotes one UN official as estimating 700,000 Egyptian workers in and around Baghdad in 1980, while Birks and Sinclair (1980:144) claim there were fewer than 600,000 in all Iraq. Socknat, Birks, and Serageldin (1981:10) estimated that by 1985 Iraq's non-national labor force would range between 3.8 and 5.5 percent of its total labor force. This would not be high relative to Arab oil-producing countries—7 of which were projected by 1985 to average 54 to 57 percent non-nationals in their labor forces and 2 others to average 24 to 27 percent non-nationals (Socknat, Birks, and Serageldin 1981:10). Nevertheless, for the expanding Iraqi economy the necessity of importing workers represented a pressure to speed up and upgrade the preparation of the country's own young for labor-force participation.

Distribution of the labor force has changed dramatically since the Ba'th party gained power. The figures are broken down by economic sectors for 1968 and 1977 in Table 1 and in greater detail for 1977 in Table 2. (Slight differences in figures for 1977 are due to different sources.) The largest change has been a drop in agricultural employment from 54 percent of the labor force (1,254,000) in 1968 to 31.5 percent (944,000) in 1977.

ECONOMY

There are many reasons for the drop in agricultural employment. First, agriculture had been declining prior to the Ba'th Revolution and has not significantly improved since. Joe Stork (1982:34) estimates a 30 percent decrease in total arable and cultivated land between 1958 and 1977. Second, while many Iraqis have benefited from agricultural reforms and a degree of land redistribution, private ownership has continued to dominate the agricultural system (Farouk-Sluglett and

Table 1

STRUCTURE OF IRAQI LABOR FORCE BY MAJOR ECONOMIC SECTOR, 1968 AND 1977

Sector	1968 Number (*Thousands of workers*)	1968 Percent	1977 Number (*Thousands of workers*)	1977 Percent
Agriculture	1254	54.0%	944	31.5%
Construction	66	2.8	322	10.7
Distribution (including commerce and finance)	280	12.0	178	5.9
Industry	174	7.5	344	11.5
Services and other	550	23.7	1213	40.4
Total	2323	100.0	3001	100.0

Source: For 1968: Adapted from Iraq, Ministry of Planning 1978a:68; for 1977: Birks and Sinclair 1982:247.

Table 2

STRUCTURE OF IRAQI LABOR FORCE BY ECONOMIC SECTOR, 1977

Sector	Number (*Thousands of workers*)	Percent
Agriculture	944	30.1%
Community, social, and personal services	958	30.6
Construction	322	10.3
Electricity, gas, and water	23	0.7
Finance, real estate, and business services	31	1.0
Manufacturing industry	284	9.1
Petroleum and mining	37	1.2
Transport, storage, and communications	178	5.7
Wholesale and retail trade	224	7.1
Other	58	1.8
Unemployed	75	2.4
Total	3134	100.1

Source: Adapted from Iraq, Ministry of Planning 1978b:38-39.

Sluglett 1981). In 1973, for example, 72 percent of the landowners held 33 percent of the land under 50 dunums and 18 percent of the landowners held 37 percent of the land between 50 and 150 dunums;* however, 3 percent of the landowners held 31 percent of the land over 150 dunums (Farouk-Sluglett and Sluglett 1981:10). Furthermore, even with redistribution peasants have continued to be dependent on merchants and landowners (Theobald and Jawad 1982:214). In addition, rural to urban migration has been significant as productivity and living conditions continue to decline in the countryside (al-Jomard 1979).

For the Ba'th industrial development has been central. The government claimed an increase in the relative contribution of the industrial sector to total domestic product from 43 percent in 1968 to 61 percent in 1976 (Iraq, Ministry of Planning 1978a). However, census records indicate that the contribution of manufacturing reached a high of 10 percent in 1973, dropped to 4.7 percent in 1974, and rose to 7.8 percent in 1976 (Stork 1982:35). Nevertheless, there has been a growth in both large (over ten workers) and small firms in the past two decades (see Table 3). Much of the industrial development has been in light industry—including food, beverages, tobacco, textiles, leather, and electronics.

By far the largest growth has been in the services sector, which has absorbed many workers from agriculture. Services accounted for over one million workers (over 40 percent of the labor force) in 1977 (Table 1).† Much of the service labor force is employed by the state.

The most significant changes in the economy have been precipitated by the development and nationalization of oil. The Iraqi Petroleum Company was nationalized in 1972 and the remaining foreign oil interests in 1975. Oil revenues rose from 10 percent of government revenues in 1952 to 35 percent in 1970 to 52 percent in 1971 to 60 percent in 1974. They have remained at approximately that level (Stork 1982:37). By 1975 oil accounted for 98 percent of all Iraqi exports and by 1976, 87 percent of government revenues

*One dunum is approximately .62 acre.

†Birks and Sinclair (1982:247) report statistics from a Ministry of Planning document indicating that personal and community services accounted for 40.4 percent of the employment in Iraq by 1977. My copy of the same document (Iraq, Ministry of Planning 1978a) does not provide figures for 1977, stating only that 21.5 percent of the labor force was employed in services in 1976. Assuming a later edition of this document has been published which I have not been able to obtain, I have used Birks and Sinclair's figures.

Table 3

LARGE MANUFACTURING IN IRAQ, 1954 AND 1976[a]

Year	Number of Firms	Number of Workers
1954	727	44,410
1976	1479	142,740

Source: Stork 1982:35.

[a]Large firms have over ten workers.

(Stork 1982:37 and 1980:187). In monetary terms oil revenues increased from $19 million in 1950 to $488 million in 1968 to $12,180 million in 1979 (Stork 1982:32). However, oil is a capital-intensive industry; thus, with mining, it claimed only 1.2 percent of the labor force (Table 2). The impact of the increased revenues from oil on the Iraqi state (discussed below) has been phenomenal.

POPULATION, LABOR FORCE, AND ECONOMY IN LEBANON

POPULATION

For political reasons which will be detailed in the following section, the last official census carried out in Lebanon was in 1932. Thus more recent demographic data have been in the form of estimates or based on sample surveys which are not officially recognized. These methods have often led to conflicting figures on population transformations.

Lebanon's population has been quite heterogeneous in religious and ethnic terms. It is divided among seventeen formally recognized religious sects, comprising Arabs and a number of ethnic minorities such as Armenians. According to the 1932 census, the Christian sects together outnumbered the Muslim sects by a 6 to 5 ratio. The census placed the Maronites at about 30 percent of the population, Sunnis at 20 percent, Shīʿites at 18 percent, Greek Orthodox at 10 percent, Greek Catholics at 6 percent, Druze at 6 percent, Armenian Orthodox at 5 percent, and the remaining groups at 5 percent. However, by the mid-1970s it was well recognized—though not officially accepted—

that the Muslims outnumbered the Christians, accounting for 55-60 percent of the population, with the Shī'ites having become the largest single sect.*

Prior to the outbreak of the war in 1975, Lebanon had an estimated population of about 3 million with an annual growth rate of about 2.8 percent. Its gross birth rate was the lowest in the Arab world in the mid-1960s (Seklani 1970:83). Given its population density of 257 persons per square kilometer, it was one of the most densely populated Arab countries, exceeded only by Bahrain and Gaza (UNESOB 1970:257). While many Arab countries exhibited high population densities in urban areas, Lebanon had high densities in rural areas as well—59 persons per square kilometer in the Bekka Valley, 144 in south Lebanon, and 231 in north Lebanon (Chasteland 1970).

Lebanon also was remarkable in the region for its high rate of urbanization. The capital, Beirut, housed just under 40 percent of the population in 1970 (Chasteland 1970). At that time, about 55 percent of the population was urban and 45 percent rural (UNESOB 1971c). Urbanization proceeded rapidly in the 1970s as many peasants were displaced from their lands and others fled to urban areas to escape the increased militarization of the Lebanese south. By 1975 according to the UN Department of International Economic and Social Affairs–UNDIESA (1982:326) 70 percent of the population

*According to a recent *New York Times* article, the Muslims are now 55 percent of the Lebanese population (not counting Palestinians). The article presented the following figures:

Group	Estimated Population	Percent of Total Population	Seats in Parliament
Shī'a Muslims	1,000,000	29%	19
Maronite Christians	600,000	17	30
Sunni Muslims	600,000	17	20
Greek Orthodox	400,000	11	11
Druze	300,000	9	6
Greek Catholic	250,000	7	6
Armenian (Orthodox and Catholic)	250,000	7	5
Protestants and other minorities	100,000	3	2
Total	3,500,000	100	99

Source: New York Times, 2 October 1983, sec. 4:1.

was concentrated in urban areas and 30 percent lived in 2,200 villages scattered across the country.

LABOR FORCE

The growth and rapid urbanization of the population in the post-World War II period was reflected in the growth and distribution of the labor force (see Table 4), which grew from 571,755 in 1970 to an estimated 748,000 in 1975. While Lebanon has traditionally exported some of its labor force, periods of economic and political crisis have witnessed far greater labor migrations. Thus Lebanon's instability and uneven economic development have contributed significantly to a heavy labor exodus, much of which has been young people. Socknat, Birks, and Serageldin (1981:18) reported 28,500 (or 5 percent of the Lebanese labor force) working in nine Arab labor-importing countries in 1975—probably before the civil war—and projected a 10-12 percent increase by 1985. However, after nine years of war, 35 percent of the Lebanese workforce is out of the country (Stork 1983:13).

While Lebanon has been exporting labor, prior to 1975 it was also importing workers, most of whom were unskilled and semi-skilled manual laborers. There were about half a million Syrians working in Lebanon, concentrated in the port areas and for seasonal agricultural harvests. The 300,000 Palestinians living there were an expanding section of the non-national labor force. There were also Egyptians and Asians, particularly females employed in domestic service.

The labor problems in Lebanon were evident in unemployment and underemployment. While the 6 percent unemployment figure in 1970 (Table 4) seems small by today's standards, it concealed employment difficulties. Lebanon was estimated to need half a million new jobs between 1965 and 1980—an annual average increase of 30,000. Between 1960 and 1964 only 4,000-6,000 new jobs were created annually (UNESOB 1971b). Most of the employment difficulties were in the rural areas, where a 69 percent underemployment rate was estimated in 1971 (UNESOB 1971a). The relatively small percent of the labor force in agriculture was striking—17 percent in 1975, down from 21.4 percent in 1970 (Table 4).

Table 4

ECONOMICALLY ACTIVE POPULATION IN LEBANON BY ECONOMIC SECTOR, 1970 AND 1975

	1970						1975	
Sector	Males	Percent of Total Labor Force	Females	Percent of Total Labor Force	Total	Percent of Total Labor Force	Total	Percent of Total Labor Force
Agriculture, hunting, forestry, fishing	80,535	17.0%	21,225	21.4%	101,760	17.8%	127,000	17.0%
Community, social, personal services	106,605	22.6	43,185	43.6	149,790	26.2	213,000	28.5
Construction	34,800	7.4	255	.3	35,055	6.1	50,000	6.7
Electricity, gas, water	5,550	1.2	60	.1	5,610	1.0	8,000	1.0
Financing, insurance, real estate, business services	15,600	3.3	2,820	2.8	18,420	3.2	26,000	3.5
Manufacturing	76,890	16.9	18,645	18.8	94,620	16.5	135,000	18.1
Mining, quarrying					915	.2	1,000	.1
Trade, restaurants, hotels	85,845	18.2	5,775	5.8	91,620	16.0	130,000	17.4
Transport, storage, communications	36,375	7.7	1,860	1.9	38,235	6.7	54,000	7.2
Not adequately defined	2,085	.4	300	.3	2,385	.4	3,000	.4
Total employed	444,285	94.0	94,125	94.9	538,410	94.2		
Unemployed	28,335	6.0	5,010	5.1	33,345	5.8		
Total labor force	472,620	100.0	99,135	100.0	571,755	100.0	748,000	100.0

Source: 1970: Based on Fisher 1982:555; 1975: Based on ILO 1982:42.

ECONOMY

Between 1972 and 1974 agriculture contributed about 9 percent of the Gross Domestic Product (GDP) (Fisher 1982:548), a decline from its 12 percent share in 1964 (Makdisi 1977:268). Its small contribution was a byproduct of the lack of attention and investment from both public and private sectors and the increased militarization of the important agricultural lands in the south after 1967. Since 1975 there has been an even greater decline in the agricultural labor force and the contribution of agriculture to the GDP–9 percent in 1970 according to Birks and Sinclair (1980:210). The decline is more dramatic when one notes that in 1960 one study reported 50 percent of the labor force worked in agriculture, although it contributed only 15.6 percent of the Gross National Product (GNP) (Lebanon, Ministry of Planning 1960:57, 87). Some sources reported that agriculture accounted for almost 50 percent of the labor force even in the 1970s (Edwards 1971:3); others credit it with as little as 19 percent (Birks and Sinclair 1980:210).

Manufacturing, mining, and quarrying accounted for over 18 percent of the labor force in 1975 (Table 4). Industry increased its share of the GDP from about 13 percent in 1964 to 19 percent in 1973 (Makdisi 1977:268). Most of the industrial output came from small firms employing ten people or less.

Most of Lebanon's industrial production has been concentrated in the Greater Beirut area. A study by the Centre d'Etudes et de Recherches sur le Moyen Orient Contemporain (CERMOC) found over two thirds of the firms and workers there. Most of these firms had fewer than twenty-four workers and low productivity per worker (cited in Lorfing 1983:3). The war apparently has been reducing Beirut's popularity as an industrial center. In 1980 other urban centers, Zahleh and the Shouf, claimed more new factories than did Beirut (Fisher 1982:550). The war has also considerably weakened Lebanon's industrial performance. Between 1975 and 1977 as a result of the war, 15 percent of the total capital invested in industry was destroyed and another 35-40 percent damaged (*ibid.*).

Rather than industry or agriculture, Lebanon's primary economic role in the region had been to provide tourism, trade, financing, and other services. The sectors of trade, restaurants, and hotels; financing, insurance, real estate, and business services; and community, social, and personal services accounted for 45.4 percent of the labor force in 1970 and 49.4 percent in 1975. The last sector alone accounted for almost 44 percent of the female labor force in 1970 (Table 4). However, this role had begun to decline prior to the 1975 war. An economic crisis, signaled by the fall of the IntraBank, the country's largest, had begun in 1966. The 1967 and 1973 Arab-Israeli wars added to Lebanon's problems. It increasingly became the confrontation zone between the Palestinians, other Arabs, and Israel and simultaneously became an internal battlefield among various domestic factions. This political instability significantly undermined its economic role in the region.

RULING ELITES, CLASS, AND STATE IN IRAQ

STRUCTURE OF RELATIONS

Since 1968 Iraq has been controlled primarily by petty bourgeois elements, or what Hanna Batatu describes as "middle classes"—i.e.,

> that composite part of society which is plural in its functions but has in common an intermediate status or occupies a middle position between the propertyless and the big proprietors and which includes, among other elements, army officers, civil servants, members of professions, merchants, tradesmen, and landowners (1979a:240).*

Batatu argues that the "middle class" character of the recent Iraqi regimes can be seen in the social origins of the ruling elite in the state and the Ba'th party, in the growth of the middle class under these regimes, and in the relatively improved condition of the middle class. He cautions that the ruling elite are acting in their own interests and not necessarily in the interests of the middle class as a whole (*ibid.*).

While the class structure of Iraq has continued to be unstable through much of the modern period, the fraction of the petty bourgeoisie that took control of the state in 1968 has been relatively homogeneous. The top leaders of the state are Arab Sunnis from

*Batatu actually contends that the character of the Iraqi regimes has been middle class since a revolution in 1958. A more thorough investigation of the state would require analysis of the Iraqi state in that and earlier periods. However (as noted), this paper focuses on the state since 1968. Space does not allow for historical coverage, which would certainly enrich this analysis; for that coverage see Batatu 1979b.

northwestern provincial towns, particularly Takrit. A number of them are consanguineal realtives from the Albun Nasir tribe or are affinally related (Batatu 1979a:243). In addition to tribal, extended kin, and family ties, the top administrators in the state share adherence to and membership in the Ba'th party. The Ba'th has a long history of underground struggle for leadership. Out of this struggle, a discipline and a degree of ideological coherence have developed that are unusual in the Arab world. While ardently anti-Communist, the Ba'th adherents have considered themselves both socialists and pan-Arab nationalists. Adherence to the party has become a necessary element for mobility in the state bureaucracy.

The homogeneity, discipline, and ideological coherence of the ruling elite have not yet transformed it into a class, however. Farouk-Sluglett and Sluglett (1980:15) contend that the state bureaucracy is not developing into a class of its own because the state is controlled by a very narrow elite acting in their own interests. Batatu (1979a: 244) sees a potential for the differentiation of a new upper class from the ruling families. Stork's position is to the point: the state in Iraq "incorporates a bourgeoisie in formation" (1982:45).

The transformation of the ruling elite into a ruling class, should it succeed, has been facilitated by the elite's ruthless crushing of opposition (Batatu 1981). The state is controlled by a handful of individuals, comprising President Saddam Husein and his close advisors, who are simultaneously the leaders of the Ba'th party. This high degree of centralization has been made possible by the resources available to the state.

RULING ELITE STRATEGIES VIS-À-VIS THE STATE

The ruling elite has turned the state into an autonomous arena of activity and the center of social action in Iraq. The prime factors which have made this possible are the huge revenues from oil and the undermining of the propertied classes following agrarian reforms in the early 1970s. As the economy became dependent on oil, the state's control over oil production and revenues gave it the central position in the economy.

The state's control over the economy following the nationalization of oil can be seen in the increased contribution of the public or "socialist" sector (as the public sector is called in Iraq) to the GDP. Between 1970 and 1978 the state's share of the GDP increased seventeen-fold (see Table 5). The rapid rate of state control can also be seen in the relative share of the socialist sector. For example, between 1968 and 1976 the socialist share in oil rose from 0.4 to 100 percent (see Table 6).

The distribution of the labor force between public and private sectors has changed as a result of state economic programs. State industrial expansion has been primarily in large establishments. The state role increased from 14 percent of the large establishments and 61 percent of the workers in 1972 to 17 and 70 percent respectively in 1977 (see Table 7). By 1978 the changes were more dramatic. The

Table 5

IRAQI STATE SHARE OF GDP BY ECONOMIC SECTOR, 1970 AND 1978
(Current prices in ID million)

Sector	1970	1978[a]
Commodities	64.0	4403.5
Distribution	59.4	402.2
Services	188.5	663.6
GDP	311.9	5469.3

Source: Farouk-Sluglett and Sluglett 1980:14.

[a]Provisional.

Table 6

SHARE OF IRAQI SOCIALIST SECTOR IN PRINCIPLE ECONOMIC ACTIVITIES, 1968 AND 1976
(Percent)

Economic Activity	1968	1976
Agriculture	1%	29%
Commerce	11	53
Manufacturing	41	51
Oil	0.4	100

Source: Adapted from Iraq, Ministry of Planning 1978a:34.

Table 7

IRAQI PUBLIC- AND PRIVATE-SECTOR LARGE INDUSTRIAL ESTABLISHMENTS, EMPLOYEES, AND VALUE OF OUTPUT AND INPUT, 1972-78

Year	Sector	Number of Establishments (*Thousands*)	Percent	Number of Employees (*Thousands*)	Percent	Value of Output (*ID million*)	Percent	Value of Input (*ID million*)	Percent
1972	Public	182	14%	71	61%	172	73%	102	69%
	Private	1107	86	45	39	64	27	45	31
1977	Public	266	17	106	70	522	72	310	68
	Private	1282	83	44	30	200	28	144	32
1978	Public	321	20	5156	93				
	Private	1333	80	369	7				

Source: Adapted from Farouk-Sluglett and Sluglett 1980:20.

public sector accounted for 321,000 of large industrial establishments (20 percent) but employed 5,156,000 (93 percent) of the workers. The private sector, on the other hand, accounted for 80 percent of the establishments but employed only 7 percent of the workers. In the small establishments, however, the private sector has remained dominant (Farouk-Sluglett and Sluglett 1980:19).

The state expanded its own bureaucracy as well under the Ba'th. State personnel increased from around 20,000 in 1958 to over 580,000 by 1977 (see Table 8). In addition, there were approximately 230,000 state personnel in the armed forces and 200,000 pensioners (Stork 1982:39).

RULING ELITE AND STATE AS ONE

With the vast resources available from oil revenues, the Ba'th elite have attempted to expand the state broadly into all avenues of economic, social, and political life. In the economic domain they have not only developed industries, agriculture, and services, but have also promulgated extensive regulations, including labor laws. In the social domain, through both state agencies and party organizations, they have established extensive programs for the young, women, the aged, and the disabled and have reformed laws concerning personal status and social welfare. In the political arena they have moved swiftly and ruthlessly to crush and eliminate opposition (Batatu 1981), leaving themselves as the only significant actors. In all these domains the Ba'th strategy has been to promulgate programs primarily through state agencies and to ensure that all these agencies

Table 8

IRAQI STATE PERSONNEL, 1958-77

Year	Personnel
1958	20,031
1968	224,253
1977	580,132

Source: Stork 1982:39.

are controlled by members of the Ba'th party. The trade unions, women's federation, student unions, and associations for the young (among others) have all been controlled by party members receiving instruction from the top levels of party and state leadership.

Similarly in their attempts to gain popular legitimacy, the ruling elite have stressed the unity of party and state. A personal cult of heroic proportions has developed around President Husein (who is also head of the party) in the traditional manner of Middle Eastern leaders. His pictures have been posted everywhere; his presence has dominated the media; schoolchildren have been taught songs in his praise; he has been presented as the father of the nation. At the same time, he has been strongly identified with the Ba'th and the state. This identity between the person of the leader, the party, the state, revolution, and society can be seen in an officially sponsored biography of Husein distributed for free by various Iraqi government ministries. In the preface the author, Amir Iskandar, an Egyptian socialist, describes this identity:

> But why Saddam Husein? Because it is Saddam Husein who is now in control of the train of the Revolution in Iraq and who has a thorough knowledge of the line and all its twists and turns, and because it is Saddam Husein whom the passengers have chosen as the engine driver to sit in the driver's cabin because of his knowledge, pugnacity, and loyalty and because they know that he will not stop halfway or maroon them at a remote station, and because Saddam Husein has brought a new dawn to all our Arab homeland and it is he who is best qualified to guide us through the perils that await us on the rough road that lies before us and bring us safely to our desired goal. He is an integral part of it, as it is of him. The story of his life and struggle is the story of the revolutionary struggle itself; an account of his ideas and attitudes is, at the same time, an account of the ideas and attitudes of the Revolution (Iskandar 1980:11).*

While domains not controlled by the state and party have continued to exist—and to offer resistance—the ruling elite clearly control

*In Iraq "Revolution"—always capitalized when referring to the Ba'th Revolution—has been glorified as the ultimate destiny of all Arab peoples. It refers to the process of unifying all Arab countries into one nation. In Iraq, therefore, Iraq is considered a "region" of the Arab nation. However, it is the spearhead of the Revolution, under the leadership of the Ba'th, led—for the present—by Saddam Husein.

political, economic, and social initiatives and define the significant trajectories for Iraqis at this point in history. By 1980 Iraq was a centralized, tightly controlled state expanding into all domains of Iraqi life. The situation was quite different in Lebanon during the same period.

RULING ELITES, CLASS, AND STATE IN LEBANON

STRUCTURE OF RELATIONS

Lebanon has been a weak state controlled by a ruling elite which, as in Iraq, cannot be said to comprise a class. Moreover, as noted, Lebanon's ruling elite is more heterogeneous in terms of class, religion, and ethnicity. It is composed of competing factions of large landowners, merchants, compradores, and some petty bourgeois families. Lebanon differs from Iraq also in that its military has not been as significant an avenue toward state power as in Iraq. Nor have the leaders of the Lebanese state attained their positions through revolutionary struggle or military coups. Some of the elite families have been in the ruling circles of Lebanon for centuries, while others have gained access to power very recently.

The ruling elite is composed of members of each of the major religious sects in Lebanon. Indeed the political system is designed to continually reproduce ethnic and religious heterogeneity at the state level. The state is formally plural, organized to represent the seventeen formally recognized religious sects in all government agencies. Representation is based on the proportional distribution of the sects in the population at the last formal census in 1932. In addition, the major positions in government have been allocated according to that census. The president of the republic has always been a Maronite, the prime minister a Sunni, the speaker of the parliament a Shī'ite, and his deputy a Greek Orthodox. Proportional representation has given an edge to the Christians—particularly the Maronites, who dominate all upper-level ministerial and military positions.*

The dominance of the Christians was further consolidated at independence in 1943 by an informal agreement among the leading families called the National Pact. According to this agreement, Lebanon was to maintain a balance between its Arab and Western

*See footnote on p. 200 above.

orientations (the former demanded by the Muslims and the latter by the Christians). Furthermore, the governmental system gives tremendous powers to the president, so the National Pact has enhanced the position of the Maronites. As the demographics have changed, the Maronites have been unwilling to carry out a new census or acknowledge the population realities which had come to favor the Muslims (and the Shi'ites in particular) by the 1970s.

Both the ideology and the sectarian structure of the Lebanese state had emerged over the past two hundred years of interaction among the Ottoman Empire, European states, and indigenous ruling families. In the competition for the Fertile Crescent, various international and local powers had used religious sects as vehicles for recruiting and mobilizing clients. The sectarian system of representation had been established gradually through repeated interventions by Europeans and Ottomans over the past century and one half. By independence the Lebanese ruling families were also recognized as the leaders of their religious sects. The pluralist state structure by then appeared to be advantageous to these families as well as to the foreign powers who had helped devise the system (Joseph 1978).

RULING ELITE STRATEGIES VIS-À-VIS THE STATE

Both formal and informal government policies in the period of the modern state have helped to reproduce the social basis of the sectarian structure of the state. Formally (as noted) positions in government agencies were allocated according to pre-set ratios of the major religious sects. Since independence, for example, parliament has changed the total number of its seats several times, but always in multiples of eleven to retain the 6 to 5 ratio of Christians to Muslims.

The zu'amā' used their formal positions to maintain a minimalist state and reproduce sectarianism. They accomplished this in part by limiting state institution-building in a number of ways. For one thing, they kept government revenues and expenditures minimal. In 1950, for example, the government's contribution to the GDP was only 6.9 percent and rose to only 8.8 percent by 1967 (UNESOB 1970:17); it was down to 8.3 percent by 1971 (Makdisi 1975:88). For another thing, the government collected relatively little revenue through income taxation. The tax system readily allowed tax evasion by those self-employed in commerce and services. In the late 1960s one estimate indicated that 75 percent of those in private business and 90 percent of those in the liberal professions did not report large portions of their incomes (Clarke 1966:8). Moreover, the encouragement of entrepreneurs and capitalists over wage and salary earners was systemic. Indicative of this favoritism were various government tax concessions. For example, in 1972 the government exempted all industries established between 1971 and 1976 from income taxes for six years and gave partial exemptions to those which expanded their enterprises. A similar law had been enacted in 1954 (Fisher 1982: 550). One Lebanese economist noted that the ratio of taxes to GNP was not high in Lebanon (11.9 percent in 1973) and called for a more progressive tax system and more systematic tax collection (Makdisi 1977:274).

The government policies resulted in increased class differentiation over the years. Clarke (1966:7; based on Lebanon, Ministry of Planning 1960) reported that in 1965, 50 percent of the population received 18 percent of the national income, 32 percent received 22 percent, 14 percent received 28 percent, and 4 percent received 32 percent. By 1975, 5 percent of the population was reported to be receiving 50 percent of the national income (Rouleau 1975).

The ruling elite also limited state institution-building by limiting the development of government social and legal services and using government monies to subsidize private provision of these services. In the private sector sectarian social service agencies received most of the public monies. In 1964, for example, there were 18 public and 120 private hospitals (Lebanon, Ministry of Planning 1969:248). Legal authority over matters of personal status remained the exclusive domain of religious courts. Marriage, divorce, inheritance, and child custody laws were created and adjudicated by the seventeen different religious sects. This gave significant power to the churches and helped reproduce different social realities within the Lebanese populace.

Particularly significant for the reproduction of different social realities was the development of the school system. Rather than building an extensive public school system in which a coherent national curriculum could have been instituted to stimulate the development of a more unified national identity and culture, the ruling elite limited public school building. However, they used public monies to subsidize the construction of private schools and the tuition of students in many of these schools. In 1968-69 a little over half of the primary, intermediate, and secondary schools were private, and about 57 percent of the country's teachers were in those schools.

However, over two thirds of the students were in private schools (Lebanon, Ministry of Planning 1969:216). The picture had changed somewhat by the early 1970s, with the public sector claiming a larger share of students, although the private sector still claimed over half of them (see Table 15 below).

The elite's emphasis on the private sector and reduction of the public sector was systematic. Public monies have subsidized not only private social service agencies and the educational system, but also charity, sports, cultural, and youth groups. In all cases there was a tendency for sectarian organizations to dominate. Thus in effect the ruling elite have used their formal position to subsidize the sectarian basis of their clientele.

Even in the critical domain of banking and finance, the ruling elite limited the role of the state. A central bank was not created until 1963. Even then strict rules limited state borrowing. It was not until the fall of the IntraBank in 1966 that the government instituted measures to regulate banking. However, these were quite limited, and the government role in regulating monetary policy remained small (Makdisi 1975:89).

A Ministry of Planning had been established in 1954, but there was little commitment to planning in either the ministry or the rest of the state. For example, one purported objective of the 1972-77 Six-Year Plan was to increase jobs. However, the plan neglected to forecast the country's employment conditions (Aly and Abdun-Nur 1975). Furthermore, despite an acknowledged need for increased employment opportunities, the 1972-77 plan would have brought about a drop in the ratio of the economically active population from .56 in 1970 to .52 in 1977 (*ibid.*). In 1970 the government recognized the need for an agency within the Ministry of Labor and Social Affairs to deal with problems of employment. Such an agency was established, but two years later it had accomplished very little (author's interviews with government officials). The government continued to encourage the development of the private sector over the public to deal with economic issues. The 1972-77 plan called for gross investments of L£ (Lebanese pounds) 7,200 million. Of this L£ 5,460 million (76 percent) was to be contributed by the private sector and only L£ 1,740 million by the public sector (*ibid.*).

Informally the government operated through patron-client relationships organized around the zu'ama' and their assistants. The ruling elite made it necessary for individual citizens to have the backing of a *za'īm* (singular of zu'amā') to secure legal protection, gain access to public positions, and avail themselves of state services. Rather than building a strong police system or army, the zu'amā' maintained private militias which they trained and armed and which were loyal to them personally. These militias were used to protect their clients against other zu'amā' and other private persons, as well as against the state; in addition, the militias served to discipline the clients into a following.

RULING ELITE AND THE STATE

By subordinating public law to personal influence, the ruling elite helped to ensure the dependence of their clients on them rather than on the state. Even when the ultimate source of services was the state, private citizens perceived—correctly—that a relationship with zu'amā' was necessary to obtain them. Through such personal provision of services and protection, the zu'amā' established and reinforced the personal loyalty of their following and their legitimacy as leaders (Joseph 1978), and they did so at the cost of allegiance to and legitimacy of the state. Such systematic limiting of state functions reflects the fragmentation of the ruling elite, which did not have a coherent conception of itself as a class and indeed did not comprise a class. It was both unwilling and unable to build a strong state with strong national institutions. Thus in 1975 the Lebanese state was stagnant. The center of social, political, and economic activity was in the private domain, where zu'amā' competed with each other—and with the state—for power and legitimacy. The strategies of the ruling elite in Lebanon vis-à-vis the state directly affected their strategies for training the young, and these differed markedly from the strategies and programs of the Iraqi ruling elite.

TRAINING THE YOUNG IN IRAQ

DEMOGRAPHIC FACTORS

The young are a growing segment of the Iraqi population. In 1977 males 0-24 years accounted for 4.1 million, or over 67 percent, of the total male population and 34 percent of the total Iraqi population (see Table 9). Females 0-24 years accounted for 3.9 million, or 66 percent, of the total female population and 33 percent of the

Table 9

IRAQ: ADJUSTED POPULATION BY AGE AND SEX, 1977

Age Group *(Years)*	Male	Percent of Total Population	Female	Percent of Total Population
0-4	1,224,058	19.5%	1,165,769	19.4%
5-9	1,063,572	16.9	1,005,294	16.7
10-14	814,204	12.9	775,432	12.9
15-19	604,000	9.6	575,866	9.6
20-24	539,714	8.6	514,014	8.6
Total population (all ages)	6,286,604		6,002,193	

Source: Based on Iraq, Ministry of Planning 1978b:27.

total Iraqi population. Those between 15-24 years—the prime ages of employment for the young—made up 2.13 million, or 18 percent of the population.

LABOR FORCE PARTICIPATION OF THE YOUNG

In 1977, 65 percent of all economically active females (as compared with 23 percent of all economically active males) were in agriculture, where they constituted 37 percent of the labor force. Of these, 42 percent were 7-24 years and 19 percent were 10-14 years (Iraq, Ministry of Planning 1978b:36). The participation of the female young in agriculture is even more dramatic when viewed in terms of each age group by economic activity. Of the economically active females 49 percent of those aged 7-9, 92 percent of those aged 10-14, 74 percent of those aged 15-19, and 50 percent of those aged 20-24 were in agriculture in 1977. (For males in those age groups the figures were 38, 27, 12, and 9 percent respectively; see Table 10). Young males tend much more to be employed in building and construction (23 percent of economically active males aged 10-14 and 18 percent of those aged 15-19) or in community, social, and personal services (38 percent of the economically active males aged 15-19 and 59

Table 10

IRAQ: LABOR FORCE PARTICIPATION OF THE YOUNG BY ECONOMIC SECTOR, 1977

Age Group (*Years*)	Sex	Total Econom-ically Active	Percent	Agri-culture, Hunting, Forestry & Fishing	Percent	Mining & Oil	Percent	Manufac-turing	Percent	Elec-tricity, Water, & Gas	Percent	Building & Con-struction	Percent
	Male	3,835	100%	1,443	38%	25	1%	841	22%			646	17%
7-9	Female	755	98	370	49	7	1	257	34	2		8	1
	Total	4,590	99	1,813	40	32	1	1,098	24	2		554	14
	Male	89,326	100	23,954	27	519	1	11,227	13	99		20,876	23
10-14	Female	71,402	99	65,367	92	126		3,127	4	2		217	
	Total	160,728	100	89,321	56	645		14,354	9	101		20,093	13
	Male	194,703	100	22,373	12	931		23,850	12	442		34,793	18
15-19	Female	56,706	100	41,902	74	157		7,756	14	70		482	1
	Total	251,409	100	64,275	26	1,088		31,606	13	512		35,275	14
	Male	511,615	100	44,477	9	4,741	1	31,125	6	2,962	1%	53,128	10
20-24	Female	79,420	100	39,315	50	572	1	10,564	13	409		1,512	2
	Total	591,035	100	83,792	14	4,313	1	41,689	7	3,371	1	54,640	9

Table 10 (cont.)

Age Group *(Years)*	Sex	Trade, Restaurants, & Hotels	Percent	Transport, Storage, & Communications	Percent	Financing, Insurance, Real Estate, & Business Services	Percent	Community, Social, & Personal Services	Percent	Unknown	Percent	Unemployed or Not Previously Employed	Percent
	Male	242	6%	55		12	1%	423	11%	148	4%		
7-9	Female	7	1	2		--		48	6	54	7		
	Total	249	5	57	1%	12		202	4	471	10		
	Male	4,419	5	1,564	2	380		6,620	7	2,587	3	17,081	19%
10-14	Female	213		31		2		623	1	1,062	1	632	1
	Total	4,632	3	1,595	1	382		7,243	5	3,649	2	17,713	11
	Male	8,926	5	5,630	3	861		73,287	38	5,449	3	18,161	9
15-19	Female	663	1	316	1	164		2,388	4	1,484	3	1,324	2
	Total	9,589	4	5,946	2	1,025		75,675	30	6,933	3	19,485	8
	Male	12,057	4	24,490	5	2,405		301,302	59	11,485	2	16,443	3
20-24	Female	2,828	4	1,797	2	1,723	2	12,867	16	2,028	3	5,805	7
	Total	21,885	4	26,287	4	4,128	1	314,169	53	13,513	2	22,248	4

Source: Based on Iraq, Ministry of Planning 1978b: 36-37.

percent of those aged 20-24). The young were also found in the furniture and fixture works, textiles, spinning, motor vehicle repair, laundries, forging and founding, woodworking, service shops, and other crafts. They did not tend to be in large places of employment.

LITERACY AND EDUCATION

The training of the growing population of young people for labor-force participation has been a central objective of the Ba'th and the Iraqi state. To achieve this goal a diversity of programs and strategies has been implemented. Foremost among these have been attempts to educate the young and eradicate illiteracy.

In the early 1970s the Ba'th embarked on a large-scale literacy and mandatory education campaign. By 1977 it was claiming that illiteracy had been reduced to 19 percent in the 15-45 age group (Iraq, Ministry of Planning 1978a:93). By 1979 it was claiming that all children 6-10 years were attending primary school. Between 1968-69 (when the Ba'th first took power) and 1978-79 there was a 142 percent increase in the number of students in primary school, an 85 percent increase in the number of primary school teachers, and a 106 percent increase in the number of primary schools (see Table 11). In 1978-79 the government reported that 1,579 academic, 45 industrial, 25 agricultural, and 39 commercial secondary schools were operating, as well as 3 fine arts institutes, 33 teachers' training schools, 16 technical institutes, and 46 colleges—almost all public. With the primary schools this amounted to 12,692 schools enrolling 3,468,137 students (40 percent of whom were female) (Iraq, Ministry of Education 1979b).

In 1978 the overall literacy rate for the Iraqi population over the age of 10 was 47 percent. Illiteracy was higher in the countryside (75 percent of the rural population), where there was a higher proportion of females. In 1977 illiteracy among women was 71 percent in the population as a whole but 93 percent among rural women (Iraq, Ministry of Planning 1978b:134). In 1978 the Ba'th instituted a massive literacy campaign for those beyond primary school age. Participation for four years was mandatory for all those 15-35 and for two years for those 36-45.*

*In 1980 as I traveled in the countryside in the northern areas of Iraq, I repeatedly observed groups of women, covered in their black *'abā'as*, walking

Table 11

EDUCATION GROWTH IN IRAQ, 1968-69 AND 1978-79
(Thousands)

Category of Growth	1968-69	1978-79
Students in primary school	1,000	2,400
Primary school teachers	47	87
Primary schools	5	10

Source: Iraq, Ministry of Education 1979a.

VOCATIONAL TRAINING

Vocational training of the young has frequently been on the job. Much of it has been in the form of apprenticeships, often with family members. On-the-job training predominates among the young because they are employed primarily in agriculture or in small shops which are often family-run.

Aware of the problems of the young in rural areas and in urban crafts, the Ba'th instituted educational programs within agricultural cooperatives, trade unions, and other economic associations (see Table 12), and the young have often been paid to engage in these programs. Numerous on-the-job training programs aimed mainly at the young are organized through state-run industries, trade unions,

together to literacy centers. However, some women I talked to did not attend, even though it was mandatory, because of family pressures.

Table 12

WORKER TRAINING CENTERS IN IRAQ BY ECONOMIC SECTOR, 1978

Sector	Number of Centers	Capacity *(Number of trainees)*
Agriculture	10	5,210
Construction	1	80
Electricity, water, and gas	1	120
Manufacturing	4	1,468
Oil	4	1,175
Transport, storage, and communications	7	4,145
Total	27	12,198

Source: Adapted from Iraq, Ministry of Planning 1978a:70.

and women's organizations.* Moreover, the unions, organized into local committees, offer not only vocational training, but also training in party principles. In discussions with some young union members, it was clear to me that those who had accepted the party ideology benefited tremendously from the union training and were enthusiastic about it. I also found resistance, often expressed in nonparticipation and silence, the main forms of opposition acceptable in the tightly controlled unions.

Despite the Ba'th's efforts, problems persist for the rural and urban unskilled and semi-skilled young.

VOLUNTARY ASSOCIATIONS AND SERVICE

The Ba'th has also established voluntary associations to train all ages of the young. For example, Ṭalīʿa (Vanguard) is a paramilitary organization for children recruited from primary schools. For high school and college students there are (among others) paramilitary organizations, party cells, student unions, sports associations, literary

*In 1980 there were seventeen unions and twelve craft unions in Iraq representing 1.25 million workers (personal interview with Salman Nejris Bayati, Secretary General, Federation of Trade Unions, 12 July 1980).

and artistic societies, and scientific and professional associations. In 1978 the Ba'th reported eighty-one youth centers, seventy-eight sports clubs, and eleven youth hostels, and it planned fifty-one more centers in the immediate future (Iraq, Ministry of Planning 1978a: 116).

SOCIAL LEGISLATION

To facilitate the participation of the young in the labor force, the Ba'th promulgated various social welfare reforms. These included free and subsidized health care, free transportation to state-run industries, subsidized housing, and even subsidized dowry payments for prospective brides. A series of laws has established equal rights to women to protect their wages; opportunities for training (including on the job), advancement, compensation, and retirement; paid maternity leaves; and state-subsidized child-care centers (Joseph 1982). The Ba'th also took tentative steps to change family laws in order to free women for labor-force participation (Joseph 1982; Rassam 1982).

RULING ELITE AND CONTROL OF THE YOUNG

Although all the Ba'th programs and legislation have offered many benefits, they have also entailed heavy costs. Among the costs has been freedom. The Ba'th maintains strict control over all the programs, institutions, resources, and agencies. It does not tolerate opposition.* Ideological training and control have been a systematic part of labor-force training of the young. Many seem to accept this, seeing the advances that the Ba'th has brought and feeling that the costs have not been great, while others, less frequently able to express their views, feel the costs have been too high.

In 1974 I had the opportunity to participate in and observe some of the Iraqi youth programs. First, invited by the General Union of Iraqi Students to join in a youth camp, I worked (along with other guests of Arab origin) to build a village for Egyptian workers and harvested potatoes from experimental fields. The program was rigorous:

*While I was there, I heard a few young people protesting the lack of choice and decision-making over their organizations.

we rose before dawn, ate a heavy breakfast, and immediately went to work for long hours. A late lunch was followed by rest because the heat of the desert sun made early afternoon work impossible. In the late afternoon the over 2,000 students in the camp returned to work until a late dinner. Following dinner, there was always a long evening of political instruction, discussion, or (at times) entertainment. Camp life was highly regimented, sharply hierarchical, and tightly disciplined by the top few leaders, who were members of the Ba'th. The discussions were dominated by Ba'th ideology and conflicting views were systematically suppressed.

During the same trip I attended a Ba'th youth cell meeting organized to explain and plan a party program. All discussion was initiated and controlled by the cell leader. The members asked questions and accepted the ideologically mandated answers without debate or argument. I also observed numerous public celebrations for the young organized by the Ba'th party and the state. The degree of discipline was as impressive as the lack of spontaneity: young Iraqis, dressed in uniforms, marched at a Germany-style military clip, chanting allegiance to the *'umma 'al-'arabiya* (the Arab nation), national unity, Arab socialism, and freedom. As always, there were the larger-than-life pictures of the Ba'th and state leaders, who were praised in highly routinized songs and chants.

Preparation of the young for labor-force participation in Iraq under the Ba'th leadership is thus multifaceted. Yet all the diverse programs, whether initiated through state or party agencies, are run by Ba'th personnel. Moreover, all of them seek to win the allegiance and loyalty of the populace—particularly the young—to the Iraqi state, the Ba'th party, particular party leaders, and the "Arab socialist revolution." In Arab terms, the outcome has been a relatively regimented, disciplined, and obedient young population which is less spontaneous, questioning, and creative.

TRAINING THE YOUNG IN LEBANON

DEMOGRAPHIC FACTORS

Like in Iraq, the young in Lebanon have been a growing segment of the population. In 1975 males aged 0-24 were estimated at 861,000, or 62 percent of the total male population. Females aged 0-24 were estimated at 830,000, or 60 percent of the total female population (see Table 13). Males and females 0-24 were about 61 percent of the Lebanese population–i.e., 6 percent less than the share of the comparable age group in Iraq in 1977. Those in the prime employment age for the young (15-24) were estimated at 552,000, or 19.9 percent of the total population.

LABOR FORCE PARTICIPATION OF THE YOUNG

Estimates of economic activity among the young in Lebanon indicated a low activity rate for those aged 0-14 relative to developing countries (see Table 14), reflecting a high rate of school enrollment for that age group. However, 26 percent of those aged 15-19 and 49 percent of those aged 20-24 were economically active. The male activity rate–36 percent for those aged 15-19 and 72 percent for those 20-24–was higher than the female (16 and 26 percent for the respective age groups). The figures reflect both the reality and the methods of measurement.

Table 13

LEBANON: ESTIMATED POPULATION BY AGE AND SEX, 1975
(Thousands)

Age Group *(Years)*	Male	Percent of Total Population	Female	Percent of Total Population
0-4	194	13.9%	187	13.6%
5-9	200	14.4	192	14.0
10-14	186	13.4	180	13.1
15-19	159	11.4	154	11.2
20-24	122	8.8	117	8.5
0-24	861	61.9	830	60.4
Total population (all ages)	1,392		1,375	

Source: Based on UNDIESA 1982:327.

Table 14

LEBANON: POPULATION BY AGE GROUP, SEX, AND ECONOMIC STATUS, c. 1981-82
(Thousands)

Population Factor	Age Group *(Years)* 0-14	15-19	20-24
Total population	1,241	313	239
Economically active population	22	81	118
Activity rate *(Percent)*	1.8%	25.9%	49.4%
Males: Total population	632	159	122
Males: Active population	10	57	88
Males: Activity rate *(Percent)*	1.6%	35.8%	72.1%
Females: Total population	609	154	117
Females: Active population	12	24	30
Females: Activity rate *(Percent)*	2.0%	15.6%	25.6%

Source: ILO 1982, vol. 42:25.

LITERACY AND EDUCATION

Consistent with their general strategy of limiting state-building, the ruling elite's approach toward planning for the young has been to encourage the private sector and constrain the public sector. Figures on educational development reveal the predominance of the private sector, although they also indicate the growing role of the government in education. In the 1964-65 school year there were 2,770 schools in Lebanon, of which 1,572 (57 percent) were private and 1,198 (43 percent) were public. Of the over 400,000 students in primary and secondary schools, 60 percent (245,738) were in private schools and 40 percent (166,769) in public schools (Clarke 1966:21). By 1972-73 the public sector claimed 54 percent of the schools and 53 percent of the teachers but 45 percent of the students (see Table 15). In 1971 there were about 140 private technical and vocational schools and only 7 such public schools (Edwards 1971). In that year Lebanon had 7 institutions of higher learning, only one of which was a state university.

Despite the limited government role in education, Lebanon had the highest literacy rate in the Arab world. In 1970, 93.2 percent of

Table 15

PRIVATE AND PUBLIC PRIMARY, INTERMEDIATE, AND SECONDARY EDUCATION IN LEBANON, 1968-69 AND 1972-73

Buildings or Personnel	1968-69		1972-73	
Schools	Number	Percent	Number	Percent
Public	1,318	47%	1,354	54%
Private	1,474	53	1,132	46
Teachers				
Public	13,014	43	17,077	53
Private	16,960	57	16,168	47
Students				
Public	242,101	32	298,314	45
Private	416,347	68	366,987	55

Source: Lebanon, Ministry of Planning 1969 and 1973.

the males and 85.4 percent of the females aged 15-24 were literate (Chasteland and Georgiou 1970). Indeed Lebanon was an educational center for the whole region. Over 12,000 students in Lebanon's institutions of higher learning were foreign, as compared with about 15,000 Lebanese (UNESOB 1971a).

PRIVATE VERSUS PUBLIC EDUCATION

The high educational achievements of Lebanon can in part be attributed to the role of private schools, which were generally superior to the public schools. However, private education affected the training of the young and the character of the labor force. The private schools were generally run by religious institutions or catered primarily to clients of one sect.* Many of them were originally run by foreign missions and stressed instruction in the language and culture

*In Borj Hammoud, an urban working-class municipality where I carried out fieldwork, there were only three public schools for the estimated population of 200,000. Most students therefore attended private schools.

of their country of origin. Schools came to be known by their language of instruction—primarily French or English but also Italian, German, and others. Often (particularly in French schools) the European language was stressed at the cost of Arabic so that students became more fluent in the foreign language than in their own. Since language instruction was a significant part of the curriculum, private schools helped to create and reproduce social differences in the populace.

The stress on languages in private schools—often two or three languages were mandatory beginning at the primary level—was at the cost of science, math, or more technical training. The emphasis on language reflected the bias toward classical education in the Lebanese school system. Inherited from the colonial period, the system focused on humanities, arts, and the social sciences. This classical preparation influenced student choices of majors at the college level. In 1971, 87 percent of those in institutions of higher learning were specializing in the humanities, education, fine arts, law, and social science, and only 12 percent were in engineering, medical and natural sciences, and agriculture (UNESOB 1971a)—disciplines which were important for Lebanon's economic development.

The impact on Lebanon's young of this dual system of public and private schooling was manifold and profound. First, it helped create and reproduce class inequities. The private schools were not only generally superior, but they also tended to serve the middle and upper classes. Second, the system tended to reinforce sectarian affiliation and identity. While the student bodies of private schools attended by children of the elite were often heterogeneous, those of the lower classes were commonly more homogeneous in religious affiliation. Thus school curriculums, activities, and holidays reinforced diverse orientations rather than national orientations among the schoolchildren. For example, Muslim schools gave students holidays on Fridays, while Christian schools gave holidays on Sundays, so children in these schools did not have the same days off to play together. Third, the curriculums of most schools did not prepare the young for positions in the Lebanese economy. It is possible that they trained them as much if not more for regional and international labor migration. Students from the better French schools not only spoke French better than Arabic, but also knew more French history and culture than Lebanese, read French literature, smoked French cigarettes, wore French clothes, and were quite knowledgeable about the streets of Paris. The English-language schools were not as successful as the

French, but they nevertheless strove to produce an English or American orientation. The comments of one Armenian school director concerned about the problem of non-Lebanese education in relation to the Armenian schools, are relevant to other schools as well:

> We are living in Lebanon and not feeling Lebanese. I am not convinced to give a Lebanese education to the children. We teach "our" language and "our" history, etc. We are misguiding our children and making them feel they do not belong. Fortunately we are now beginning to teach Arabic language and history and to feel a bit Lebanese. But we still teach them that they don't belong here, so they travel away and leave Lebanon (Joseph 1975:139).

VOLUNTARY ASSOCIATIONS AND SERVICE

Lebanon had no mandatory youth service or state training programs as did Iraq, but it had volunteer programs to train youths or offer them an opportunity to contribute to the development of their country. Youth volunteer service in the early 1970s was handled by the Office of Social Development (OSD) in the Ministry of Labor and Social Affairs (MLSA), the Directorate of Youth and Sports (DYS) in the Ministry of Education, and the Ministry of Tourism through a nongovernmental agency, the Youth Reception Center. The MLSA licensed all social service agencies in Lebanon and therefore had the authority to regulate youth volunteer service programs in the private sector; however, it did not make use of its authority.*

The government did not have an explicit program for youth volunteers, but it trained youths in various capacities. The MLSA ran a Rapid Occupational Training Office for teaching youths such skills as watchmaking, electrical work, and radio and television repairs. Each training session was for six months and enrolled thirty individuals. The OSD, in conjunction with UNICEF, cosponsored the Center for Training in Social Service and Development, a school designed to train youths from junior high school levels and above to do both paid and unpaid social-service work. The OSD also subsidized a nongovernmental program, the Lebanese Center for Training in Methods of Active Education, to train youths for summer work camps in the villages.

*The MLSA also housed an Office of Employment, but it was largely inoperative.

The DYS had four units organizing youth activities: the Departments of Boy Scouts, Popular Education, Outdoor Activities and Summer Camps, and Female Activities. Only the first of these had a full staff, while the others each had only one staff person. The entire DYS employed only thirty people to work with youths in the early 1970s. However, under the supervision and pay of the DYS were five hundred sports teachers in public schools, fifty teachers in sports schools, and thirty "sports monitors" working with nongovernmental organizations to train personnel in sports.

The DYS worked with youth more than any other government agency. In 1970 it organized the following activities: civil defense education camps (250 youths participated in 21-day periods); vocational training courses (250 youths for 10-day periods); training programs for new scout leaders (250 youths for 10 days); Red Cross training (3-month periods); arts and crafts courses (3- and 6-month periods); agricultural sciences training (150 boys for 15 days); training programs for summer work camp leaders (50 trainees); work camps (500 youths for 15-day periods); and leadership training courses for voluntary organizations. In 1969 the DYS had organized 1,000 students to work with the army on irrigation projects in the south. In 1971 the army, in conjunction with the Ministry of Education, replaced its mandatory 2-week training for secondary school boys with the DYS work camp program in the villages. However, it was reported that the program was not well planned.

In the early 1970s one section of the DYS, the Popular Education Service, subsidized sixty-four private organizations throughout Lebanon involved in training youths and adults. Together with the government, these organizations supported programs such as the Boy and Girl Scouts, founded in 1962, which recruited children from the public schools—and therefore was primarily made up of children from poorer families. The Scouts were most popular in the villages, where they often were the only youth organization. They trained youths not only in scouting activities, but in public service activities, as well as work in some development projects. In 1971 there were twenty-one Boy Scout organizations in Lebanon—most of them private. Each religious group organized its own scouts. (Sectarian scouts were called *ḍalīlāt*, while lay scouts were *murshīdāt.*)

SOCIAL LEGISLATION

Social legislation concerning youth work was limited in Lebanon, although prior to the war some advances had been made. There were no regulations for youth work in the agricultural sector. For most jobs in industry the minimum work age was eight years; for dangerous, strenuous, or unhealthy jobs the minimum work age was sixteen (Clarke 1966). The maximum legal work load for those under seventeen was seven hours a day. Apprentices were supposed to be paid a minimum of two thirds of the fixed adult minimum wage. However, even these limited regulations were often not implemented by employers and rarely enforced by the government.

The minimum daily wage for adults was 683 piasters in 1970. Young workers actually received anywhere between 80 and 640 piasters, and very young apprentices often worked without wages (UNESOB 1971a). While adults working in agriculture received an average of L£6-9 daily in 1970, those under 16 earned L£2-6 (*ibid.*).* Workers were often fired summarily, and they found it difficult to collect the legally required wage compensation when they left work. For the few who were covered by the medical benefits of the social security law, collection of reimbursements involved a time-consuming process at the expense of wages. With worker protections rarely enforced, job turnovers were very high—particularly among the young. Government employment offices were never effective, and most government protections to workers were nonoperative. Indeed the means to enforce even the minimal social legislation on the books were practically nonexistent; in 1966 Lebanon had only 13 inspectors, 13 assistant inspectors, 1 doctor, and 1 engineer to enforce the labor code (Clarke 1966).

CONTROLLING THE YOUNG THROUGH FRAGMENTATION

While the Lebanese government offered youths various training and volunteer programs after a fashion, there was very little planning concerning these programs. Certainly there was no attempt to link them with development planning, human resource development, or labor needs.

*In 1972 the Lebanese pound equaled about $.31.

In interviews with officials of the MLSA and DYS in 1971, I learned that each ministry and each agency within the ministries operated almost autonomously. All the officials interviewed maintained that there was no national plan in Lebanon, and they did not receive guidelines from their ministries concerning their work. When I contacted officials in the Ministry of Planning concerning their planning for youth and labor, I was told it would be a waste of time to seek interviews because the Ministry of Planning had no plans.

Among the government officials I interviewed, there was a sense of frustration concerning planning for youth and development. One official commented as follows:

> We need to admit and feel that our country is backwards. Our government should honestly say to its people that we are underdeveloped. Youth should feel this underdevelopment. They should feel their responsibility. The summer camps are giving this feeling, but it is not enough. Many youths think that all Lebanon is Hamra.*

The assistant director of the Center for Training in Social Service and Development was more direct:

> We encourage volunteers to stop being volunteers and get professional know-how. . . . Youths do conceive of themselves as doing something for national development, but they are not able to because of the dilemma between private and public sectors. The main problem is the complete lack of information in the private sector about the public sector and vice versa. There is a complete separation. The main problem in the public sector is the lack of continuity. The personnel keeps changing because of the political system. The amazing isolated structure of the public sector is another problem. The OSD, Ministry of Health, the DYS are all doing the same projects and the villagers are getting fed up. The private sector has the same problem in reverse. One person at the head of a society or agency remains until he dies. You get ossification of the structure and centralization of authority. When the person dies, there is a collapse of the structure because no one is prepared to take his place. Because there are so many private organizations working there is overlapping and conflict and so there is no development. All this is bound up with confessional

*Hamra was the fashionable shopping street of Beirut.

boundaries. One confessional group cannot see the overall situation so they concentrate on their own problems which may not benefit the national picture. Many of the agencies do not have their base in Lebanon. Most of these social welfare agencies started as a technique of infiltrating the country by Europeans (Joseph 1971:51, 65-66).

As noted above, nongovernmental agencies were primarily sectarian. Every religious group organized youth programs—from the scouts to sports to cultural organizations. In 1971 I interviewed officials from many private youth and volunteer organizations.* Almost all the groups received some subsidies from the government. Most of them served a specialized clientele—usually one religious sect. There was constant duplication of activities among them. Since none were large organizations, budgetary considerations limited their programs. Their accomplishments—particularly of such organizations as the YWCA vocational school for girls—were quite remarkable given those limitations. However, it was also apparent that a pooling of resources and coordination from the government (impossible given the structure of the state and ruling elite) could have produced far more effective programs.

Between the late 1960s and early 1970s I participated in and observed a number of training programs for the young operated by both governmental and private agencies. In 1968 I participated in a YWCA summer camp for girls, who attended in two-week, age-graded sessions. Most of the girls were from upper middle- and upper-class families, although there was one subsidized session for children of poorer families. Set in the beautiful mountain town of Dhour el Choueir, the camp was organized almost exclusively for play. I was struck by the girls' spontaneity and creativity. By comparison to comparable American schoolchildren, they were unruly; by Iraqi standards they probably would have been considered wild. They initiated programs on their own, questioned projects of the camp leaders, and regularly played tricks on the leaders, who had to coddle and persuade them to obey. The camp leader consulted lower-level leaders and was in charge largely because of personal charisma.

*Among these were the following: the YWCA, YMCA, Red Cross, Youth Reception Center, Youth and Volunteers, Social Movement, Ecumenical Youth and Student Secretariat for the Middle East, Orthodox Youth Movement, Committee for Social Activity, Maqasad Secondary School for Girls, Social Center of the Qarantina, University Christian Center, Social Welfare Institution of Lebanon, and Jabal 'Amil Women's Association.

Also in the summer of 1968, for a research project for the YWCA in a southern Lebanese village, I engaged a number of young students to assist me. As in the camp, the local YWCA leader had to use persuasion and cajolery to elicit the students' participation and cooperation. On the whole, it was quite a task to make them follow instructions and work in a sustained fashion.

In 1971, while doing a study on youth volunteer service for the United Nations, I had the opportunity to observe private and public programs for the young. The government-run summer training camps had a minimal hierarchical structure and were poorly organized and undisciplined. The government scouts were more organized and hierarchical but nevertheless allowed for a relatively high degree of spontaneous, unruly behavior.

The diverse volunteer programs I observed had a common theme of minimal hierarchy and discipline. Many seemed to be held together by persuasion and caretaking rather than authority and discipline. In addition, they were all highly personalized in their leadership management strategy—that is, the leaders who managed to lead successfully did so by evoking a personal commitment from the young. There was close contact between the leaders and the young, including much caretaking from the former to the latter.

One striking feature of most of the programs was that the leaders seemed to have a relatively high tolerance of disobedience among their charges; some even seemed to encourage it. One YWCA national leader reported that she loved to see a child be an *'az'ar* (scoundrel). I found this attitude in both public and private programs. The main exception was among Armenians, who in both their family setting and social organizations created a relatively more disciplined and regimented environment for the young.

Another striking feature of these programs was that there was a very small degree of political ideological coherence among or within them. (Again the main exception was the Armenian programs.) They did little to evoke national allegiance. Their primary underlying message was identification with the social constituency from which the members were drawn. Since most of the private programs were run by sectarian groups, they reinforced primarily sectarian identities (true for the Armenian programs as well). Some of the government programs also reinforced sectarian identities since they were drawn primarily from one sect or another. Thus these programs elicited personal loyalty to the leaders and to primarily sectarian constituencies.

CONCLUSION

The ruling elites in Iraq and Lebanon, having faced repeated internal and external challenges to their power and authority, have sought to gain control over the allegiance and behavior of the young. The striking differences in their programs and policies are related to their different strategies vis-à-vis their states.

In Iraq the ruling elite, which has been relatively homogeneous, has organized itself into an ideological political party and uses the party as the conduit into the state. The ruling elite controls the party; uses the party to control the state; and fosters identity between itself, the party, and the state. Thus allegiance to the ruling elite is deemed equivalent to allegiance to the Ba'th party, the Iraqi state, and the socialist revolution. Through control over the massive resources of the state, the ruling elite has generated a centripetal force, pulling all social action into the state arena, including the struggle for control over the young.

In Lebanon, on the other hand, the ruling elite has been heterogeneous and fragmented. Numerous political "parties" have largely sectarian clienteles who owe personal allegiance to individual zu'amā'. They have drained the minimalist state, with its limited resources, to subsidize their separate power bases outside of the state. The centrifugal force generated by the ruling elite has pushed significant social action into the private arena, where it is dominated by individual elite and affiliated sectarian organizations. As a result, the struggle to gain control over the young has been significantly shaped outside the state.

Whereas in Iraq there has been a strong state initiative to train and prepare the young, in Lebanon the state has encouraged the private sector to undertake the major responsibility. In Iraq there has been an attempt to build a coherent national curriculum, creating a national identity and a national culture, but in Lebanon regional and sectarian programs, identities, and cultures have been encouraged. Iraq in recent years has stressed gaining the allegiance of the young to the ruling elite, the state, and party; in Lebanon there has been little stress on state loyalty, no identification of one party with the state, and pressure to align with individual zu'amā'. Iraq has attempted to orient a new school curriculum toward its industrial and other economic development programs, but Lebanon has continued to focus on a classical education. Iraq tightly controls unions, social services, and voluntary organizations through the Ba'th party and uses them to train the young and mobilize their support for the state; Lebanon has initiated few programs for the young and has permitted a proliferation of unions, social services, and voluntary organizations in the private sector which at times have organized against the state and have been vehicles to mobilize support for the zu'amā' and sectarian organizations.

The outcome of these different strategies is mixed in balance. The strategies of the Iraqi elite, emphasizing discipline, obedience, and loyalty to the party and the state, have necessitated a brutal suppression of dissidents in the country which has increased during the current war. It would seem apparent that the strategies of the Lebanese ruling elite have helped create the conditions for the present war, including the collapse of national institutions such as the army, the immobilization of the state, the plurality of sectarian militias, and the exodus of Lebanese—particularly the young—from the country.

A more difficult factor to measure is the quality of education and the degree of creativity encouraged among the young. There would probably be much agreement that the Lebanese labor force is among the best educated and probably one of the more creative and entrepreneurial of the Arab region. Some of that creativity is undoubtedly a factor of training. Schooling in Iraq allows for less diversity and less consideration of social and intellectual alternatives. Both creativity and options are to some degree a reflection of the greater heterogeneity in the political structure of the Lebanese state. On the other hand, the more focused, directed, and controlled Iraqi program might allow for the fulfillment of the Ba'th development plans for economic growth. Such planning was absent in Lebanon, which has depended on the private sector to respond to economic, political, and social needs.

The current wars in both countries will undoubtedly affect their needs and thus their strategies toward the young. In Iraq the survival of the regime is at this point unclear. Should it survive, it apparently will continue to move in the direction of centralization. In Lebanon the survival of the state is problematic. It appears that a Lebanese state—should one survive—will be more decentralized than it was before the war. In either case the strategies of the ruling elites toward their states will significantly shape the strategies toward the young and the degree to which the young are trained for national or fragmented polities and economies.

REFERENCES

al-Alusi, Manal. 1980. Speech delivered at the Ninth Conference of the General Federation of Iraqi Women. Baghdad.

Aly, Hamdi F., and Abdun-Nur, Nabil. 1975. "An Appraisal of the Six-Year Plan of Lebanon (1972-1977)." *Middle East Journal* 29:151-64.

Barakat, Halim. 1977. *Lebanon in Strife: Student Preludes to the Civil War.* Austin: University of Texas Press.

Batatu, Hanna. 1979a. "Class Analysis and Iraqi Society." *Arab Studies Quarterly* 1, 3:229-44.

__________. 1979b. *The Old Social Classes and the Revolutionary Movements of Iraq*. Princeton: Princeton University Press.

__________. 1981. "Iraq's Underground Shī'i Movements: Characteristics, Causes and Prospects." *Middle East Journal* 33, 4:578-94.

Birks, J. S., and Sinclair, C. A. 1980. *Arab Manpower: The Crisis of Development.* London: Croom Helm.

__________. 1982. "The Challenge of Human Resource Development in Iraq." In Niblock, ed. 1982.

Centre d'Etudes et de Recherches sur le Moyen Orient Contemporain (CERMOC). 1978. *Etat et perspectives de l'industrie au Liban.* Beirut.

Chasteland, Jean-Claude, and Georgiou, Ylande. 1970. "Demographic Characteristics of Youth in the Arab Countries. Present Situation and Growth Prospects 1970-1990." In *Children and Youth in National Planning and Development in the Arab States*. Beirut: UNICEF.

Clarke, Joan. 1966. *Labor Law and Practice in Lebanon.* Washington, D.C.: U.S. Department of Labor.

Edwards, John P. 1971. "Basic Data on the Economy of Lebanon." Washington, D.C.: U.S. Department of Commerce, Overseas Business Reports.

Farouk-Sluglett, Marion, and Sluglett, Peter. 1981. "Notes Towards the Definition of the Post-Revolutionary State: Iraq 1958-1977." Presented at symposium on Iraq: The Contemporary State. University of Exeter, England.

Farsoun, Samih. 1973. "Student Protests and the Coming Crisis in Lebanon." *Middle East Research and Information Project (MERIP) Reports* 19:4-8.

Farsoun, Samih, and Carroll, Walter. 1976. "The Civil War in Lebanon: Sect, Class, and Imperialism." *Monthly Review* 28:12-37.

Fisher, W. B. 1982. "Lebanon." In *The Middle East and North Africa 1981-82.* Europa Publications Ltd. London: Staples Printers Rochester Ltd.

Gotlieb, Yosef. 1981. "Sectarianism and the Iraqi State." In *Religion and Politics in the Middle East*, ed. Michael Curtis. Boulder, Colo.: Westview Press.

International Labour Organization (ILO). 1982. *Yearbook of Labour Statistics.* Geneva.

Iraq, General Federation of Iraqi Women (GFIW). 1978. *Iraqi Women*. Baghdad.

__________, __________. 1980. "A Practical Translation to the Objectives of the Revolution in Work and Creativity." Beirut: Dar al-Afaq al-Jadidah.

__________, General Federation of Trade Unions (GFTU). 1979. *The Role of the Working Woman in Economic and Social Development in the Region of Iraq*. Baghdad.

__________, Ministry of Education. 1979a. *Compulsory Education*. Baghdad.

__________, __________. 1979b. *Education in Iraq in Figures*. Baghdad.

__________, Ministry of Planning. 1972. *National Income of Iraq 1964-1971*. Baghdad.

__________, __________. 1973. *Annual Abstract of Statistics*. Baghdad.

__________, __________. 1976. *Annual Abstract of Statistics*. Baghdad.

__________, __________. 1978a. *Man: The Object of Revolution*. Baghdad.

__________, __________. 1978b. *Annual Abstract of Statistics*. Baghdad.

Iskandar, Amir. 1980. *Saddam Hussein: The Fighter, The Thinker and The Man*. Paris: Hachette Réalités.

al-Jomard, Atheel. 1979. "Internal Migration in Iraq." In *The Integration of Modern Iraq*, ed. Abbas Kelidar. London: Croom Helm.

Joseph, Suad. 1971. "Youth Volunteer Service in Lebanon." Beirut: UN Economic and Social Office in Beirut. Unpublished ms.

__________. 1975. "The Politicization of Religious Sects in Borj Hammoud, Lebanon." Ph.D. dissertation, Columbia University.

__________. 1978. "Muslim-Christian Conflict in Lebanon: A Perspective on the Evolution of Sectarianism." In *Muslim-Christian Conflicts: Economic, Political and Social Origins*, ed. Suad Joseph and Barbara L. K. Pillsbury. Boulder, Colo.: Westview Press.

__________. 1982. "The Mobilization of Iraqi Women into the Wage Labor Force." *Studies in Third World Societies* 16:69-90.

Lebanon. Ministry of Planning. 1960. *Besoins et possibilités de développement du Liban*, vol. 1. Beirut. Prepared by Mission IRFED.

__________. 1969 and 1973. *Recueil de statistiques libanaises: Année 1969/Année 1973*. Beirut.

Lorfing, Irene. 1983. "Women Industrial Workers in Lebanon." In *Women and Work in the Third World: The Impact of Industrialization and Global Economic Interdependence*, ed. Nagat M. el-Sanabarry. Berkeley: University of California, Center for the Study, Education, and Advancement of Women.

Makdisi, Samir A. 1975. "Lebanon: Monetary Developments, Management and Performance in the Post-War Period up to 1972." *Middle East Journal* 29, 1:81-92.

__________. 1977. "An Appraisal of Lebanon's Postwar Economic Development and Look at the Future." *Middle East Journal* 31, 3:267-80.

Niblock, Tim, ed. 1982. *Iraq: The Contemporary State.* London: Croom Helm, and Exeter: Center for Arab Gulf Studies.

Rassam, Amal. 1982. "Revolution Within the Revolution? Women and the State in Iraq." In Niblock, ed. 1982.

Rouleau, Eric. 1975. "Civil War in Lebanon." *Le Monde* (Paris), 20-25 September 1975. Translated in SWASIA, 17 October 1975.

Seklani, Mahmoud. 1970. "Demographic and Socio-Cultural Environment in the Arab Countries." In *Children and Youth in National Planning and Development in the Arab States.* Beirut: UNICEF.

Socknat, James; Birks, Stace; and Serageldin, Ismail. 1981. "International Labor Migration in the Middle East and North Africa." Presented at the Conference of Social Legislation and Social Structure in the Contemporary Middle East. American Council of Learned Societies and Social Science Research Council, Rabat.

Stork, Joe. 1980. "Oil and the Penetration of Capitalism in Iraq." In *Oil and Class Struggle*, ed. Petter Nore and Terisa Turner. London: Zed Press.

__________. 1982. "State Power and Economic Structure: Class Determination and State Formation in Contemporary Iraq." In Niblock, ed. 1982.

__________. 1983. "Report from Lebanon." *MERIP Reports* 13, 8:3-15.

Theobald, Robin, and Jawad, Sa'ad. 1982. "Problems of Rural Development in an Oil-Rich Economy: Iraq 1958-1975." In Niblock, ed. 1982.

United Nations, Department of International Economic and Social Affairs (UNDIESA). 1982. *Demographic Indicators of Countries: Estimates and Projections as Assessed in 1980.* New York.

__________, Economic and Social Office in Beirut (UNESOB). 1970. *Studies on Selected Development Problems in Various Countries in the Middle East, 1970.* New York.

__________, __________. 1971a. "The Socio-economic Situation of Youth in Selected Countries in the Middle East." Beirut. June.

__________, __________. 1971b. "Situation and Prospects of National Youth Policies, Programs, and Services in Selected Countries of the Middle East." Beirut. June.

__________, __________. 1971c. "Population Distribution and Urbanization in Selected Countries in the Middle East." Beirut.

Part IV

INTERNATIONAL ECONOMIC FACTORS AND LAW

Chapter 7

FOREIGN INVESTMENT AND LEGISLATIVE EXEMPTIONS IN EGYPT: NEEDED STIMULUS OR NEW CAPITULATIONS?

Jeswald W. Salacuse

In order to encourage capital formation many developing countries give some role to foreign investment in their plans for economic development. Toward this end their governments enact investment laws or investment codes whose purpose is to create a legal framework for the entry and operation of foreign capital. In the Middle East Egypt's Law No. 43 of 1974, "Concerning the Investment of Arab and Foreign Funds and the Free Zones" (Egypt, *Garida Rasmia*, no. 26, 27 June 1974), as amended by Law No. 32 of 1977 (Egypt, *Garida Rasmia*, no. 23 [bis], 9 June 1977), has attracted significant attention (Salacuse 1975; Salacuse and Parnall 1978; McLaughlin 1978; Bushnell 1980); but one can also find investment laws in Jordan, Syria, the Sudan, Iraq, Tunisia, and Morocco (Abdel-Rahman 1976). Indeed the "investment law" or "investment code" seems to be a basic element in the legal systems of virtually every developing country in the world (see International Center for the Settlement of Investment Disputes 1972).

Although the form and content of such legislation demonstrate exceptional diversity, every investment law has basically two objectives: to attract foreign investment and to control its activities and effects within the host country. These two objectives often create tensions in the formulation and application of these laws as the government and interested parties struggle to determine the appropriate balance between attraction and control. In surveying investment legislation throughout the Third World, one finds that the degree of emphasis placed on attraction or control varies from country to country. Thus one study conducted by the UN Center on Transnational Corporations (1978) concluded that the investment laws of Africa tended to emphasize attraction while those in Latin America tended to stress control. There are similar divergences in the Middle

East–for example, between the Egyptian approach centering on attraction and the Algerian approach centering on control. Numerous factors may account for the difference in emphasis, including a country's prevailing economic policies, its previous experience with foreign investment, and its current level of capital accumulation.

One of the principal techniques used by host countries to attract foreign capital is to grant investors exemptions from local legislation to which they would otherwise be subject. Such exemptions take a wide variety of forms, including exemptions from taxation, customs duties, foreign exchange regulations, price controls, the jurisdiction of local courts, certain social and business legislation, and various other laws that host governments are willing to waive to attract an investment project.

With the exemptions, the host government implicitly accords foreign investors and projects a privileged status. In this respect the exemptions enjoyed by foreign investors in the Middle East today may appear, at least superficially, to resemble the capitulations granted to foreigners in the Ottoman Empire. The capitulations, which included immunity from the Ottoman courts as well as fiscal and commercial privileges, originally applied to a few visiting foreign merchants but eventually grew into a full-blown system of extraterritorial privilege and immunity that benefited not only all foreigners, but a select group of Ottoman subjects as well (Lewis 1968:455). Applying to all Ottoman provinces (including Egypt), the capitulations were a symbol of the inferiority and subservience of local institutions and individuals, and they facilitated European domination of Middle Eastern economies of that time (see Issa 1970:58-61). In this instance (as well as in many others) law had a direct impact on the social structure of the countries concerned.

The purpose of this chapter is to examine the modern-day exemptions arising under investment laws and codes and to determine their impact, actual or potential, upon the legal systems and social structures of the Middle East. It will focus on Egypt and its open-door policy because Egypt, to a far greater extent than any of its neighbors, has actively sought to attract foreign capital through the use of exemptions, and because its dominant position in the region has meant that its social and economic innovations have attracted the attention of–and sometimes influenced–other Middle Eastern countries (see Waterbury 1975).

It must be acknowledged at the outset that the subject of foreign investment, in Egypt and elsewhere in the Third World, is emotionally and ideologically charged. On the one hand, its proponents view foreign investment as indispensible to economic development since it facilitates capital formation, the introduction of new and needed technology, and linkage to world markets. On the other hand, its opponents see it as a dangerous form of imperialism which will result in foreign domination of the economy and the loss of national resources without equivalent benefit to the people of the host country. This argument certainly took place in Egypt as the government formulated its open-door policy during the first half of the 1970s, and it has sharpened since the death of President Anwar Sadat in October 1981.

This chapter will not advocate either one side of the ideological debate or the other. Based largely on Egypt's experience during the 1970s, it will merely attempt to analyze the actual and potential consequences of granting legislative exemptions to foreign investment projects. After describing Egypt's attempts to attract foreign investment by granting various exemptions, it will seek to examine the effect of such exemptions on (1) the foreign investor, (2) national institutions, and (3) social groups within the host country.

EGYPTIAN LAW ON FOREIGN INVESTMENT

One cannot fully understand the significance of Egypt's foreign investment laws without a brief glance at modern Egyptian history. Prior to the Free Officers' Revolution of 1952 and the advent of President Gamal Abdel Nasser, the economic door to Egypt had also been open—so much so that foreign interests controlled major sectors of the economy, including banking, insurance, transportation, and commercial trade. To service these interests Egypt accepted a variety of essentially foreign institutions, such as the Mixed Courts, European mortgage law, legal codes from France, and commercial banking methods from Britain.* As a result of the introduction of European law and institutions, one may argue that Egypt, following the classic generalization of Sir Henry Maine, experienced a profound movement from "status to contract" as the source of legal rights (see Salacuse 1980).

*The mortgage law provisions of the Mixed Civil Code of 1876 proved to be a particularly effective means to facilitate European penetration of the Egyptian economy, for they enabled foreign companies to obtain a significant ownership interest in Egyptian land. Between 1876 and 1883 the mortgage debt of Egyptian farmers rose from E£ 500,000 to 7 million (Issawi 1963:25-26).

Egyptian capitalists, particularly through the Bank Misr Group, played an increasing economic role after World War I. However, such indigenous participation did not bring about a significant change in the structure of the Egyptian economy. By and large, land remained the principal investment for Egyptians with capital.

The Free Officers' Revolution did not immediately overturn the prevailing economic order. For four years after the coup, the government appeared to follow a policy of creating conditions favorable to private enterprise. It granted tax incentives, increased tariffs, facilitated credit, and made improvements in infrastructure; however, the Egyptian investing and entrepreneurial class, cautious and relatively small in size, did not respond to these incentives with major investments in sectors desired by the government. A major shift in traditional policy took place in 1956, when, as a result of the Suez War, the Egyptian government sequestrated the property of British and French citizens, thereby gaining control over major foreign banking interests. This action eventually led to a drive to "Egyptianize" the main arteries of the national economy, and all foreign banks, insurance companies, and commercial agencies were ultimately forced to convert themselves into nationally owned joint stock companies.

Beginning in 1960, the Egyptian government initiated a series of nationalizations which effectively curtailed private enterprise and fostered a great expansion of the public sector of the economy (see O'Brien 1966:124-47). These measures not only struck at European interests, but they also affected Arab and Egyptian investors. The resulting pronounced orientation toward state ownership of all major enterprises, government regulation of the remaining private sector, and strong efforts at central economic planning led to the growth of a new group of institutions, while those which had formerly serviced the free-enterprise, foreign-dominated economy underwent a major transformation. In the ensuing years a complex system of planning organizations, regulatory bodies, economic legislation, and extensive controls evolved to buttress the socialist policy of the government. Moreover, the law increasingly granted workers and peasants new and greater economic benefits. During this period little foreign investment entered Egypt, and that which did tended to concentrate in oil prospection and the drug industry.

After the death of President Nasser in 1970, the severity of Egypt's economic problems and the growth of Arab capital eventually led the government of President Sadat to reexamine past policies with regard to foreign investment and the private sector. This reexamination resulted in the adoption of Law No. 65 of 1971, "Concerning the Investment of Arab Funds and the Free Zones" (Egypt, *Garida Rasmia*, no. 39, 30 September 1971), which was basically designed to encourage the oil-producing Arab states to place a portion of their surplus funds in Egypt. The response to this legislation was far from overwhelming, and few significant investments entered the country, largely because of Egypt's continuing confrontation with Israel, its history of hostility to foreign investment during the Nasser era, and the fact that Arab investors generally lacked the experience and know-how to undertake the kind of industrial projects which Egypt needed.

Following the October War of 1973 and a more pronounced diplomatic shift toward the West, Egypt widened the opening for foreign capital by enacting Law No. 43 of 1974, which made virtually no distinction between Arab and other foreign investors. Nonetheless, the law continued a major restriction on foreign investment: for all practical purposes it allowed only export-oriented projects capable of earning foreign exchange and virtually prohibited those aimed at the Egyptian domestic market alone. But owing to strong pressure from investors conscious of the potential rewards to be gained from one of the largest markets in the Middle East, the government extensively revised the foreign investment law in 1977 and lifted even this restriction by allowing the establishment of import-substitution projects to serve the local market. Thus the open-door policy, known in Arabic as *infitah*, evolved incrementally to create a substantial opening for the entry of foreign capital into the Egyptian economy.

The Egyptian efforts to attract foreign capital were not intended to tear down completely the law, institutions, and regulations that had emerged during the Nasser era. Instead, by granting numerous exemptions, the government sought to create special enclaves within which foreign investment projects might operate without the legal restrictions that would otherwise be applicable. Law No. 43 of 1974, as amended, provided for numerous exemptions, including those from income and commercial taxes, foreign exchange regulations, customs duties, certain rules of corporation law, and selected labor law provisions. It allowed investment disputes to be settled by international arbitration, thus exempting investors to a limited extent from the jurisdiction of the Egyptian courts, and it established "free zones," special areas which had even greater freedom from taxes, foreign exchange rules, and customs laws. To implement the provisions of Law No. 43, a new government agency was created—the

General Authority for Investment and Free Zones, whose principal function was to attract foreign investors to Egypt, negotiate and evaluate investment proposals, and supervise their implementation.

EFFECT OF EXEMPTIONS ON FOREIGN INVESTORS

Egypt's aim in granting legislative exemptions is essentially to influence investor behavior–i.e., to induce a foreign enterprise to undertake an investment in Egypt that it would not otherwise make. Obviously if an investor would undertake desirable projects without exemptions, it would be pointless for Egypt or any host country to grant them nonetheless.

Investor reluctance to undertake a particular project in a given country stems from a judgment that the potential rewards are too small or that the potential risks are too great when compared to the investor's requirements and alternative investment opportunities. In theory, therefore, the purpose of an exemption is to change the investor's evaluation of the risks and rewards to the point where a project in question meets investor requirements. Thus with the passage of Law No. 43 of 1974 Egypt hoped that investors would view exemptions from taxation and customs duties as tending to increase the rewards to be gained from a project and exemptions from exchange control laws and the jurisdiction of local courts as reducing the risks (see Lessard and Hansen 1982). In this respect at least investment law exemptions are unlike the capitulations of the Ottoman Empire: the latter did not grant capitulations in order to encourage the establishment of Europeans in the empire but rather to accommodate their presence within an existing system of laws.

Theoretically, of course, an exemption granted to investors ought to bear some relationship to the nature and magnitude of the benefits that the host country expects to derive from a given project. Most investment laws embody the notion that projects yielding great benefits to the country in terms of employment, technology transfer, and capital infusion should receive greater privileges than projects yielding few benefits. For example, Law No. 43 of 1974, as amended, offered an approved project an exemption from taxes on commercial and industrial profits for a period of five years following the commencement of its activities; however, projects having special importance by reason of their geographic location, volume of capital, and importance to economic development might obtain an exemption for eight years, while projects involving reconstruction, establishment of new cities outside agricultural areas, and land reclamation might receive "tax holidays" of up to fifteen years with the approval of the president (Law No. 43 of 1974, Art. 16; as amended by Law No. 32 of 1977).* Today large or important projects will very often obtain exemptions and concessions beyond those specifically offered by a host country's investment laws. For example, a gigantic Kenana Sugar Company project in the Sudan received special tax exemptions in addition to those provided in the country's general investment law, and a Union Carbide project to establish a dry cell battery plant in Egypt, because of its "strategic" status as one of the first manufacturing ventures undertaken by an American multinational corporation under the auspices of the open-door policy, also received a concession not specifically found in Law No. 43—i.e., the imposition of a conditional quota on competing imported batteries (see below).

The application of foreign investment laws in Egypt may perhaps be best examined within the context of a specific investment project. One of the largest projects established under the auspices of the open-door policy is Union Carbide Egypt, a company created to manufacture dry cell batteries. Formed in 1977, the company, 75 percent of whose shares are owned by Union Carbide and the remainder by local private investors, built a modern plant at Alexandria and by 1981 had invested, through both debt and equity, $13.5 million in the venture. At the time the project was proposed in 1976, the total Egyptian battery market amounted to 135 million AA, D, and C dry cells a year; however, the government-owned General Company for Batteries (Genbat), the local producer, was manufacturing only between 84 and 95 million batteries a year.† Consequently Egypt had to import at least 35 million batteries a year to satisfy local demand. Not only were local batteries produced in insufficient quantity, but their quality was also considered inferior to that of imported batteries.

The Egyptian government desired the Union Carbide project in order to gain modern battery technology and to produce enough batteries to meet local demand. It did not view dry cell batteries as a luxury item, but as an essential element in communicating with

*In this respect too modern-day exemptions differ from Ottoman capitulations, which applied to all foreigners regardless of their importance and contribution to the economy.

†Genbat had a theoretical capacity of 200 million cells a year.

the population, whose radios are powered principally by dry cell batteries.

Union Carbide viewed the project as potentially highly profitable because of Egypt's large and growing population and because Union Carbide technology would allow it to produce a battery that would be far superior to any being produced locally. Nonetheless, according to its managers, Union Carbide would not have been interested in undertaking the project without Law No. 43—and specifically the concessions and exemptions it offered because they served to increase profitability and reduce the risks of the project. After lengthy negotiations, Union Carbide Egypt received twenty-one specific concessions and privileges. Embodied in a letter from the General Authority on Foreign Investment and Free Zones, the principal concessions included the following: (1) Guarantees that capital could be transferred at the highest prevailing rate of exchange; (2) A tax holiday of five years, which was later extended to eight years; (3) An agreement by the Egyptian government not to license another dry cell battery plant for a period of four years from the commencement of production of the Union Carbide Egypt plant; (4) A guarantee to make foreign exchange available for payment of technical assistance fees to Union Carbide USA (which amounted to 4 percent of annual net sales of batteries sold, regardless of whether the Egyptian project made a profit); (5) Authorization to obtain foreign currency for the project's needs from the free market, with a commitment by the Egyptian government to use its best efforts to make foreign currency available; (6) A commitment by the Egyptian government not to impose restrictions on profit margins on the project or price controls on its product; (7) Exemptions from customs duties on the importation by the project of its capital equipment; and (8) A commitment by the Egyptian government to limit the importation of foreign batteries to the extent local production was sufficient to meet local needs.

Instead of providing such an array of benefits, a host government could of course seek to alter an investor's risk-reward calculus by other means, such as offering a direct subsidy—for instance, low-cost leases on land, inexpensive power, or guarantees for investor loans. But the "beauty" of legislative exemptions in the eyes of most governments is that they are "cheap" because they do not involve an immediate and direct expenditure of state resources. For example, a tax exemption is seen merely as giving up tax revenues which the host government never had in the first place.

In addition to attempting to affect investor decision-making, exemptions serve to "announce" to the international investment community that the host country is serious in seeking foreign investment and to show that government policy truly welcomes the entry of foreign capital. Moreover, the promise of legislative exemptions gives the foreign investment policy an aura of stability and permanency that it would not have were it merely enunciated in speeches by the president or a minister. Clearly the passage of Egypt's Law No. 43 of 1974 represented a powerful signal to members of the international business community that Egypt was open to investment. They in turn responded with numerous visits and missions, although relatively few resulted in major investment projects.

The use of exemptions to influence investor behavior may encounter a variety of unexpected problems. First, a host country may make erroneous assumptions about what will influence investor decision-making. For example, an income tax exemption may have little or no effect on an investor if the resulting gain from the exemption is subsequently taxed by the investor's home country. In such a situation the tax exemption is in effect a transfer of wealth from the host country's treasury to that of the investor's home country, and the value of the exemption as an incentive to investment may be nullified completely. Thus the utility to the host country of a tax exemption may depend very much on the tax laws of the investor's home country.

Second, while an exemption may indeed influence an investor to undertake a project, it may at the same time induce perverse and undesirable investor behavior. For example, an exemption from customs duties on raw materials may give the investor little incentive to use local goods and services, and exemptions from import duties on capital goods may encourage a project that is capital-intensive rather than one which uses local labor to greater advantage.

Third, the granting of exemptions has the effect of affirming the legitimacy of a special—and in most cases superior—status for foreign enterprises in the host country. With such legitimacy affirmed, the response of foreign enterprises is to seek yet additional exemptions and to urge that the legal system be further adjusted to meet their particular needs. For example, following the passage of Law No. 43 of 1974 in Egypt, foreign interests lobbied for increased exemptions and clarifications, which ultimately led to the enactment of Law No. 32 of 1977, amending Law No. 43. Thereafter, they pushed for the reform of the tax code and company law. As a result, the tax law has undergone significant changes during the period of infitah and a new company law (No. 159) was adopted in 1981. A similar phenomenon has taken place in other countries that have pursued a strong open-door policy.

One gains the impression that exemptions engender the belief among foreigner investors that the legal system of a host country should be redesigned for their special needs. In truth, many government officials eagerly courting foreign capital sometimes appear to convey the attitude that their law is "for sale."* If the local population perceives this to be government policy, one may ask what effect such perception will have upon their attitudes toward the legal system and the legitimacy of the institutions of the state.

EFFECT OF EXEMPTIONS ON HOST COUNTRY INSTITUTIONS

While exemptions may appear to be an inexpensive and easy way to attract foreign capital, they can have significant and sometimes costly consequences for the institutions of the host country. The most elementary consequence of the adoption of an investment code is the need to build new state institutions to evaluate investment proposals and to decide which projects will receive exemptions. In addition, if exemptions are granted subject to certain conditions, specialized state institutions must supervise approved projects to ensure that they continue to meet the conditions and therefore remain entitled to the exemptions. Invariably the development of such institutions will require significant human and material resources which the host government may be able to secure only at the expense of other essential state activities. For example, the Egyptian government has made major efforts during the past decade to develop the General Authority for Foreign Investment and Free Zones.

To grant an investor an exemption from state laws and charges is to grant him a valuable property right. For example, the right to

*The term "law for sale" was previously affixed to the efforts of the state of Delaware to shape its corporation law to favor business interests and thus encourage large enterprises to incorporate within the state. This effort, which is not unlike the effort of developing countries to attract foreign investment through the adoption of investment laws, has been successful: approximately one third of the companies listed on the New York Stock Exchange are chartered in Delaware. (See Comment, "Law for Sale: A Study of the Delaware Corporation Law of 1967," *University of Pennsylvania Law Review* 117 [1969]:861-98.)

import raw materials without the payment of duty into an economy which is otherwise protected by high tariffs affords the opportunity for guaranteed profits. Generally exemptions under most foreign investment laws are at the discretion of the administering agency and are shaped by negotiation with a prospective investor rather than by the automatic application of fixed rules. Such a situation provides useful flexibility in balancing the importance of a project to a host country's development. At the same time, it presents the possibility of administrative abuse or corruption, particularly because negative decisions on investment applications are not ordinarily subject to review by higher authorities or the courts. In Egypt many Egyptians as well as foreigners claim to perceive widespread corruption within the bureaucracy as a result of the open-door policy. Nonetheless, one must temper such assertions with the fact that corruption anywhere is extremely difficult to locate and measure, that corruption in Egypt existed long before foreign investment, and that other factors, such as inflation, may be powerful forces for inducing corrupt behavior by government officials. Even if abuse or corruption does not take place, vesting power in administrative officials to grant exemptions may foster an attitude in the bureaucracy and population that law may be manipulated for the benefit of special interest groups, rather than applied on the basis of equality to all groups within a society.

While host country investment policy officials may wield considerable power, one must at the same time acknowledge their difficult position in implementing a policy. Having announced such a policy with great fanfare—which in the case of Egypt represented an implicit rejection of many policies of the Nasser era—a host government usually feels itself under increasing pressure with the passage of time to "produce results"—that is, to secure investment projects. But it is the investor, not the host country, who ultimately controls where he will invest. As the host country fails to attract major projects, it may lower its evaluation standards and grant exemptions beyond its original intentions, often justifying its position on the grounds that once a few projects have been established in the country, other investors will rapidly follow suit.

A lowering of evaluation standards occurred in Egypt for the reasons noted above. In the very early days of the open-door policy the Egyptian government claimed that it wanted only "industrial" projects which used significant local resources, employed large numbers of Egyptian workers, and produced primarily for export. Such lofty objectives were probably unrealistic in view of Egypt's limited economic advantages and foreign investors' strategies and goals. In the ensuing years both law and policy were modified to permit a greater variety of foreign enterprises. This process probably reached its culmination in November 1980, when the government announced that it would approve, under the terms of Law No. 43, a joint venture to manufacture chewing gum, using imported gum base, for sale to the Egyptian market ("U.S., Egypt Announce Gum Deal"; *Washington Post*, 16 November 1980:F1).

The investment legislation of most developing countries seems to assume that the state may secure foreign capital and its benefits while at the same time preserving indigenous economic and social institutions untouched. If foreign investment constitutes a special enclave by virtue of its privileges and exemptions, government planners appear to believe that it will remain an enclave isolated from the other institutions and policies of the host country. However, the experience of developing countries with foreign investment demonstrates that such isolation is not possible and that foreign capital will ultimately have a significant impact, both positive and negative, on national institutions.

Host countries often hope that the introduction of foreign capital and technology will modernize and stimulate major industrial sectors, if not the entire economy. In certain cases a new project will indeed cause existing enterprises to improve their operations. For example, the financial services sectors in Egypt have undergone extensive modernization as a result of the open-door policy. These sectors have received the largest number of foreign investment projects, and they in turn have influenced a transformation of Egyptian public banking, which had to modernize if it was to compete successfully with the foreign enterprises. On the other hand, the introduction of foreign investment rarely occurs without some social and economic costs. In Egypt the foreign banks have been criticized severely because of their suspected speculation in foreign exchange, their unwillingness to finance productive long-term projects, and their placement of Egyptian deposits outside the country through the Eurodollar market.*

Instead of acting as a stimulus for constructive change, foreign investment projects armed with exemptions from taxation, customs

*For example, a 1977 report of the Central Bank of Egypt criticized the failure of the foreign banks in the country to contribute to the national economy (*Mideast Markets,* 12 September 1977:7).

duties, certain labor laws, and financial controls may constitute a destructive competitive force for local public and private enterprises that do not benefit from similar privileges. Such competition is obvious when the foreign investment project operates in the same area of economic activity as an existing local enterprise, as where a foreign investor's battery plant competes with a local battery manufacturer in the local market. The foreign plant could drive the local plant out of business—unless the host government also provides assistance to the local manufacturer. In Egypt, Union Carbide did not drive Genbat out of business primarily because Genbat, unlike Union Carbide, was required to sell its batteries subject to price controls. As a result, although Genbat produced an inferior battery, its low prices permitted it to retain an important segment of the Egyptian market. Moreover, as a state-owned enterprise, Genbat was not forced to adhere to the same standards of profitability and return on capital that would be applicable to a privately owned project.

The destructive effects of special exemptions may be felt even if the foreign investor and the local manufacturer operate in totally different economic domains. For example, a local foundry in a developing country may find that it is in competition with a foreign battery manufacturing project, not for customers, but for human and financial resources in an economy of scarcity. By virtue of its exemptions, the foreign investment project can command scarce foreign exchange for needed imports and has the ability to pay high salaries to attract skilled workers in a way that the foundry cannot. In Egypt new foreign investment projects have drawn large numbers of skilled and talented Egyptians away from the public sector and civil service, a phenomenon that appears to have had a negative impact on government enterprise.

One method of attempting to protect local companies from the destructive effects of such competition is to require that foreign investment take the form of a joint venture with a local public or private enterprise. For example, Egypt's Law No. 43 of 1974 establishes the general principle that foreign capital participate in joint ventures with Egyptian public or private capital.* The stated purpose of the joint venture requirement is to allow national enterprises to share the benefits of foreign investment, to facilitate a more effective

*It should be noted, however, that Article 4 of Law No. 43, as amended, provides that all investment projects except for banks engaging in local currency may obtain a special exemption from the requirement of local participation.

transfer of technology, and to ensure that the project will conduct its operations in the national interest. Whether the joint venture structure in fact achieves these objectives is open to question. Numerous devices, including majority share ownership, management contracts, and technology transfer agreements, may permit the foreign partner to dominate the operation of the enterprise despite substantial local participation.

The joint venture concept raises the question of whether exemptions granted to purely foreign projects are also to be granted to joint ventures, thus extending the benefit of the exemptions not only to the foreigner but to the local participant as well. Generally most countries grant exemptions to joint ventures. The Egyptian law (Art. 9, Law No. 43, as amended) specifically provides that even where public enterprises are participants, joint ventures are to be considered "private," thereby exempting them from the restrictive public sector legislation on such matters as employment, salaries, procurement, and financial procedures. In effect, the law offers the possibility of shifting existing state resources from the domain of public decision-making to that of private decision-making–i.e., from the domain of state planning to that of private contract (see Salacuse 1980). Public sector managers have been quick to see the advantages of being exempted from the public sector legislative regime; consequently by the end of 1978 Egyptian public enterprises had agreed to enter into over 130 joint ventures with foreign partners (Egypt 1978:45). One possible danger in this phenomenon is that profitable components of public sector enterprises may be diverted to joint ventures with foreign firms, leaving the unprofitable but socially useful components to disappear eventually or to exist on government subsidies.

Granting exemptions to foreign or joint projects may lead to growing pressure by local enterprises that they be treated equally with foreigners. In truth, it is difficult to justify more favorable treatment to a foreign investment project than to a project that is locally owned. Eventually indigenous entrepreneurs will challenge the legitimacy of a system where some enterprises must bear the burdens and costs of social and tax legislation while others do not. Consequently granting exemptions to foreigners, particularly on a broad basis, may set in motion a process that leads to major changes in a country's social legislation and economic system. Once again Egypt is a good example of such a process of change, for the 1977 amendment to Law No. 43 of 1974 allows Egyptian investors to obtain some of the incentives and exemptions previously accorded only to foreigners.* On the other hand, a country which attracts only a few special investment projects--such as a steel plant or aluminum smelter (which are not likely to have local equivalents)--may be able to grant concessions without engendering significant pressure for equal treatment by local enterprises.

The host country government must also recognize that the granting of certain exemptions will sometimes provoke fundamental conflicts with well-settled national policies; therefore it must determine how far it is willing to place foreign investment projects outside the scope of national legislation and policies, not only with respect to taxation, but also with respect to such sensitive matters as labor and social legislation. The Egyptian government faced precisely such a decision when it drafted its own investment law. The Nasser era had brought about new legal rights for workers and peasants, but the Sadat government feared that the costs to employers of meeting these rights might discourage the entry of foreign capital. A major problem concerned the extent to which approved foreign investment projects would be exempted from two important laws: Law No. 26 of 1954, requiring business enterprises to distribute a legally specified percentage of net profits annually to workers and employees, and Law No. 73 of 1973, governing the representation of labor on the board of directors of a company.

Recognizing that foreign investors might find the requirements of both laws highly objectionable, the authors of the investment law sought to accommodate the imperatives of foreign capital with those of Egyptian socialism. In the end, they adopted a superficial compromise. Article 10 of the foreign investment law states that approved projects will be exempt from Law No. 26 of 1954 "provided that *a* percentage of the net profits of such companies shall be distributed annually among employees and workers in accordance with the rules proposed by the company's Board of Directors and approved by the general meeting of the stockholders" (emphasis added). The investment law thus appears to preserve the principle of worker participation in profits, but in practice it permits the company to minimize the financial burdens that such a principle entails. Similarly Article 10 also exempts approved enterprises from Law No. 73 of 1973; however, it preserves the principle of worker participation—at least in

*Similarly the Ottoman Empire at the beginning of the nineteenth century instituted the sale of *berats* (certificates), thus extending to local merchants the possibility of obtaining some of the privileges previously enjoyed exclusively by foreigners.

theory—by requiring the company by-laws to specify the way in which labor is to participate in the management of the project.

It is interesting to note that following the enactment of the foreign investment law, the Egyptian private sector actively sought to reform Egyptian company law so as to obtain equal treatment with foreign companies with respect to worker participation in profits and management.

EFFECT OF EXEMPTIONS ON INDIGENOUS SOCIAL GROUPS

While the intent of a host government in granting an exemption may be to influence solely the foreign investor, various indigenous social groups may also be affected. Because of their power and benefits, foreign investors are able to attract host country nationals, who assist in the project's activities and eventually come to share a favored position within their society. In Egypt observers have pointed to a "new class" that has emerged as a result of infitah—i.e., Egyptians who have benefited in various ways from the increased foreign presence in the country.

The phenomenon of a new class is not new. In the time of the Ottoman capitulations, certain local subjects had a "protected" status as a result of their association with a foreign embassy, concern, or household, and they enjoyed many of the exemptions granted to foreigners under the capitulary system (Lewis 1968:455-56). Today in Egypt and in other developing countries, local joint venture partners, employees, and professionals associated with foreign investment projects gain in status, as well as in financial benefits, because of their association with a foreign investment project. In many cases, these persons become the clients of the foreign investors, sharing and defending the interests of their foreign employers. Although they do not have a special legal status, as did the *protégés* during the Ottoman era, their emergence as a distinct privileged group nonetheless presents serious problems for host governments seeking to pursue policies of social and economic equality.

The pursuit of foreign investment also leads to the development of a professional and service class to provide for the needs of foreign firms. One clear example of this phenomenon has been the change in the legal profession in Egypt as a result of infitah. The nationalization of private commercial and industrial interests during the time of President Nasser dealt a severe blow to lawyers because it ended the very lucrative support of such interests to the private practice of law. Thereafter the best opportunities for the legally educated lay in government service, the judiciary, and the Council of State (Ziadeh 1968:159). The policy of infitah has brought about a resurgence of the private practice of law, particularly in the business and commercial area. New law firms have emerged to service the needs of foreign investors and the newly revived Egyptian private sector, and many talented Egyptians have left the judiciary and the government to enter private practice. The accounting profession has experienced a similar change, as has consulting in economics, business, engineering, and management. Indeed in most developing countries the pursuit of foreign capital invariably stimulates the growth of the legal, accounting, and other service professions necessary for the operation of foreign investment projects. In Egypt it has been Western-educated professionals who have primarily benefited from the open-door policy rather than those who received their degrees from Eastern bloc institutions and who have tended to gravitate toward the public sector.

While benefiting some groups, foreign investment may negatively affect others. Since inflation often accompanies the introduction of significant foreign capital, low-level workers, as well as civil servants and others on relatively fixed wages, may sustain a decline in their standard of living as a result of an open-door policy. Such was the case in Egypt. For example, while the Egyptian government actively sought Arab investment in real estate projects, the result in the view of most Egyptians has been an astronomical rise in the cost of urban middle-class housing, despite the construction of numerous new high-rise apartment buildings in Cairo.

Many developing country governments are pursuing or claim to be pursuing a policy of social equality. Special legislative exemptions for particular individuals or groups are of course a negation of equality. The inherent contradiction between a declared policy of equality, on the one hand, and vested privilege by reason of legislative exemptions, on the other, may set in motion forces that ultimately lead to instability and conflict within the host country. At the very least, it introduces social tensions and the potential for hostility between those who benefit from exemptions (directly or indirectly) and those who do not. In Egypt some observers consider that special exemptions to attract foreign capital present the dangers of a return to foreign domination of important sectors of the economy, an increased likelihood of exploitation of the poor, and a diversion of national resources to purposes that in the end will not serve Egyptian development. Should these dangers come to pass, the exemptions, which at first seemed a cheap means to attract foreign capital, may engender long-term social and economic costs that make them an expensive development strategy indeed.

CONCLUSION

In view of the truly difficult problems which face an investor undertaking an investment project in most developing countries, a host country must usually grant some exemptions or concessions if it is to attract foreign capital to any significant extent. Political instability, the risk of nationalization, the shortage of foreign exchange, and the existence of pervasive controls on economic activity represent genuine obstacles to any rational investor, and they cannot be eliminated by soothing words of host country officials and colorful brochures exaggerating the country's economic prospects. Egypt had a history of nationalizing foreign enterprises, an apparently monolithic public sector, and a complex regulatory system which seemed designed to curtail rather than encourage private enterprise.

When a government begins a policy of attracting foreign capital, its officials often are not realistic about the economic attractions of their country; consequently they may sometimes argue that few if any concessions are needed. In the early days of the open-door policy Egyptian officials saw their country as an ideal place from which to export to Europe, Africa, and the rest of the Middle East—a view no doubt influenced by the country's extreme shortage of foreign exchange at the time. On the other hand, potential foreign investors, concerned primarily with opportunities for profit rather than solutions to a national balance-of-payments problem, viewed Egypt as the largest potential market in the Middle East, and they therefore sought to establish enterprises to serve that market rather than to export.

Even if it is assumed that Egypt would have to grant exemptions if it was to attract foreign capital, one may ask whether the Sadat government was correct in attempting to follow any type of open-door policy in the first place. It has become common—indeed fashionable—to criticize the open-door policy, but one must recall the terrible economic and political stagnation which afflicted Egypt in the early 1970s. Faced with an apparently endless stalemate with Israel ("no war, no peace"), having experienced an overwhelming military humiliation in 1967, and staggering under an enormous international debt, a deteriorating infrastructure, and a grossly inefficient public sector, the Sadat government clearly had to seek new policy options. Even to the most optimistic, the policies and institutions inherited from the Nasser era did not seem to offer ways to revive the economy. In those circumstances, the development of an open-door policy, coupled as it was with a political alliance with the West, did indeed seem a plausible way out of Egypt's difficulties.

More than a decade after its inception, Egypt's open-door policy has both ardent defenders and ferocious opponents. A comprehensive, objective evaluation of its effects remains to be undertaken. At this point, one can say that the policy has had both positive and negative effects, and that neither early portents of great prosperity nor subsequent prophesies of terrible doom have come to pass. On the one hand, the open-door policy has restored international business confidence in Egypt, has revived and stimulated certain sectors of the Egyptian economy, and has facilitated a political alliance with the West which has brought the country large amounts of foreign aid. On the other hand, the policy has introduced significant inflation into the economy and new distortions of income distribution accompanied by disquieting displays of conspicuous consumption among a relatively few.

The suggestion that the exemptions represent a new form of capitulations remains to be proved. Yet one must not underestimate the risks which the open-door policy poses for Egyptian society. It may indeed resurrect some of the social and economic ills that eventually gave rise to the 1952 revolution. As many Egyptians fear, the policy raises the spectre of a return to foreign domination of the economy, of the exploitation of the mass of Egyptians (who are poor), and of the inadequate and ineffective allocation of resources for developmental purposes. The increasing *visible* disparity in wealth between the relatively few who have reaped rewards from the new policy and the great mass who have yet to benefit creates the potential for dangerous social conflict. Yet these consequences may be an inevitable part of the process of capital formation and economic liberalization. With time, their harsher aspects may abate as the policy takes hold. Perhaps what the open-door policy requires even more than the skills of the economist and the legislative draftsman is the art of a consummate politician to "keep the lid on," to persuade the mass of Egyptians that the policy will bring tangible economic benefits to their lives while at the same time seeking to channel the energies and capital of the "open-door class" toward activities and projects that will advance the development of Egypt. With the death of Sadat in October 1981, President Hosni Mubarak now faces that challenge.

REFERENCES

Abdel-Rahman, A.M. 1976. "A Survey of the Investment Laws of Selected Members of the Council of Arab Economic Unity." IMF internal paper.

Bushnell, George E. 1980. "The Development of Foreign Investment Law in Egypt and Its Effect on Private and Foreign Investment." *Georgia Journal of International and Comparative Law* 10:301-24.

Egypt. 1979. *Annual Report for the Period Ending 31 December 1978 of the General Authority for Investment and Free Zones.* Cairo.

__________. *Garida Rasmia.* Official gazette in which all Egyptian legislation is printed and the official source of Egyptian laws. Appears at least weekly.

International Center for the Settlement of Investment Disputes. 1972. *Investment Laws of the World*, 10 vols. Dobbs Ferry, N.Y.: Oceana Publications.

Issa, Hossam M. 1970. *Capitalisme et sociétés anonymes en Egypte.* Paris: Librairie Générale de Droit et de Jurisprudence.

Issawi, Charles. 1963. *Egypt in Revolution.* London and New York: Oxford University Press.

Lessard, Donald, and Hansen, Eric. 1982. "Host Government Regulations and Incentives for Direct Foreign Investment." *Negotiating Foreign Investments: A Manual for the Third World*, vol. 1, sec. 1B. Washington, D.C.: International Law Institute, Georgetown University Law School.

Lewis, Bernard. 1968. *The Emergence of Modern Turkey*, 2d ed. Oxford: Oxford University Press.

McLaughlin, Gerald T. 1978. "Infitah in Egypt: An Appraisal of Egypt's Open-Door Policy for Foreign Investment." *Fordham Law Review* 46:885-906.

O'Brien, Patrick. 1966. *The Revolution in Egypt's Economic System: From Private Enterprise to Socialism, 1952-1965.* London and New York: Oxford University Press.

Salacuse, Jeswald W. 1975. "Egypt's New Law on Foreign Investment: The Framework for Economic Openness." *International Lawyer* 9:647-60.

__________. 1980. "Back to Contract: Implications of Peace and Openness for Egypt's Legal System." *American Journal of Comparative Law* 28:315-33.

Salacuse, Jeswald W., and Parnall, Theodore. 1978. "Foreign Investment and Economic Openness in Egypt: Legal Problems and Legislative Adjustments of the First Three Years." *International Lawyer* 12:759-77.

UN Center on Transnational Corporations. 1978. *National Legislation and Regulations Relating to Transnational Corporations*. New York.

Waterbury, J. 1975. "The Opening," parts 1-4. *American Universities Fieldstaff Reports, North Africa Series* 20.

Ziadeh, Farhat J. 1968. *Lawyers, The Rule of Law and Liberalism in Modern Egypt*. Stanford: Hoover Institution.

Chapter 8

TECHNOLOGY TRANSFER AND SOCIAL STRUCTURE IN THE ARAB WORLD

Ali E. Hillal Dessouki

Since the choice of technological alternatives is central to the overall strategy of development in less developed countries (LDCs), technology transfer has been extensively dealt with in the literature on modernization, development, and social change.* The subject has been approached from the perspectives of pricing policies, the legal framework of transfer, the role of transnational corporations, and the impact of technology upon society. Particular emphasis has been placed on the notion of *appropriate technology*. Proponents of this idea start from the premise that technology is socially and culturally conditioned. A technological model developed in response to the needs of a given socioeconomic context is primarily suited to that context. Thus the choice of a certain technology developed for one society has obvious social, economic, and political implications when transferred to another (al-Zaim 1978:29).

A review of the literature on appropriate technology for LDCs shows little consensus on what technologies can be considered appropriate or the criteria of their appropriateness. Different authors have emphasized different aspects, such as the use of local resources, labor-intensive techniques as opposed to capital-intensive ones, distributive justice, self-reliance, and decentralization (Evans and Adler 1979:35-72). From my perspective appropriate technology refers to an orientation, a logic of technological evaluation and choice rather than a specific mix of equipment or know-how. The appropriateness of a technological alternative can be measured only in relation to specific social, economic, and cultural referents. The

*Technology transfer is a broad concept including not only the importation and acquisition of machinery and equipment, but also the technical skills and management techniques that go with them.

choice depends not only on the overall development goals of a society, but also on other factors such as population density, per capita natural resources, and the particular sector of the economy for which the technology is being considered. Hence appropriate technology is that technology which makes optimum use of available resources in a given society.

It is to be noted, however, that the needs of LDCs are diverse. In some countries capital-intensive methods are preferable. In others, adaptation of existing technologies is essential, while sometimes the situation calls for the development of a totally new technology. Despite the diversity, in all cases it is crucial to consider seriously issues such as a greater use of unskilled labor, local resources, and existing technologies; national self-reliance; and adaptation to local conditions. Finally, as Eckaus argues (1977:10), since technology is not an end in itself but a means to achieve development goals, the ultimate criteria of appropriateness of a particular technology are to be found in the goals sought by development. More specifically, Winner notes that "Different ideas of social and political life entail different technologies for their realization" (1977:325).*

This chapter deals with one aspect of technology transfer to LDCs, focusing on the impact of technological choice on social structure in the Arab world and analyzing the relationship between technological alternatives and the changing position of different socioeconomic groups and the distribution of income in society.

TECHNOLOGY TRANSFER AND SOCIAL STRUCTURE: A THEORETICAL PERSPECTIVE

As it has developed in the West, technology is a form of property protected by a system of patents and licenses and is considered the private property of the patentee. It follows that technology transfer constitutes a form of transnational transfer of property rights and values, similar to the transfer involved in labor migration from one country to another. The transfer takes place either through official institutions of the states concerned, such as ministries and

*It is surprising to read in a Soviet book the following statement: "Technology is socially neutral. Similar equipment can be produced in countries with different social systems. It can also be used in countries with differing social systems, as witnessed by the scientific and technical links between socialist and capitalist countries" (Tygunenko 1976:139).

public corporations, or is made by private companies and enterprises. In all countries, notwithstanding differences in economic structure, ideological orientation, and level of development, governments control and regulate the transfer process. Technology transfer has always been used as an instrument of foreign policy and a means of expressing political positions and sentiments. Indeed, contrary to the naive image of a free market, technology is "a monopoly, and the developed countries have endeavored to keep that monopoly secure through retaining control over technology secrets, management and higher technical staff, raw materials supplies, research and development, and patents" (Nayar 1980:33).

The sociopolitical impact of technology transfer can be analyzed at two levels: between states and within a society. In the first case, the transfer is closely associated with the politically sensitive issues of ownership and control, and governments are usually concerned with the legal framework within which the transfer takes place and the resulting relations of interdependence and dependence. In the second case, governments are also concerned with the relative gains and losses accruing to different social groups due to the introduction of a particular technology—that is, they wish to know how the adoption of a particular technology will affect power relations, patterns of social conflict, and distribution of wealth and income.

Despite a great deal of literature on appropriate technology and technology assessment, we know little of the effects of a particular technological alternative on the social structure and income distribution in a society. For instance, Eckaus writes that "while income distribution is an isssue of increasing social concern, the relations between technical decisions and the achievements of this particular goal are seldom clear" (1977:10-11). Goulet (1977:128) also notes that there are few empirical studies to help us determine who truly gains from a particular technological choice.

The linkage between technological decisions and social structure in terms of relative benefits or losses to various social groups can be established in at least two areas. One is the volume and kind of employment provided by a particular technological choice; another is the accessibility of technology. In most LDCs new jobs in the agricultural sector are unable to keep pace with the increase of the labor force, and new employment opportunities have to be created elsewhere. Thus the benefits of alternative technological choices can be judged according to the volume of employment opportunities they create and whether these new opportunities go mainly to low- or high-income groups, to the unskilled and the many, or to the highly educated few (Eckaus 1977:43). Moreover, as Singer (1977: 50) has pointed out, there is a complementary relationship between more equal income distribution and a shift to more labor-intensive technologies. In a study done in Indonesia Wells argued that labor-intensive technologies "can provide more than ten times as many jobs as the capital intensive plants for the same outputs" (1973:64). The argument for labor-intensive technologies, however, must not always be accepted uncritically, for it is possible that creating employment in the short run will result in the sacrifice of investment that would create greater job opportunities in the long run (Colman and Dixson 1978:265). Another difficulty is that labor-intensive technologies require sophisticated personnel management skills which are not usually available.

Some sectors such as road construction, which could create significant employment opportunities for the unskilled, appear to be highly mechanized in most LDCs, with little impact on total employment (Irvin 1975:1). Irvin's study, prepared for the International Labour Office (ILO) on the economic and technical feasibility of labor-intensive methods of road construction in Iran, recommended the adoption of labor-intensive methods as socially feasible. In each of the cases investigated "it was found that equipment can be reduced and employment significantly increased" without delay in construction time (p. 7). However, it also found that the adoption of labor-intensive methods is uneconomical from the point of view of private enterprise. Thus a shift to labor-intensive methods is likely to occur only as a result of purposeful governmental action or through the public sector of the economy.

Bhalla (1975:33) suggests that labor intensity, together with the absolute size of the labor market, is a useful indicator in defining priorities for the choice of technologies. If employment opportunity is given high priority—as it is in Algeria and Egypt, for instance—labor-intensive technologies, even when they are not the least costly in terms of market prices, may be considered socially desirable. The implication is that technologies that seem uneconomical based on the calculations of private enterprises may be favored on the basis of social cost-benefit criteria. ILO studies on road construction in Iran, the Philippines, and Thailand confirm this conclusion (Bhalla 1976: 192).

The second linkage between technology and social structure,

the accessibility of technology and who uses its outputs, is what some (e.g., Eckaus 1977:43) call the consumption criterion—i.e., whether the technology output will increase the consumption of high- or low-income groups. The advocates of appropriate technology favor the development of products suited to the broadest sectors of a population rather than luxury consumption goods for the few; that is, they stress a technology that satisfies the basic needs of the masses. Goulet (1977:128-29) observes that when technology transfer does not benefit the masses, it is probably because that technology was not designed to do so, but rather was designed to create marketable products for those whose basic needs are already satisfied. In this case technology transfer tends to enhance the position of those already privileged and favored.

The wholesale adoption of modern capital-intensive technology may enhance social and economic inequality in a number of ways. In most cases modern technology benefits primarily individuals and institutions already in control of resources. Expensive technology is beyond the reach of poor individuals and firms alike. Many of its consumer products are available only to the rich in LDCs. Unless a free and equitable educational system exists, technological opportunities tend to be monopolized by the educated elite. Singer (1977: 25) notices a circular relationship between technology and income distribution in LDCs. Where income distribution is unequal and where high-income groups have access to scarce resources in a free-enterprise system, the products in demand are likely to be similar to those produced in the more industrialized societies and will therefore tend to encourage a basically capital-intensive technology. In this case, it would be difficult to change to more "appropriate products" geared to low-income groups because such products would lack a sufficient market. A shift to more appropriate products by means of increased employment—i.e., through the use of more labor-intensive techniques—would help to create and support a more equal distribution of income.

Our discussion of technology transfer and social structure is better understood within a larger political context which involves the important issues of ownership, power, and control. A significant question is who *owns* and *controls* the new technologies. Here the issues are public versus private interests and national versus foreign interests. Another question is the role of an exporting country in influencing the technological choices of the importing countries, especially in the area of technical assistance. For instance, the

U.S. Agency for International Development requires a recipient country to use American technologies, technical skills, consulting firms, and industrial products. Thus the assistance is tied to the use of particular technologies which have probably not been developed to suit the circumstances of developing countries. In addition to restrictions on sources of inputs such as capital equipment, spare parts, and intermediate components, a formal contract for technology transfer may impose restrictions on access to market outlets. Other restrictions may include the unnecessary use of expensive foreign personnel in key positions and prohibitions on the diversification of product lines by domestic firms (Zahlan 1978: 117).

A most important consequence of ownership and power is the loss of control over critical decisions related to a national economy. With the increasing desire of developing countries to own their own resources, the crucial issue has become effective control rather than legal ownership. For instance, in the negotiations leading to Saudi Arabia's takeover of ARAMCO, the four U.S. oil companies that were partners in ARAMCO were less concerned with ownership per se than with "who retains control over management, the rate and form of payment of management fees (commission) and the share of U.S. partners in the allocation of crude oil quotas on a preferential basis" (Zahlan 1978:118).

TECHNOLOGY TRANSFER IN THE ARAB COUNTRIES

There is a striking absence in most Arab countries of clear policies for technology transfer or for the development of appropriate technology at home. Technology is perceived in most of these countries as a marginal component of development planning, and there is a shortage of technological evaluations of the effectiveness of policies. In many of the countries it is difficult to find out which governmental unit is responsible for technological decision-making. Scientific and technological policies are fettered by a multiplicity of organizations involved in research, lack of coordination between their activities, absence of communication between research centers and production units such as factories, meager budgets (in Egypt the share for scientific research in the 1960s was 0.1 percent of the GNP), organizational uncertainty and reshuffles, and shortages of scientific personnel (Ayubi 1981). In a worldwide directory of research centers and institutes dealing with appropriate technology published by the Organization for Economic Cooperation and Development (OECD) (Jequier 1979), only five such centers are listed for twenty-three Arab states (one in Egypt, one in Lebanon, one in Oman, and two in Tunisia), as opposed to fourteen in India, eleven in Indonesia, seven in the Philippines, six in Kenya, four in Sri Lanka, and three in Israel.

In the Arab world one finds an almost mystical faith in science and in the ability of modern technology to solve the problems of underdevelopment. Somehow science and technology are perceived as capable of providing the solution for all economic and social ills. Many leaders, political and otherwise, closely associate development with the adoption of the most modern and up-to-date technology, which happens to be primarily Western and capital-intensive. Both planned-economy revolutionary and market-oriented moderate regimes share this attitude. For instance, revolutionary regimes such as Algeria, Iraq, and Nasser's Egypt embarked upon massive transfers of modern capital-intensive technology. The Rabat Declaration, adopted in 1976 by the conference of ministers of Arab states responsible for the application of science and technology to development, shared a similar belief in science and technology. Why is there such faith in science and modern sophisticated technology? In some countries it is a function of a slavish orientation which some ruling classes have toward almost everything Western. In others it is related to the consumption patterns and tastes of these classes and their ability to convert their interests into national policies. Moreover, an emphasis on science and technology allows ruling elites to avoid facing the need to transform social organizations and political structures and to restrict the debate on development to technicist terms. Not only that, but technology provides them with new instruments of control and manipulation.

In the 1970s the value of technology imported into Arab countries reached astronomical proportions. Zahlan (1978:52) reported that twelve Arab states imported machinery and transport equipment at a cost of $8 billion in 1975 alone.* According to a U.S. Library of Congress document (1976:16), during 1970-75 Iran most vigorously pursued technology, followed by Algeria, Iraq, Egypt, and Libya. In 1980 the value of ongoing engineering projects

*The twelve states were Bahrain, Iraq, Jordan, Kuwait, Lebanon, Oman, Qatar, Saudi Arabia, Syria, the United Arab Emirates, South Yemen, and North Yemen.

by foreign companies in all Arab states was estimated at $400 billion; most of the projects involved transfers of products and machinery rather than know-how or patents (Zahlan 1980:8-10). UN specialists estimated in 1979 that Middle Eastern countries were allocating some $50 billion a year for the design, planning, and implementation of projects, 90 percent of which were carried out by foreign contractors (Vandervort 1979:3).

Zahlan (1978:116) showed that in the 1970s consulting fees in Iraq ranged between 3 and 11 percent of the total costs of technology projects (average: 7 percent). Similar costs, royalty payments, and management fees for developing countries in 1968 were estimated at 8 percent of the imports of machinery and capital equipment. If we know that the Arab world's imports of machinery and capital goods in 1973-74 totaled $7.167 million, then the direct costs of technology (applying the 8 percent estimate) must have been on the order of $573 million. If we assume a yearly cost increase of 20 percent, in the early 1980s Arab countries must have been paying some $1.7 billion per year in the form of royalty and management fees. For oil-producing countries, which have a faster than average rate of growth in technology imports, this figure must be adjusted by a factor of two.

Technology transfer to the Arab countries, as in most of the Third World, takes place within a context of technological dependence. This dependence exists when the primary source of a country's technology is foreign and when the mode of transfer does not increase the indigenous capability for science and technology but rather creates new relations of dependence on the outside. Whether we take the percentage share for research and development in GNP, the number of scientists and engineers engaged in research and development per 10,000 of a population, or capital goods imports as a percentage of gross fixed capital formation, all indicators signify technological dependence (Zahlan 1978:115).

Three case studies will illuminate how technology transfer relates to social structure in the Arab world. The first, an example of technological dependence between countries, involves a contract signed in 1974 between GTE International, Inc. (GTEI), a subsidiary of General Telephone and Electronics Corporation (U.S.), and the Algerian state enterprise SONELEC for the construction of a $232 million consumer electronics manufacturing plant. The *produits en main* contract was similar to a turnkey project, in which the supplier provides training at all levels as well as all the equipment.

It seemed on the surface that Algeria had purchased the capacity to become a potential electronics exporter, but in reality the new plant also enhanced its technological dependence:

> The terms of the contract call for the transfer of technologies limited to the design and engineering of a specific manufacturing facility, and production of specific products. The contract is executed over a finite period and tied to an existing state of the art technology. Although the agreement requires GTEI to keep SONELEC informed about new technical developments, they will not necessarily be incorporated into the plant (Baranson 1978: 101).

Given the rapid advances in the consumer electronics field which GTEI incorporated into its own products, the Algerian products had a much less competitive position in the world market. (For instance, the television design provided to Algeria by GTEI was not in compliance with U.S. standards.) Moreover, for several years SONELEC depended on GTEI for some of the key parts needed in its manufacturing process.

A second case study, showing how technology transfer can affect social groups within a society, concerns the Wadi Zabid project in North Yemen. Reports by the UN Economic Commission for Western Asia (ECWA) and the FAO Joint Agricultural Division (Zahlan 1978:325-26) show how unequally the benefits of technology transfer were distributed. For centuries the floodwaters of the wadi (valley) were the only source of irrigation, and scarce water availability imposed severe limits to agricultural growth. The total irrigable area of the wadi was 16,900 hectares served by sixteen ancient canals without any regulatory structures.* The area is inhabited by 10,000 families, of which 8,000 depend upon agriculture (4,400 families are agricultural workers, 2,000 small owners, 1,400 private tenants, and 160 state tenants). The pattern of land ownership is unequal: 1 percent of the owners control 60 percent of the land, and 60 percent of the owners control 10 percent of the land. In the mid-1960s lift pump technology was introduced to extract groundwater, and since it was obviously profitable, it was seized upon by a few entrepreneurs. During the following ten years they installed 268 lift pumps on the land they managed in return for a half share in the produce. As a result of increased water availability,

*A hectare is 10,000 square meters, or 2.4711 acres.

crop yields improved. In 1965-75 the overall cropping intensity increased from 82 to 125 percent, the gross production value per cropped hectare rose by 43 percent, and the annual growth rate was 6.5 percent.

The gains in Wadi Zabid, however, were denied to most of the population of the wadi. The technology was capital-intensive, so it remained beyond the reach of the small owners. The benefits went almost exclusively "to the large farm sector managed by the intermediaries [entrepreneurs] now turned pump owners" (Zahlan 1978: 326); 35 percent of the land and 92 percent of the owners did not receive any of the benefits generated by the new technology. The outcome was an uneven pattern of growth. The sector that did not gain from the new technology continued its state of near-zero growth. The increases in output were monopolized by the large farm sector, where the cropping intensity rose from 82 to 146 percent and productivity in terms of gross product value per cropped hectare rose by 60 percent. The gross value added in this sector rose from 8 to over 19 million Yemeni riyals—a yearly growth rate of 9.5 percent. Marked changes in income distribution favored the rich as a result of the introduction of technology. Out of the total output of 11 million Yemeni riyals generated by the new technology, 60 percent went to the owners of capital, 21 percent to the state as taxes, 16 percent to agricultural workers, and 3 percent to tenants. A corresponding change took place in the shares of the different groups in the total income. Owners of capital increased their share from 43 to 58 percent at the expense of agricultural workers, whose share fell from 57 to 42 percent.

A third case, from Sadat's Egypt, relates to the government's policy of mechanizing agriculture. In the section on manpower in the agricultural part of the five-year plan for 1978-82 is the following statement: "Agricultural mechanization must be expanded to relieve demands for workers." Imported tractors jumped from a yearly average of 1,200 in 1965-73 to 6,000 in 1977, most of them privately owned. In 1979 it was estimated that privately owned tractors outnumbered by four to one those owned by agricultural cooperatives (Era 2000, 1979: ch. 3:15-18). The government gave a push to the development of the private farm machinery industry by approving a private sector joint venture between Massey Ferguson and NASCO (an Egyptian farm machinery firm) for domestic production.

In Egypt most of the owners of farm machines rent them to

others, resulting in the rise of a group of private machine owners who happen in most cases to be big landowners as well. Ownership of at least ten feddans of land is almost a condition for buying an imported tractor because the agricultural credit banks apply this criterion in considering applications for tractor loans.* The rise of this favored group of machine-and-land owners appears to have led to an increase of class consciousness in the countryside. In a survey conducted as part of a feasibility study on mechanization, it was reported that farmers made frequent references to the "big people," the "poor people," and the like (Era 2000, 1979:ch. 8:25-28). Iliya Harik (1974) reported a similar attitude in his study, noting that Egyptian farmers referred to private tractor owners in particular as the "rich people."

The social impact of mechanization on Egypt's countryside is an unsettled question. In other countries mechanization has led to an increase in farm size, a decrease in the agricultural workforce and farm population, reduction of grain supplies and increase of milk and wheat production, rural-urban migration, less work for women and children, more commercialization of agriculture, and displacement of tenants. In Turkey, for instance, small landowners have developed a pattern of client relations with tractor owners in what has become known as the *ortakci* system, according to which the management of a crop is under the control of the tractor owners, not the landowners. The tractor owners provide all tractor services and take half the crop (Mann 1980:198-209).

It seems that further commercialization of agriculture in Egypt will enhance class differentiation and awareness. In the absence of governmental intervention, those best able to profit from the process are usually the rich since they own the means for adopting efficiency-increasing techniques of production. Thus mechanization will tend to increase the role and influence of those owning farm machines who also own more than ten feddans. The authors of the Era 2000 study concluded that from an economic and production standpoint substantial benefits to Egypt and to individual farmers would accrue "if a comprehensive program [of mechanization] were undertaken" (Era 2000, 1979:iii). How these benefits would be distributed would "depend in large part upon what happens outside the agricultural sector, especially with respect to off-shore employment opportunities and government policy vis-à-vis farm product prices and food subsidies" (ch. 24:49).

*A feddan is 1.038 acres.

CONCLUSIONS

The case studies discussed above raise three important issues about the impact of technology transfer on social structure. The first is the need for a comprehensive policy on technology transfer and therefore of development objectives. For instance, the mechanization of agriculture in Egypt may be a desirable objective from a production point of view in order to meet the demands for food from a population increasing by one million every ten months. Mechanization, however, has a social impact that favors the rich. Here the issue should not be approached in terms of mechanization versus traditional methods of production, but rather from the overall social and economic policies, rural and urban, within which mechanization would be introduced. It is exactly at the level of overall policies that most Arab and other LDC governments do not fare well because of the prevalence of eclectic, selective, and incremental orientations.

The second issue relates to private enterprise economic calculations versus social cost-benefit analyses. The use of particular labor-intensive technology may seem uneconomical from a private entrepreneurial perspective, but it could be socially desirable. Thus the socioeconomic and legal framework within which technology transfer occurs is crucial in determining its impact on social structure.

Finally, technological dependence requires an integrated policy on the part of developing countries. A policy is needed that controls technology imports in order to offset their high cost and undesirable effects and to reduce LDC dependence through the strengthening of collective indigenous technical capabilities.

REFERENCES

Ayubi, Nazih N.M. 1981. "Technology Policies in Egypt: Scientists, Technocrats, and Public Policy." Paper prepared for a seminar on Technology Policies in the Arab States, organized by the UN Economic Commission for Western Asia. May. Mimeo.

Baranson, Jack. 1978. *Technology and the Multinationals*. Lexington, Mass.: Lexington Books.

Bhalla, A.S., ed. 1975. *Technology and Employment in Industry*. Geneva: International Labour Office.

__________. 1976. "Technology and Employment: Some Conclusions." *International Labor Review* 113:189-203.

Colman, D., and Dixson, F. 1978. *Economics of Change in Less Developed Countries.* New York: John Wiley.

Eckaus, R.S. 1977. *Appropriate Technologies for Developing Countries.* Washington, D.C.: National Academy of Sciences.

Era 2000, Inc. 1979. *Further Mechanization of Egyptian Agriculture.* Report submitted to USAID, Gaithersburg, Md.

Evans, D.D., and Adler, L.N., eds. 1979. *Appropriate Technology for Development: A Discussion and Case Histories.* Boulder, Colo.: Westview Press.

Goulet, D. 1977. *The Uncertain Promise.* Washington, D.C.: Overseas Development Council.

Harik, Iliya F. 1974. *The Political Mobilization of Peasants: A Study of an Egyptian Community.* Bloomington, Ind.: Indiana University Press.

Irvin, G.W. 1975. *Roads and Redistribution: Social Costs and Benefits and Labor-Intensive Road Construction in Iran.* Geneva: International Labour Office.

Jequier, N. 1979. *Appropriate Technology Directory.* Paris: Development Center of the Organization for Economic Cooperation and Development.

Mann, Charles. 1980. "The Effects of Government Policy on Income Distribution: A Case Study of Wheat Production in Turkey Since World War II." In *The Political Economy of Income Distribution in Turkey,* ed. Ergun Ozbudun and Aydin Ulusan. New York: Holms and Meier.

Nayar, B.R. 1980. "Independence, Development and Technology: Third World Quest for Technological Independence." Mimeograph in files of author, Department of Political Science, McGill University, Montreal.

Singer, H. 1977. *Techniques for Basic Needs.* Geneva: International Labour Office.

Tygunenko, V.L., ed. 1976. *The Third World and Scientific and Technical Progress.* Moscow: Central Department of Oriental Literature.

UNESCO. 1976. "National Scientific and Technological Policies in the Arab States." *Science Policy Studies and Documents,* No. 38. Paris.

U.S. Library of Congress. 1976. *Technology Transfer to the Middle East OPEC Nations and Egypt, 1970-75.* Washington, D.C.: U.S. Government Printing Office.

Vandervort, Bruce. 1979. "Technology Transfer Talks Take Forward Step." *Middle East Economic Digest.* 9 March, p. 3.

Wells, L.T. 1973. "Man and Machines in Indonesia's Light Manufacturing Industries." *Bulletin of Indonesian Economic Studies* 9:62-72.

Winner, L. 1977. *Autonomous Technology.* Cambridge, Mass.: MIT Press.

Zahlan, A.B. 1980. "Al-Sūq al-'Arabīya lil-tiknūlūjīyā" (The Arab market for technology). *Al-Mustaqbal al-'Arabī* (The Arab future) 22:6-29.

__________, ed. 1978. *Technology Transfer and Change in the Arab World.* New York: Pergamon Press.

al-Zaim, I. 1978. *Problems of Technology Transfer: A Point of View of the Third World.* Vienna: Institute for Development, Occasional Papers.

Chapter 9

INTERNATIONAL LABOR MIGRATION IN THE MIDDLE EAST AND NORTH AFRICA: CURRENT AND PROSPECTIVE DIMENSIONS, 1975-85

James Socknat, Stace Birks, and Ismail Serageldin

International labor migration in the Middle East and North Africa (MENA) has become a factor of major economic and social significance for virtually every country in the region. In the Mashreq (eastern Arab region) the phenomenon of crossing national boundaries for employment has been closely linked with the discovery of commercially exploitable quantities of oil, and the subsequent expenditure of oil revenues on economic diversification, social welfare improvements, development of infrastructure, and modernization of the public administration apparatus. Thus, for example, Kuwait had become a significant importer of foreign workers by the mid-1950s. By the early 1970s foreign workers were a feature, but not always a dominant one—and certainly not the nearly preoccupying one they have now become—in Saudi Arabia, Bahrain, Qatar, the United Arab Emirates (UAE), and Oman, as well as their neighbor, Iran, across the Gulf. For nationals of the Maghreb (western Arab region) countries, the lion's share of the labor migration has been to Western Europe, particularly France. The job opportunities in the oil-endowed states of the Gulf did not significantly attract nationals of the Maghreb states until the late 1970s.

The oil price increases of 1973-74 triggered a change in scale of international labor migration that proved to be of such magnitude that the phenomenon took on a substantively different meaning to both the labor-importing and labor-exporting countries of the MENA region. The impact of rising oil prices was very quickly felt in West European economies. As employment demand slackened in these

---

The opinions expressed in this paper are those of the authors and should not be attributed to any organization with which they are or have been affiliated.

economies, Western Europe's "guest workers" were quickly affected. By 1976 there was a net reduction in the number of guest workers in Europe, and the Maghreb countries began receiving return migrants on a heretofore unexperienced scale.

In contrast to the woes of Europe and the Maghreb, the 1973-74 and subsequent oil price rises brought to Libya and the oil-endowed Gulf states an economic boom of staggering proportions. As observers tried to assess whether the oil states had the absorptive capacity to handle the resource transfers implicit in the higher oil prices, these states were busily spending their greatly increased incomes. The felt needs of these countries for improved social welfare services, economic diversification, and extensive infrastructure additions were great. Not surprisingly, veritable droves of individuals, institutions, and governments proved to be quite ready and willing to supply the array of goods and services required in their burgeoning economies and in the process help reduce the petrodollar surpluses of these states.

LITERATURE ON MENA INTERNATIONAL LABOR MIGRATION

The body of literature on labor migration in the MENA region has grown substantially since the mid-1970s. A commendably thorough compilation of available data on nine Arab countries was presented in Farrag (1975). The increasingly significant impact of labor migration was assessed—albeit on the basis of scanty and often contradictory data—from a variety of specific, and sometimes parochial, viewpoints in the late 1970s. For example, Halliday's 1977 article is an essentially politically normative assessment coupled with a mix of basic summary and illustrative migration and labor-force statistics. Choucri (1977) is an especially striking example of an ethnocentric perception of the migration phenomenon. Shaw (1979) focused on the construction sector in his analysis.

Under an International Labour Office (ILO) research grant, Birks and Sinclair (1980) carried out an extremely valuable and insightful series of country case studies. One of the cardinal features of their book was its treatment of the numbers of migrants within a matrix framework showing countries of origin and destination in 1975. This means of reconciliation of source and destination numbers of migrants is especially helpful to migration-scene observers, who are continuously confronted with estimates which are typically exaggerated by labor-exporting countries and understated by labor-importing countries. Another relatively comprehensive publication on labor migration in the region was Pennisi (1981). Particularly notable in that work is an appendix review of the theoretical bases for assessment of international labor migration.

By the late 1970s the literature shifted from descriptions of the process and dimensions of labor migration and began to focus on the impact of MENA labor migration on both labor-exporting and labor-importing countries within the region and on the impact on non-MENA countries of their labor exportation to the Middle East. Examples of the former include Socknat (1979), Birks and Sinclair (1979), Ibrahim (1982), and Sherbiny and Serageldin (1982). Examples of the latter include Ali et al. (1981), Gilani et al. (1981), and Ranesh (1978).

The scale of labor migration in the MENA region has been of such proportions that various schemes of compensation by labor-importing countries to labor-exporting countries have been proposed. A principal analyst and proponent of compensation or recompense has been W. R. Bohning of the ILO (1977, 1978, 1982).

A recently completed World Bank research project (1981) differs from the other works on international labor migration in the region in that it includes computer modeling of manpower requirements and supply by sector, occupation, and nationality for nineteen countries, as well as an assessment of the implications of the projections for the period 1975-85.* In this chapter we draw primarily on the World Bank 1981 study; unless otherwise noted, references are to that study.

EXPLANATION OF DATA AND CAVEATS

In the assessment of international labor migration in MENA, 1975 has been found to be the most feasible benchmark year. It is close to the 1973-74 period of key oil price increases, and data are generally available for that year, particularly from population

*The nineteen countries in the study are the following: Algeria, Bahrain, Egypt, Iran, Iraq, Jordan, Kuwait, Lebanon, Libya, Morocco, Oman, Qatar, Saudi Arabia, Sudan, Syria, Tunisia, UAE, Yemen Arab Republic (YAR), and the People's Democratic Republic of Yemen (PDRY). It should be noted that Birks and Sinclair were also among the principal researchers on this study, which obviously benefited extensively from Birks and Sinclair (1980).

censuses in a number of MENA countries. Considerable time and effort were expended in settling upon a set of 1975 labor-force statistics (including migration data) most persuasive to the authors. The matrix reconciliation of origin and destination countries for migrants was a key feature of this process. A variety of consistency checks was employed to ensure as far as possible the creditability of the data set. For example, if the often exaggerated claims of labor-exporting countries were accepted, one would not only have to reject even the order of magnitude of accuracy of labor importers' population censuses, but (unless the national accounts data of the labor-importing countries were disbelieved as well) one would also implicitly have to believe that productivity levels in many economic sectors in the labor-importing countries were incredibly low. Another source of data was immigration arrivals and departures; due allowance was made for illegal migration, whether across unpatrolled borders or unsanctioned stays by legal entrants to a labor-importing country—e.g., arrivals on a visitor's visa or Hajj visa. In some cases, vigorous examination of the conventional claims by labor-exporting countries of the numbers and characteristics of their workers abroad revealed their improbability. Such a case was the preliminary estimate of 1,234,000 migrants abroad from the YAR, most of whom were thought by YAR officials to be prime-working-age males, almost all residing in Saudi Arabia and unaccompanied by dependents. Careful reference to the YAR September 1974 census showed that if this claim and YAR de facto census results (confirmed by air photo and on-ground verification work) were both accepted, the YAR de jure population would have a sex ratio of 139 males to 100 females. The authors did not give serious weight to such a biological improbability.

To borrow from legal parlance, the data set adopted for 1975 seemed to the authors to be supported by a preponderance of the evidence, but not so persuasive as to be beyond reasonable doubt—particularly in that the base year position comprises sector-occupation-nationality-specific employment figures for such a large number of countries. Projections to 1985 have been made using the International Labor Migration Model, a computer model developed by the World Bank's Technical Assistance and Special Studies Division.* To project manpower requirements, two sets of sectoral output and productivity growth rates were postulated for each year of the

*For information on the International Labor Migration Model and its application in the study, see World Bank (1981:15-29 and Appendices A and B).

projection period for each of the countries. The two sets represent the "high" and "low" ends of a realistic spectrum of growth expected for each country based upon past performance, country plans, and authors' professional judgment. Table 1 provides a summary of the economic growth rates used for the projections.

In addition to the caveats noted above and the normal hazards of projecting total and sectoral economic output and productivity growth for each country, two other factors must be added which are essentially political. First, the virtual certainty that the relationships among the MENA countries and between any one of them and the other countries of the world will change and affect any projections is easy to state as a generality but next to impossible to accurately translate into specifics. Events in Iran, for example, were such that we assumed that Iran would not be a significant labor importer during the 1975-85 period. The war between Iraq and Iran, however, was not anticipated. Second, the very projection of the scale and composition of labor migration in the MENA region may contribute to labor migration policy formulation by various countries in the region, the results of which could alter the actual size and shape of the migration. It must be emphasized, therefore, that the projections are meant to be indicative orders of magnitude, subject to alteration by a wide variety of social, economic, and political factors. They are nonetheless useful as a point of departure for the assessment of broad, general trends and impacts.

TOTAL LABOR REQUIREMENTS IN MENA

Total labor requirements in MENA are projected to rise from just under 42 million in 1975 to 50.7 million (low growth scenario) or 55.7 million (high growth scenario). Table 2 shows the labor requirements under the two scenarios for each country.

Over the 1975-85 period a significant change is projected in the sectoral composition of employment in MENA. Most striking is a decline in the share of employment in agriculture—from 44.5 percent in 1975 to about 35 percent by 1985. The composition by sector is summarized in Table 3, and details are shown in Table 4.

The occupational composition of total employment in MENA is also expected to markedly change over the 1975-85 period. The combination of changing sectoral composition of employment and the changing composition within each sector results in a pronouncedly

Table 1

AVERAGE ANNUAL ECONOMIC GROWTH RATES: HIGH AND LOW SCENARIOS, 1975-85
(Percent)

Country	High Growth Rate Scenario	Low Growth Rate Scenario
Algeria[a]	9.7%[b]	6.8%
Bahrain[a]	11.2	8.6
Egypt	8.4	6.1
Iran[a]	4.2	1.8
Iraq[a]	11.3	10.3
Jordan	7.2	5.4
Kuwait[a]	6.0	5.6
Lebanon	1.1[c]	1.1
Libya[a]	11.6	8.7
Morocco	5.4	4.2
Oman[a]	4.7[c]	4.7
Qatar[a]	8.6	7.4
Saudi Arabia[a]	10.6	8.6
Sudan	4.8	3.7
Syria	6.1	4.4
Tunisia	6.3	4.1
UAE[a]	11.6	9.4
YAR	7.8	5.6
PDRY	9.9	5.9

[a]Oil-exporting state. In the calculations here its mining and quarrying sector (predominantly hydrocarbons) has been excluded. In subsequent tables, however, employment and manpower requirements in this sector are tabulated in full. It is to avoid economic growth rate distortions that the sector is not included in this table.

[b]The fractions of a percent in the growth rate values tend to reflect the methods of calculation rather than growth rates which are postulated to be accurate to 0.1 percent. All rates are calculated in local currency deflated to constant prices.

[c]Only one scenario calculated.

Table 2

TOTAL LABOR REQUIREMENTS IN MENA BY COUNTRY AND GROWTH RATE, 1975 AND 1985 (HIGH AND LOW GROWTH RATE SCENARIOS)

	1975		1985							
			High Economic Growth Rate				Low Economic Growth Rate			
Country	Labor Requirements (Thousands)	Percent Shares	Labor Requirements (Thousands)	Percent Shares	Annual Average Compound	Overall Percent Increase	Labor Requirements (Thousands)	Percent Shares	Annual Average Compound	Overall Percent Increase
Algeria	3,083	7.4%	4,511	8.1%	3.9%	46.3%	3,954	7.8%	2.5%	28.3%
Bahrain	79	0.2	150	0.3	6.7	89.9	129	0.3	5.0	63.3
Egypt	9,433	22.5	13,006	23.3	3.3	37.9	11,836	23.3	2.3	25.5
Iran	8,789	20.9	10,646	19.2	1.9	21.1	9,579	18.9	1.1	9.0
Iraq	3,008	7.2	4,566	8.2	4.3	40.2	4,302	8.5	3.6	32.3
Jordan	374	0.9	439	0.8	1.6	17.4	425	0.8	0.8	13.6
Kuwait	297	0.7	414	0.7	3.4	39.4	393	0.8	2.8	32.3
Lebanon	550	1.3	599	1.1	0.8[a]	8.9	599	1.2	0.8	8.9
Libya	735	1.7	1,414	2.5	6.7	92.4	1,260	2.5	5.5	71.4
Morocco	4,308	10.3	5,145	9.2	1.8	19.4	4,93[illegible]	9.7	1.4	14.5
Oman	192	0.5	257	0.5	3.0[a]	33.9	257	0.5	3.0	33.9
Qatar	74	0.2	136	0.2	6.3	83.8	135	0.3	6.1	79.7
Saudi Arabia	1,968	4.7	3,245	5.8	5.1	64.9	3,055	6.0	4.5	55.2
Sudan	3,700	8.8	3,898	7.0	0.5	5.4	3,502	6.9	-0.6[b]	-5.4
Syria	1,794	4.3	2,605	4.7	3.8	45.2	2,162	4.3	1.9	20.5
Tunisia	1,599	3.8	2,242	4.0	3.5	40.2	1,973	3.9	2.2	23.7
UAE	292	0.7	632	1.1	8.0	116.4	570	1.1	6.9	95.2
YAR	1,361	3.1	1,312	2.4	-0.4[b]	-3.6	1,220	2.4	-1.1[b]	-10.4
PDRY	357	0.8	510	0.9	3.5	42.9	407	0.8	1.2	14.0
Total	41,993	100.0	55,727	100.0	2.8	31.9	50,693	100.0	1.9	20.0

[a]Only one scenario projected.

[b]The overall reduction in manpower requirements projected for the Sudan under the low growth rate scenario and for the YAR under both the high and low growth scenarios results from a decline in agricultural requirements which is larger than the increase in the nonagricultural growth in manpower requirements. The nonagricultural manpower requirements for the Sudan (low growth) rise by 2.3 percent per annum (annual average compound), giving an overall increase of 27 percent over the projection period. In the YAR (high growth) nonagricultural manpower requirements are projected to rise at 4.8 percent per annum (annual average compound) with an overall increase of 61 percent. Under the low growth rate scenario, the figures are 3.2 percent and 38 percent respectively.

Table 3

TOTAL LABOR REQUIREMENTS IN MENA BY ECONOMIC SECTOR, 1975-85 (HIGH AND LOW GROWTH RATE SCENARIOS)

	High Economic Growth Rate		Low Economic Growth Rate	
Economic Sector	Increase in Manpower Requirements *(Thousands)*	Percent Shares	Increase in Manpower Requirements *(Thousands)*	Percent Shares
Agriculture	844.0	6.1%	-1,011.0	-11.6%
Mining and quarrying	389.0	2.8	360.0	4.1
Manufacturing	2,304.0	16.8	1,691.0	19.5
Utilities	388.0	2.8	266.0	3.1
Construction	2,494.0	18.2	1,897.0	21.8
Trade and finance	1,977.0	14.4	1,698.0	19.5
Transport and communications	987.0	7.2	751.0	8.6
Services	4,342.0	31.7	3,048.0	35.0
Total	13,725.0	100.0	8,700.0	100.0

higher skill requirements profile in 1985 compared with 1975. This is most dramatically seen in the "Percent Increase" columns for the 1985 projections in Table 5.

Of the nineteen MENA states, ten may be classified as "oil-endowed": Algeria, Bahrain, Iran, Iraq, Kuwait, Libya, Oman, Qatar, Saudi Arabia, and the UAE. While some of the other states—e.g., Egypt and Syria—are in fact oil producers, their oil export and/or oil revenue relative to population are not of a scale to put them in the same league with the oil-endowed. In contrast, Iran is clearly an oil-endowed state, but the unsettled conditions in Iran would seem to preclude the resumption of significant labor imports for some years at least. Thus for purposes of this analysis, Iran does not belong in the group of labor-importing countries. The remaining nine oil-endowed states in 1975 accounted for 23 percent of MENA's total labor requirements. By 1985 their share will rise to approximately 28 percent (under both the high and low economic growth scenarios).

Table 4

TOTAL LABOR REQUIREMENTS IN MENA BY ECONOMIC SECTOR, 1975 AND 1985 (HIGH AND LOW GROWTH RATE SCENARIOS)

	1975		1985					
			High Economic Growth Rate			Low Economic Growth Rate		
Economic Sector	Labor Require-ments *(Thousands)*	Percent Shares	Labor Require-ments *(Thousands)*	Percent Shares	Percent Increases	Labor Require-ments *(Thousands)*	Percent Shares	Percent Increases
Agriculture	18,703	44.5%	19,547	35.2%	4.5%	17,692	35.0%	-5.7%
Mining and quarrying	425	1.0	823	1.5	93.6	785	1.5	84.7
Manufacturing	4,882	11.6	7,185	12.8	47.2	6,573	13.0	34.6
Utilities	451	1.1	839	1.5	86.0	717	1.4	60.0
Construction	3,488	8.3	5,982	10.7	71.5	5,385	10.6	54.4
Trade and finance	3,762	9.0	5,739	10.3	52.6	5,460	10.8	45.1
Transport and communications	1,856	4.4	2,843	5.1	53.2	2,607	5.1	40.5
Services	8,426	20.1	12,768	22.9	51.5	11,474	22.6	36.2
Total	41,993	100.0	55,727	100.0	32.7	50,693	100.0	20.7

Table 5

TOTAL LABOR REQUIREMENTS IN MENA BY OCCUPATION AND PERCENTAGE GROWTH, 1975 AND 1985 (HIGH AND LOW GROWTH RATE SCENARIOS)

	1975		1985					
			High Economic Growth Rate			Low Economic Growth Rate		
Occupational Category[a]	Labor Requirements *(Thousands)*	Percent Shares	Labor Requirements *(Thousands)*	Percent Shares	Percent Increase	Labor Requirements *(Thousands)*	Percent Shares	Percent Increase
Professional and technical (A-1)	412	1.0%	1,034	1.9%	150.0%	950	1.9%	130.6%
Other professional (A-2)	943	2.2	1,797	3.2	90.0	1,664	3.3	76.5
Sub-professional and technical (B-1)	956	2.3	1,813	3.3	89.0	1,636	3.2	71.1
Other sub-professional (B-2)	1,290	3.1	2,391	4.3	85.3	2,167	4.3	68.0
Skilled office and manual (C-1)	3,595	8.6	5,968	10.7	66.0	5,460	10.8	51.9
Semi-skilled office and manual (C-2)	8,379	19.9	12,631	22.6	50.7	11,534	22.7	37.7
Unskilled (D)	26,421	62.9	30,093	54.0	13.9	27,282	53.8	3.3
Total	41,996	100.0	55,727	100.0	32.7	50,693	100.0	20.7

[a]The categories presented here are according to the International Standard Classification of Occupations three-digit listings (1968 ed.). Their presumed correspondence with education/training is as follows:

A-1: Science/mathematics-based university degree;
A-2: Fine or liberal arts-based university degree;
B-1: One to three years' science/mathematics-based post-secondary or technical-secondary education;
B-2: One to three years' non-science/mathematics-based post-secondary or vocational-secondary education;
C-1: General secondary education completion;
C-2: Intermediate-level education or literacy at least;
D: No specific education or training.

Details for the categories are shown in World Bank (1981: ap. A, annex 3, pp. 4-5).

More dramatically, under the high growth scenario these nine states would account for about 41 percent of the region's net growth in labor requirements, or 50 percent under the low growth scenario.

MENA DEPENDENCE ON NON-NATIONAL WORKERS

Of the net 1975-85 employment increase accounted for by the nine oil-endowed states, roughly one half is attributable to Algeria and Iraq. The relatively large populations of these two countries enable them to be generally self-sufficient in meeting their labor requirements. In contrast, the remaining seven states–hereafter referred to as the major labor importers–continue and in most cases increase their heavy reliance upon imported manpower. Table 6 clearly shows the different orders of dependence of the two subcategories of oil-endowed labor-importing countries. Algeria and Iraq together, with less than a one percent share of non-national employment in 1975, are projected to have imported only between 282,000 (low growth) and 512,000 (high growth) non-nationals by 1985, accounting for 3.4 or 5.7 percent respectively of their combined labor force. However, for the major labor importers as a group, the non-national share of employment rises from 44.0 percent in 1975 to 53.7 percent (low growth) or 56.8 percent (high growth) in 1985. Foreign labor-dependence is extreme for the UAE and Qatar, where non-nationals are projected to reach 90 percent and 86 percent of employment respectively. Only Kuwait and Oman are likely to reduce their relative dependence on foreign workers, although the absolute level of foreign labor is projected to increase.

FACTORS ACCOUNTING FOR LABOR IMPORTS

Several factors contribute to the oil-endowed states' current and projected reliance upon imported workers. First, the indigenous populations of the seven major labor-importing states are relatively small. Second, the labor-force participation rates are low due to the states' youthful population structures and low female labor-force participation. In principle, it is important to be precise about female labor-force participation in these countries. It is becoming increasingly clear that female labor-force participation is a nearly direct function of educational attainment–i.e., rates are very high for university

Table 6

LABOR-IMPORTING COUNTRIES: EMPLOYMENT OF NATIONALS AND NON-NATIONALS, 1975 AND 1985 (HIGH AND LOW GROWTH RATE SCENARIOS)
(Thousands)

	1975				1985							
					High Economic Growth Rate				Low Economic Growth Rate			
Country	Nationals	Non-Nationals	Total	Percent Non-Nationals	Nationals	Non-Nationals	Total	Percent Non-Nationals	Nationals	Non-Nationals	Total	Percent Non-Nationals
Major labor importers												
Bahrain	49.6	29.1	78.7	37.0%	69.5	81.4	150.9	53.9%	69.4	59.8	129.2	46.3%
Kuwait	86.9	210.6	297.5	70.8	140.4	273.4	413.8	66.1	140.4	252.4	392.8	64.3
Libya	454.1	280.4	734.5	38.2	695.1	719.3	1,414.4	50.9	676.2	583.8	1,260.0	46.3
Oman	88.9	103.2	192.1	53.7	149.8	107.0	256.8	41.7	151.1	105.7	256.8	41.2
Qatar	12.5	61.3	73.8	83.1	18.9	116.7	135.6	86.1	18.9	114.6	133.5	85.8
Saudi Arabia	1,300.0	668.4	1,968.4	34.0	1,565.2	1,679.9	3,245.1	51.8	1,565.2	1,489.6	3,054.8	48.8
UAE	44.6	247.8	292.4	84.7	61.6	570.7	632.3	90.3	61.6	508.0	569.6	89.2
Subtotal	2,036.6	1,600.8	3,637.4	44.0	2,700.5	3,548.4	6,248.9	56.8	2,682.8	3,113.9	5,796.7	53.7
Algeria	3,073.1	9.8	3,082.9	0.3	4,247.5	263.1	4,510.6	5.8	3,831.4	122.1	3,953.5	3.1
Iraq	3,007.6	0.0	3,007.6	0.0	4,253.2	248.4	4,501.6	5.5	4,097.9	159.7	4,257.6	3.8
Subtotal	6,080.7	9.8	6,090.5	0.2	8,500.7	511.5	9,012.2	5.7	7,929.3	281.8	8,211.1	3.4
Total	8,117.3	1,610.6	9,727.9	16.6	11,201.2	4,059.9	15,261.1	26.6	10,612.1	3,395.7	14,007.8	24.2

graduates, high for secondary school graduates, moderately high for those who did not finish secondary school, but very low for those with less or no education. Those in the last group are engaged primarily in traditional agriculture. Thus in most Gulf states, where agriculture is a minute sector, few females with little or no education are economically active. The somewhat higher labor-force participation rates in Algeria and Iraq are largely accounted for by their more sizable agricultural sectors, in which females (typically with little education) and youths traditionally work. Table 7 summarizes the contrasts in population, employment, and labor-force participation in the oil-endowed states when they are subdivided as City States (Bahrain, Kuwait, Qatar, and the UAE), Desert States (Libya, Oman, and Saudi Arabia), and Standard Developing Countries (Algeria and Iraq).* In the states with the smallest populations the reliance on imported labor is greatest, but because migrant workers often are not accompanied by nonworking dependents, the total labor-force participation rates are higher than in states with larger populations.

In addition to these essentially quantitative factors for reliance on imported workers, there is a qualitative factor—i.e., a mismatch between education/training and job requirements. Despite the enormous strides made in recent years in increasing the enrollments of nationals in the education/training systems in the oil-endowed states, the full impact of these efforts will not be felt in the labor market for some years to come. Table 8 will confirm that the projections for the education/training systems in the major labor-importing states should be a source of pride for these states, but, as Table 9 shows, the efforts will be inadequate to cope with the projected manpower requirements. For example, in Table 8 it can be seen that in 1976-80 about 46 percent of labor-importing countries' nationals entering the labor force would have neither enough education to be literate nor any special training, and that by 1981-85 only 26 percent would be so unqualified. At the other end of the spectrum, the share of labor-force entrants with a scientific-based university degree is projected to more than double—from 1.1 percent in 1976-80 to 2.4 percent in 1981-85. Nonetheless, these highly qualified nationals will be able to fill only 18 percent of the new professional and technical jobs that are projected to be created in the 1976-85 period.

*The concept and terminology for so dividing the oil-endowed states is borrowed from Halliday (1977). It proves to be a particularly suitable division for illustrating the population size and labor-force relationship, as shown in Table 7.

Table 7

LABOR-IMPORTING COUNTRIES: POPULATION, EMPLOYMENT, AND LABOR-FORCE PARTICIPATION RATES, 1975

	Population			Employment			Labor-Force Participation Rates (*Percent*)	
Category of Countries[a]	Total (*Thousands*)	Nationals (*Thousands*)	Percent National Shares	Total (*Thousands*)	Nationals (*Thousands*)	Percent National Shares	Total	Nationals
City States	2,022	934	46.2%	743	195	26.2%	36.7%	20.9%
Desert States	10,859	8,824	81.3	2,895	1,843	63.7	26.7	20.9
Standard Developing Countries	26,938	26,907	99.9	6,091	6,081	99.8	22.6	22.6

[a]Countries within each category are identified on the preceding page.

Table 8

EDUCATION/TRAINING FOR EMPLOYMENT BY OCCUPATIONAL CATEGORY IN MAJOR LABOR-IMPORTING COUNTRIES: PROJECTIONS FOR 1976-80 AND 1981-85

			Occupational Category[a]							
Country	Years	Qualified Personnel	Professional and Technical	Other Professional	Sub-Professional and Technical	Other Sub-Professional	Skilled Office and Manual	Semi-Skilled Office and Manual	Unskilled	Total
Bahrain	1976-80	Number	460	1,210	1,250	700	4,780	7,760	1,810	17,970
		Percent	2.5	6.7	7.0	3.9	26.6	43.2	10.1	100.0
	1981-85	Number	1,010	2,140	1,020	810	5,750	8,210	1,980	20,920
		Percent	4.8	10.2	4.8	3.9	27.5	39.3	9.5	100.0
Kuwait	1976-80	Number	1,060	3,290	680	3,590	6,170	15,540	6,460	36,790
		Percent	2.9	8.9	1.8	9.8	16.8	42.2	17.6	100.0
	1981-85	Number	2,870	3,860	900	5,460	9,640	19,000	7,400	49,130
		Percent	5.8	7.9	1.8	111.1	19.6	38.7	15.1	100.0
Libya	1976-80	Number	1,130	4,200	5,440	8,100	14,130	82,790	22,540	138,340
		Percent	0.8	3.0	3.9	5.9	10.2	59.9	16.3	100.0
	1981-85	Number	1,680	2,950	15,810	27,120	27,630	135,720	16,430	228,340
		Percent	0.7	1.3	7.4	11.9	12.1	59.4	7.2	100.0
Oman	1976-80	Number	200	470	50	30	3,720	9,060	17,210	30,740
		Percent	0.6	1.5	0.2	0.1	12.1	29.5	56.0	100.0
	1981-85	Number	400	750	450	50	7,950	19,110	9,330	38,040
		Percent	1.1	2.0	1.2	0.1	20.9	50.2	.24.5	100.0
Qatar	1976-80	Number	430	890	170	300	750	1,500	1,300	5,340
		Percent	8.1	16.7	3.2	5.6	14.0	28.1	24.3	100.0
	1981-85	Number	550	790	180	240	1,270	1,660	1,360	6,050
		Percent	9.1	13.1	3.0	5.0	20.9	27.4	22.5	100.0
Saudi Arabia	1976-80	Number	3,110	10,510	3,550	20,980	23,410	59,220	209,920	330,700
		Percent	0.9	3.2	1.1	6.3	7.1	17.9	63.5	100.0
	1981-85	Number	11,510	21,570	9,320	48,820	50,270	102,690	162,290	406,470
		Percent	2.8	5.3	2.3	12.0	12.4	25.3	39.9	100.0
UAE	1976-80	Number	70	500	270	190	1,010	7,100	3,530	12,630
		Percent	0.6	3.9	2.1	1.5	8.0	56.0	27.9	100.0
	1981-85	Number	220	580	230	70	1,590	11,050	2,490	16,230
		Percent	1.4	3.6	1.4	0.4	9.8	68.1	15.3	100.0
Total	1976-80	Number	6,460	21,070	11,410	33,900	53,970	182,970	262,770	572,550
		Percent	1.1	3.6	2.0	5.9	9.4	32.0	45.9	100.0
	1981-85	Number	18,240	32,660	28,910	82,570	104,100	297,440	201,280	765,180
		Percent	2.4	4.2	3.8	10.8	13.6	38.9	26.3	100.0

[a]The categories are defined and described in Table 5.

Table 9

PROJECTED NET GROWTH IN MANPOWER REQUIREMENTS AND NATIONAL LABOR-FORCE ENTRANTS FOR MAJOR LABOR-IMPORTING COUNTRIES, 1976-85

	Net Growth in Manpower Requirements		National Labor-Force Entrants		
Occupational Category[a]	Number (*Thousands*)	Percent	Number (*Thousands*)	Percent	Supply of Nationals as Percent of Requirements
Professional and technical	136.7	5.2%	24.7	1.9%	18.1%
Other professional	197.0	7.6	53.7	4.0	27.3
Sub-professional and technical	151.8	5.8	40.3	3.0	26.5
Other sub-professional	234.8	9.0	116.5	8.7	49.6
Skilled office and manual	446.4	17.1	158.1	11.8	35.4
Semi-skilled office and manual	676.3	25.9	480.4	35.9	71.0
Unskilled	768.8	29.4	464.0	34.7	60.4
Total	2,611.8	100.0	1,337.7	100.0	51.2

[a]The categories are defined and described in Table 5.

A fourth factor is also at play—i.e., the attitudinal and motivation nexus regarding work in the oil-endowed countries. There is a wide variety of views on this issue among Middle East observers, ranging from prejudice through bias to academic conclusions. One extreme view is that nationals of the oil states do not and will not do manual work. Small employers and vocational training center administrators often have formed this view based on their practical experience. This view is also on occasion advanced by commentators who look to the nomadic tradition and make an analogy between the role of the Sulubba* and the skilled and semi-skilled craftsmen of today's modern sector economic activity. The statistical evidence from sector/occupation matrixes of population censuses and employment surveys confirms that oil state nationals have to a very great extent avoided manual jobs in construction and manufacturing (see Table 10). Another extreme view is that oil state nationals will do any job if the financial and career incentives are right, the opportunities appropriately broadcast, and certain sociological realities reckoned with (e.g., winning the influence of the father, uncle, and community in persuading a son of the appropriateness of a particular type of employment). The hardest evidence available in support of this view is the success of the oil companies, the airlines, and the major (usually parastatal) industrial concerns in recruiting nationals of the oil states. These employers are among the most prestigious in their countries because of their size, stability, "modernity," and importance in the efforts to diversify the economy. They have high wage structures and career development systems, often including opportunities for travel and training abroad. Consequently they have attracted nationals for all types of jobs—including the blue-collar occupations which nationals so shun in most private-sector establishments.

The occupational avoidance-preference issue of oil state nationals is not really of great relevance to our projections for migration size or composition. The quantitative labor needs of oil states are so severe that their nationals need not choose between "unattractive" jobs and unemployment. In part, they have not had to make a choice because government employment has been an attractive and de facto guaranteed opportunity. Should governments eliminate the "guaranteed employment" components of their public-sector payrolls, this issue would become of prime importance.

CHANGING OCCUPATIONAL REQUIREMENTS FOR NON-NATIONALS

Because of the quantitative and qualitative factors discussed above, the oil-endowed states will require between 3.4 and 4.1 million non-national workers by 1985; 3.1 to 3.5 million will be needed in the seven major labor-importing countries (see Table 6). This represents

*Although the camel-herding nomads depended upon the Sulubba tribe for virtually all tinkering services, the Sulubba were looked down upon by the "true nomads" and social segregation was the norm.

Table 10

NON-NATIONALS' SHARE OF EMPLOYMENT IN MAJOR LABOR IMPORTING COUNTRIES BY ECONOMIC SECTOR AND OCCUPATIONAL CATEGORY, 1975 AND 1985
(HIGH GROWTH RATE SCENARIO)
(Percent)

Occupational Category[a]	Economic Sector																	
	Agriculture		Mining and Quarrying		Manufacturing		Utilities		Construction		Trade and Finance		Transport and Communications		Services		Total	
	1975	1985	1975	1985	1975	1985	1975	1985	1975	1985	1975	1985	1975	1985	1975	1985	1975	1985
Professional and technical	56.3%	74.6%	79.6%	83.2%	89.5%	84.3%	80.7%	79.5%	93.3%	91.4%	62.4%	78.8%	79.8%	82.7%	75.5%	81.2%	80.6%	83.2%
Other professional	30.7	61.7	74.0	77.2	80.4	80.1	51.3	71.8	85.3	86.5	57.5	70.6	60.6	72.4	66.7	73.5	66.7	74.6
Sub-professional and technical	51.2	75.9	79.2	80.5	80.1	76.3	88.6	82.8	88.8	83.2	78.5	80.6	69.3	78.1	76.4	75.4	79.7	78.4
Other sub-professional	15.5	45.5	47.1	71.4	80.5	65.5	57.8	66.3	74.2	67.5	61.8	67.0	58.9	60.6	44.7	50.8	50.1	56.3
Skilled office and manual	77.4	70.5	51.4	64.3	73.5	70.3	58.3	67.3	74.1	74.4	64.7	71.4	59.7	67.8	51.2	67.1	62.8	70.3
Semi-skilled office and manual	30.2	42.3	16.0	37.4	61.1	39.9	35.7	43.1	79.9	55.3	52.9	54.8	43.7	51.7	33.5	46.0	47.4	48.3
Unskilled	6.1	36.9	30.2	50.5	63.4	71.5	37.4	56.4	73.0	69.9	52.4	49.6	44.3	50.4	43.6	55.5	35.2	51.2
Total	9.2	38.5	36.8	54.8	66.8	61.3	46.2	58.9	73.6	69.7	57.5	62.5	48.9	58.3	45.7	36.7	44.0	56.8

[a]The categories are defined and described in Table 5.

a projected increase during the 1975-85 period of 1.5-1.9 million non-national workers in these seven states. Although the majority of migrant workers will continue to be employed in unskilled and semi-skilled jobs, the need for non-nationals to fill professional, sub-professional, and skilled jobs is growing considerably faster than for unskilled and semi-skilled occupations (see Table 11). Table 12 provides details on the projected degree of reliance upon non-nationals by occupational category in each of the seven major labor importers.

NATIONALITY COMPOSITION OF MIGRANT WORKERS

Until the economic boom of the mid-1970s (induced by the rise in oil prices) the overwhelming majority of non-national workers in the oil-endowed states had been drawn from other Arab countries. In 1975 the ethnic composition of migrants was as follows: Arabs—65 percent; Iranians—4 percent; Indian subcontinent nationals—22 percent; Southeast Asians—a little over one percent; the remaining 8 percent mainly from Europe, Africa, and North America. By 1985 it is projected that Arabs will account for about one half of the migrant workers and the Iranian share will decline to 2-3 percent. The shares for the Indian subcontinent will remain relatively stable. Migrants from Southeast Asia are projected to grow most quickly (34 percent per annum) and will account for about 10 percent of the migrants by 1985. Table 13 provides details of the projected evolution of nationality composition of migrants to the oil-endowed countries.

EXTENT OF LABOR-EXPORTING COUNTRIES' WORKERS ABROAD

Even though a decline is projected in the share of Arab migrants among total non-national workers in the major labor-importing countries, their absolute number will increase significantly. More important for almost all of the major Arab labor-exporting countries, by 1985 a higher portion of the total national workforces (i.e., nationals employed at home and abroad) will be employed in oil-endowed Arab states. Table 14 shows the wide variations in numbers of migrant workers among the major Arab labor-exporting countries. Jordan in 1975 had already exported 40 percent of its total national workforce, and roughly that share will continue to work abroad. Similarly, the YAR is projected to continue to export about one quarter of its total

Table 11

MAJOR LABOR-IMPORTING COUNTRIES: EMPLOYMENT OF NATIONALS AND NON-NATIONALS BY OCCUPATIONAL CATEGORY, 1975 AND 1985 (HIGH AND LOW GROWTH RATE SCENARIOS)

	1975			1985									
				High Economic Growth Rate					Low Economic Growth Rate				
Occupational Category[a]	Total Employment *(Thousands)*	Percentages per Category	Percent Shares	Total Employment *(Thousands)*	Percentages per Category	Percent Shares	Increase 1975-85 *(Thousands)*	Annual Increase *(Percent)*	Total Employment *(Thousands)*	Percentages per Category	Percent Shares	Increase 1975-85 *(Thousands)*	Annual Increase *(Percent)*
Professional and technical													
Nationals	10.5	19.4%	0.5%	32.1	16.8%	1.2%	21.6	11.8%	32.1	17.8%	1.2%	21.6	11.8%
Non-nationals	43.5	80.6	2.7	158.7	83.2	4.5	115.2	13.8	148.1	82.2	4.8	104.6	13.0
Other professional													
Nationals	47.6	33.3	2.3	86.5	25.4	3.2	38.9	6.1	86.6	27.0	3.2	39.0	6.1
Non-nationals	95.4	66.7	6.0	253.6	74.6	7.1	158.2	10.3	234.5	73.0	7.5	139.1	9.4
Sub-professional and technical													
Nationals	13.8	20.3	0.7	47.6	21.5	1.8	33.8	13.2	47.6	22.5	1.8	33.8	13.2
Non-nationals	54.3	79.7	3.4	173.6	78.5	4.9	119.3	12.3	163.6	77.5	5.3	109.3	11.7
Other sub-professional													
Nationals	66.3	49.9	3.3	161.1	43.7	5.9	94.8	9.3	161.1	45.7	6.0	94.8	9.3
Non-nationals	66.6	50.1	4.1	207.7	56.3	5.9	141.1	12.0	191.1	54.3	6.1	124.5	11.1
Skilled office and manual													
Nationals	161.2	37.2	7.9	262.1	29.8	9.7	100.9	5.0	262.1	31.4	9.8	100.9	5.0
Non-nationals	271.9	62.8	17.0	618.6	70.2	17.4	346.7	8.6	573.1	68.6	18.4	301.2	7.7
Semi-skilled office and manual													
Nationals	347.2	52.6	17.0	691.4	51.7	25.6	344.2	7.1	672.5	53.6	25.1	325.3	7.1
Non-nationals	313.3	47.4	19.6	645.5	48.3	18.2	332.2	7.5	583.2	46.4	18.7	269.9	6.4
Unskilled													
Nationals	1,390.0	64.8	68.3	1,419.7	48.8	52.6	29.7	0.2	1,420.5	53.8	52.9	30.5	0.2
Non-nationals	755.9	35.2	47.2	1,490.5	51.2	42.0	734.6	7.0	1,220.4	46.2	39.2	464.5	4.9
Total													
Nationals	2,036.6	56.0	100.0	2,700.5	43.2	100.0	663.9	2.9	2,682.5	46.3	100.0	645.9	2.8
Non-nationals	1,600.9	44.0	100.0	3,548.2	56.8	100.0	1,947.3	8.3	3,114.0	53.7	100.0	1,513.1	6.9

[a]The categories are defined and described in Table 5.

Table 12

NON-NATIONALS' SHARE OF EMPLOYMENT IN MAJOR LABOR-IMPORTING COUNTRIES BY OCCUPATIONAL CATEGORY, 1975 AND 1985
(HIGH GROWTH RATE SCENARIO)
(Percent)

Country	Occupational Category[a]															
	Professional and Technical		Other Professional		Sub-Professional and Technical		Other Sub-Professional		Skilled Office and Manual		Semi-Skilled Office and Manual		Unskilled		Total	
	1975	1985	1975	1985	1975	1985	1975	1985	1975	1985	1975	1985	1975	1985	1975	1985
Bahrain	84.4%	62.2%	38.7%	54.9%	51.8%	51.9%	38.4%	82.5%	33.2%	57.2%	40.0%	37.4%	38.5%	57.7%	37.0%	53.9%
Kuwait	89.9	66.7	66.5	69.8	83.0	85.5	55.5	61.6	71.5	75.1	68.8	41.4	77.1	67.3	70.8	66.1
Libya	71.3	90.2	55.7	78.0	58.5	53.4	25.8	45.8	38.1	57.2	43.2	20.1	35.6	60.2	38.2	50.9
Oman	68.1	82.1	59.6	69.8	85.3	92.0	77.2	92.7	87.5	72.3	83.5	47.4	29.6	14.5	53.7	41.7
Qatar	92.3	84.5	84.7	84.3	89.0	93.1	82.4	88.1	67.6	84.8	75.4	31.0	88.2	89.0	83.1	86.1
Saudi Arabia	70.0	74.1	61.3	65.3	75.3	80.5	48.8	44.8	68.0	69.4	35.2	55.0	26.9	44.7	34.0	51.8
UAE	95.1	97.9	86.4	94.3	91.5	96.5	74.6	94.9	76.7	91.3	77.0	80.5	88.4	90.9	84.7	90.3
Total	80.6	83.2	66.7	74.6	79.7	78.5	50.1	56.3	62.8	70.2	47.4	48.3	35.2	51.2	44.0	56.8

[a] The categories are defined and described in Table 5.

Table 13

MIGRANT WORKERS IN OIL-ENDOWED COUNTRIES BY NATIONALITY, 1975 AND 1985 (HIGH AND LOW GROWTH RATE SCENARIOS)

	1975		1985							
			High Economic Growth Rate				Low Economic Growth Rate			
Nationality	Number (*Thousands*)	Percent Shares	Number (*Thousands*)	Percent Shares	Percent Increase	Percent Share of Total Change	Number (*Thousands*)	Percent Shares	Percent Increase	Percent Share of Total Change
Arab										
Egyptian	353.7	22.0%	761.7	18.8%	8.0%	16.7%	616.9	18.2%	5.7%	14.7%
Iraqi	18.7	1.2	12.4	0.3	-4.0	-0.3	11.6	0.3	-4.7	-0.4
Jordanian	139.0	8.6	263.4	6.5	6.6	5.1	267.0	7.9	6.7	7.2
Lebanese	28.5	1.8	86.1	2.1	11.7	2.4	71.7	2.1	9.7	2.4
Moroccan	2.2	0.1	12.5	0.3	19.0	0.4	9.8	0.3	16.1	0.4
Omani	30.8	1.9	46.0	1.1	4.1	0.6	44.6	1.3	3.8	0.8
Sudanese	26.0	1.6	88.1	2.2	13.0	2.5	80.0	2.4	11.9	3.0
Syrian	38.1	2.4	113.0	2.8	11.5	3.1	91.8	2.7	9.2	3.0
Tunisian	29.8	1.8	94.0	2.3	12.2	2.6	62.2	1.8	7.6	1.8
Yemeni (YAR)	328.5	20.4	400.8	9.9	2.0	3.0	381.0	11.2	1.5	2.9
Yemeni (PDRY)	45.8	2.8	84.7	2.1	6.3	1.6	80.9	2.4	5.9	2.0
Subtotal	1,041.1	64.7	1,962.7	48.4	6.5	37.7	1,717.5	50.6	5.1	37.8
Iranian	70.0	4.3	115.6	2.8	5.1	1.9	98.1	2.9	3.4	1.6
South Asian										
Indian	141.9	8.8	364.4	9.0	10.0	9.1	291.2	8.6	7.5	8.4
Pakistani	205.7	12.8	555.1	13.7	10.4	14.3	446.0	13.1	8.0	13.5
Subtotal	347.6	21.6	914.5	22.7	10.2	23.4	737.2	21.7	7.8	21.9
Southeast Asian	20.5	1.3	383.9	9.5	34.0	14.8	369.9	10.9	33.5	19.6
Other	130.8	8.2	677.9	16.6	17.9	22.2	472.8	13.9	13.7	91.1
Total	1,610.0	100.0	4,059.6	100.0	9.7	100.0	3,395.5	100.0	7.7	100.0

Table 14

ARAB LABOR-EXPORTING COUNTRIES: DOMESTIC EMPLOYMENT OF NATIONALS AND NATIONALS EMPLOYED IN MAJOR LABOR-IMPORTING COUNTRIES, 1975 AND 1985 (HIGH AND LOW GROWTH RATE SCENARIOS)

Exporting Country	1975				1985							
					High Economic Growth Rate				Low Economic Growth Rate			
	Domestic Employment of Nationals[a] (*Thousands*)	Employment Abroad (*Thousands*)	Percent of Workforce Abroad	Percent Share of Arabs Abroad[b]	Domestic Employment of Nationals[a] (*Thousands*)	Employment Abroad (*Thousands*)	Percent of Workforce Abroad	Percent Share of Arabs Abroad[b]	Domestic Employment of Nationals[a] (*Thousands*)	Employment Abroad (*Thousands*)	Percent of Workforce Abroad	Percent Share of Arabs Abroad[b]
Egypt	9,070	353	3.7%	34.6%	12,127	712	5.5%	39.2%	11,154	616.9	5.2%	36.4%
Jordan	207	139	40.2	13.6	413	237	38.3	14.1	385	267.0	41.0	15.7
Lebanon	522	28	5.0	2.9	587	70	10.6	3.8	587	71.7	10.9	4.2
Oman	89	31	25.8	3.0	150	46	23.4	2.5	151	44.6	22.8	2.6
Sudan	3,674	26	0.7	2.6	3,704	88	2.2	4.8	3,361	79.9	2.3	4.7
Syria	1,741	38	2.1	3.7	2,311	96	4.0	5.3	1,936	91.8	4.5	5.4
Tunisia	1,599	29	1.8	2.8	2,122	63	2.9	3.5	1,914	62.2	3.1	3.7
YAR	1,033	329	24.1	32.3	1,155	401	25.8	22.1	1,087	381.0	25.9	22.5
PDRY	311	46	12.9	4.5	439	85	16.2	4.7	354	80.9	18.6	4.8
Total	18,246	1,019	5.3	100.0	23,008	1,818	7.9	100.0	20,928	1,696.0	7.5	100.0

[a]Excludes labor surpluses at home.

[b]Excludes Iraqis, Mauritanians, and Somalis.

national labor force. The numbers of nationals working abroad are projected to double for Egypt and triple for Sudan, but the shares of their total national workforces employed abroad will remain rather small–i.e., about 5 percent and 2 percent respectively.

Because of the occupational selectivity of the labor migration process, the aggregate figures just cited only begin to portray the significance of the projected increases in out-migration from the major Arab labor-exporting countries. For example, only 0.7 percent of Sudan's total national workforce was working abroad in 1975 (Table 14). Yet this minute share included some 44 percent of Sudan's professional-technical personnel. By 1985 the share of Sudanese working abroad in the MENA region in that occupational category is projected to be 67 percent. In Jordan's case some two thirds to three fourths of professional-technical and other professionals were employed abroad in 1975, and these figures are projected to continue through 1985. Although only about 4 percent of Egypt's total national workforce was employed abroad in 1975, 21 percent of Egyptian workers in the construction sector were employed abroad. It is such severely high losses of manpower in key occupational categories that have most alarmed officials of labor-exporting countries. Tables 15 and 16 provide further details on the occupational and sectoral composition of employment at home and abroad for the major Arab labor-exporting countries.

Earlier it was rather naively assumed and glibly asserted that international labor migration was particularly beneficial to labor-exporting countries because it provided at least a temporary outlet for the unemployed of these generally labor surplus economies. The experience of recent years has shown that not all migrants were either unemployed or of low marginal value to their domestic economies. Even migrants with little formal education or training tend to have some on-the-job experience. In some cases, workers have left domestic economies already short of adequately educated or trained manpower. Table 17 illustrates the range of domestic shortfalls and surpluses that may be expected in the major Arab labor-exporting countries by the various occupational categories under the high growth scenario. For example, by 1985 Egypt is projected to export 352,000 unskilled workers, but it will still have a surplus of nearly two million such workers. Jordan is projected to export 48,000 workers in this category and experience a shortfall of about 31,000. Were it not for the migration of Jordanian unskilled workers, the shortage would not be likely to occur. Oman is projected to export nearly 6,000 skilled office and manual workers and suffer a deficit of nearly 30,000 workers in that category. This is an example in which labor migration aggravates a domestic manpower shortage but is not its sole cause. In the Jordanian and Omani cases the labor shortages will be filled by "replacement migrants." This phenomenon is of particular importance in Jordan, Oman, and the YAR, where replacement migrants will come chiefly from Egypt, Syria, India, and Pakistan.

The recent experience in Jordan is a good illustration of the volatility of international labor migration in the MENA region (and of the hazards of attempting migration projections). Jordanian data show that there were especially heavy population outflows of nationals in 1976 (83,000) and 1977 (104,000). Then net returns of Jordanians to the East Bank amounted to a few thousand in 1978, about 17,000 in 1979, and fell to around 1,000 in 1980. Prompted by concern that domestic development would be impeded by labor shortages, Jordan in the mid-1970s opened its labor market to all Arab nationals (with no work permits required in advance of entry) and to non-Arabs (with valid work permits required in advance of entry). The number of work permits issued to non-Jordanians has grown rapidly: about 19,000 in 1978, over 26,000 in 1979, nearly 80,000 in 1980, and over 53,000 in the first half of 1981. With indications of net return migration of Jordanians and rising unemployment rates among Jordanians, the open labor market policy may be in for serious review.

MIGRANT POPULATIONS IN LABOR-IMPORTING COUNTRIES

In 1975 the 1.6 million migrant workers in the seven major labor-importing countries were accompanied by 1.5 million dependents. By 1985 the migrant workers required by these countries (3.1-3.5 million) will be accompanied by as many as 6.5-7.4 million dependents. These projections of dependents are based upon assumptions of declining crude economic activity (labor-force participation) rates for the various non-national populations (see Table 18). The expected decline in crude activity rates is in line with experience in the region (as well as elsewhere in the world). Typically a male migrant arrives to take up work in a host country; after settling into the job and securing housing, he brings other members of the family. The pace of settlement of the migrants may vary from one host country to another, and there are distinct differences among the

Table 15

ARAB LABOR-EXPORTING COUNTRIES: DOMESTIC WORKFORCE AND FRACTION OF TOTAL NATIONAL WORKFORCE EXPORTED TO MENA IMPORTERS BY OCCUPATIONAL CATEGORY, 1975 AND 1985 (HIGH GROWTH RATE SCENARIO)

		Occupational Category[a]							
		Professional and Technical		Other Professional		Sub-Professional and Technical		Other Sub-Professional	
Exporting Country	Year	Domestic Workforce *(Thousands)*	Percent Exported[b]	Domestic Workforce *(Thousands)*	Percent Exported	Domestic Workforce *(Thousands)*	Percent Exported	Domestic Workforce *(Thousands)*	Percent Exported
Egypt	1975	168.7	5.2%	267.5	9.6%	228.7	3.6%	255.0	7.2%
	1985	295.8	10.1	498.2	13.3	388.7	6.6	398.3	14.3
Jordan	1975	1.8	79.0	11.8	65.0	7.4	65.0	22.6	52.7
	1985	9.0	74.7	31.6	62.6	25.5	53.5	54.0	26.7
Lebanon	1975	8.3	34.6	45.0	10.0	29.0	9.0	64.8	7.9
	1985	14.0	50.5	49.3	21.6	37.9	20.9	77.5	20.2
Oman	1975	0.8	20.0	1.0	14.1	1.4	10.5	1.1	34.0
	1985	1.0	28.6	1.9	17.4	1.4	22.2	0.7	56.2
Sudan	1975	3.3	44.1	29.9	9.5	32.6	5.2	92.8	3.4
	1985	3.6	67.2	37.7	21.1	33.9	13.1	76.8	12.1
Syria	1975	16.1	12.1	25.7	21.0	11.2	15.1	35.2	12.3
	1985	56.9	12.2	71.7	23.3	54.7	10.8	58.7	20.3
Tunisia	1975	9.0	4.1	17.3	2.0	46.7	0.5	58.7	1.6
	1985	20.0	27.3	27.0	22.2	84.0	8.7	52.3	18.1
YAR	1975	0.3	31.7	2.1	22.3	1.1	14.8	9.6	7.6
	1985	1.9	13.6	9.9	13.1	2.0	20.0	9.9	16.1
PDRY	1975	0.6	40.0	4.6	9.2	1.1	25.8	15.7	6.0
	1985	1.4	46.1	5.1	17.7	2.7	25.0	18.3	11.2
Total	1975	208.9	12.7	404.9	15.1	359.2	7.5	555.5	8.7
	1985	403.6	19.7	732.4	20.2	630.8	12.3	746.5	18.8

Table 15 (cont.)

Exporting Country	Year	Skilled Office and Manual: Domestic Workforce (*Thousands*)	Skilled Office and Manual: Percent Exported[b]	Semi-Skilled Office and Manual: Domestic Workforce (*Thousands*)	Semi-Skilled Office and Manual: Percent Exported	Unskilled: Domestic Workforce (*Thousands*)	Unskilled: Percent Exported	Total: Domestic Workforce (*Thousands*)	Total: Percent Exported
		Occupational Category[a]							
Egypt	1975	1,357.8	2.5%	1,781.3	3.4%	5,011.2	3.8%	9,070.2	3.8%
	1985	1,471.2	0.5	2,985.1	10.5	6,089.1	5.4	12,126.4	5.9
Jordan	1975	20.2	52.0	60.9	12.7	81.9	33.3	206.6	40.3
	1985	46.6	50.0	96.1	6.8	150.5	24.3	413.3	38.9
Lebanon	1975	56.5	9.1	100.2	2.6	217.8	1.0	521.6	5.2
	1985	72.4	16.4	117.6	14.8	217.9	4.9	586.6	12.8
Oman	1975	3.6	49.1	6.2	53.4	74.7	20.4	88.8	25.8
	1985	11.4	74.7	28.1	33.6	105.3	16.3	149.8	23.5
Sudan	1975	102.0	2.7	187.2	2.2	3,226.3	0.3	3,674.1	0.7
	1985	162.6	4.6	291.4	6.1	3,098.0	0.6	3,704.0	2.3
Syria	1975	128.4	5.1	470.4	1.3	1,054.0	2.2	1,741.0	3.0
	1985	193.3	3.7	690.0	3.7	1,186.0	2.2	2,311.3	4.7
Tunisia	1975	94.8	6.3	306.7	3.6	1,065.7	1.0	1,598.9	1.9
	1985	174.5	8.4	516.0	3.2	1,248.1	1.4	2,121.9	4.2
YAR	1975	10.2	68.1	10.9	65.0	998.5	22.2	1,032.7	24.1
	1985	8.2	90.9	41.3	86.5	1,081.6	19.7	1,154.8	25.8
PDRY	1975	6.3	77.9	9.6	65.0	272.9	4.8	310.8	14.5
	1985	8.1	91.0	51.6	11.6	352.2	1.9	439.4	16.1
Total	1975	1,779.8	7.1	2,933.4	6.0	12,003.0	4.3	18,244.7	5.4
	1985	2,148.3	12.6	4,817.2	6.1	13,528.7	5.3	23,007.5	7.7

[a]The categories are defined and described in Table 5.

[b]"Percent exported" of total national workforce (domestic plus exported). The workers exported are to all MENA countries—i.e., all nine labor-importing oil-endowed states—*and* there is some "replacement migration," such as Egyptians working in Jordan to replace Jordanians working in Saudi Arabia.

Table 16

ARAB LABOR-EXPORTING COUNTRIES: DOMESTIC WORKFORCE AND FRACTION OF TOTAL NATIONAL WORKFORCE EXPORTED TO MENA IMPORTERS BY ECONOMIC SECTOR, 1975 AND 1985 (HIGH GROWTH RATE SCENARIO)

		Economic Sector									
		Agriculture		Mining and Quarrying		Manufacturing		Utilities		Construction	
Exporting Country	Year	Domestic Workforce *(Thousands)*	Percent Exported[a]	Domestic Workforce *(Thousands)*	Percent Exported	Domestic Workforce *(Thousands)*	Percent Exported	Domestic Workforce *(Thousands)*	Percent Exported	Domestic Workforce *(Thousands)*	Percent Exported
Egypt	1975	4,173.5	2.0%	36.0	14.3%	1,114.1	1.7%	17.1	9.6%	353.4	21.0%
	1985	4,677.0	2.3	50.8	18.7	1,672.7	22.0	65.4	14.8	541.6	32.3
Jordan	1975	41.8	31.0	3.0	10.4	16.0	15.4	1.1	49.6	18.1	20.6
	1985	89.8	18.0	4.4	56.4	24.1	34.1	2.4	78.0	39.2	5.2
Lebanon	1975	103.5	0.4	17.2	2.4	77.3	3.1	4.9	10.7	31.1	12.9
	1985	126.3	3.0	18.0	9.0	86.4	6.8	5.3	32.0	43.9	26.2
Oman	1975	69.5	14.2	2.4	12.1	0.3	60.4	0.1	55.2	9.0	49.1
	1985	77.8	8.4	2.0	23.1	21.6	8.5	3.8	19.1	21.7	15.9
Sudan	1975	2,603.7	–	23.1	1.7	135.1	0.9	39.8	0.9	79.2	9.0
	1985	2,378.6	0.5	29.8	4.5	156.2	2.5	41.1	3.3	117.6	11.5
Syria	1975	900.0	1.8	11.2	5.0	207.7	1.4	8.9	6.9	120.6	7.0
	1985	1,120.6	1.2	24.2	8.0	261.4	2.6	11.0	23.6	216.3	6.0
Tunisia	1975	722.0	0.3	18.3	3.9	267.2	0.8	12.0	5.8	140.0	10.3
	1985	727.2	1.3	22.2	5.9	389.4	2.2	16.5	7.3	275.8	7.1
YAR	1975	900.5	12.0	1.5	9.7	25.4	31.7	0.5	58.3	16.0	65.1
	1985	820.8	16.4	2.9	6.4	41.3	28.2	1.6	74.6	82.2	32.2
PDRY	1975	169.7	0.3	0.6	92.2	14.6	16.3	3.4	42.9	18.3	15.2
	1985	205.0	3.0	1.0	60.0	29.0	11.3	4.9	32.9	36.0	19.1
Total	1975	9,645.2	3.1	113.3	6.9	1,857.7	2.3	107.8	8.4	785.7	17.1
	1985	10,223.1	0.3	155.3	16.8	2,682.1	8.4	152.0	19.4	1,374.3	18.0

Table 16 (cont.)

		Economic Sector							
		Trade and Finance		Transport and Communications		Services		Total	
Exporting Country	Year	Domestic Workforce (*Thousands*)	Percent Exported	Domestic Workforce (*Thousands*)	Percent Exported	Domestic Workforce (*Thousands*)	Percent Exported	Domestic Workforce (*Thousands*)	Percent Exported
Egypt	1975	941.1	2.7%	375.4	7.1%	2,078.7	4.7%	9,070.3	3.8%
	1985	1,466.2	5.1	666.6	6.3	2,986.4	9.1	12,126.7	5.9
Jordan	1975	10.4	56.7	8.0	42.5	108.3	45.9	206.7	40.3
	1985	23.7	60.6	17.1	50.0	212.5	38.6	413.2	38.9
Lebanon	1975	107.4	4.3	37.3	4.5	142.9	8.5	521.6	5.2
	1985	114.0	10.2	39.5	71.0	153.4	19.8	586.8	12.8
Oman	1975	0.5	65.0	0.9	58.8	6.1	55.1	88.8	25.8
	1985	1.2	88.9	1.8	69.4	19.7	47.2	149.6	29.5
Sudan	1975	217.0	1.4	146.6	1.2	429.7	2.3	3,674.2	0.7
	1985	289.4	4.3	194.2	4.7	497.0	5.9	3,703.9	2.3
Syria	1975	192.2	3.6	75.8	3.2	224.5	5.8	1,740.9	3.0
	1985	262.0	6.5	101.7	7.4	313.8	13.0	2,311.0	4.7
Tunisia	1975	99.0	1.7	53.0	4.2	287.3	2.1	1,598.8	1.9
	1985	165.2	5.6	74.1	5.5	451.1	8.0	2,121.5	4.2
YAR	1975	33.0	55.4	14.7	42.8	41.2	58.9	1,032.8	24.1
	1985	53.1	44.0	31.0	53.0	122.1	44.3	1,155.0	25.8
PDRY	1975	17.8	41.0	10.3	46.4	76.1	22.7	310.8	14.5
	1985	27.3	44.0	20.8	18.6	115.2	19.2	439.2	16.1
Total	1975	1,618.4	6.3	722.0	7.9	3,394.8	8.6	18,244.9	5.4
	1985	2,402.1	9.2	1,146.8	10.8	4,871.2	13.1	23,006.9	7.7

[a]"Percent exported" is of total national workforce (domestic plus exported). The workers exported are to all MENA countries—i.e., all nine labor-importing oil-endowed states—*and* there is some "replacement migration," such as Egyptians working in Jordan to replace Jordanians working in Saudi Arabia.

Table 17

ARAB LABOR-EXPORTING COUNTRIES: TOTAL NATIONAL WORKFORCE, WORKERS EXPORTED, AND DOMESTIC SHORTFALLS AND SURPLUSES BY OCCUPATIONAL CATEGORY, 1985 (HIGH GROWTH RATE SCENARIO)

Exporting Country	Occupational Category[a]: Professional and Technical		Other Professional		Sub-Professional and Technical		Other Sub-Professional		Skilled Office and Manual		Semi-Skilled Office and Manual		Unskilled		Total	
	Number *(Thousands)*	Percent	Number *(Thousands)*	Percent	Number *(Thousands)*	Percent	Number *(Thousands)*	Percent	Number *(Thousands)*	Percent	Number *(Thousands)*	Percent	Number *(Thousands)*	Percent	Number *(Thousands)*	Percent
Egypt																
Total national workforce	329.2		574.5		416.4		464.8		1,588.2		3,073.5		6,441.3		12,887.9	
Workers exported	33.4	10.1%	76.3	13.3%	27.7	6.6%	66.5	14.3%	117.0	7.4%	88.4	2.9%	352.2	5.5%	761.5	5.9%
Shortfall	0	0.0	0	0.0	0	0.0	57.9	12.5	820.9	51.7	0	0.0	0	0.0	878.8	6.8
Surplus	53.0	16.1	1.7	0.3	298.7	71.7	0	0.0	0	0.0	1,291.4	42.0	1,982.9	30.8	3,627.7	28.1
Jordan																
Total national workforce	35.7		84.5		54.8		98.1		87.2		117.6		198.6		676.5	
Workers exported	26.7	74.8	52.9	62.6	29.3	53.5	44.1	44.9	40.6	46.6	21.5	18.3	48.3	24.3	263.4	38.9
Shortfall	5.8	16.2	18.4	21.8	11.2	20.4	20.5	20.9	17.3	19.8	7.0	5.9	30.6	15.4	110.8	16.4
Surplus	0	0.0	0	0.0	0	0.0	0	0.0	0	0.0	0	0.0	0	0.0	0	0.0
Lebanon																
Total national workforce	28.3		62.9		47.9		97.2		84.5		122.6		229.2		672.6	
Workers exported	14.3	50.5	13.6	21.6	10.0	20.9	19.7	5.1	12.1	14.3	5.0	4.1	11.3	4.9	86.0	12.8
Shortfall	4.4	15.5	8.0	12.7	0	0.0	0	0.0	0	0.0	0	0	0	0.0	12.4	1.8
Surplus	0	0.0	0	0.0	1.4	2.9	0.4	0.0	8.3	12.0	69.5	56.7	32.5	14.2	112.1	16.7
Oman																
Total national workforce	1.4		2.3		1.8		1.6		17.2		45.7		125.8		195.8	2
Workers exported	0.4	28.6	0.4	17.4	0.4	22.2	0.9	56.2	5.8	33.7	17.6	38.5	20.5	16.3	46.0	23.5
Shortfall	4.6	328.5	4.4	191.3	16.1	6.2	8.9	556.2	29.8	173.3	25.3	55.4	17.9	14.2	107.0	54.6
Surplus	0	0.0	0	0.0	0	0.0	0	0.0	0	0.0	0	0.0	0	0.0	0	0.0
Sudan																
Total national workforce	11.0		47.8		39.0		87.4		176.8		313.2		3,116.8		3,792.0	
Workers exported	7.4	67.3	10.1	21.1	5.1	13.1	10.6	12.1	14.2	8.0	21.8	7.0	18.8	0.6	88.0	2.3
Shortfall	28.8	261.8	25.9	54.2	38.0	97.4	77.4	88.6	23.9	13.6	0	0.0	0	0.0	194.0	5.1
Surplus	0	0.0	0	0.0	0	0.0	0	0.0	0	0.0	634.8	202.6	214.4	6.9	849.2	22.4

Table 17 (cont.)

Exporting Country	Occupational Category[a]															
	Professional and Technical		Other Professional		Sub-Professional and Technical		Other Sub-Professional		Skilled Office and Manual		Semi-Skilled Office and Manual		Unskilled		Total	
	Number *(Thousands)*	Percent	Number *(Thousands)*	Percent	Number *(Thousands)*	Percent	Number *(Thousands)*	Percent	Number *(Thousands)*	Percent	Number *(Thousands)*	Percent	Number *(Thousands)*	Percent	Number *(Thousands)*	Percent
Syria																
Total national workforce	64.8		93.5		61.3		73.7		208.8		709.8		1,212.4		2,424.3	
Workers exported	7.9	12.2	21.8	34.0	6.6	10.8	15.0	20.3	15.5	7.4	19.8	2.8	26.4	2.2	113.0	4.7
Shortfall	0	0.0	4.2	4.5	0	0.0	30.8	41.8	29.0	13.9	0	0.0	0	0.0	64.0	2.6
Surplus	7.2	11.1	0	0.0	29.4	48.0	0	0.0	0	0.0	524.0	73.8	257.5	21.2	818.1	33.7
Tunisia																
Total national workforce	27.5		34.7		92.0		63.9		207.8		524.6		1,265.5		2,216.0	
Workers exported	7.5	27.3	7.7	22.2	8.0	8.7	11.6	18.1	33.3	16.0	8.6	1.6	17.4	1.4	94.1	4.2
Shortfall	21.6	78.5	21.8	62.8	14.1	15.3	62.1	97.2	0	0.0	0	0.[illegible]	0	0.0	119.6	5.4
Surplus	0	0.0	0	0.0	0	0.0	0	0.0	24.2	11.6	199.0	37.[illegible]	104.3	8.2	327.5	14.8
YAR																
Total national workforce	2.2		11.4		2.5		11.8		42.7		137.7		1,347.2		1,555.5	
Workers exported	0.3	13.6	1.5	13.2	0.5	20.0	1.9	16.1	34.5	80.8	96.4	70.[illegible]	265.6	19.7	400.7	25.8
Shortfall	8.5	386.4	4.7	41.2	10.3	412.0	15.3	129.7	46.5	108.9	27.1	19.[illegible]	0	0.0	112.4	7.2
Surplus	0	0.0	0	0.0	0	0.0	0	0.0	0	0.0	0	0.[illegible]	34.8	2.6	34.8	2.2
PDRY																
Total national workforce	2.6		6.2		3.6		20.6		44.8		87.1		359.0		523.9	
Workers exported	1.2	46.1	1.1	17.7	0.9	25.0	2.3	11.2	36.7	31.9	35.5	40.8	6.8	1.9	84.5	16.2
Shortfall	6.9	265.4	9.0	145.2	7.2	200.0	12.5	60.7	34.6	77.2	0	[illegible]0	0	0.0	70.2	13.4
Surplus	0	0.0	0	0.0	0	0.0	0	0.0	0	0.0	67.0	7[illegible]9	172.0	47.9	239.0	45.6
Total																
Total national workforce	502.7		917.8		719.3		919.1		2,485.0		5,131.8		14,295.8		24,944.5	
Workers exported	99.1	19.7	185.4	0.2	88.5	12.3	172.6	18.8	309.7	12.6	314.6	[illegible].1	767.3	5.4	1,937.2	7.8
Shortfall	80.6	16.0	96.4	0.5	96.9	13.5	285.4	31.0	1,002.0	40.8	59.4	[illegible].2	48.5	0.3	1,669.2	6.9
Surplus	60.2	12.0	1.7	0.2	329.5	45.8	0.4	0.0	32.5	1.3	2,785.7	5[illegible].3	2,798.4	19.6	6,008.4	24.1
Net shortfall	20.4	4.1	94.7	10.3	0	0.0	285.0	31.0	969.5	39.4	0	[illegible].0	0	0.0	0	0.0
Net surplus	0	0.0	0	0.0	232.6	32.3	0	0.0	0	0.0	2,726.3	5[illegible].1	2,749.9	19.2	4,339.2	17.2

[a]The categories are defined and described in Table 5.

Table 18

NON-NATIONAL POPULATION AND WORKFORCE IN MAJOR LABOR-IMPORTING COUNTRIES, 1975 AND 1985 (HIGH AND LOW GROWTH RATE SCENARIOS)

	1975			1985					
				High Economic Growth Rate			Low Economic Growth Rate		
Country or Area of Origin of Migrants	Population *(Thousands)*	Workforce *(Thousands)*	Crude Activity Rate *(Percent)*	Population *(Thousands)*	Workforce *(Thousands)*	Crude Activity Rate *(Percent)*	Population *(Thousands)*	Workforce *(Thousands)*	Crude Activity Rate *(Percent)*
Algeria	0.5	0.3	60.0%	0.4	0.3	75.0%	0.4	0.2	50.0%
Egypt	620.3	353.3	60.0	2,318.6	711.5	30.7	2,016.1	603.4	29.9
India	205.7	141.9	69.0	1,055.4	360.7	34.2	819.8	289.3	35.3
Iran	142.4	69.9	49.1	418.3	115.6	27.6	364.6	98.1	26.9
Iraq	47.0	18.7	39.8	57.2	12.4	21.7	54.9	11.6	21.1
Jordan	503.0	139.0	27.6	1,138.9	257.4	22.6	1,145.9	263.9	23.0
Lebanon	52.6	28.4	54.0	278.7	70.4	25.3	267.1	67.6	25.3
Morocco	4.7	2.2	46.8	52.5	12.5	23.8	41.7	9.8	23.5
Oman	56.9	30.8	54.1	145.4	46.0	31.6	142.5	44.6	31.3
Pakistan	353.8	205.7	58.1	1,935.6	541.3	28.0	1,591.1	442.7	27.8
Southeast Asia	21.6	20.5	94.9	397.8	370.5	93.1	398.1	368.7	92.6
Sudan	64.5	26.0	40.3	362.0	88.1	24.3	342.0	79.9	23.4
Syria	104.6	38.1	36.4	412.4	96.1	23.3	381.2	86.9	22.8
Tunisia	52.4	29.3	55.9	215.7	62.8	29.1	183.4	52.5	28.6
YAR	607.6	328.5	54.1	773.9	400.8	51.8	751.2	381.0	50.7
PDRY	123.3	45.8	37.2	374.4	84.7	22.6	362.6	80.9	22.3
Rest of world	166.9	122.4	73.2	974.5	317.3	32.6	701.5	232.7	33.2
Total	3,127.4	1,600.8	51.2	10,911.5	3,548.4	32.5	9,564.1	3,113.8	32.6

various ethnic and nationality groups; however, the trend toward higher dependency rates (or lower crude activity rates) is general.

This demographic evolution of non-national communities has given officials of the major labor-importing countries a number of causes for concern. First is the question of the population balance. In 1975 the nationals of Kuwait, Qatar, and the UAE were already a minority in their own countries. For the major labor-importing countries as a whole, non-nationals accounted for just under one quarter of the total population. By 1985 non-nationals are projected to account for a little over four out of ten in the total population of these countries. Table 19 presents population figures for the nineteen states of the MENA region in 1975 and alternative projections for 1985. These projections could be significantly affected by labor-importing countries' policies on allowing dependents to accompany workers. Such policies, however, have proven very difficult to enforce.

A second cause for concern is the ethnic composition of the non-national population. In 1975 Arabs represented about 72 percent of the non-national populations in the major labor-importing countries, but by 1985 they are projected to account for only 56-60 percent. A little over one quarter of the non-national population will be South Asian, and another 4 percent Southeast Asian. (Table 20 summarizes the population compositions in 1975 and projections for 1985.) Cultural pluralism has not—to date at least—been set as an objective in any of the oil-endowed states.

A third cause for concern is the growing requirement in the oil states for social, administrative, and security services attendant upon the increasing size and changing composition of the non-national populations. The provision of education to the children of migrants illustrates the challenge of providing social services. Already in 1975 over one quarter of a million non-national students were enrolled in the school systems of the oil-endowed states. In Kuwait, which has the most "mature" non-national demographic profile of the labor-importing states, non-nationals accounted for 40 percent of all enrollments (see Table 21). The demand for education and other social services for non-nationals in the oil states will surely increase dramatically as the demographic evolution runs its course.

The impact upon lifestyles and social values of the growing non-national communities is not easy to quantify, but the provision of administrative and security services is (if anything) of greater concern than the provision of education and welfare services.

Table 19

NATIONAL POPULATIONS AND SHARES IN MENA COUNTRIES, 1975 AND 1985 (HIGH AND LOW GROWTH RATE SCENARIOS)

	1975			1985					
				High Economic Growth Rate			Low Economic Growth Rate		
Country	Total (*Thousands*)	Nationals (*Thousands*)	Nationals' Share (*Percent*)	Total (*Thousands*)	Nationals (*Thousands*)	Nationals' Share (*Percent*)	Total (*Thousands*)	Nationals (*Thousands*)	Nationals' Share (*Percent*)
Major labor importing countries									
Bahrain	267	209	78.3%	578	293	50.8%	505	293	58.1%
Kuwait	1,027	472	46.0	1,817	663	36.5	1,744	663	38.0
Libya	2,680	2,179	81.3	5,404	3,218	59.6	5,007	3,218	64.3
Oman	845	709	83.9	1,287	1,008	78.3	1,292	1,011	78.2
Qatar	180	53	29.4	474	78	16.6	464	78	16.9
Saudi Arabia	7,334	5,936	80.9	13,711	8,757	63.9	13,112	8,757	66.8
UAE	551	200	36.3	1,961	295	15.0	1,764	295	16.7
Subtotal	12,884	9,758	75.7	25,232	14,312	56.7	23,888	14,315	59.9
Other labor-importing countries									
Algeria	15,865	15,834	99.8	22,905	22,022	96.1	22,461	22,022	98.0
Iraq	11,073	11,073	100.0	16,697	15,749	94.3	16,465	15,751	95.7
Iran	32,602	32,602	100.0	43,871	43,871	100.0	43,923	43,923	100.0
Replacement migration countries									
Jordan	2,237	2,189	97.9	2,965	2,956	99.7	2,965	2,957	99.7
YAR	4,152	4,152	100.0	7,189	6,956	96.8	7,153	6,982	97.6
Labor-exporting countries									
Egypt	35,443	35,443	100.0	44,870	44,870	100.0	44,442	44,442	100.0
Lebanon	2,828	2,828	100.0	3,332	3,332	100.0	3,376	3,376	100.0
Morocco	17,150	17,150	100.0	23,716	23,716	100.0	23,727	23,727	100.0
PDRY	1,528	1,528	100.0	2,099	2,099	100.0	2,111	2,111	100.0
Sudan	15,929	15,929	100.0	22,284	22,284	100.0	22,303	22,303	100.0
Syria	7,176	7,176	100.0	9,632	9,632	100.0	9,693	9,693	100.0
Tunisia	5,554	5,554	100.0	6,925	6,925	100.0	7,019	7,019	100.0
Total	164,421	161,216		231,717	218,724		229,526	218,621	

NOTE: A small number of non-nationals resided in Iraq, Iran, and the YAR, as well as the labor-exporting countries, in 1975, but for purposes of this table the figures were not significant enough to warrant inclusion.

Table 20

POPULATION IN MAJOR LABOR-IMPORTING COUNTRIES BY MAJOR ETHNIC GROUP, 1975 AND 1985 (HIGH AND LOW GROWTH RATE SCENARIOS)

	1975		1985					
			High Economic Growth Rate			Low Economic Growth Rate		
Major Ethnic Group	Population (*Thousands*)	Percent	Population (*Thousands*)	Percent	Annual Increase, 1975-85 (*Percent*)	Population (*Thousands*)	Percent	Annual Increase, 1975-85 (*Percent*)
Arab non-nationals	2,237.3	71.5%	6,130.0	56.2%	10.6%	5,688.8	59.5%	9.7%
South Asians	559.5	17.9	2,991.0	27.4	18.2	2,410.6	25.2	15.7
Southeast Asians	20.3	0.7	399.0	3.6	33.9	398.0	4.2	33.8
Other	309.3	9.9	1,391.5	12.8	16.2	1,066.3	11.1	13.2
Subtotal	3,126.4	100.0	10,911.6	100.0	13.3	9,563.7	100.0	11.8
Nationals	9,758.3	75.7	14,313.3	56.7	3.9	14,313.3	60.0	3.9
Total	12,884.7	100.0	25,224.9	100.0	6.9	23,877.0	100.0	6.4

Table 21

STUDENTS ENROLLED BY NATIONALITY GROUP AND SEX IN MAJOR LABOR-IMPORTING COUNTRIES, 1975-76

Country[a]	Enrollments *(Thousands)*					
	Total	Nationals	Non-Nationals	Arabs	Non-Arabs	Nationality Unspecified
Saudi Arabia						
Male	637.2	566.8	70.5	63.2	7.3	
Female	325.4	282.9	42.5	38.7	3.7	
Total	962.6	849.7	113.0	101.9	11.0	
Percent	100.0	88.3	11.7	10.6	1.1	
Bahrain						
Male	36.1	33.3	2.9	0.7	2.1	
Female	29.6	26.8	2.9	0.7	2.2	
Total	65.7	60.1	5.8	1.4	4.3	
Percent	100.0	91.3	8.7	2.2	6.5	
UAE[b]						
Male	30.3	22.5	7.7	7.5	0.2	
Female	22.1	16.9	5.2	5.1	0.1	
Total	52.4	39.4	12.9	12.6	0.3	
Percent	100.0	75.3	24.7	24.2	0.5	
Kuwait						
Male	112.4	66.2	46.2	33.1	0.8	12.3
Female	95.4	57.9	37.5	31.8	0.5	5.2
Total	207.8	124.1	83.7	64.9	1.3	17.6
Percent	·100.0	59.7	40.3	31.2	0.6	8.5
Qatar						
Male	17.1	11.4	5.7	4.6	1.1	
Female	15.3	10.9	4.4	3.7	0.7	
Total	32.4	22.3	10.1	8.3	1.8	
Percent	100.0	68.9	31.1	25.6	5.5	
Oman						
Male	41.0	40.6	0.4	0.3	0.1	
Female	15.2	14.9	0.3	0.2	0.1	
Total	56.2	55.5	0.7	0.5	0.2	
Percent	100.0	98.8	1.2	0.9	0.3	
Total						
Male	874.1	740.8	133.4	109.4	11.6	12.3
Female	503.0	410.3	92.8	80.2	7.3	5.2
Total	1,377.1	1,151.1	226.2	189.6	18.9	17.6
Percent	100.0	83.6	16.4	13.7	1.4	1.3

Source: Educational and statistical yearbooks of the countries tabulated.

[a]Data for Libya were not available.

[b]Figures for 1974-75.

Increasingly policymakers in the oil-endowed states are taking the foreign labor and population factors into account in setting their economic growth targets. However, the existing momentum of the oil economies, the pressures for continued rapid growth which makes easier individual financial reward (e.g., construction contracts, housing rentals, etc.), and the nearly inevitable increase of the non-national populations even if migrant worker imports were to be severely curtailed will almost certainly ensure that the issues outlined above will be of increasing importance and concern to officials of the oil states in the coming years.

SOME COSTS AND BENEFITS OF MIGRATION

The perceptions of the labor-exporting countries will also change as the ramifications of international labor migration become clearer. Nothing approaching a full-fledged cost-benefit assessment of labor exporting has yet been made. Several of the factors to be taken into account have been identified, however. For the labor-exporting countries as well as individual migrants, the most visible and tangible reward has been remittances. Table 22 provides remittance data for selected countries for 1974-78. Remittances have been welcomed as a source of foreign exchange to offset adverse trade balances. But the expenditure patterns of remittances have been far from a development economist's dream. Much remittance money goes for consumption, some of it conspicuous; little goes to investment. This has led to the inclusion of the following statement in the Egyptian National Plan for 1978-82: "Growing numbers of Egyptians work abroad for very high wages, if compared with domestic salaries. These individuals return to Egypt with huge purchasing powers, which they individually direct not to savings and investment, but to flagrant and luxurious consumption."

A growing number of studies provide insight into the patterns of remittance expenditures. For example, when a sample of migrant Egyptian construction workers was asked about the way they would like to use their savings, 78 percent indicated first preference for future spending; when asked about the type of commodities they would like to buy on their way back home, consumer goods—especially durables—ranked high on their preference scale (Mohie-Eddin 1980:149). A study of Bangladeshi migrants to the Middle East concluded the following about remittances:

Table 22

REMITTANCES: NET TRANSFERS BY COUNTRY OF RECEIPT, 1974-78
(*US$ millions,* current prices)

Country of Receipt	1974	1975	1976	1977	1978
Algeria	$ 352.4	$ 397.0	$428.3	$309.4	$ 330.6
Bangladesh	N.A.	15.3	18.1	78.3	115.1
Egypt	268.2	365.5	755.1	896.7	1,761.2
India	234.5	414.0	633.8	910.7	–
Jordan	75.4	166.6	411.0	455.3	520.2
Morocco	319.9	489.3	498.8	535.9	699.9
Pakistan	178.0	275.6	409.9	866.3	1,303.3
Syria	44.5	52.2	53.1	140.2	93.9
Tunisia	107.0	126.3	121.2	144.8	191.6
Turkey	1,410.7	1,293.1	940.4	823.1	980.3
YAR	135.5	279.0	676.5	914.3	866.6
PDRY	41.1	55.9	115.2	172.6	254.8

Source: Data compiled by G. Swamy of the Development Economics Department, World Bank.

> A look at the use of remittance money itself reveals that nearly half of it is spent for the purchase of land and the construction, repair and improvement of houses. A substantial part of it is also used for the repayment of earlier debts. Very little, however, is invested in activities like agriculture, industry or business. It is clear, therefore, that the remittance received by the households contributes very little (at least directly) towards the creation of productive employment opportunities (Ali et al. 1981:137).

A recent study of Pakistani migrants to the Middle East found that 62 percent of remittance expenditure goes into current consumption, 22 percent into real estate purchases, 11.5 percent into real physical investments, and 1.4 percent into financial investments (Gilani et al. 1981:143). In Jordan a purposive sample showed that 52.4 percent of households with return migrants did not make any type of investment, and 27 percent of households with a member currently abroad as a migrant invested in real estate, 7.8 percent bought land for speculative purposes, 5.9 percent invested in agriculture or industry, and 6.3 percent bought some government bonds. Some households made more than one type of investment since only 39.6 percent of the sample had made some investment (Saket 1981:18).

The rapidly rising volume of remittances in the mid- to late 1970s contributed substantially to the severe inflation experienced by the labor-exporting countries. These countries often did not have either adequate domestic production capacity or sufficient imports infrastructure to quickly meet the demand generated by remittance flows.

Of longer term significance may be the changes in taste and consumption patterns acquired in the course of the migration experience—e.g., the shift from consumption of domestically produced millet and sorghum to imported wheat and rice in the YAR. These changes already have resulted in some significant alterations in production patterns such as the abandonment of marginal agricultural land, crop shifts, and some decline in terrace maintenance in the YAR, and failure to maintain the *falaj* (underground stone-lined canals) irrigation system in Oman. Agricultural production in the YAR decreased significantly in the late 1970s, and wage rates have risen to about two thirds the level of wages in Saudi Arabia; both outcomes are mainly attributable to international migration. The wage rates now prevalent in the YAR may well preclude the development of many export industries. It may be extreme to characterize these changes as distortions in the YAR economy, but they would clearly pose major readjustment problems were international migration and remittances to quickly decline.

The export of migrant workers and accompanying dependents produces benefits in that certain services are provided to the migrant communities abroad which the home country would otherwise have to or wish to provide. The example noted above of non-national student enrollments in the labor-importing countries is a case in point. Of the 226,000 non-nationals enrolled in the labor-importing countries in 1975-76, some 190,000 were Arabs. As Table 23 shows, the 27,000 Yemenis (YAR) enrolled in six labor-importing countries were equivalent to 10 percent of total domestic enrollments. At the secondary school level (grades 10-12), Yemeni enrollments abroad were equivalent to 33 percent of domestic secondary enrollments, and at the intermediate level (grades 7-9), 21 percent. This represents a substantial savings for the YAR and the preparation of a significant

Table 23

EDUCATIONAL ENROLLMENT AT HOME AND ABROAD BY EDUCATIONAL LEVEL IN SEVEN MIDDLE EAST COUNTRIES, 1975-76
(Thousands)

	Country													
	Egypt		Jordan[a]		Lebanon		YAR		PDRY		Sudan		Syria	
Educational Level	Home	Abroad[b]	Home	Abroad[b]	Home[c]	Abroad[b]	Home	Abroad[d]	Home	Abroad[d]	Home	Abroad[d]	Home	Abroad[d]
Primary														
Total	3,871.4	14.6	430.4	51.4	613.2	3.2	252.6	20.7	203.5	12.7	1,134.8	1.9	1,212.0	5.0
Percent		0.4		12.0		0.5		8.2		6.2		0.2		0.4
Intermediate														
Total	1,340.4	5.4	128.9	14.2	180.0	1.0	16.8	3.4	34.3	2.9	188.9	4.0	314.3	1.3
Percent		0.4		11.0		0.5		20.5		8.4		0.2		0.4
Secondary and Vocational[e]														
Total	808.8	3.7	59.9	11.4	48.6	0.9	7.7	2.6	12.9	1.6	61.0	0.2	155.0	1.0
Percent		0.5		19.0		1.8		33.0		12.6		0.4		0.6
University														
Total	474.5	0.8	44.7	2.5	48.2	0.2	4.3	0.4	0.7	0.4	14.9	0.1	67.9	0.2
Percent		0.2		5.6		0.3		10.3		60.7		0.8		0.3
Grand total														
Total	6,495.1	24.5	663.9	79.5	890.0	5.3	281.4	27.1	251.4	17.6	1,399.6	2.6	1,749.2	7.5
Percent		0.4		12.0		0.6		9.6		7.0		0.2		0.4

Source: Educational statistics yearbooks of the countries.

[a] Enrollment includes Jordanians and Palestinians.

[b] Enrollments in Saudi Arabia, Kuwait, Bahrain, Qatar, Oman, and the UAE.

[c] Enrollment is for 1973-74; taken from Educational Center for Research and Development, "Educational Statistics 1973/74."

[d] Enrollments in Saudi Arabia, Kuwait, and Qatar.

[e] Includes other types of education in Saudi Arabia (mostly vocational).

portion of future middle-level personnel for the labor force. A matrix showing Arab non-national student enrollments by country of study and origin is presented in Table 24.

SOME FURTHER ISSUES FOR CONSIDERATION

As should be clear even from this severely abbreviated review of international labor migration in MENA, the social structure of the region has been and will continue to be affected by the phenomenon. In addition to the issues already touched upon, a wide range of other questions should be addressed, such as the following:

(i) *Acquisition of Citizenship.* The oil states have not extensively offered opportunities for naturalization. A limited number of long-time residents, usually advisors or other professionals (almost always Arabs) working in the public sector, have been given citizenship. Another group receiving citizenship has been non-national women upon marriage to a national. Finally, certain tribal affiliations have from time to time been recognized as adequate for entitlement to citizenship. In the absence of significant opportunity for naturalization, will the large and growing non-national populations remain content with the higher standards of living they enjoy in the oil states, or will their aspirations extend to political as well as material participation in their society of residence? Possibly even more serious is the question of the attitudes and aspirations of those who are and will be born and raised in the oil states, have only a limited personal knowledge of and attachment to their parents' home country, but have no chance for complete integration into the society of their native oil states.

(ii) *Terms and Conditions of Employment.* In most labor-importing countries, trade unions are not allowed. As the oil states move from the infrastructure/construction phase to the plant or project operation phase of development, the average duration of the employee-employer relationship may be expected to increase. It is in such situations that some form of collective bargaining is most likely. Pressures for some revision of labor legislation may therefore be anticipated, with very sticky questions inevitable as to the coverage of non-nationals. It is also likely that officials of the countries of origin of migrants will become increasingly concerned over the terms and conditions of recruitment, employment, housing, and repatriation

Table 24

NON-NATIONAL ARAB STUDENT ENROLLMENTS IN MENA BY COUNTRY OF STUDY, COUNTRY OF ORIGIN, AND SEX, 1975-76

		Country of Origin or Nationality							
Country of Study	Total MENA	Egypt	Palestinian	Jordan	Syria	Lebanon	Iraq	Sudan	Saudi Arabia
Saudi Arabia									
Male	63,200	9,600	10,100	6,300	2,500	800	200	1,300	
Female	38,700	7,800	8,800	5,300	2,100	700	200	1,100	
Total	101,900	17,400	18,900	11,600	4,600	1,500	400	2,400	
Bahrain									
Male	700	100	100	100		*	*		100
Female	700	100	100	100		*	*		100
Total	1,400	200	200	200		100	*		200
UAE[a]									
Male	7,500	500	700	600		100			
Female	5,100	400	700	700		100			
Total	12,600	900	1,400	1,300		200			
Kuwait									
Male	33,100	2,400	2,200	18,300	1,500	1,600	2,000	100	2,100
Female	31,700	2,400	2,300	18,300	1,400	1,600	1,800	100	1,700
Total	64,800	4,800	4,500	36,600	1,900	3,200	3,800	200	3,800
Qatar									
Male	4,600	400	1,300	1,200	100	100			200
Female	3,700	500	1,200	1,100	100	100			100
Total	8,300	900	2,500	2,300	200	200			300
Oman									
Male	300	200	*	*		*		*	*
Female	200	100	*	*		*		*	*
Total	500	300	*	100		*		*	*
Total									
Male	109,300	13,200	14,400	26,500	4,000	2,600	2,300	1,300	2,400
Female	80,200	11,400	13,100	25,500	3,500	2,500	2,000	1,200	2,000
Total	189,500	24,600	27,500	52,000	7,500	5,100	4,300	2,500	4,400

Table 24 (cont.)

Country of Study	Country of Origin or Nationality									
	YAR	PDRY	Bahrain	Qatar	Oman	UAE	Kuwait	Gulf Countries	Tunisia, Algeria, Mauritania, Morocco, Somalia	Other
Saudi Arabia										
Male	20,400	9,900	500	100	400	*	100		400	600
Female	5,700	6,000	300	100	100	*	*		200	300
Total	26,100	15,900	800	200	500	*	100		600	900
Bahrain										
Male					200					100
Female					200					100
Total					400					200
UAE[a]										
Male								3,700		2,000
Female								1,700		1,600
Total								5,400		3,600
Kuwait										
Male	500	800	300	*	900	300			*	
Female	200	400	500	*	600	400			*	
Total	700	1,200	800	*	1,500	700			100	
Qatar										
Male	200	300						800		
Female	200	200						300		
Total	400	500						1,100		
Oman										
Male										*
Female										*
Total										*
Total										
Male	21,100	11,100	800	100	1,500	300	100	4,500	400	3,700
Female	6,100	6,500	800	100	900	400	*	2,000	300	1,000
Total	27,200	7,600	1,600	200	2,400	700	100	6,500	700	4,700

Source: Educational statistics yearbooks of the countries.

[a]Figures for 1974-75.

*Less than 50.

NOTE: Figures are rounded to nearest 100.

of their increasingly numerous nationals in the labor-importing countries.

(iii) *Family Cohesion and Family Member Roles.* In the initial stage of migration, a male job-seeker ventures forth to take up employment; later he brings family members. In some cases (e.g., the YAR), migration is rotational, with an average stay abroad as short as six months. During such absences from home of the male migrant, females are often increasingly called upon to play roles they traditionally did not play. For example, much more farm work in the YAR is now carried out by females. One may also speculate that the authority role of females may change in such situations, and that such roles may survive, to some extent at least, the return of the male migrant (or the move by the female to join the migrant worker abroad).

(iv) *Parochialism, Nationalism, and Pan-Arabism.* It is interesting to speculate on the impact that migration may have on the migrants in their attitudes toward home and host country and peoples. For example, employment in Saudi Arabia may produce quite different reactions from a Yemeni (almost certainly of rural origin), for whom the exposure to the lifestyle of Riyadh or Jeddah may be an initial contact with a "big city," as compared with a Lebanese, Egyptian, or Jordanian professional, who might conceivably find the lifestyle in Saudi Arabia confining and dull in contrast to Beirut, Cairo, or Amman. And what of the contact between migrants and host country nationals? Will the experience foster a sense of identification or at least empathy with the host country and its nationals? Or will the impression be formed that the host country nationals "use" and "discard" migrants at will in the interest of the chosen few who were fortunate enough to be born to citizenship? Will the contact by Arab migrants with other Arab migrants and host country nationals instill or strengthen a pan-Arab view of a single Arab nation in which Arab labor "circulates" (as the Arab Labor Organization prefers to view and term migration within the region)?

CONCLUSIONS

Since 1975 international labor migration has become a major economic and social phenomenon within MENA. It has enabled the oil-endowed states of the region to launch a major transformation of their economies. For the labor-exporting states, out-migration has alleviated unemployment and generated flows of remittances that have been valuable as sources of foreign exchange to offset adverse trade balances. For the individual migrants, the process is clearly highly rewarding.

There are, however, significant costs, especially to the societies. For the labor-importing countries, the prospect of becoming or remaining dependent upon foreign labor is increasingly perceived as a critical issue. With foreign laborers and their dependents come ideas and lifestyles, not all of which are welcome, as well as requirements for facilities and services that are not all that easy to provide. For the labor-exporting countries, the losses of manpower have been from key categories of employment as well as from the ranks of the unemployed. The remittances have contributed to inflationary pressures and have often been expended conspicuously on luxuries unaffordable by the general population. As prices of goods and services have adjusted to the economic order of the region at the present level of migration, concern has grown over the possibility of having to readjust to an order in which a particular labor-exporting country may not be as full a participant.

Governments of both the labor-importing and labor-exporting countries have so far responded on an ad hoc basis to the challenges posed by international labor migration. From the projections we have discussed, it would appear that the scale of labor migration will continue to rise for some years at least, with accentuated consequences for all parties concerned. At least some of the more adverse consequences could be mitigated and some of the more beneficial consequences could be enhanced by increased cooperation among the labor importers and exporters. A realistic first step might be for the countries of the region to share information on prospective manpower requirements and supplies. Development of such an "early warning" system would be a logical initial move toward a much more ambitious system of joint planning and regulation of the migration process within the region. In this broader context, one has added reasons for hoping that the spirit of cooperation rather than conflict will dominate the search for appropriate mechanisms for dealing with the challenges and opportunities of the labor migration phenomenon.

REFERENCES

Ali, Sayed Ashraf; Arif, Abu Ahmed; Habibullah, A. K. Md; Hussain, A. R. M. Anwar; Islam, Rizwanul; Mahmud, Wahiduddin; Osmani, S. R.; Rahman, Q.M.; and Siddiqui, A. M. A. H. 1981. *Labor Migration from Bangladesh to the Middle East.* Washington, D.C.: World Bank. Staff Working Paper no. 454.

Birks, J. S., and Sinclair, C. A. 1979. "Migration and Development: The Changing Perspectives of the Poor Arab Countries." *Journal of International Affairs* 33, 2 (Fall-Winter): 285-309.

__________, and __________. 1980. *International Migration and Development in the Arab Region.* Durham: Department of Economics, University of Durham. (Some of these case studies were clustered and issued by the ILO as working papers. The project, including the final, published book, was commissioned by the ILO as part of the Migration for Employment of the World Employment Program.)

Bohning, W. R. 1977. *Compensating Countries of Origin for the Out-Migration of Their People.* Geneva: ILO. December.

__________. 1978. *Elements of a Theory of International Migration and Compensation.* Geneva: ILO. November.

__________. 1982. *Towards a System of Recompense for International Labor Migration.* Geneva: ILO. February.

Choucri, Nazli. 1977. "The New Migration in the Middle East: A Problem for Whom?" Cambridge, Mass.: Migration and Development Study Group, Center for International Studies, MIT. January.

Farrag, Abdelmegid M. 1975. "Employment and Regional Cooperation (Including Migration)." Paper presented to the Seminar on Manpower and Employment Planning in the Arab Countries; Beirut, 12-14 May. Sponsored by the ILO and the UN Economic Commission for Western Asia. Working paper no. E/ECWA/ILO/WG.4/4.

Gilani, Ijaz; Khan, M. Fahim; and Iqbal, Munawar. 1981. "Labor Migration from Pakistan to the Middle East and Its Impact on the Domestic Economy." Final Report for General Distribution of Research Project on Report of Manpower from Pakistan to the Middle East. Washington, D.C.: World Bank. June/July.

Halliday, Fred. 1977. "Migration and the Labor Force in the Oil Producing States of the Middle East." *Development and Change* 8: 263-91.

Ibrahim, Saad Eddin. 1982. "Oil, Migration and the New Arab Social Order." In Kerr and Yassin, eds. 1982.

Kerr, Malcolm H., and Yassin, El Sayed, eds. 1982. *Rich and Poor States in the Middle East: Egypt and the New Arab Order.* Boulder, Colo.: Westview Press.

Mohie-Eddin, Amr. 1980. "External Migration of Egyptian Labour." Paper submitted to ILO Strategic Employment Mission to Egypt. Mimeo.

Pennisi, Giuseppe. 1981. *Development, Manpower and Migration in the Red Sea Region: The Case for Cooperation.* Hamburg: Deutsches Orient-Institut.

Ramesh, Jairam. 1978. "Indian Labor in the Middle East: A Preliminary Analysis." Cambridge, Mass.: Center for International Studies, MIT. Mimeo; 27 December.

Saket, Bassam K. 1981. "Remittances and Their Uses: The Case of Jordan." Paper submitted to the Conference on International Migration in the Arab World; Beirut, 11-16 May.

Shaw, R. Paul. 1979. "Migration and Employment in the Arab World: Construction as a Key Policy Variable." *International Labor Review* 118, 5 (September-October).

Sherbiny, Naiem A., and Serageldin, Ismail. 1982. "Expatriate Labor and Economic Growth: Saudi Demand for Egyptian Labor." In Kerr and Yassin, eds. 1982.

Socknat, James. 1979. "The Potential Relationship of International Migration for Employment and a Middle East Peace Settlement: An Assessment." *Middle East Review* 11, 4 (Summer): 58-64.

World Bank. 1981. "Manpower and International Labor Migration in the Middle East and North Africa." Final Report for General Distribution of the Research Project. Prepared by Ismail Serageldin, James Socknat, Stace Birks, Bob Li, and Clive Sinclair. Washington, D.C., 30 June.

Chapter 10

TURKISH MIGRATION TO EUROPE AND THE MIDDLE EAST: ITS IMPACT ON SOCIAL STRUCTURE AND SOCIAL LEGISLATION

Nermin Abadan-Unat

Migration is a universal phenomenon. In the past there were four major types of human migration: migration forced by poor geographic or climatic conditions; migration owing to conquest; group migration for sociological reasons; and migration for religious reasons. Today, however, migration has acquired a new character. Franklin D. Scott (1968:2-3) correctly observes that the day of individually motivated, uncontrolled international migrations has passed; "laissez-faire" no longer regulates large-scale migratory movements. The change is evident both in the case of migration to Europe over the past quarter century and of migration within Middle Eastern countries during the last decade. Instead of a shift of populations, we are now facing an increasingly important shift of manpower.

The traditional role of Europe as a source of settlers for North and South America, Australia, and southern Africa dramatically and systematically changed in the decade that followed the establishment of the European Economic Community—EEC (Abadan-Unat 1976:2). Through the Treaty of Rome (1957) legal and institutional arrangements were established to encourage the intra-European movement of labor. Northwestern Europe quickly became a magnet for immigrants from the less developed regions of the EEC and the Mediterranean. Five countries—the Federal Republic of Germany (FRG, or West Germany), France, the Netherlands, Belgium, and Switzerland—attracted the majority of these new immigrants. On a smaller scale Sweden, Denmark, Norway, and Austria also became targets for job-seekers from Mediterranean countries.

In a closer examination of what has come to be called the "European South"—i.e., the less developed countries encircling the Mediterranean—a basic distinction has to be made. Marios Nikolinakos (1973) classifies the region into three groups: (1) The countries of southern Europe proper (Portugal, Spain, Italy, Greece); (2) Turkey and Yugoslavia—countries which emerged in the twentieth century through the liquidation or dismantling of empires; (3) Countries which experienced some kind of European colonialism: Algeria, Morocco, Tunisia, Syria, Lebanon, Jordan, Egypt, and Libya (pp. 142-43). A number of the countries from the second and third groups, such as Turkey and the countries of the Maghreb, have organized large-scale migration not only to northern Europe, but also to the oil-rich countries of the Middle East.

In this chapter we shall analyze Turkish migration in an effort to evaluate the pattern and effects of migration from the European South on the social structure of both sending and host countries, as well as the role of social legislation on both sides. It should be emphasized that while rapidly increasing external migration has forced legislatures to enact some new laws, existing rules and regulations have also contributed to migratory trends. Thus the causal role of law appears to rest upon interdependence, in spite of the fact that external migration is heavily subjected to a dependence relationship. (Concrete examples will be presented below.)

TURKISH MIGRATION TO EUROPE

In present-day Turkey migration has become a commonly accepted alternative for employment, ranging from the "brain drain" to the export of excess manpower to the encouragement of entrepreneurship to settling abroad, but this practice has a very short history. Legally, free exit started with the adoption of the Constitution of 1961, whereby leaving or entering the country became a fundamental right and freedom (Abadan-Unat 1976:14). By 1984, 2,404,031 Turkish citizens had taken up permanent residence in five continents, showing the rapidity with which this new type of lifestyle has been adopted. (See Table 1 for a distribution of Turkish migrants by host country; breakdown figures by years, sex of workers, and children in selected host countries are presented in Tables 2-4.) Rapid migration becomes even more significant if one considers that at the beginning employment abroad—especially in West Germany—was principally considered as a form of twelve-month apprenticeship based on a system of rotation (i.e., short-term recruitment).

Turkish migration to Europe, beginning in the late 1950s, has undergone five major phases, which we shall discuss below.

Table 1

DISTRIBUTION OF TURKISH MIGRANTS BY HOST COUNTRY: MAY 1984

Host Country	Workers	Workers' Children	Total Citizens Abroad
EEC countries			
West Germany	542,512	623,700 (0-18 years)	1,552,328
France	64,070	61,610 (0-16 years)	144,790
Netherlands	55,000	74,633 (0-19 years)	154,201
Belgium	25,000	29,579 (0-14 years)	63,587
England	11,648	4,272 (0-10 years)	28,480
Denmark	8,496	7,952 (0-18 years)	17,240
Subtotal	706,726	801,746	1,960,626
Non-EEC countries			
Austria	27,733	24,979 (0-18 years)	75,000
Switzerland	24,751	19,638 (0-18 years)	48,485
Sweden	10,000	9,974 (0-19 years)	20,900
Norway	1,400	1,346 (0-19 years)	3,086
Subtotal	63,884	55,937	147,471
Subtotal, all European countries	770,610	857,683	2,108,097
Australia	20,000	N.A.	60,000
North Africa and Middle East			
Libya	75,500	2,500 (0-18 years)	80,000
Saudi Arabia	120,000	1,000 (0-18 years)	126,000
Iraq	9,144	90	9,284
Jordan	8,000	N.A.	8,000
Lebanon	7,000	N.A.	7,000
Kuwait	3,000	–	3,000
Syria	230	N.A.	–
United Arab Emirates (UAE)	60	N.A.	150
Subtotal	222,934		233,434
Other countries	2,000	N.A.	2,500
Total	1,015,544		2,404,031

Source: Turkey, Ministry of Labor 1984b:150, table 1.

Table 2

NUMBER OF WORKERS SENT ABROAD THROUGH TURKISH EMPLOYMENT SERVICE, 1961-80

Host Country	1961-73	1974	1975	1976	1977	1978	1979	1980
West Germany	648,029	1,228	640	2,101	2,413	1,333	933	764
France	45,366	10,577	25	6	15	13	11	21
Austria	34,461	2,501	226	672	583	54	23	944
Netherlands	23,359	1,503	32	98	83	48	40	32
Belgium	15,309	555	59	72	45	41	27	35
Switzerland	6,360	770	229	281	246	326	406	536
Libya	664	1,015	2,121	4,098	8,582	7,726	9,825	15,090
Saudi Arabia	4	—	251	1,832	4,722	5,769	8,522	5,643
Australia	4,668	1,133	491	339	542	549	407	409
Other	12,069	924	435	1,059	1,853	2,993	3,436	5,029
Total	790,289	20,206	4,509	10,558	19,084	18,852	23,630	28,503

Source: Turkey, Ministry of Labor 1982.

Table 3

TURKISH MIGRANT WORKERS IN SELECTED EUROPEAN HOST COUNTRIES ACCORDING TO SEX, 1980

Host Country	Men	Women	Total
West Germany	431,623	159,000	590,623
Netherlands	36,126	11,200	47,326
Austria	21,702	8,428	30,130
Switzerland	12,992	7,127	20,119
Total	502,443	185,755	688,198

Source: Turkey, Ministry of Labor 1982.

Table 4

TURKISH WORKERS' CHILDREN BY HOST COUNTRY AND AGE, 1980

	Age of Children			
Host Country	0-6 Years	7-18 Years	Total	Percent of Migrant Children
West Germany	201,500	382,900	584,400	78.8%
Netherlands	16,465	20,555	37,000	5.0
France	14,257	17,820	32,027	4.3
Belgium	12,478	17,780	30,258	4.1
Austria	7,796	9,743	17,539	2.4
Switzerland	6,047	7,557	13,604	1.8
Sweden	3,636	4,545	8,181	1.1
Denmark	2,351	2,747	5,098	0.7
Saudi Arabia	223	277	500	–
Libya	400	500	900	0.1
Australia	4,445	5,555	10,000	1.4
Other	889	1,111	2,000	0.3
Total	270,487	471,090	741,507	100.0

Source: OECD 1981:127.

PHASE 1: EXPERIMENTAL MIGRATION; RECRUITMENT BY NOMINATION (1956-61)

This first phase is characterized by the recruitment efforts of private businessmen and (later) semi-official labor-recruiting institutes, predominantly in West Germany. An official effort came in 1956 from the Institute of World Economy of the University of Kiel, which requested that the Turkish Foreign Affairs Ministry send volunteer migrants who needed vocational training. These early-comers were mostly recruited by shipbuilding companies in Hamburg, Bremen, and Kiel. Having been solicited on a private basis by receiving personally addressed letters of invitation (the legal form of nominated recruitment)—mostly through the good services of German spouses of well-to-do Turkish businessmen in Istanbul—these people were able to bring their families with them, and after the completion of their apprenticeship, instead of returning home, settle down for good. Indeed these skilled workers preferred to stay, putting an end to an idea launched in Hamburg by the Chamber of Commerce: "The middle class helps the middle class." It had been thought that by promoting time-bound technical training on the spot for labor exchange and sending skilled migrant manpower home, the growth of industrialism could be promoted in the country of origin. Facts did not confirm this premature assumption (Abadan-Unat 1964:121, table 108).

PHASE 2: UNCONTROLLED EXPANSION; GOVERNMENTAL MEDIATION; OBLIGATORY SINGLE EMIGRATION (1961-72)

External migration prior to 1961 remained confined to individuals or small groups, but the adoption of Turkey's first Five-Year Development Plan (1962-67) and the building of the Berlin Wall (which cut off the labor supply from East Germany) drastically changed the situation. Viewing existing domestic employment possibilities realistically, the first five-year plan states that "The export of excess, unskilled labor to Western Europe represents one of the possibilities for alleviating unemployment" (Turkey 1963:456). This new outlook and the growing needs of the West German labor market led to an explosion in emigration. While in 1960 only 2,700 workers had left Turkey, the number rose to 27,500 in 1963 and reached the dramatic high point with 615,827 in 1973 (Abadan-Unat 1976:7, table 1).

During this phase external migration proceeded mostly in two ways. The most common was a system called "anonymous recruitment," according to which employers seeking Turkish workers applied to the authorities in their own countries for the specific number of recruits they required. Their requests would be transferred to the Turkish Employment Service, which, in collaboration with the German Recruitment Bureau in Istanbul, would then choose a sufficient number of applicants from waiting lists. In order to avoid favoritism toward metropolitan areas with long waiting lists and to permit less developed areas to share the benefits of external migration, available jobs were distributed from the headquarters of the Employment Service all over the country. When waiting lists grew longer, priority was given to prospective migrants from the least developed regions of Turkey, to members of Village Development Cooperatives (see below), and to inhabitants of officially designated "disaster areas"—i.e., regions affected by earthquakes, droughts, plant diseases, etc.

The second method of migration during this phase was known as "nominated recruitment." An employer abroad would file an application for a specific individual. The Employment Service in Turkey would then arrange for his dispatch as an officially recognized migrant, whether or not his name already appeared on the waiting list. Normally nominated recruits depended on a network of friends or relations already established abroad who could locate vacancies in nearby workplaces and arrange with the employers to nominate them.

This unprecedented expansion of migrant workers abroad forced Turkey (as well as other Mediterranean countries) to sign bilateral agreements with host countries. Accordingly in 1961 Turkey signed its first bilateral agreement with West Germany, followed in 1964 by agreements with Austria, Belgium, and the Netherlands. In 1965 it signed a bilateral agreement with France, and in 1967 with Sweden (Onulduran and van Renselaar 1976:29-30). All these agreements have removed the implementation of migration from the initiative of the individual and transferred it to the appropriate government bureaucracies of the concerned countries. Thus recruitment became a monopoly to be exercised only by the Turkish Employment Service and its counterpart in a host country. All the agreements covered the terms and procedures for final selection of migrants (including a rigorous health examination), transportation costs, and cases of workers who desired or were compelled to return before their contracts expired.

The bilateral agreements also contributed to the creation of auxiliary organizations aimed at facilitating the adjustment of foreign workers to their new home and work environments. Thus in West Germany each ethnic group was assisted by a social welfare organization—mostly church organizations in the case of Catholic or Protestant migrants. For Turks the Social Democratic party, through a branch organization called Arbeiterwohlfahrt, offered Türk-Danış, a team of Germans and Turks employed solely to solve the personal grievances, legal requests, and issues pertaining to Turks in West Germany. One could conclude, as does Rist (1978:111), that from this phase on, foreign workers were in West Germany as the result of policies made at the highest levels of the German government.

From the Turkish end, the most important government policy during this phase was the introduction of a special rate of exchange available only to holders of "workers' passports." The policy had two purposes: to prevent a further growth of a permanent black market, and to induce migrant workers to send more of their savings home.

Finally, in this period cultural and social associations for migrant workers began to emerge in the host countries. Viewed by some Turkish workers as a kind of compensation for trade union activities, these associations, in line with the pluralistic structure of the host country, obtained important subsidies. In 1963 West Germany had 20 such associations; by 1974 there were 112 in West Germany and 156 in all of Western Europe (Abadan-Unat 1979:22). As of 1980 there were 573 in West Germany and 117 in the rest of Western Europe (see Table 5).

During this phase little attention was devoted to the problem of how to bring the families of migrant workers to join them in the host country, even though the notion of returning home after one year of work abroad had been quickly abandoned. Most migrants were men who went abroad alone, leaving their families behind. A more important discussion which predominated at this time concerned the ghetto-like, mostly male communities of workers in host countries, as well as the compulsory, regimented lifestyle which was imposed on workers' dormitories set up by the employers.

The fast tempo of recruitment suddenly slowed down during the recession of 1966-67, but this did not last. In spite of the discharge in 1966 of approximately 70,000 Turkish workers in West Germany, very few returned to their home country. Those who were not able to find a job in another part of West Germany or in a country

Table 5

DISTRIBUTION OF TURKISH RELIGIOUS AND SOCIAL ASSOCIATIONS BY HOST COUNTRY, 1980

Host Country	Religious Associations	Social Associations
West Germany	312	261
Netherlands	24	15
France[a]	19	30
Belgium	11	29
Austria	7	15
Switzerland	7	31
Denmark[b]	3	6
Sweden	–	17
Total	386	404

Source: Turkey, Ministry of Labor 1984a: 34, table 14.

[a]Figures for Strasbourg and Marseilles only.

[b]Figures are for 1979.

neighboring their new home country (such as the Netherlands and Belgium) began to enquire about unemployment insurance. Thus the abrupt economic crisis made Turkish workers aware of the scope and uses of social legislation. It also led to a heated debate about the economic and social role of the foreign labor class as a "conjunctural buffer" (*Konjunkturpuffer*)—in other words, a reserve labor army. At this point special units for migrant workers were established in the European national trade unions.

PHASE 3: CONSOLIDATION AND REDEFINITION OF GOALS IN REGARD TO EMPLOYMENT OF FOREIGN WORKERS AND LEGITIMATION OF ILLEGAL (TOURIST) MIGRANTS (1972-75)

This phase reflects major developments in both host and home countries. By 1973 the host countries had slowly realized that the "temporary" employment of foreign manpower was questionable.

Strongly pressured by their respective national trade unions, the host countries started to sign with Turkey a series of social security agreements providing coverage to migrant workers for preventive health, illness, accidents and work-related diseases, unemployment, retirement, maternity, child allowances, death and permanent injury, and aid to survivors.

From 1973, however, world economic events changed the manner in which foreign workers came to be viewed in West Germany. The oil embargo of 1973-74, a subsequent fourfold increase in the price of crude oil, a recession, and the unemployment of more than one million German workers resulted in the following policies: no new foreign workers were to be allowed to come; those that were already in the country could either continue to work or leave the labor force permanently. The economic situation led to a sharp polarization of opinion in regard to migratory policies. On one side the German employers association, the Bund der Deutschen Arbeitgeber (BDA), and communal organizations, concerned that German infrastructures (hospitals, schools, social services) were overburdened, began to support the principle of "rotation" (i.e., short-term recruitment). On the other side, the major workers' organization, the Deutscher Gewerkschaftsbund (DBG—the German Federation of Trade Unions), anxious that wage levels would be lowered if low-paid job categories were permitted for foreign labor and wishing to oppose further illegal immigration, started after 1968 to attack the discriminatory Alien Act of 1965 and to promote the principle of "full integration" (Zur Reform der Auslaenderpolitik 1973; Ahrendt 1973:689-93).

The discussions which ensued led to an important modification of the official labor policies of West Germany. Government decisions of 6 June 1973 were made public by the Federal Minister of Labor and Social Affairs. According to these decisions, the ultimate goal of employing foreign labor was to achieve a harmony between the needs for continuity in production and a full integration of foreign manpower into society. Thus the following drastic measures were made possible: (a) A German worker had the option of taking over a position held by a foreign worker when the latter's labor permit expired; (b) Work permits for family members who came to Germany after 30 November 1974 could be refused; (c) The recruitment of each new foreign worker would depend upon the availability of adequate and decent housing facilities, to be provided by employers in conformity with standards established in April 1974; (d) The permission for newcomers to settle in already heavily concentrated regions would depend on the absorption capacity of the existing social structure; (e) Employers would have to pay DM 1,000 for each non-EEC worker—an increase of DM 700 over the old figure; (f) Any obligatory or coercive measures tending to abruptly terminate the prevailing employment arrangements of foreign labor were to be rejected on "social and humanistic" grounds. These measures deeply affected the migratory flow. While in 1973, 103,753 new workers came from Turkey to West Germany, in 1975 only 640 received a first-time German labor permit (Rist 1978:113).

These drastic measures also explain a sudden swell of illegal migrants. Already in 1970-71 the waiting list in Turkey stood at over one million. Prospective migrants who were not willing to wait in vain for six or seven years sought to avoid a seemingly endless delay by emigrating unofficially. With limited exceptions, a Turkish citizen is entitled to apply for a tourist passport valid for three, six, or twelve months. Particularly in the 1970s unofficial migrants hoped to slip into a country of destination as "tourists" and find jobs with employers willing to turn a blind eye to the lack of a work permit. Sometimes unofficial migrants crossed frontiers over rarely frequented mountain paths to evade control. Another popular channel was to undertake a bus trip through socialist countries (Bulgaria, Rumania, East Germany), enter East Germany in East Berlin, and take a subway heading to West Berlin. (This channel has been closed.)

Inevitably unscrupulous brokers established themselves. For a hefty fee they would undertake to shepherd clandestine migrants to their destination. Of course unofficial migrants constantly face problems: they can always be deported, and they are wide open to exploitation. A case study reflects the ordeal such "tourist" migrants have experienced. A returnee relates the following:

> I applied to the Employer Service in Yozgat in 1965, but was never called. I waited 3 years and in 1968 decided to go as a tourist. I borrowed 4,000 TL [Turkish lira] with 25 dönüm as a guarantee.*
>
> We went with a bus from Istanbul. In Italy we crossed the Italian-Austrian border at night through the forest with an Italian guide. We were 15 then and everyone had to pay 900 TL to that guide.
>
> In Austria I found work for 1,000 schillings a month. The farmer liked me much but the payment was too low. After two months we found work in a lumber factory; this time we were paid 500

*One dönüm is approximately one acre.

> sch. each. I worked two and a half years in that factory for 4,000 schillings a month. There were 8 workers from my village in that area then.
>
> Later all the workers from the village passed from Austria to Germany. There was a Turk who "organized" these nominated calls to Germany for a payment of 1,000 schillings. I did not know the language and they profited from the situation.
>
> In Germany I got work in a big construction firm in Sigmar, where I worked 8 months. But the payment was low for the hard work I had to do. So I wrote a letter to my cousins in Munich; they found me work in the same firm where they worked. When I came there, there were 4 migrants from the village working in Munich.
>
> After one and a half year's work in that firm I fell ill from hard work. I stayed some days in the hospital and found an easier job afterwards, which paid somewhat less. In 1974 I fell ill again, appendicitis. I went to the hospital, but they did not want to help me; they sent me home. I was very upset and decided to return to Turkey immediately. I had had enough! (Penninx and van Velzen 1976:184-86).

The same empirical survey from which this case study is taken revealed that out of a group of five hundred migrants, as many as 42.4 percent had originally gone abroad on a tourist passport (Penninx and van Velzen 1976:180). The higher earnings for unskilled workers in Western Europe still made the risks worthwhile for many migrants.

As the protection of illegal workers became urgent, some governments offered amnesty and issued the migrants official permits. Such amnesty has been granted by Belgium (in 1966 and 1974), some West German state governments (Hessen and the Palatinate in 1972), France in 1973, and Holland in 1975 (Hale 1978:43).

In the third phase both Turkey and the major host countries gained "consciousness" in regard to the manifold problems of foreign workers. As a result, much larger audiences were made aware of the problems in recent years. This awareness is partly reflected in the large number of articles published in the Turkish and European press, as well as the coverage by the mass media of labor shortages, foreign manpower, and its impact on social life. In addition this phase marks the beginning of the interaction of migration on the arts—particularly literature—both in Europe and at home. A short example comes from Nevzat Üstün, a writer living in West Germany:

> What the Germans are expecting is totally opposed to existence in contemporary civilization. They demand only additional manpower. . . . Workers will come, sweep the streets, build the houses, weld the electric fixtures, but will not be visible. . . . They are not supposed to live in houses, to go to parks, to eat, to make love. . . . If they could, they would send all foreigners home after five o'clock in the afternoon and bring them back at five o'clock in the morning!

PHASE 4: SETTLING ABROAD FOR INDEFINITE PERIODS; MIXED MARRIAGES; FAMILY MIGRATION; EDUCATIONAL PROBLEMS (1975-78)

This period reflected an ambivalence among many migrant workers. On the one hand, most of them wanted to cling to the illusion that they would return home and realize their dreams; on the other, the persistent unemployment at home, along with growing violence and political instability, induced a significant number of them to postpone their return at least until they retired. Thus they began to bring their families, and united families became the prevailing pattern. This trend was indirectly or inadvertently reinforced by legislation in the host country. An important step in this direction was a decision not to grant work permits to spouses and children who entered West Germany after December 1974. The most blatant example of indirect consequences comes from a new child allowance policy. Prior to 1 January 1975 a taxpayer could deduct child support from his gross income (as in the United States). In 1973, 60.5 percent of all child allowances–i.e., DM 357 million–had been paid for 515,161 Turkish children left in the home country. With the reforms, the deductions were eliminated and a new family allowance was instigated. Child allowances were now available to all children in the country at a uniform rate and payable regardless of parent income; the idemnity was adjusted to the cost of living. Lower allowances were paid to migrant workers whose children were outside of West Germany. The different schedules are shown in Table 6.

This child allowance legislation affected Turkish workers most, for despite the trend toward united families, they still had the highest proportion of married workers (86 percent) but the lowest proportion of united families–only 46 percent. As a result of the legislation, even more workers brought their families. This situation induced the

Table 6

MONTHLY CHILD ALLOWANCES IN WEST GERMANY
BEFORE AND AFTER 1975
(DM)

Number of Children	Allowance for German and Foreign Children Irrespective of Residence, 1964-74	Allowance for Turkish Children Residing Outside West Germany after 1975	Allowance for German and Foreign Children Residing in West Germany from 1975
1	–	10	50
2	25	25	70
3	50	60	120
4	60	60	120
5	70	70	120

Source: Abadan-Unat 1976:35.

German lawmakers to change their policies in order to discourage foreign workers from bringing their families. Regulations were enacted in late 1975 to provide that foreign workers whose children remained in the home country would receive a different child allowance, on the assumption that the foreign workers would not bring their children to West Germany due to the high cost of living (Abadan-Unat 1976: 34-35; see also Rist 1978:85). However, Turkish migrants were not deterred from bringing their families—even if they had to pay a surcharge to be with their families (which the native workers did not). Their attitude is easy to understand: child allowances were paid in cash, while tax deductions could be obtained only after careful accounting. Thus after 1975 airplanes loaded with as many as fifty young children would arrive in West Germany. This was the period of the "imported baby boom." Moreover, the child allowance policy also seriously affected the fertility pattern of migrants. In 1984 Turks had a fertility rate of 3.5 per 1,000 women of reproductive age—compared to 1.3 for the West Germans. Between 1974 and 1980 the number of Turkish children under the age of 16 living in West Germany increased 129.8 percent; the increase for 1978-79 alone was 15.7 percent. In 1980, 40 percent of the Turkish migrant population of West Germany, Switzerland, Sweden, and Norway was under 18 years old.* The rapid increase in the migrant population under 18 has amplified the existing social problems. Ignorance of the host country's language, difficulties in adapting to a different society, and the impossibility of benefiting from an educational system fraught with complications only reinforced segregation and the migrants' preference for ghetto life.

The strong desire of migrants to remain in West Germany led to a noticeable increase in mixed marriages after 1973. Article 6 of the German Constitution states that marriages are to enjoy special protections—most notably the protection from interference by the state. While mixed marriages were one of the desired consequences of full integration, in West Germany there has been much substantial evidence that they were performed only for a migrant to obtain a permanent residence permit. To prevent the misuse of this institution the German civil law was changed. Prior to 1973 the civil law (section 13.54) granted a husband the sole right to determine where his family was to live; this rule obviously prevented deportations. After 1973 the right was given to both partners. However, in order to deport the foreign spouse of a mixed marriage, specific and important reasons based upon evidence had to be presented in an open hearing. A continued increase in mixed marriages is reflected in the most recent statistics: in 1979 there were 25,023 marriages between Germans and foreign nationals (16,246 German women married foreign men)—an increase over 1978 of 7.2 percent (*Der Spiegel* 1982).† In addition to the increase in mixed marriages, there was an increase in children born out of wedlock.

Migrant workers were also affected by large-scale legislative measures to decongest cities with heavy foreign populations. Between 1975 and 1977 cities with more than 6 percent foreigners in their total population could apply to their state government to be designated "overburdened settlement areas." In consequence a ban would be placed on further foreign settlement. As of 1977 five of the largest cities in West Germany—Cologne, Frankfurt, Hannover, Munich, and

*The figures for West Germany were as follows: 0-6 years—201,500 (13.8 percent); 7-10 years—142,600 (9.8 percent), 11-15 years—146,100 (10.0 percent); 16-18 years—94,200 (6.4 percent) (Turkey, Ministry of Labor 1982:19).

†According to *Der Spiegel* (1982), there were 526 marriages between Turks and Germans in 1965, 586 in 1970, 964 in 1975, and 3,765 in 1980. (See also OECD 1981:43.)

West Berlin—had obtained such bans.* By seeking to control the urban foreign populations, the various city and state governments aimed at keeping down the "social costs" of migrants. However, conflicting interests arose from these measures, and the policy was abandoned (*Bildung und Wissenschaft* 1/2:10).

In this phase the problems connected with providing a satisfactory education to the children of Turkish migrants became more severe. Although equality of educational opportunities has been greatly stressed in West Germany, the federal system applied many alternative models which resulted in a bewildering array of segregated or integrated classes. Confused by the complicated requirements of various school systems, many parents decided to take their children out of school after five years—the compulsory schooling period in Turkey; it differs substantially from that of West Germany, where school attendance until the age of 16 is compulsory. In addition to the bewildering school system in West Germany, some parents sent their children to privately supported Koran schools for religious education on Saturdays and Sundays, forcing upon the children totally opposite pedagogical methods. The discrepancy lies in the fact that the regular West German schools emphasize creative thinking and mental curiosity, while Islamic religious teaching relies totally upon memorizing texts in Arabic which the children do not understand. Thus the migrants' offspring had to cope not only with the most important obstacle—the language barrier—but also with a clash of cultural values.

As Rist (1978:201) observes, the German school system has traditionally been selective, elitist, and rigid. It has effectively excluded some 90 percent of its students from the opportunity for a university education. The situation bears particularly on foreign children. So far 60 percent of the children of foreign workers have not completed any of the three alternatives for secondary education (Bodenbender 1976:9). Despite measures to facilitate vocational training, only 18 percent of Turkish youngsters between the ages of

*In West Germany as a whole there was a foreign population of 6.4 percent in 1977. For individual cities the proportions were as follows: Frankfurt—19.4 percent; Stuttgart—16.3 percent; Munich—15.8 percent; Cologne—12.6 percent; Düsseldorf—12.5 percent; West Berlin—9.5 percent; Hamburg—7.4 percent. According to *Der Spiegel* (1982), the proportions in 1981 were as follows: Frankfurt—23.2 percent; Stuttgart—18.3 percent; Munich—17.3 percent; Cologne—15.2 percent; West Berlin—12.0 percent; Hamburg—9.9 percent.

15 and 21 attended vocational schools in 1979 (Turkey, Ministry of Labor 1982:109; see also Hecker 1980:51).

In addition to the major difficulty—an insufficient knowledge of German—Turkish children face the following problems:

(a) The tendency in some *Laender* (states) to keep the children out of regular German schools and segregate them in separate classes (the Bavarian model);

(b) The decision on who should teach the children their mother tongue;

(c) The total integration model, in which the mother tongue is not taught, thus alienating the children from their home and parents (the Berlin model);

(d) The emphasis upon continual evaluation of students.

Conflicts also arise between the methods of teaching by two different groups of Turkish teachers, one appointed by the Turkish National Education Ministry and the other recruited by German school authorities and placed on the German payroll (Abadan-Unat 1975:314-16). Furthermore, some Turkish parents discriminate against their eldest daughters, using them as "mother substitutes." As a result, the girls' school attendance is poor or they drop out entirely. This situation, which in brief can be described as the cultivation of "bilingual illiteracy," requires fast and effective policy correctives (Boos-Nünning et al. 1976).

PHASE 5: EXCESSIVE ASSOCIATIONAL ACTIVITIES: INCREASED REQUESTS FOR ASYLUM; INTRODUCTION OF VISA REQUIREMENTS; ENCOURAGEMENT OF INTEGRATION AND REINTEGRATION (1978-)

Until September 1980—when there was a military intervention in Turkey—the political turmoil shaking the foundations of the country's civil society created a boomerang effect in the form of excessive associational activities and political polarization among migrant workers in host countries. In the early 1960s Turkish workers' associations were mainly supported by the host country and served on a limited scale as surrogate trade unions and supportive networks among Turks. Their number and functions grew very rapidly. (The distribution of associations was presented in Table 5.)

Gradually these associations became involved in ideological controversies. Both leftist oriented, internationally linked ones and fanatically rightist religious associations started to recruit members in large cities and became the satellites of extremist political parties in the home country. Thus on the one hand, as early as 1973 the fascist-leaning National Action Party had established six autonomous sections in Berlin, Hannover, Cologne, Mannheim, Munich, and Stuttgart which had militia-like commandos called the Gray Wolves. Following sharp criticism in the Bundestag, these sections were closed down in November 1976. Similarly ultra-conservative religious associations not only supported the National Salvation Party at home, but also established private schools in all major urban centers in which a blend of missionary zeal and ideological warfare was propounded (Abadan-Unat 1979:23). After the military intervention of 1980 some of these extremist associations engaged in European-wide hunger strikes, sharply condemning the incumbent governments, and thus becoming the mouthpieces for prosecuted or escaped Turkish political activists. Subsidies were still being granted by the German government to these associations, partly explaining their continued growth, and creating serious political problems—especially in regard to the secessionist claims of Kurds. One could say that the deprivation of political rights to migrant workers in a host country created excessive political polarization among the minority groups. (Sweden was an exception: it had granted political rights on the communal level since 1975.) It can be argued that migrants who are compelled to live under such a system of deprivation show two kinds of tendencies: either they fall into a state of complete political disinterest, or their political interest grows so much that they seek "buffer" institutions such as associations for the fulfillment of their aspirations (Abadan-Unat 1979:27).

In addition to the growing impact of associational activities, this phase witnessed another unexpected development. In 1978 the ban on further recruitment in Europe had been reinforced. The authorities in West Germany were then suddenly confronted with an enormous increase of so-called "political refugees" who requested asylum. In reality these people were mostly job-seeking potential migrants who through the efforts of some German lawyers were helped to articulate their demands. Owing to a special constitutional provision, until 18 June 1980 every person seeking asylum was admitted into the country, housed at government expense (sometimes in very good hotels), granted a weekly monetary allowance, and given a work permit until his case was settled—a procedure which in the past had sometimes taken seven or eight years. Table 7 indicates the sudden growth of these disguised economically motivated migrants.

The German authorities, concerned with the rapid increase in migrants seeking political asylum, enacted measures in June 1980 to cut down the numbers of applications for asylum based on economic rather than political reasons. Among other things, these compelled applicants to take up residence in camps and put an end to the issuing of work permits and social security rights (OECD 1981:19). There was a decline in the number of candidates seeking asylum each month—from 10,932 in May 1980 (of which 6,685, or 61.2 percent, were Turks) to 2,338 in April 1981 (of which 405, or 17.3 percent, were Turks).

Finally, during this phase West Germany—followed by all European countries except Great Britain and Italy—introduced a visa requirement for Turks. It was a cumbersome bureaucratic formality which largely reduced the visits between migrants and the families they had left behind; it contributed to a growing tension between the host countries and their foreign manpower.

Xenophobia has grown, mostly due to the increases in unemployment in European countries. It has led to dramatic incidents

Table 7

TURKS SEEKING ASYLUM IN WEST GERMANY, 1976-83

Year	Number	Percent of Total Asylum Seekers
1976	809	7.3%
1977	1,168	7.1
1978	7,419	22.4
1979	13,246	25.7
1980	57,913	53.7
1981	6,302	12.8
1982	3,688	9.9
1983[a]	980	

Source: Turkey, Ministry of Labor 1984b:7, table 2.1.1.10.

[a]Until August.

among Turkish migrants, such as suicides, homicides of young children, and increasing graffiti in Germany's large cities calling for a quick exit of "Jews and Turks." The negative climate of opinion, with openly racist tendencies, has received additional intellectual support by anti-migrant manifestos like the Heidelberg Declaration, signed by sixteen West German university professors who call for the fast evacuation of all migrant workers while stressing their duty to preserve the "Christian/Occidental values of Europe" (*Die Zeit*, 26 February 1982:61). These tendencies become particularly noticeable during pre-election and pre-convention periods, and they are increasingly contributing to intolerance and racial and religious discrimination. The American press recently reported the following:

> The new prime minister of West Germany aims at defining a new "humane immigration policy." This policy is based on integrating foreigners into German society, limiting how many foreigners would be admitted to settle in the country and providing incentives for those wishing to return. In contrast to the system in the U.S. where children born of foreign residents are automatically eligible for citizenship, children born to foreign workers in West Germany are subject to the same visa and registration restrictions as their parents. If they wish to become citizens, they must apply. According to German officials, most foreign workers prefer permanent resident alien status to citizenship. Due to increasing xenophobia about 120,000 Turkish workers returned in 1983 to their homeland ("A New Racism in West Germany"; *San Francisco Chronicle*, 29 August 1984).

TURKISH MIGRATION TO THE MIDDLE EAST

A major shift in the migration of Turkish manpower from Western Europe to the Middle East and North Africa began in 1979 and continued in 1980 and 1981. Before we attempt to compare European and Middle Eastern host countries, a short structural overview of the region will be helpful.

DEMOGRAPHIC CHARACTERISTICS OF MIDDLE EASTERN COUNTRIES

One of the most striking characteristics of the Middle East is that the most populous countries are the poorest in natural resources, while the richest countries have the smallest populations. In addition, there are vast differences in technological development and manpower availability. In terms of manpower the countries can be classified into three major categories:

1. Countries that export largely skilled or professional labor (Egypt, Lebanon, Jordan, Turkey);
2. Countries that import a large portion of their labor force, particularly skilled workers (Kuwait, Saudi Arabia, Libya, Bahrain, Oman, Qatar, the United Arab Emirates (UAE), Jordan, Algeria, Iraq, Yemen [YAR]),
3. Relatively self-sufficient countries which neither import nor export labor extensively (Tunisia, Morocco, Syria).

As pointed out by a World Bank report (1981:8), Iraq, Algeria from 1976, and in more recent years Jordan, the YAR, and Oman have a dual role in the international labor market in which they both export and import labor.

A second feature of almost all of the Middle Eastern countries is that they have a distinctly different distribution of the labor force from that of Western Europe (see Table 8). In general labor is concentrated in agriculture and services rather than in industry. This is mostly due to internal migration and fast depeasantization, which produces an informal or marginal sector, as well as overemployment in public sectors.

A third important and distinctive feature of labor-importing Middle Eastern countries is that the share of migrant labor in total employment exceeds 50 percent in the case of Kuwait, the UAE, and Qatar. For the remaining labor-importing countries, the share is close to half of total employment (see Table 9). The non-national labor force is concentrated in construction and manufacturing. As in Europe labor in the construction sector is predominantly foreign—60 percent in Kuwait, 64 percent in Libya, 48 percent in Saudi Arabia, 82 percent in Qatar, and 96 percent in Abu Dhabi (Labib 1980:3). The distribution of the Turkish labor force in selected countries is shown in Table 10.

By 1975—i.e., within 20 years since substantial labor migration had begun in the Middle East—the number of migrants in the oil-rich countries had reached nearly 3.5 million, 1.82 million of whom were actively employed. The number of migrants for 1985 is estimated at 10 million. However, it is estimated that only 55 percent of the migrant workers will come from Arab or other Middle Eastern countries

Table 8

STRUCTURE OF THE LABOR FORCE IN THE MIDDLE EAST BY ECONOMIC SECTOR, 1977
(Percent)

	Economic Sector		
Country	Agriculture	Services	Industry
Turkey	64%	27%	9%
Saudi Arabia	63	23	14
Morocco	55	28	17
Syria	49	28	23
Iraq	43	32	25
Tunisia	39	39	22
Algeria	30	53	17
Jordan	28	33	39
Libya	23	52	25
Lebanon	13	60	27
Kuwait	2	73	25

Source: Statistical, Economic, and Social Research and Training Center for Islamic Countries (Ankara) 1981a:8, table 4.

Table 9

EMPLOYMENT OF NATIONALS AND NON-NATIONALS IN MAJOR LABOR-IMPORTING MIDDLE EASTERN COUNTRIES, 1975

Importing Country	Number Employed	Nationals *(Percent)*	Non-Nationals *(Percent)*
Saudi Arabia	1,799,900	57.0%	43.0%
Libya	781,600	57.5	42.5
Kuwait	299,800	30.6	69.4
UAE	296,500	15.2	84.8
Oman	207,700	66.0	34.0
Bahrain	75,800	60.4	39.6
Qatar	66,200	18.9	81.1
Total	3,527,600	51.3	48.7

Source: Statistical, Economic, and Social Research and Training Center for Islamic Countries (Ankara) 1981a:20, table 8.

Table 10

DISTRIBUTION OF TURKISH LABOR FORCE IN SAUDI ARABIA, IRAQ, AND LIBYA BY ECONOMIC SECTOR, 1983

Sector	Saudi Arabia	Iraq	Libya
Agriculture	6,300	3,176	2,000
Construction	111,600	4,719	72,000
Services	2,100	1,249	1,500
Total	120,000	9,284	75,500

Source: Turkey, Ministry of Labor 1984a: 91, 98, 104.

such as Turkey, and the rest will come from Asia (predominantly Pakistan and Sri Lanka for unskilled work and Korea for highly skilled jobs).

It is important to note the following additional features about foreign manpower in the Middle East.

1) It is predominantly male; except for teaching, employment for women is extremely limited;
2) With the exception of highly skilled foreigners, workers are obliged to live quite celibate lives;
3) Recruitment is usually through firms operating in the host country; local agents; unofficial middlemen; or within the framework of a larger "package deal" by a multinational corporation, sometimes through advertising;
4) Work and residence permits are strictly confined to times stipulated in work contracts; a change of work place is possible only through written permission (*tenezzül*);
5) Bilateral agreements are not the rule;
6) Unless migrant workers belong to highly skilled professional groups, they cannot formally be granted permission to settle in a host country for an indefinite period unless they are accompanied by their families; however, some host countries have begun to disregard this ban.

TURKISH MANPOWER IN THE MIDDLE EAST

As the opportunities for emigration to Western Europe gradually narrowed during the mid-1970s, Turkish workers directed their aspirations to Middle Eastern oil-exporting countries. The scarcity of reliable statistics in this region poses some difficulty in properly assessing the scope of the "second Turkish wave." According to the OECD's SOPEMI reports, in 1980, 28,443 Turkish workers were sent abroad through the placement services. The Arab countries absorbed about 73 percent of the flow, with Libya alone taking 15,090 workers. The great majority of these workers were male, most of them highly skilled, and with contracts of limited and usually short duration. Doctors, engineers, architects, and accountants were the most common of the highly specialized professionals. The Turkish Employment Service supplied only about 15 percent of the workers—mostly those going to non-Arab countries. The rest were recruited by Turkish entrepreneurs themselves. According to the 1983 report of the Ministry of Labor, the total number of Turkish workers in Arab countries is around 215,284; roughly 37 percent are employed in Libya, 59 percent in Saudi Arabia, and 4 percent in Iraq. No exact figures are available for the UAE. Of the Turkish workers in the Middle East 60 percent are unskilled, 35 percent are skilled, and 5 percent belong to the highly skilled technical manpower group (Adler 1981:34).

Table 11 gives the estimated number of Turkish workers in North Africa and the Middle East in recent years. The projections for 1985 may not be realized due to political events such as the Israeli invasion of Lebanon and the Iran/Iraq war. However, the estimated increase in migration to Libya and Saudi Arabia is likely to prove accurate. A major reason for this increase is a significant growth in the number of Turkish firms established in the Middle East by Turkish entrepreneurs, who in 1981 alone signed contracts for infrastructure projects for over $7 billion. (For a distribution of these firms by country, see Table 12.) In spite of the steady growth of Turkish entrepreneurial initiative, there seems to be a limit to the potential increase in Turkish migration to the Middle East because in recent years there has been an official policy to reduce the numbers of workers from Arab and Middle Eastern Moslem countries in favor of workers from Asian countries. Thus in 1980 the proportion of migrant workers to the Middle East and Africa from Arab countries fell from 71.2 to 54.8 percent, while the proportion of Asian migrant workers rose from

Table 11

ESTIMATED NUMBER OF TURKISH WORKERS IN NORTH AFRICA AND MIDDLE EAST, 1980-85

Country	1980	1981	1985[a]
Libya	38,000	60,000	150,000
Saudi Arabia	45,000	56,000	80,000
Iraq	8,000	16,000	80,000
UAE	3,000	4,000	10,000
Kuwait	2,000	2,500	5,000
Jordan	1,500	2,500	7,000
Qatar	1,000	2,500	5,000
Bahrain	500	1,000	2,000
Lebanon	1,000	1,000	1,000
Other[b]	1,000	4,500	10,000
Total	101,000	150,000	350,000

Source: Turkey, Ministry of Labor 1982:98, table 21.

[a]Figures are projections.

[b]Iran, Oman, YAR, Nigeria, Tunisia, and Sudan.

Table 12

TURKISH FIRMS ESTABLISHED IN ARAB COUNTRIES, 1979-81

Country	1979	1980	1981[a]
Libya	17	30	38
Saudi Arabia	6	13	15
Iraq	3	7	8
Kuwait	1	2	3
UAE	1	1	1
Jordan	–	1	2
Total	28	54	67

Source: Turkey, Ministry of Labor 1982:94, table 19.

[a]Figures are for January-March only.

25.6 to 33.7 percent. (The share of Turkish migrant workers increased from 0.5 to 3.1 percent [Turkey, Ministry of Labor 1982:94; see also World Bank 1981:112].)

The influx of Asian workers is mostly due to their willingness to work for relatively low wages. For example, a typical Turkish worker will accept a month-long contract to work six days per week and eight hours a day for no less than $300. Asian workers will sign such a contract for less: Thais for $225, Indians for $210, Filipinos for $208, and Pakistanis for $193 (Turkey, Ministry of Labor 1982: 95-96).

SOCIAL LEGISLATION IN MIDDLE EASTERN COUNTRIES

One of the major differences between migrant work in Europe and the Middle East lies in the application of social security to migrant workers. In principle almost all Islamic countries have established some kind of social security system inspired by the European model, but in practice the system has not been carried out. Libya has ratified Convention No. 118 of the Equality of Treatment for All Sectors agreement, an inter-Arab pact (Statistical, Economic, and Social Research and Training Center for Islamic Countries 1981b:39). Furthermore, Libya is the first—and so far the only—country which has signed a bilateral agreement with Turkey. This agreement (signed 5 January 1975) was followed by a specific social security agreement in 1976. These agreements provide Turkish workers all the social security rights and duties stipulated in Libyan legislation—i.e., equal treatment. The agreements specify the proportion of earnings that Turkish workers are allowed to transfer to the home country: 90 percent for unmarried workers and 60 percent for married workers living with their families. However, thus far Libyan authorities have permitted transfers of only 30 percent. Similarly the stipulation on pension rights (whereby a worker's employment in both Turkey and Libya would be considered) has not been implemented. Moreover, schools for Turkish children, to be established according to the agreements, have not been set up. Finally, some employers have been reluctant to issue workers a service certificate enabling them to change their workplace; such certificates represent the major subject of current negotiations (*Günaydın* [Istanbul], 2/9/81; Çölaşan 1980).

TURKEY'S MAJOR SOCIAL LEGISLATION RELATING TO EXTERNAL MIGRATION

REMITTANCES

Remittances are the most widely recognized benefit of labor exportation. Not only are they beneficial to the balance of payments, but also they alleviate traditional foreign exchange bottlenecks. Arguments in favor of remittances inspired the architects of the First Five-Year Development Plan to encourage and organize the "export of excess manpower" (including skilled labor) on a governmental level. Stephen Adler (1981) has analyzed the impact of remittances on Turkey's economy, distinguishing among macro, regional, and family/individual levels, as well as between "consumption" and "investment." Much of the discussion below draws on Adler's work.

In an assessment of the contribution of remittances to the economy as a whole, there is a tendency to compare them to foreign aid and direct foreign investment. Although the impact of these flows on the balance of payments is essentially the same, their contributions to capital outlays and economic growth are not identical. Foreign aid and foreign investment are frequently earmarked for specific investment by government or private sectors. Remittances, on the other hand, are transfers of personal income which are used partly for consumption by the immediate family of the migrant worker at home or by the worker himself upon his return; therefore they are only partly for savings and investment. Furthermore, remittances very often have some negative effects, as has been observed in Egypt. The preface to the Egyptian national plan for 1978-82 states that "a growing number of Egyptians work abroad for very high wages. These individuals return home with huge purchasing powers, which they direct toward flagrant and luxurious consumption" (Egypt, Ministry of Planning 1978:214). The tendency toward conspicuous consumption has been closely observed in Turkey. It is partly related to a desire to acquire prestige and achieve upward mobility. Two examples might help to illustrate the point. One case is of a returned migrant who had very little land:

> Even before he went abroad Mehmed had an investment plan for what he would save: "I thought of building a new house; we had no house then. I dreamed that my daughter would become a tailor and that I would buy a tractor, if Allah permits me. I thought, I will bring my daughter-in-law to my new house with my own tractor. And,

> Allah be thanked, in 1973 I brought my daughter-in-law to my new house with my own tractor!" (van Velzen and Penninx 1976:218).

Tractors acquired for such purposes usually stayed idle or were from time to time offered for rent elsewhere.

In the other case family members who are left behind have used the remittances in useless conspicuous consumption:

> Şahap has been employed for 11 years in the Netherlands. He lives in the largest house in his village. The guestroom, furnished with modern city furniture, was overflowing with machines and gadgets. Nothing looked used. There were 2 electric blankets, 2 lamps, an electric juice squeezer, an electric knife sharpener, 5 or 6 clocks, a vacuum cleaner, plastic party decorations hanging from the ceiling, a breakfront full of cups and plates and a teflon pan, even a sunlamp for someone's rheumatic pains. There was also a washing machine with dryer of Turkish manufacture. Şahap's wife said she used it, but that, too, did not look used. They also had a brand new refrigerator which was stored in the bedroom for the time being (Yenisey 1976:363-64).

One may say that on the macro level remittances in Turkey have had a beneficial impact, particularly in regard to bridging the gap in the balance of trade and in filling the need for foreign exchange. On the regional and macro levels, the increased wealth and spending power of migrants have had a "spinoff" effect on the local economy especially in regard to the housing industry. A number of authors–particularly Penninx and van Velzen (1976)–have pointed to the disappointing effects on the regional level.

The role of remittances in the Turkish economy can be easily inferred from Table 13. It should be noted that Turkey's remittances were $45 million in 1964 and had reached more than $2 billion by 1980. The increase in remittances in 1980/81 is closely related to the relative stability after the military takeover in September 1980. Another important factor has been the special interest rate given by Turkish banks to savings accounts established in foreign currencies.

It should be emphasized that remittances do not always come through official channels, but also informally through visiting migrants or the black market. The country's dependence on external sources of energy (such as the import of gasoline), as well as the increased import of consumer goods, have strengthened the prevailing asymmetric relationship between sending and host countries.

Table 13

WORKERS' REMITTANCES TO TURKEY, SEPTEMBER 1979-SEPTEMBER 1983

(U.S. $ billion)

Year	Remittances
1979/80	$1.693
1980/81	$2.476
1981/82	$2.186
1982/83	$1.553

Source: Turkey, Ministry of Labor 1984a:155, table 6.

In consequence, Turkey has passed social legislation in an attempt to make better use of the remittances. For example, laws geared to support the domestic car industry guarantee immediate delivery of domestic automobiles if they are paid for in foreign currency. The most recent legislation shortens the duration of compulsory military service in exchange for foreign currency. According to Law No. 2299, which entered into force on 1 December 1980 and was amended in June 1984, Turkish citizens up to the age of 32 who pay the equivalent of TL 600,000 need to serve in the military for only 2 months.* This law is justified on the grounds that compulsory military service should not cause Turkish workers abroad to lose their jobs and deprive the country of future remittances (Turkey, Ministry of Labor 1982:198).

SPECIAL CREDIT ALLOCATIONS

From the very beginning of its citizens' exodus to foreign labor markets, Turkey has attempted to channel their savings into productive areas of the national economy. These efforts have not been particularly successful as migrants have been mostly interested in using their savings to acquire houses, condominiums, land, or small

*The exemption fee is calculated according to the value of foreign currency as of 1 March 1981. At that time, $1 was equal to TL 170. Thus the fee amounts to $5,174.

businesses such as restaurants, coffee shops, taxi services, barbershops, and repair shops. The investment patterns of migrants have changed in recent years for two major reasons: (a) As migrants abroad have increasingly opted for a semi-permanent stay in the host country, they have begun to invest there; (b) In Turkey brokers, banks, and investment corporations have competed intensely to offer special high interest rates for foreign currency and have attracted a substantial amount of workers' savings. This source of remittances might significantly decline following the bankruptcy of both small and large brokers in the late 1970s and early 1980s; Turkey's largest broker, Kastelli, fled the country in June 1981.

Domestic Credit Allocations. Efforts to channel migrants' savings into productive economic areas go back as far as 1964. Special legislative measures were designed to encourage Turkish workers abroad to remit their savings home. For example, one law (no. 499) allocated special credits to migrants who opened accounts in foreign currencies in any of several state banks. The Emlâk Kredi Bankası (Real Estate Bank), the most important mortgage bank in Turkey, offered mortgages on the condition that an applicant kept at least 40 percent of the desired loan in a savings account for three years. This scheme did not become popular at all. Another state bank, the Ziraat Bankası (Agricultural Bank), offered migrants loans to purchase land or farm machinery. These loans were also not much used. The most popular credit offered by national banks has been that of the Halk Bankası (People's Bank). Founded in 1938 as a credit source for artisans and small-scale industrialists, after 1960 this bank started to provide managerial and technical assistance to small enterprises. After 1975 it offered a special credit plan for migrant workers: whoever opened an account with foreign currency of at least DM 20,000 could obtain a loan after one year of TL 1,250,000. Yet even this scheme in its first year attracted only 173 Turkish workers abroad ("Development of Small Scale Industry, Emergence of a New Economic Class and Role of Türkiye Halk Bankası"; *Turkish Daily News*, 2/1/75).

Turkey's provisions for the State Industry and Workers' Investment Bank (DESIYAB) deserve special attention. Law No. 1877 (17 April 1975) empowered the government to establish a bank within two years which would (a) consolidate the savings of citizens abroad and use these savings productively; and (b) channel these savings into countrywide enterprises, especially industrial investments in accordance with the aims of national development. Thus far, however, the bank is still in the building phase and has not had a decisive role in regard to workers' savings (Turkey, Senate 1980:24).

The balance sheet of the past twenty years indicates that attracting remittances for productive home investment by central authorities has proved awkward and elusive (in other labor-exporting countries as well as Turkey). A similar conclusion can be drawn in regard to investment programs for returning migrants. These can best be seen in terms of credit arrangements with host countries.

Bilateral Credit Arrangements. The bilateral agreement between Turkey and West Germany signed in 1972 was conceived in order to create a special credit fund for migrants. In July 1972 the German Ministry of Economic Cooperation made over DM 2.5 million available for initial deposit in the fund. The beneficiaries were to be migrants definitely returning to Turkey who wished to establish small businesses. A prerequisite for applying for credit from the fund was a training program in West Germany and a follow-up program in business administration in Turkey. This project, which was supposed to become an essential part of a reintegration policy for returnees, has not been successful. The number of returnees has thus far remained below all estimates, even in periods of recession (Abadan-Unat 1971: 26)—mainly because of an extraordinarily high rate of unemployment in Turkey. According to the Fourth Five-Year Development Plan, in 1978, 2,286,000 were unemployed out of an economically active population of 16,411,000. In addition, inflation has continued to grow. After the Christian Democratic party took power in West Germany in 1982, the government offered foreigners without "valid" jobs about $3,600 per adult and $500 per child to leave the country; the offer expired 30 June 1984 ("A New Racism in West Germany"; *San Francisco Chronicle*, 29 August 1984).

VILLAGE DEVELOPMENT COOPERATIVES

In spite of a poor record on government-sponsored investment schemes, Turkey attempted to develop "participatory" investment projects. First launched in 1962 by the Ministry of Village Affairs, the objective of the Village Development Cooperatives (VDCs) was to generate employment and use potential savings productively. At the same time, these institutions tried to establish priority ranking for their members for job vacancies abroad; this aim was vitally important, as the number of migrant candidates was constantly swelling and reached 1.5 million by the late 1970s (Geray 1981:80-87).

The preliminary requirement to enter the VDCs during 1963-65 was a membership pledge of TL 8,000, only TL 2,000 of which was requested as a down payment. During the initial period the coops were used almost uniquely to bypass the disproportionally long waiting lists for migration. In 1965 the Ministry of Village Affairs undertook a critical reappraisal of the VDCs and developed a blueprint for their use (van Renselaar and van Velzen 1976:105-6). The blueprint comprised the following essential points:

(a) As of March 1966 for three succeeding years at least 20,000 individuals from the 150 village cooperatives already in existence would be allocated jobs abroad. Every migrating member would contribute between TL 5,000 and 15,000 to the cooperative;

(b) The government would increase the contributions of the individual migrants by making up to TL 900 million available in credit;

(c) In addition to awarding quotas to VDCs for priority placement of members abroad, the Employment Service would see that members met their obligations;

(d) A special department for cooperatives would be set up in the Ministry of Village Affairs.

By 1966 there were 382 VDCs, and in 1967, 1,349. The Ministry of Village Affairs had not foreseen the "success"(!) of this program (van Renselaar and van Velzen 1976:107). In reality the VDC project was implemented solely to assure coop members priority in finding work in Europe. Detailed information about the cooperatives was distributed by some MPs who were anxious to secure employment opportunities for their constituents in return for electoral support (Abadan-Unat and Ünsal 1976:88-89).

A change in government in Turkey in 1965, its reluctance to back the cooperative movement, as well as an economic recession in 1966-67 in West Germany, slowed down the movement. Between 1967 and 1968 there was hardly any increase; the total number rose to 1,381. After 1973, with the labor ban in Western Europe, initiatives to found new cooperatives came totally to an end.

Evaluating the VDC program, we find that the majority of its projects were not successfully or effectively realized for the following reasons: (a) Political and administrative inertia and excessive red tape; (b) Inability of the Ministry of Village Affairs to control the projects; (c) Lack of expertise and leadership among the members. A few examples will illustrate the point. The cooperative of Yenifakıllı in Yozgat, one of the initial "pilot projects," built a flour mill in 1973. Shortly after, control of the mill passed into the hands of local grain merchants. In 1975 the mill was closed (van Velzen and Penninx (1976:240). The Çandır cooperative in Yozgat undertook to build a factory to produce sunflower oil; it was backed by the State Planning Organization. However, it selected an inappropriate site and in addition it was unable to collect the necessary supply of seed; thus it could produce only 0.24 percent of Turkey's total sunflower oil (Geray 1981:80-87).

Thus far comprehensive studies on village development, such as that by Sevin Osmay (1975) have all shown that the disguised purpose of the VDC program (i.e., filling job vacancies abroad) explains their failure. The cooperatives could certainly have been of great benefit for rural areas with heavy out-migration if properly prepared, implemented, and controlled.

WORKERS' COMPANIES

A second major instrument for channeling the savings of Turkish workers toward employment-generating investments is the Turkish Workers' Companies (TWCs). (Penninx and van Renselaar [1976] call them "workers' joint stock corporations," and Suzanne Paine [1974:114-15] calls them "work ventures.") The essential features of this type of investment scheme are the following:

1) TWCs are economic self-help initiatives of Turkish migrants, who invest their savings in the form of shares to establish a firm;
2) The number of founding members is usually small; they are strongly dependent on other participants and local leaders;
3) In their charters TWCs exclude takeovers by large-scale investors;
4) TWCs are primarily regionally oriented;
5) Shares are usually transferable only after a certain time period;
6) The average capital investment amounts to about TL 50-75 million and creates about 100 jobs, which are supposed to be instrumental for the reintegration of returnees;

7) TWCs are supported by governmental policies such as exemptions from duties for imported machinery, exemptions from taxes, and the establishment of the State Industry and Workers' Investment Bank;
8) TWCs have been linked through bilateral agreements with other countries—e.g., the Ankara Agreement between Turkey and West Germany (Werth and Yalçintaş 1978).

The exact number of TWCs in existence is not certain. An interim report concerning the development of economic initiatives in Turkey, prepared jointly by the universities of Istanbul/Turkey and Saarbrücken/West Germany (cited as ISOPLAN), reported 125 such companies in 1977, of which 78 were in operation. Adler (1981), referring to a 1978 report undertaken by the International Labor Organization (ILO), reports 141 cases, of which 42 were operational. Penninx and van Renselaar (1978) took a sample of 64 companies, of which 24 were in production. Şen (1980:233) analyzed 32 TWCs in 15 locations, 11 of which had not yet passed into production. The most recent report of the Turkish Ministry of Labor (1982:313-28) reports about 100 TWCs in the production stage, with a total personnel of 10,972; 63 TWCs are in the investment stage and have an estimated 8,143 job openings.

There have been two major responses to the TWC experiment. On one hand, a number of authors (Gitmez, Penninx, van Renselaar, Paine, Adler, Abadan-Unat) consider that it has had only a marginal impact on Turkish employment. They point to (a) a high proportion of failures, (b) the small scale of the TWCs, (c) their vulnerability in competition, and (d) their irrelevance to Turkey's development priorities. On the other hand, some authors (Yasa, Bozkurt, Güven, Yalçintaş) have responded optimistically, placing more importance on regional diversification, the creation of employment, and small- or medium-scale industries. They defend the thesis that TWCs represent a genuine entrepreneurial initiative whose potential power is far from being realized and for which new policies are required. A slightly different point of view is offered by Şen, who emphasizes the important function of social change which emanates from these ventures, although he (among others) is seriously worried about new conflict situations which are bound to emerge between the private sector properly speaking and the "people's sector" represented by these investments.

In brief, the majority of TWCs are in a precarious position. Many projects became irrelevant due to serious delays in feasibility studies, allocation of credits, inflation, and devaluation. TWCs suffer from inadequate management at the top, high debt ratios, and shortages of working capital. Furthermore, one of the major causes of failure has been the strong motivation to choose sites less on the basis of rentability, adequate communication networks, and transport facilities and more for what could be defined as "local patriotism."

When TWCs are considered as a means of reintegrating returning workers into their society, it should be kept in mind that psychological motives play a major role. Returning workers are strongly determined to set up businesses of their own for which they alone are responsible ("bazaar capitalism"). However, this inclination does not prevent them from contributing to projects from which their home town or region could benefit. Their virulent local patriotism causes them to identify with the problems of their home regions. In press interviews of TWC shareholders the following kind of argument is often expressed: "Why did I invest in local industry? Our sultans spent billions, built mosques and palaces in Istanbul, but no factories; that's why we are underdeveloped. Only industrialization can save us!" Unfortunately most of those who hold these ideas are unable to exercise the rational thinking necessary for the functioning of highly developed technologies.

The assumption that the good will of investors and modest starting capital are sufficient to overcome the hurdles of economic underdevelopment is doubtlessly extremely naive. Innovative entrepreneurs are the products of a certain level of economic growth and technological progress. Thus the most rational way to attract the savings of Turkish workers (estimated at DM 6 billion in German banks) would lie in an ability to conceive, design, and realize a bold, motivating, promising public policy. In spite of all their shortcomings, the TWCs appear to be the most imaginative device to channel savings into productive investment. The number of TWCs and the capital transferred and accumulated deserve sincere admiration. According to the most recent statistics (Turkey, Ministry of Labor 1982:33), 104,773 shareholders living and working abroad have invested TL 18 billion (approximately $1.8 million) to create 20,753 jobs.

MIGRATION AND SOCIAL STRUCTURE

The exodus of almost two million Turks over the past twenty years to nearly thirty countries of the globe has no doubt created a deep, lasting effect on Turkey. Contrary to the findings of D. Lerner in the early 1950s (when he attempted to describe the transition from traditional society toward modernization and gauge the impact of urbanization, education, and exposure to mass media), the empathy among Turks, which was then quite low, has increased remarkably since that time. The willingness—or better said the eagerness—of Turkey's rural population to envisage life in any part of the world indicates that migration has become an accepted lifestyle alternative for the majority of Turks. Nevertheless, this new outlook to life and career has created important changes in both the host and home countries.

IMPACT OF MIGRANTS ON THE SOCIAL STRUCTURE OF THE HOST AND HOME COUNTRIES

The most visible and measurable impact of foreign workers in highly industrialized countries is their predominant share in labor market "dirty work"—jobs that are dangerous, temporary, dead end, undignified, and menial. The presence of the migrant workers to do these jobs frees the domestic workforce to take higher paying and "cleaner" jobs that tend not to be dangerous, dirty, or temporary. In short, as Castles and Kosack (1973) point out, the migrant workers provide an underclass which of itself generates social and economic mobility for the domestic labor force.

The clearest theoretical interpretation of this process is provided by Hoffmann-Nowotny (1981), who refers to the creation of a new societal stratum beneath the existing social structure of the host country as an example of *Unterschichtung* (undercasting). The concept is one of the major elements of Hoffmann-Nowotny's theory of societal systems. He asserts that migration is a process of societal interaction whose effect is to reduce tension. Emigration from a home country exports tension. Through immigration tension can be localized in the lower economic strata. As a result of undercasting, the host system provides greater opportunities for its members to climb into higher positions of the employment structure. Upward mobility takes place intra- as well as intergenerationally. However, immigrants, as a result of a negative status ascription ("foreigners"), have little opportunity for mobility and remain for the most part at the bottom (pp. 74-77). The migrant worker is in an ambivalent position. In the host country his educational background, culture, and religion force him into the lower social echelons: the majority of Turkish workers are unskilled, have relatively little education, and have contributed to the growth of unemployment; moreover, increasing xenophobia is nurtured by the fact that they are Moslem. Indeed the Turkish worker is a kind of "industrial pariah." At the same time, in his community at home he gains unanimous approval as someone who has moved up the social echelon.

SOCIAL MOBILITY

Among the Turkish migrant population in host countries there is a noticeable amount of intergenerational mobility, specifically from agricultural occupations to industrial or tertiary occupations (Abadan-Unat 1974:392-93). However, the relatively high percentage of semi-qualified Turkish workers in Europe has not achieved upward mobility; on the contrary, noticeable downward mobility has taken place because a large number of primary school teachers, accountants, and the like have opted (for higher wages and a different lifestyle) to leave their white-collar jobs and become industrial workers. Downward mobility has also produced what Lenski (1966) calls "status inconsistency." Lenski suggests that status inconsistency offers an explanation for the dissatisfaction of migrants with both host and home country and their constant search for a "better future" (p. 88). In some cases it may lead to support for radical political movements.

LOSS OF SKILLED LABOR

As a labor-exporting country, Turkey has lost considerable skilled labor, and the loss has been accentuated by a parallel loss owing to a "brain drain." Indeed Turkey continues to export a higher percentage of its skilled labor force than any other labor-exporting Mediterranean country. Turkey has restricted emigration only by miners from the Zonguldak district. Other Mediterranean countries have been much more reluctant to give up their skilled labor force while Turkey has not hesitated to export an important part of its qualified manpower (see Table 14). Between 1964 and 1971 nearly 17 percent of Turkey's skilled workers emigrated. (High-level manpower is excluded.) Such an outflow no doubt had a negative impact on output: the Second Five-Year Plan estimated shortages of skilled

Table 14

SKILLED TURKISH WORKERS SENT BY EMPLOYMENT SERVICE TO EUROPE, 1964-71

Year	Number of Workers Abroad	Skilled Labor *(Percent)*
1964-66	152,106	35.4%
1967	8,947	31.2
1968	43,205	28.1
1969	103,075	31.2
1970	129,575	27.0
1971	88,442	37.7

Source: Turkey: Employment Services 1964-71, and State Planning Organization 1973:676.

workers in 1970 and 1975 at 337,000 and 885,000 respectively (Aydınoğlu 1976: 109-10).

The policy of allowing skilled labor to emigrate has been sharply criticized by the Turkish Union of Chambers of Commerce, the Ministry of Industry and the State Planning Organization (among others), but it has continued in order to maintain a continuous flow of remittances. It may be argued that the high skill levels of Turkish migrants have helped host countries to realize their own development programs.

IMPACT OF MIGRATION ON AGRICULTURAL OUTPUT

Predominantly agrarian regions with a high rate of external migration are witnessing a number of changes, such as the erosion of the adult male population and the creation of a population of women, small children, and the elderly. Furthermore, regions with high out-migration are not willing to engage in traditional agrarian activities, thus becoming centers of secondary migrant outflow. Intense migration may also cause a phasing-out of animal-based tilling, as the following case study shows:

> Around 1965 in Müftükişla [village] there were more than 80 teams of horses in the village. Nearly everyone tilled his own fields

> with his own animals. There was one tractor. With the advent of migration, workers leaving the village entered into an agreement of sharing the crop with the owner of the tractor. In 1975 no horses were left in the village. Farmwork is performed by the seven tractors now owned there (van Velzen and Penninx 1976:231-32).*

This case study also shows the indirect impact of legislation which accorded special import rights to migrant workers. Lawmakers thought that encouraging investment in farming machinery would lead to higher productivity. Instead it has led to overmechanization and attempts to build personal prestige.

INCREASE OF FEMALE/MALE MIGRATION AND ITS EFFECT ON SEX ROLES

External migration has encouraged women as well as men to seek employment abroad. In West Germany alone the number of gainfully employed Turkish women—which was 173 in 1960—reached 143,611 in 1975 (Abadan-Unat 1977:33). In 1981 there were 597,827 men 16 years and older, 393,216 women 16 years and older, and 555,268 children under 16 years. Out of the total female population in West Germany in that period, 177,143 were gainfully employed (OECD 1982:41, 66). In Austria in 1978 there were 12,450 Turkish women with work permits, representing 25.5 percent of the gainfully employed Turkish worker population. Not only were more Turkish women taking up employment in industry or services, but also more wives were joining their husbands in Europe. This exodus of women induced a great number of changes. The most important one seems to concern the economic independence of women. Due to the entrance of women into the labor market, nuclear families increased as dependency relationships to members of the extended family became redundant. Moreover, the responsibilities within families concerning breadwinning, bank accounts, saving, investing, and spending changed. The emancipation of women became more noticeable. It also caused a substantial amount of marital strain and conflict. The ones who suffered most in this framework were the elder daughters in a family; as noted, they had to shoulder heavy responsibilities as mother

*In a similar vein Magnarella has observed the following: "Foreign earnings have brought a high degree of economic equality to Hayriye village as former peasants with insufficient land must no longer work for others" (1979:161).

substitutes. Under the circumstances, the entry into industry and services of conventionally trained women (especially from rural backgrounds) may lead to isolation for the daughters and the reinforcement of traditional values and attitudes. Thus external migration may be an isolating as well as a liberating process.

The mixture of positive and negative consequences faced by migrating women can also be observed among the family members left behind. For women who stay with their in-laws, interfamily control increases. However, approximately half of the wives and/or mothers decide to set up independent households, and for them there is a noticeable increase in decision-making and authority (Abadan-Unat 1981:27-28, and 1982: 207-34).*

TREND TOWARD CONSPICUOUS CONSUMPTION

The most visible effect in Turkey of external migration is the high value placed on conspicuous consumption. Migrants and their families are extremely anxious to acquire an image of affluence and prestige in their communities. This involves (for example) purchasing new styles of furniture, which results in simulated city rooms in villages—even displaying electrical appliances where there is no electricity. This strong tendency toward conspicuous consumption is very eloquently described by Bekir Yıldız, one of Turkey's best known writers:

> Give up eating, Ahmets, give up eating Jales. Load your stuff on trains, Osman and Ayshes. . . . Fly to Turkey, your marks weigh little, but their value goes a long way. Fly home with your marks. Buy plots in our big cities. Even the cemeteries have been uprooted in recent years. These days, second-rate and third-rate cemeteries for those who have died of hunger are going for a song. . . . For those who don't care for farming, there are some other fields of investment. Buy stocks and shares, buy into new industries. When you return to your country, you could become industrialists, no less. What's wrong? Haven't you worked long enough? In this mortal life, it should now be your turn to hire others, to put others to work! (Yıldız 1974:103).

*Kiray emphasizes—correctly—that the "separate-house-in-village syndrome has to be considered as one of the most important functional changes in the role of women, brought by migration in Turkey, as no law of the republican era could bring in such a scale" (1976:223-24).

A NEW ELEMENT IN TURKISH SOCIETY: THE "*ALAMANYALI*"

Turkish migration has no doubt led to the emergence of a new social stratum. Those living in Europe, regardless of their place of employment, are called *Alamanyalı*—those from Germany. Those who migrated to Middle Eastern countries are labeled "migrating citizens." Both types are rooted in two countries—the host country which provides them employment and a place to live, and the country of their birth and heart. Predominantly employed in industry in Europe, they tend to behave as a privileged group at home. Their preference to live off of rental income or small business produces a type one might call the "proletarian bourgeois" (Abadan-Unat 1972: 293).

These permanently mobile people rank themselves higher at home than in the past. One mother who had three sons employed in Holland stated the following: "Previously the grocer of our village did not even let me enter his shop. Now, if I wish, I could buy out all his staple merchandise!" (Abadan-Unat 1977:46). They feel relatively secure due to their jobs, savings, purchasing power, life experience, and anticipated pensions. Yet most of them face a dilemma in terms of their cultural identity. Their self-imposed isolation from the culture and mores of the host country results from a dislike of integration, changing nationalities, and learning the language of the host country. Nonetheless, the Alamanyalı represent a new generation of those who dare to look for a future outside the national boundaries. As such, they have made a permanent impact on Turkey's economic life and political choice.

In sum, migration has been one of the most powerful vehicles of social change in Turkey (as in other countries). However, unrealistic assessments of it have caused political and economic leaders to believe in unproven assumptions such as "Migration has served to train skilled industrial manpower." Such a contention seems to be much more a case of wishful thinking and a convenient social and political myth than a quantitatively measurable assertion.

A lack of foresight and adequate planning have so far led to a waste of human and financial resources. Yet international migration has in the last quarter of the twentieth century become an essential part of almost all economic systems. In order to reverse the shortcomings of the past, one of the most effective solutions would seem to be well-designed and rationally conceived social legislation in both the host and home countries, particularly stressing educational policies for the second generation.

REFERENCES

Abadan, Nermin. 1964. *Bati Almanya'daki Türk İşçileri ve Sorunlari* (Turkish workers in the Federal Republic of Germany and their problems). Ankara: State Planning Organization.

Abadan-Unat, Nermin. 1971. "La Récession de 1966/67 en Allemagne Fédérale et ses répercussions sur les ouvriers turcs." *Turkish Yearbook of International Relations 1971,* pp. 39-61. Ankara: Institute of International Relations, Faculty of Political Science, University of Ankara.

__________. 1972. "Le Non-retour à l'industrie, trait dominant de la chaine migratoire turque." *Sociologie du travail,* Special Edition—*Les Travailleurs immigrés*, pp. 278-93.

__________. 1974. "Turkish External Migration and Social Mobility." In *Turkey: Geographic and Social Perspectives*, ed. P. Benedict, E. Tümertekin, and F. Mansur, pp. 362-402. Leiden: E. J. Brill.

__________. 1975. "Educational Problems of Turkish Migrant Children." In UNESCO, Institute for Education, *International Review of Education*, 21, 3; Special Edition—*Education for Children of Migrant Workers*, pp. 311-22. The Hague: Martinus Nijhoff.

__________. 1976. "Turkish Migration to Europe (1960-1975): A Balance Sheet of Achievements and Failures." In Abadan-Unat, ed. 1976, pp. 1-44.

__________. 1977. "Implications of Migration on Emancipation and Pseudo-Emancipation of Turkish Women." *International Migration Review* 11 (Spring): 31-57.

__________. 1979. "Die politischen Auswirkungen der turkischen Migration im In und Ausland." *Orient* 20, 1: 1-22.

__________. 1981. "Social Change and Turkish Women." In *Women in Turkish Society*, ed. N. Abadan-Unat et al., pp. 5-31. Leiden: E. J. Brill.

__________. 1982. "The Effect of International Labor Migration on Women's Roles: The Turkish Case." In *Sex Roles, Family and Community in Turkey*, ed. Ç. Kâğitçibaşi, pp. 207-34. Bloomington: Indiana University Press.

__________. 1984. "International Labour Migration and Its Effect upon Women's Occupational and Family Roles: A Turkish View." In UNESCO, *Women on the Move: Contemporary Changes in Family and Society*, pp. 133-58.

Abadan-Unat, N., and Ünsal, A. 1976. "Migration through the Eyes of Political Parties, Trade-Unions, Employers' Associations and Bureaucracy." In Abadan-Unat et al., eds. 1976, pp. 43-99.

Abadan-Unat, N., ed. 1976. *Turkish Workers in Europe, 1960-1975.* Leiden: E. J. Brill.

Abadan-Unat, N., et al., eds. 1976. *Migration and Development: A Study of the Effects of International Labor Migration on Boğazliyan District.* Ankara: Institute of Housing, Urban and Regional Development, Faculty of Political Science, Ankara University.

Adler, Stephen. 1981. *A Turkish Conundrum: Emigration, Politics and Development 1961-1980.* Geneva: ILO. WEP 2-26/WP 52.

Ahrendt, W. 1973. "Aktionsprogram für Auslaenderbeschaeftigung." *Bulletin*, no. 70. Bonn.

Aydinoğlu, Ismail. 1976. "Manpower and Employment Policies under the Five Year Plans and Emigration." In Abadan-Unat, ed. 1976, pp. 104-34.

Bodenbender, W. 1976. "Zwischenbilanz der Auslaenderpolitik." In *Bildungsprobleme und Lebenserwartungen der Kinder türkischer Gastarbeiter.* Munich: Südosteuropa.

Boos-Nünning, U., et al. 1976. *Schulbildung auslaendischer Kinder.* Bonn: Studienreihe des Instituts fur Kommunalwissenschaften der Konrad Adenauer Stiftung, Bd. 14.

Castles, Stephen, and Kosack, Godula. 1973. *Immigrant Workers and Class Structures in Western Europe.* London: Oxford University Press.

Çölaşan, Emin. 1980. "Gelişen Libya ve Türk İşçileri" (Developing Libya and the Turkish workers). *Milliyet* (March).

Egypt, Ministry of Planning. 1978. *National Plan, 1978-1982*, vols. 1-12. Cairo. Vol. 1, English typescript from World Bank 1981.

Geray, Cevat. 1981. *Kirsal Türkiye'de Toplum Kalkinması ve Kooperatifçilik* (Community development and cooperatives in rural Turkey). Ankara: Tuna Publishing House.

Hale, W.M. 1978. "Country Case Study: The Republic of Turkey." University of Durham, International Migration Project. Mimeo.

Hecker, U. 1980. *Representativ-Untersuchung über die Bildungs und Beschaeftigungssituation der auslaendischen Jugendlichen in der BDR.* Berlin: Bundesinstitut für Berufsbildung, vol. 30.

Hoffmann-Nowotny, H.J. 1983. "A Sociological Approach toward a General Theory of Migration." In *Global Trends in Migration*, ed. M.M. Kritz, C. B. Keely, and S.M. Tomasi. New York: Center for Migration Studies.

ISOPLAN (Interim report concerning Turkish Workers' Companies). 1973. *Türkischer Arbeitnehmergesellschaften in der BDR. Struktur, Legistungen und Aktivierungsmöglichkeiten.* Bonn: Saarbrucken.

Kiray, Mübeccel B. 1976. "The Family of the Immigrant Worker." In Abadan-Unat, ed. 1976, pp. 210-35.

Labib, Ali. 1980. "Elements pour une émigration tunisienne dans les pays arabes." Tunis: Direction de l'Emploi. Mimeo.

Lenski, G. 1966. *Power and Privilege: A Theory of Social Stratification.* New York: McGraw-Hill.

Magnarella, P.J. 1979. *The Peasant Venture: Tradition, Migration, and Change among Georgian Peasants in Turkey*. Cambridge, Mass.: Schenkman.

Nikolinakos, Marios. 1973. *Politische Ökonomie der Gastarbeiter.* Hamburg: Rowohlt Verlag.

Onulduran, Ersin, and van Renselaar, H. 1976. "International Relations, Legal and Political Dimensions." In Abadan-Unat et al., eds. 1976, pp. 27-43.

Organization for Economic Cooperation and Development (OECD). 1981. *SOPEMI 1980* (Continuous Reporting System on Migration). Paris.

__________. 1982. *SOPEMI 1981.* Paris.

__________. 1983. *SOPEMI 1982.* Paris.

__________. 1984. *SOPEMI 1983.* Paris.

Osmay, Sevin. 1975. *Türkische Dorfentwicklungsgenossenschaften.* Bonn: Ministry of Economic Cooperation.

Paine, Suzanne. 1974. *Exporting Workers: The Turkish Case.* Cambridge: Cambridge University Press.

Penninx, Rinnus, and van Renselaar, H. 1976. "Evolution of Turkish Migration before and during the Current European Recession." In Abadan-Unat et al., eds. 1976, pp. 5-27.

__________, and __________. 1978. *A Fortune in Small Change.* The Hague: Nuffic/Remplod Project.

Penninx, Rinnus, and van Velzen, L. 1976. "Migratory Labour—Boğazliyan District." In Abadan-Unat et al., eds. 1976, pp. 163-95.

Rist, R.C. 1978. *Guestworkers in Germany: The Prospects for Pluralism.* New York: Praeger.

Scott, Franklin D. 1968. *World Migration in Modern Times.* Englewood Cliffs, N.J.: Prentice-Hall.

Şen, Faruk. 1980. *Türkische Arbeiternehmergesellschaften.* Frankfurt: Verlag P. Lang.

Statistical, Economic and Social Research and Training Center for Islamic Countries. 1981a. *Manpower Exchange and Social Security in Islamic Countries.* Ankara.

__________. 1981b. "Report 1981." Ankara. Mimeo.

Turkey, Employment Service. *Annual Reports.* Various years.

__________, Ministry of Labor. 1982. *Yurtdişi İşçi Sorunlari '81* (Problems of migrant workers '81). Ankara.

__________, __________. 1984a. *Yurtdişi İşçi Sorunlari '83* (Problems of migrant workers '83). Ankara.

__________, __________. 1984b. *1983 Yili Yurtdişi İşçi Hizmetleri Raporu* (Report on services to workers employed abroad). Ankara.

__________, Senate. 1980. *Yabanci Ülkelerde Çalişan Yurttaşlarimizin Sorunlari hakkında Cumhuriyet Senatosu Araştirma Komisyonu Raporu* (Investigative report by special senatorial investigation concerning Turkish citizens working abroad). Cumhuriyet Senatosu: 918. Ankara.

——————, State Planning Organization. 1963. *Birinci Beş Yil Kalkinma Plani* (First five-year development plan). Ankara.

——————, ——————. 1973. *Third Five-Year Development Plan, 1973-78.* Ankara.

van Renselaar, H., and van Velzen, L. 1976. "Public and Private Initiatives aimed at Using External Labour Migration for Development." In Abadan-Unat et al., eds. 1976, pp. 104-39.

van Velzen, L., and Penninx, Rinnus. 1976. "The Economic Effects of Migration in Boğazliyan District." In Abadan-Unat et al., eds. 1976, pp. 105-267.

Werth, M., and Yalçintaş, N. 1978. *Migration and Re-integration: Transferability of the Turkish Model of Return Migration and Self-Help Organisations to Other Mediterranean Labour-Exporting Countries.* Geneva: ILO. WEP 2-26/WP 29.

World Bank. 1981. "Manpower and International Labor Migration in the Middle East and North Africa." Prepared by Ismail Serageldin, James Socknat, Stace Birks, Bob Li, and Clive Sinclair. June.

Yenisey, Leyla. 1976. "The Social Effects of Migrant Labour on the District Left Behind: Observations in Two Villages of Boğazliyan." In Abadan-Unat et al., eds. 1976, pp. 327-71.

Yildiz, Bekir. 1974. *Alman Ekmeği* (German bread). Istanbul: Cem Kitabevi.

Zur Reform der Auslaenderpolitik. 1973. *Theorie und Praxis der Socialen Arbeit.* Special issue no. Z 21441 (April). Bonn.

INDEX

Abu Dhabi, 345
Abu Dharr, 28. *See also* Shari'ati, Ali
Accounting profession, 257
Aflaq, Michel, 64-66
Agrarian reform: of Iranian Islamic Republic, 41-48, 56; in Tunisia, 162-69, 172, 186-88. *See also* Land reform
Agrarian Reform Law of 1958 (Tunisia), 165
Agricultural and Cooperative Bank (Syria), 88-89
Agricultural development. *See* Agrarian reform; Agriculture; Land reform
Agricultural Education Centers (Tunisia), 172
Agriculture: bureaucratization in Tunisia of, 175-77; decentralization in Tunisia of, 161, 174-75, 178; decline in Iraq of, 196, 198; and labor migration in Turkey, 362-63; in Lebanon, 203; mechanization in Egypt of, 272-74; reorganization of in Syria, 88-92
Agro-Combinat (Tunisia), 172, 177, 187
al-Ahmar, Abdullah, 95
Albun Nasir (Arab tribe), 205
Algeria, 128-29, 148, 150, 266, 269, 289; education in, 144-45; employment in 134-44; industry in, 149; labor in, 126-28, 287; Ministry of Labor of, 117; population growth of, 134; strikes in, 117, 127-28; state electronics company of (SONELEC), 270-71; Statute of Workers of 1978 of, 126-28; technology transfer and social structure of, 270-71; urbanization in, 134-35; workers' protection legislation in, 117
'Ali b. Abi Talib, 18n, 19
Alien Act of 1965 (FRG), 334
Alouites, 74, 76
Amul, 41
Anjuman-i Mahana-yi Dini (Monthly Religious Society), 27
Apter, David, 63
Arab-American Oil Company (ARAMCO), 268
Arab Ba'th Socialist Party. *See* Ba'th regime (Iraq); Ba'th regime (Syria); Ba'th Socialist Party (Iraq); Ba'th Socialist Party (Syria)
Arab states. *See* Arabs and Arab world; Oil-Producing Countries
Arabs and Arab world: effects of technology transfer on, 268-74; and labor migration, 295, 300-301, 309; in Lebanon, 199. *See also* Egypt; Middle East and North Africa (MENA); Oil-producing countries; Syria
Arab unity, 69
Arak, 41
ARAMCO. *See* Arab-American Oil Company
Ardabili, Ayatullah Musavi, 51, 53n
Armenians, 195, 199, 232
Artisans, 97
Asad, Hafiz, 76, 84, 95
Asghari (Minister of Justice, Iran), 51
Assyrians, 195
Asylum, political, 342-43
Ataturk, 6
Avicenna, 28
Azarbayjan, 41

Bab al-ijara (Islamic law of rentals), 50
Ba'ir (uncultivated) lands, 42-43, 45-46
Band-i jim (large private holdings), 42-43, 44
Bani Sadr, Abu 'l-Hassan, 32-33
Banking, 213

Bank Misr Group (Egypt), 244
al-Baqir, Imam Muhammad, 22
Batatu, Hanna, 204-5
Ba'th regime (Iraq): and education and control of youth, 218-22; industrial development, 198; strategy of state expansion, 208-10; voluntary service associations, 220-21
Ba'th regime (Syria): as challenge to Western interests, 83; consolidation of, 77-78; domestic constituency of, 80-81; economic policies of, 79-80, 100; effects of 1967 defeat on, 83-84; external environment of, 83; Islamic opposition to, 82; labor and welfare policies of, 93-95, 99-101; lack of public support for, 82-83; liberal opposition to, 82; and obstacles to reform, 78-79; and Palestinian cause, 83; policies toward opposition of, 82-83; problems implementing socialism of, 72-73; reorganization of agriculture under, 88-92; struggle against Israel of, 83-84; success and failure of, 101-5; urban opposition to, 82-83; and working class, 92-101
Ba'th Socialist Party (Iraq): domination of state by, 209-10; economic program of, 195-96; elite of, 204-5; and elite control of the state, 205-6, 208-10; ideology and leadership of, 192
Ba'th Socialist Party (Syria): character of elite of, 75-76; cleavages in, 74-75; constitution of, 66-67; contradictions in program of, 67; dissolution of party organization of, 73; domestic politics of, 81-83; economic model of, 81; ideology of, 62-64, 72-73, 75-77; imposition of socialism of, 71-72; institutionalization of, 74; in leadership of General Federation of Workers' Syndicates, 94-95; loss of constituency of, 73; organization of General Federation of Peasant Syndicates of, 87; performance in countryside of, 77; performance in cities of, 77; phased program of, 70-71; radicalization of doctrine of, 68-73; political model of, 70; rejection of capitalism of, 71; rural policy of, 84-92; seizure of power of, 73-74; Sixth National Congress report of, 70-71; socioeconomic order of, 78-81; social roots of, 63-64; social thought of, 67-68; structure of, 76-77; and syndicalists, 95; world-view of, 64
Bazargan, Mehdi, 25, 41
BCUPN. *See* Bureau de Contrôle des Unités Coopératives de Production du Nord
Ben Salah, Ahmed, 167, 181-82
Berlin Wall, 330
Bernard, Chantal, 131
Bihbahan, 41
Bihishti, Ayatullah Muhammud Husayn, 27, 41, 43-44, 49, 53-54
Bordj El Habib Pre-Cooperative (Tunisia), 183
Bourdieu, Pierre, 119
Bourguiba, Habib, 161-63; 170-71, 181-82
Boy Scouts (Lebanon), 228
Bund der Deutschen Arbeitgeber (BDA), 334
Bureau de Contrôle des Unités Coopératives de Production du Nord (BCUPN; Tunisia), 176, 183-84, 186
Burujirdi, Ayatullah Husayn, 26

Cairo, 257
Capitalism: critique by Talaqani of, 26; rejection by Ba'th of, 71
Capitulations, The, 242, 246, 256
Cave Viticole de Chouigui (Tunisia), 180
Center for Training in Social Service and Development (Lebanon), 230
Central Intelligence Agency (CIA), 23
Chouigui (Tunisian village), 161; cooperative problems of, 184-86; cooperative status of, 183-86; French

settlement in, 178-80; and Ten-Year Perspectives, 180-83
Christian Democratic Party (West Germany), 355
Christians in Lebanon, 199-200, 210-11
CIA. *See* Central Intelligence Agency
CMVVM. *See* Commissariat de la MVVM
Commissariat de la MVVM (Tunisia), 164
Communism/Communists, 24, 65, 93-94
Constantine (Algeria), 116
Cooperatives: in Syria, 89-91; in Tunisia, 167-68, 170-73, 180-88; in Turkey, 355-57
Council of Guardians (Iran), 46, 52, 56
Craft industry in the Maghreb, 150-51

Da'ir (cultivated) lands, 42-43, 45-46
Daoud, Zakiya, 131
Démocratie (Tunisia), 175, 177
Dependence and technology transfer, 270-71
DESIYAB. *See* State Industry and Workers' Investment Bank
Deutscher Gewerkschaftsbund, 337
Developing nations. *See* Third World
Dhour el Choueir (Lebanon), 231
Directorate of Youth and Sports (DYS; Lebanon), 227-28, 230
Druze, 199
DYS. *See* Directorate of Youth and Sports (DYS)

Economy: of Iraq, 195-96, 198-99; of Lebanon, 203-4; of the Maghreb, 118-19, 130, 148-49, 150-51. *See also* Private sector; Public sector
Education: in Algeria, 145; in Iraq, 218-21; in Lebanon, 224-27; in the Maghreb, 132-34, 144-47, 153; and MENA, 289, 309; in Tunisia, 172, 174-75; of Turks in West Germany, 340-41
EEC (European Economic Community), 325
Egypt, 8, 241-61 passim, 284, 300, 351; effects of exemption policies of, 246-50, 255-58, 259-69; exemption policies of, 241-45, 249-50, 257-58; foreign banks in, 252; foreign investment in, 245-46, 251-52, 256-57; joint ventures in, 253-56; and labor migration, 196; legal and accounting professions in, 256-57; nationalizations in, 244; National Plan for 1978-82, 313; open-door policy of 250, 252, 259-60; and technology transfer for agricultural mechanization, 272-74
Elites: in Iraq, 192, 204-6, 208-10; in Lebanon, 192-93, 210-14; and the young in Iraq and Lebanon, 191-234
Emlâk Kredi Bankası (Real Estate Bank; Turkey), 354
Employment: in Algeria, 134-44; in Libya, 124; in the Maghreb, 116, 118-21, 132-34, 146, 149-50; under Syrian Ba'th, 100
Employment Service (Turkey), 331, 348
Entrepreneurs in the Maghreb, 151
Europe: and bilateral migration agreements with Turkey, 331-32; Turkish migration to, 325-26, 330-44
European Economic Community (EEC), 325
Exemption legislation. *See under* Egypt

Farm reorganization (Tunisia), 172, 173; education of farmers, 175
Fars, 41, 44-45
Farsi, Jalal ad-Din, 33
Fayziya Madrasa (religious college), 35
Federal Republic of Germany (FRG), 330; and asylum of Turkish workers, 342-43; and bilateral credit for Turkish migrants, 355; education of Turkish migrants in, 340-41; migrant social welfare organizations in, 332; modification of policies toward Turkish migrants in, 334-37; Recruitment Bureau in Istanbul of, 331; and Turkish women migrants, 363; xenophobia against migrants in, 343-44

Fida'iyan-i Islam, 24-25
Fiqh (Islamic jurisprudence), 34, 52-55
Foreign investment. *See under* Egypt
Free Officers' Revolution of 1952 (Egypt), 243, 244
Free zones (Egypt), 245
French Protectorate in Tunisia, 178-80
FRG. *See* Federal Republic of Germany
Fuqaha (religious scholars), 36-37

General Authority for Investment and Free Zones (Egypt), 246, 248, 250
General Company for Batteries (Genbat; Egypt), 247, 253
General Federation of Peasant Syndicates (Syria), 87-88
General Federation of Workers' Syndicates (Syria), 93-97
General Telephone and Electronics Corporation, 270
General Telephone and Electronics International, Inc. (GTEI), 270-71
General Union of Iraqi Students, 221-22
Germany. *See* Federal Republic of Germany
Gerodius, Commandant, 180
Ghafuri, 'Ali Gulzada, 34
Girl Scouts (Lebanon), 228
Gray Wolves, 342
Greek Catholic, 199
Greek Orthodox, 199
Green Book, 125
Guftar-i Mah (Words for the Month), 27
Gulf states, 78, 277, 289

Habous (pious endowments), 162
Hadid, Muhammad, 95
Halk Bankası (People's Bank; Turkey, 354
Heidelberg Declaration, 344
House of justice (*'adalatkhana*), 23
House of the Worker (Khana-yi Kargar), 49, 57-58
Housing Foundation (Bunyad-iMaskan; Iran), 39
Husayn b. 'Ali, 20-21, 30-31
Husayniya-yi Irshad (Center for Religious Guidance; Iran), 27, 33

Ideological "movement regimes," 62-63
Imams. *See under* Shi'ism
Incentives in Syrian industry, 93-99
Income equality under Ba'th, 101
Indian subcontinent, 295
Indians, 195
Indonesia, 266
Industry: in Algeria, 149; in Iraq, 198; in Lebanon, 203; in Tunisia, 174
Infitah, 256-57. *See also* Open-door policy
International Labour Office (ILO), 266, 278-79
Iqtisad-i Tauhidi (The economics of *Tauhid*), 32-33
Iqtisaduna (Our economics), 32, 32n
Iran, 17-60 passim; Constitution of Islamic Republic of, 37-38; Constitutional Revolution of, 23; Cultural Revolution of, 39; Islamic Republic of, 17-60, 266, 269, 281, 284; Islamic Revolution of, 20; labor reform in, 49-50, 51-53, 56-58; land reform in, 45-47; role of justice in, 37-41
Iranian National Oil Company, 39
Iraq, 44, 194-222 passim, 269, 289, 348; agriculture in, 196, 198; bureaucracy in economy of, 208; education and youth in, 218-21; Egyptians in labor force of, 196; elites in, 204-6, 208-10, 233-34; establishment of, 192; ethnic and religious makeup of, 194-95; industry in, 198; labor demand of, 287; labor force in 195-96; oil revenues of, 192, 198-99; population trends in, 194-95; private sector in, 205-6, 208; public sector in, 205-6, 208; service associations for youth in, 220-21; social legislation in, 221; spending on imported technology of, 270; urbanization in, 195; women in labor force of, 196; youth in labor force of, 214-18
IRP. *See* Islamic Republic Party
Irrigation, 174
Isfahan, 23

Iskandar, Amir, 209
Islam: in Ba'th thought, 68; in Farsi's writings, 33; in Ghafuri's writings, 34; opposition to Ba'th of, 82; and occulted Imam, 22; political and socioeconomic dimensions of, 17-18, 25; in Shari'ati's writings, 28-29; and social justice, 34-36
Islamic economy, 26-27, 32, 48
Islamic government, 35-36, 40
Islamic law, 18, 52-54
Islamic Republic Party (IRP; Iran), 21n, 38, 54
Islamic Rural Councils (Iran), 47
Islamic Students' Association (Iran), 25
Islamic Workers' Councils (Iran), 48-51, 56-58
Israel, 83-84
Istanbul, 331
Izadi, 'Ali, 41

Jews, 195
Jordan, 295, 300-301, 314
Jumhuri-yi Islami (Iran), 51-52
Junbish-i Musalmanan-i Mubariz (Movement of Militant Muslims), 32
al-Jundi, Khalid, 95

Kamali, Husayn, 57
Kani, Ayatullah Mahdavi, 56
Kar va Malikiyat dar Islam (Labor and ownership in Islam), 26-27
Karbala, 20-21, 30
Karrubi, Hujjat al-Islam, 56
Kashani, Ayatullah Abdu'l-Qusim, 23-24
Kashani, Muhtasham, 19n
Kashf al-Asrar, 35
Kenana Sugar Company (Sudan), 247
Khadimi, Ayatullah Husayn, 42, 43n
Khomeini, Ayatullah Ruhallah: beliefs of, 34-37; and Islamic government, 40; and land law, 41, 42, 44-45; position in Islamic Republic of, 55; and revolutionary ideology in 1960s, 26; view of 'ulama of, 37
Khurramabad, 41
Khutut-i Asli dar Nizam-i Iqtisadi-yi Islam (An outline of the economic system of Islam), 34
Khuzistan, 36, 41
Kurds, 195
Kuwait, 277, 287, 309, 345

Labor force: in Iraq, 195-96; in Lebanon, 201; in the Maghreb, 118-19, 145-47; participation of Iraqi youth in, 215-18; participation of Lebanese youth in, 223; and participation of women in MENA, 287, 289
Labor migration: and citizenship, 317; costs and benefits of, 313-17; and data on for MENA, 279-81; and employment in MENA, 317; impact of oil price rise on, 277-78; and labor-exporting countries, 300-301; and labor-importing countries of MENA, 301, 309, 313; from the Maghreb, 118; in MENA, 277-321, 344-45, 347; and MENA labor importations 287, 289, 292-93; and political identification, 320; and remittances, 313-15; requirements in MENA for, 281-87; shifting patterns of, 325-26; and workers' families 320. *See also* Workers, migrant
Labor recruitment in the Maghreb, 149-51
Labor unions, 66, 92-94, 124, 220. *See also* individual unions
Land grants in Tunisia, 163
Landowners: in Syria, 91; in Tunisia, 165-66, 171, 188
Land ownership: in Islamic law, 43-44; legal regulation in Iran of, 41; reforms in Tunisia of, 165, 187-88. *See also* Land reform; Agrarian reform
Land reform: in Syria, 46, 66, 78, 85-86, 91; and Tunisification program, 164-65. *See also* Agrarian reform
Land surveys in Tunisia, 168-70
Law in the Middle East, 3-9. *See also* Legislation; Social legislation

Law, investment: application in Egypt of, 247-48; and compromise with socialism, 255; of Egypt on foreign investment, 233-34, 243-46; nature of in Middle East, 241-42
Law for the Reassignment and Revival of Land (Iran), 41-42
Law No. 21 of 1967 (Syria), 97-98
Law No. 26 of 1954 (Egypt), 255
Law No. 31 of 1964 (Syria), 93
Law No. 32 of 1977 (Egypt), 241, 249
Law No. 43 of 1974 (Egypt), 241, 245-46, 248-49, 252-54
Law No. 65 of 1971, "Concerning the Investment of Arab Funds and the Free Zones" (Egypt), 245
Law No. 73 of 1973 (Egypt), 255
Law No. 1877 (Turkey), 354
Law No. 2299 (Turkey), 353
Lebanese Center for Training in Methods of Active Education, 227
Lebanon, 222-34 passim; agriculture in, 203; censuses of, 199; dominance of Christians in, 216; economy of, 203-4; education in, 224-27; elites in, 210-14, 233-34; establishment and political structure of, 192-93, 210-11; industry in, 203; labor force in, 201; militia role in, 214; population of, 199-200; sectarianism in youth organizations in, 231-32; social legislation for youth in, 229; taxation in, 211-12; unemployment in, 201; urbanization in, 200-201; voluntary associations in, 227-28; wages and workers in, 229; weakness of the state in, 210-11; youth in, 221-23, 229-32; *zu'amā'* role in, 213-14
Legislation: for attracting foreign investment, 241-60; changes after Islamic Revolution in, 38-39, 48-53; stages of in the Maghreb, 121-22. *See also* Agrarian reform; Social legislation
Legitimacy, 9, 35; of Iraqi Ba'th regime, 192; of Ba'th ruling elite, 209; of Lebanese elite, 193
Liberalization, economic, 78, 80
Libya, 269, 278, 345, 348; ideology of, 125; labor law of 1970 of, 123-25; social security law of 1980 of, 125; trade unions in, 127; and Turkish migrants, 350
Line of the Imam, 35n, 37
Literacy: in Iran, 39-40; of youth in Iraq, 218; of youth in Lebanon, 224-25

Madina, 19
Maghreb, the, 113-59 passim; advances in education in, 153; craft industries in, 150-51; economy in, 148-49; employment in, 116, 146, 149-50; entrepreneurs in, 151; impact of oil boom on labor migration from, 278; manpower distribution in, 147-49; sources of social legislation in, 116-18; state in, 122-23, 128-32; uses of social education in, 153-54; youth of, 145
Mahallati, Ayatullah Baha ad-Din, 43
Majlis, 40, 44, 45, 51, 56
Maktab-i Tashayyu' (The school of Shi'ism), 26-27
Malikiyat, Kar va Sarmaya az Didgah-i Islam (Ownership, labor and capital from the viewpoint of Islam), 31
Maronites, 199, 211
Martyrs' Foundation (Bunyad-i Shahid; Iran), 39
Marxism-Leninism, 26, 69-70. *See also* Communism
Mashhad, 23, 27
Mauzi'giri-yi Tabaqat-i Ijtima'i dar Qur'an (The attitudes of social classes in the Qur'an), 31
Medjerda Valley, 161-62, 164, 175
MENA. *See* Middle East and North Africa
Middle East and North Africa (MENA): Arab migrant workers in, 295, 300-301; assessment of labor migration in, 279-81, 320-21; costs and benefits of labor migration in, 313-17; demand for foreign workers in, 293, 295; demographic characteristics of, 344-45, 347; dependence

on non–national workers in, 287-93; education of migrant workers in, 309; effects of labor migration on, 300-301; and international labor migration, 277-321; investment law in, 241-42; labor migration to, 344-45, 347; labor requirements in, 282-87; leadership and law in, 9; migrant labor sources in, 348, 350; migrant worker populations in, 295, 301, 309, 313; and migrant worker remittances, 313-15; participation of women in labor force of, 287, 289; and social legislation for Turkish migrants, 348, 350

Migrant workers. *See* Workers, migrant

Migration: effects on sex roles of, 363-64; effects on Turkish economy and agriculture of, 351-53, 361-63; effects on Turkish social structure of, 359-66; and growth of Turkish population in West Germany, 330-33, 337-41; and marriages of Turks in West Germany, 339; in MENA, 277-321; modifications of policies toward, 333-37; and political asylum, 342-43; and problems of Turkish migrants in host countries, 332-33, 335-37, 340-41; shifting patterns of, 325-26; and social legislation in Turkey, 351-59; and social legislation for workers in MENA, 350; of Turks to Europe and Middle East, 325-66; and West German welfare organizations, 332; and workers' families, 337-39; and xenophobia, 343-44

Militias, 214

Ministry of Agriculture (Iran), 42,46

Ministry of Agriculture (Tunisia), 166, 177, 186

Ministry of Economic Cooperation (FRG), 335

Ministry of Foreign Affairs (Turkey), 330

Ministry of Health (Lebanon), 230

Ministry of the Interior (France), 178

Ministry of the Interior (Iran), 42

Ministry of Labor (Iran), 50, 52

Ministry of Labor and Social Affairs (Lebanon), 213, 227, 230

Ministry of Labor and Social Affairs (Libya), 123

Ministry of National Education (Turkey), 341

Ministry of Planning (Lebanon), 213, 230

Ministry of Reconstruction Jihad (Iran), 56

Ministry of Tourism (Lebanon), 227

Ministry of Village Affairs (Turkey), 355-57

Mishkini, Ayatullah, 41

Morocco, 132, 144-45, 150-52

Movement for Instruction in Literacy (Nihzat-i Savad Amuzi; Iran), 39-40

Mubarak, Hosni, 26

Muhammad, 19, 22

Muntaziri, Ayatullah, 41

Muslim Brotherhood of Syria, 96

Muslim Brothers of Egypt, 23

Mustaz'af, 30

Mustaz'afan Foundation (Bunyad-i Mustaz'afan), 39

Mustaz'afin, 30n, 31, 34, 37-39

Mustaz'afin, Day of the, 38

Mutahhari, Ayatullah Murtaza, 27, 33-34

Najaf, 36

Nasser, Gamal Abdel, 243, 244, 255, 256, 259, 269

Nasserism in Syria, 69, 82, 93-94

National Action Party (Turkey), 342

Nationalization, 78, 93

National Pact (Lebanon), 210-11

Neo-Destour Party (Tunisia), 163

Nizamat-i Ijtima'i-yi Islam (The social institutions of Islam), 34

North Africa. *See* Maghreb; Middle East and North Africa

North Yemen. *See* Yemen Arab Republic (YAR)

October War, 245

OECD. *See* Organization for Economic Cooperation and Development

Office of Social Development (OSD; Lebanon), 227, 230
Oil price rises of 1973-74, 277-78
Oil-producing countries, 8, 277, 284, 289, 326
Office de la Mise en Valeur de la Vallée de la Medjerda (OMVVM; Tunisia): and Agrarian Reform Law of 1958, 165; and cooperativization, 172, 180; and land redistribution, 164-65; and land surveys, 168-70; in Medjerda Valley, 175; and private parcel regrouping, 188; role under agrarian reforms of, 165-66
Office des Terres Domainales (OTD; Tunisia): and cooperatives, 173; creation of, 167; and land surveys, 168-70; problems of bureaucratization of, 175-77; and public land management, 172-73; reorganization of, 177
Oman, 287, 300, 301, 315
OMVVM. *See* Office de la Mise en Valeur de la Vallée de la Medjerda
Open-door policy (Egypt), 8, 243, 245, 251-52, 256-57, 259-60
Organization for Economic Cooperation and Development (OECD), 269
OSD. *See* Office of Social Development
OTD. *See* Office des Terres Domainales
Ottoman Empire, 192, 242

Pahlavi, Riza Shah, 23, 35
Palestinians, 201
"Parallel" economy, 130
Parliamentarianism, 70
Payman, Habibullah, 31-32
Peasants: appeal of Ba'th to, 68; and *band-i jim* land, 44; and Islamic Rural Councils, 47; links with Ba'th party of, 77; and Majlis land law, 46; participation in Islamic Revolution of, 41; political mobilization in Syria of, 87; and village cooperatives in Syria, 89-90
Pension plan, 47-48
Pilot farms (Tunisia), 172, 187
Popular Education Service (Lebanon), 228
Population: in Algeria, 134; in Iraq, 194-95; in Lebanon, 199-201; in the Maghreb, 145; and migrant workers in MENA, 309
Pre-cooperatives (Tunisia), 168, 178-86
Private sector: in Algeria, 143-44; in Egypt, 244-45, 256; in Iraq, 196, 198, 205-6, 208; in Lebanon, 213; in Syria, 66, 79
Profit-sharing, 98-99
Public sector: in Algeria, 143-44; under Islamic Republic, 48; in Iraq, 205-6, 208; in Syria, 66, 78-79, 81

Qaddafi, Muammar, 125
Qajars, 21
Qatar, 287, 309, 345
Qazvin, 41
Qum, 23
Qur'an and concept of justice, 18-22

Rabat Declaration of 1976, 269
Rafsanjani, Hashimi, 46-47
Rahnavard, Zahra, 31
Raja'i, Muhammad 'Ali, 48
Rasht, 41
Reconstruction Jihad (Jihad-i Sazandagi; Iran), 39, 42, 44, 47
Revolutionary Council (Iran), 40-41, 45, 49
Revolutionary Council (Libya), 123
Ruhani, 46

Sadat, Anwar, 8, 243-45, 255, 258-260, 272
al-Sadr, Ayatullah Muhammad Baqir, 32
Safavi, Navvab, 24
Salamati, Muhammad, 56-57
Salamati, Riza, 45
Saudi Arabia, 268, 315, 345, 348
Sayyid Qutb, 28n, 32
Sazman-i Mujahidin-i Khalq (Organization of People's Mujahidin), 33n
Schools. *See* Education
Science in Arab world, 268-69
Sectarianism, 74, 192, 211-12, 231-32
Service associations, 39-40, 220-21, 227-28

Sex roles, 363-64
Shari'a, (Islamic religious law), 24
Shari'ati, Ali: career and thought of, 27-31; comments on *ta'ziya* by, 21; influence on others of, 31-34
Shari'atmadari, Ayatullah Kazim, 42
Shi'ism: association with Imams of, 20-22, 31, 38; concept of justice in, 18-22, 35; exegesis of Qur'an of, 20; and implications of Karbala, 20-21; in Islamic Revolution, 17; quietism of, 22; in Shari'ati's writings, 30-31
Shi'ites, 19-21, 195, 199-200
Shirazi, Ayatullah 'Abdullah, 43
Sistan, 44
Socialism: under Ba'th, 66-67, 71-73; experiments in Tunisia with, 168-70; and foreign investment in Egypt, 255-56; in thought of Aflaq, 65-66
Social legislation: debates about nature of, 5-6; definition of, 4-5, 113-16; and migrant workers, 337-39, 350; political uses in the Maghreb of, 151-54; popular perception in the Maghrcb of, 152-53; process in Iran of, 53-54; relationship with political and economic sector of, 115; sources in the Maghreb for, 116-18; and state control in the Maghreb, 122-28; in Turkey for external migration, 351-59; and worker remittances in Turkey, 353; for youth in Iraq, 221; for youth in Lebanon, 229
Social structure: effects of migration on, 359-66; and links to technology, 264-68; and ownership of technology, 267-68; and technology transfer, 270-74
Société d'Agriculture (Tunisia), 180
Société Foncière et Agricole de Chouigui (Tunisia), 180
SONELEC (Algeria), 270-71
Southeast Asia, 295, 309
Soviet Union, 8, 69
State Industry and Workers' Investment Bank (DESIYAB; Turkey), 354
Sudan, 247, 300, 301
Suez War, 244
Sunnis, 19, 195
Syria, 61-109 passim; agrarian relations legislation of, 86; under Ba'th rule, 61-105; Economic Penal Code of, 98; migrant laborers from, 201; oil production of, 284; and regional congresses of Ba'th Party, 83-84; Second Five-Year Plan (1966-70) of, 90; and worker legislation, 93, 97-98. *See also* Ba'th regime

Tabriz, 23
Takrit, 205
Talaqani, Ayatullah Mahmud, 25-26, 27, 32
Tauhid (divine unity), 28-29
Tavakkuli, Ahmad, 49, 51, 56
Taxation, 211-12, 249
Ta'ziya, 21
Technology: capital-intensive, 267; labor-intensive, 266, 274
Technology transfer, 263-74; definition of, 263-64; dependence of Arab world on, 270-71; impact on Egyptian agriculture of, 272-73; impact on social structure of, 263-74; and indigenous social groups, 271-72; lack of policy in Arab world on, 268-69; monetary cost in Arab world of, 270; and ownership, 267-68; process of, 264-65
Tehran, 27, 36
"Third" economy, 130
Third World, 8; investment law in, 241-42; planning in, 193; technology transfer to, 263-68
Treaty of Rome, 325
Tunisia, 132, 151, 162-89 passim; agrarian reform communities of, 163-64; agricultural development in, 161; centralization policies of, 166-68; education in, 144-45; Fourth National Plan of, 174; land laws and rural development policies of, 161-88; Sixth Plan of; 186-87; Ten Year Perspectives of, 167, 168, 180; and Tunisification, 164-65.

See also Agrarian reform; Land reform
Turcomans, 195
Turkey, 273, 326, 350; and bilateral agreements on migration, 331-32; and bilateral credit with West Germany, 355; constitution of (1961), 326; five-year development plans of, 330n, 351, 355, 361; impact of migration on, 359-66; investment and credit allocations of migrants' savings, 353-59; loss of skilled labor in, 361-62; military exemptions for migrants in, 353; remittances in, 351-53; social change in, 365-66; social legislation for external migration in, 351-59; and village development cooperatives, 355-57; and women under Ataturk's reforms, 6
Turkish Workers' Companies (TWCs), 357-59
Turks: associations in West Germany of, 341-44; asylum in West Germany of, 342-43; education in West Germany of, 340-41; effects of migration on sex roles of, 363-64; illegal migration to West Germany of, 335-37; integration in host countries of, 332-33; manpower in MENA of, 348-350; marriages in West Germany of, 339; migrant families of, 337-39; migration to Middle East of, 344-45, 347; modification of migration policies toward, 333-37; phases of migration to Europe of, 326, 330-44; recruitment to West Germany of, 330, 331; settlement in West Germany of, 337-41; and social mobility of migrants, 361; and West German welfare organizations, 332; xenophobia against, 343-44
TWCs. *See* Turkish Workers' Companies
Twelfth Imam, 21-22, 31, 38

UAE. *See* United Arab Emirates
UCPs. *See* Unités Coopératives de Production
UCPA. *See* Unités Coopératives de Production Agricole
'Ulama, 22-23, 36-37, 54
'Umar ibn al-Khuttab, 19
Union Carbide, 247-48, 253
Union Carbide Egypt, 248
Union Générales des Travailleurs Algériens (UGTA; Algeria), 117
United Arab Emirates (UAE), 287, 309, 345
United Nations Center on Transnational Corporations, 241
United States, 44
United States Agency for International Development (USAID), 268
Unités Coopératives de Production (UCPs; Tunisia), 173, 175-76, 183-85
Unités Coopératives de Production Agricole (UCPAs; Tunisia), 168
University Jihad (Jihad-i-Danishgahi; Iran), 39
University of Kiel, Institute of World Economy, 330
University of Tehran, 25
Urbanization: in Algeria, 134-35; in Iraq, 195; in Lebanon, 200-201; in the Maghreb, 145-46
USAID. *See* United States Agency for International Development

VDCs. *See* Village Development Cooperatives
Vieille, Paul, 33
Vilayat-i faqih (Governance of the faqih), 37
Village Development Cooperatives (VDCs; Turkey), 355-57

Wadi Zabid project (YAR), 271-72
Wages: in Algeria, 126-27, 142; in Lebanon, 229
West Germany. *See* Federal Republic of Germany
Women: in Iraqi labor force, 196; in MENA labor force, 287, 289; in Turkey, 6; and Turkish migration, 363-64

Workers: in Algeria, 127, 136-42, 144; and Ba'th labor policies, 99-100; in Lebanon, 229; in public sector in Syria, 97-99; role in Islamic Revolution of, 48

Workers, migrant: associations in West Germany for, 341-44; and citizenship in MENA, 320; demography in MENA of, 345, 347; in educational systems of MENA, 309; effects of West German social legislation on, 339-40; employment in MENA of, 317; extent of, 295, 300-301; families of, 320; investment and credit allocations in Turkey for, 353-55; nationality composition in MENA of, 295; occupations in MENA of, 293, 295; participation in Turkish Workers' Companies of, 357-59; permanent settlement abroad of, 337-41; political identification of, 320; populations in MENA of, 301, 309, 313; remittances of, 313-15, 351-53; social legislation in MENA for, 350; social mobility of, 361; and social structures of host and home countries, 360-61; and Turkish population in West Germany, 330-33. *See also* Labor migration

World Bank, 279; Technical Assistance and Special Studies Division of, 280

Yemen Arab Republic (YAR), 271-72, 280, 295-301, 315

Young Women's Christian Association (Lebanon), 231-32

Youth: and Ba'th control in Iraq, 221-22; control by elites in Iraq and Lebanon of, 233-34; control in Lebanon of, 229-32; definition of, 193-94; education and literacy of, 218-21, 224-27; impact of Lebanese education on, 226-27; in Iraqi population and labor force, 214-18; in Lebanese population and labor force, 222-23; sectarian organizations in Lebanon for, 231-32; and social legislation in Lebanon, 229; vocational training in Iraq of, 219-20; and voluntary service associations in Lebanon, 227-28; workload and wages in Lebanon of, 229

Youth Reception Center (Ministry of Tourism; Lebanon), 227

Ziraat Bankası (Agricultural Bank; Turkey), 354

Zu'amā', 192-93, 211-12, 213-14

INSTITUTE OF INTERNATIONAL STUDIES
UNIVERSITY OF CALIFORNIA, BERKELEY

215 Moses Hall | Berkeley, California 94720

CARL G. ROSBERG, *Director*

Monographs published by the Institute include:

RESEARCH SERIES

1. *The Chinese Anarchist Movement.* R.A. Scalapino and G.T. Yu. ($1.00)
7. *Birth Rates in Latin America.* O. Andrew Collver. ($2.50)
16. *The International Imperatives of Technology.* Eugene B. Skolnikoff. ($2.95)
19. *Entry of New Competitors in Yugoslav Market Socialism.* S.R. Sacks. ($2.50)
20. *Political Integration in French-Speaking Africa.* Abdul A. Jalloh. ($3.50)
21. *The Desert & the Sown: Nomads in Wider Society.* Ed. C. Nelson. ($5.50)
22. *U.S.-Japanese Competition in International Markets.* J.E. Roemer. ($3.95)
23. *Political Disaffection Among British Students.* J. Citrin and D.J. Elkins ($2.00)
24. *Urban Inequality and Housing Policy in Tanzania.* Richard E. Stren. ($2.95)
25. *The Obsolescence of Regional Integration Theory.* Ernst B. Haas. ($6.95)
26. *The Voluntary Service Agency in Israel.* Ralph M. Kramer. ($2.00)
27. *The SOCSIM Microsimulation Program.* E. A. Hammel et al. ($4.50)
28. *Authoritarian Politics in Communist Europe.* Ed. Andrew C. Janos. ($8.95)
30. *Plural Societies and New States.* Robert Jackson. ($2.00)
31. *Politics of Oil Pricing in the Middle East, 1970-75.* R.C. Weisberg. ($4.95)
32. *Agricultural Policy and Performance in Zambia.* Doris J. Dodge. ($4.95)
34. *Housing the Urban Poor in Africa.* Richard E. Stren. ($5.95)
35. *The Russian New Right: Right-Wing Ideologies in USSR.* A. Yanov. ($5.95)
36. *Social Change in Romania, 1860-1940.* Ed. Kenneth Jowitt. ($4.50)
37. *The Leninist Response to National Dependency.* Kenneth Jowitt. ($4.95)
38. *Socialism in Sub-Saharan Africa.* Eds. C. Rosberg & T. Callaghy. ($12.95)
39. *Tanzania's Ujamaa Villages: Rural Development Strategy.* D. McHenry. ($5.95)
40. *Who Gains from Deep Ocean Mining?* I.G. Bulkley. ($3.50)
41. *Industrialization & the Nation-State in Peru.* Frits Wils. ($5.95)
42. *Ideology, Public Opinion, & Welfare Policy.* R.M. Coughlin. ($6.50)
43. *The Apartheid Regime: Political Power and Racial Domination.* Eds. R.M. Price and C. G. Rosberg. ($12.50)
44. *Yugoslav Economic System in the 1970s.* Laura D. Tyson. ($5.95)
45. *Conflict in Chad.* Virginia Thompson & Richard Adloff. ($7.50)
46. *Conflict and Coexistence in Belgium.* Ed. Arend Lijphart. ($8.95)
47. *Changing Realities in Southern Africa.* Ed. Michael Clough. ($12.50)
48. *Nigerian Women Mobilized, 1900-1965.* Nina E. Mba. ($12.95)
49. *Institutions of Rural Development.* Eds. D. Leonard & D. Marshall. ($11.50)
50. *Politics of Women & Work in USSR & U.S.* Joel C. Moses. ($9.50)
51. *Zionism and Territory.* Baruch Kimmerling. ($12.50)
52. *Soviet Subsidization of Trade with East Europe.* M. Marrese/J. Vanous. ($14.50)
53. *Voluntary Efforts in Decentralized Management.* L. Ralston et al. ($9.00)

LIST OF PUBLICATIONS *(continued)*

54. *Corporate State Ideologies.* Carl Landauer. ($5.95)
55. *Effects of Economic Reform in Yugoslavia.* John P. Burkett. ($9.50)
56. *The Drama of the Soviet 1960s.* Alexander Yanov. ($8.50)
57. *Revolutions and Rebellions in Afghanistan.* Eds. M. Nazif Shahrani & Robert L. Canfield. ($1[illegible].95)
58. *Women Farmers of Malawi.* D. Hirschmann & M. Vaughan. ($8.95)
59. *Chilean Agriculture under Military Rule.* Lovell S. Jarvis. ($11.50)
60. *Influencing Political Behavior in Netherlands and Austria.* J. Houska. ($11.50)
61. *Social Policies in Western Industrial Societies.* C.F. Andrain. ($12.95)
62. *Comparative Social Policy.* Harold Wilensky et al. ($7.50)
63. *State-Building Failure in Ireland and Algeria.* I. Lustick. ($8.95)

POLICY PAPERS IN INTERNATIONAL AFFAIRS

1. *Images of Detente & the Soviet Political Order.* K. Jowitt. ($1.25)
2. *Detente After Brezhnev: Domestic Roots of Soviet Policy.* A. Yanov. ($4.50)
3. *Mature Neighbor Policy: A New Policy for Latin America.* A. Fishlow. ($3.95)
4. *Five Images of Soviet Future: Review & Synthesis.* G.W. Breslauer. ($4.50)
5. *Global Evangelism: How to Protect Human Rights.* E.B. Haas. ($2.95)
6. *Israel & Jordan: An Adversarial Partnership.* Ian Lustick. ($2.00)
7. *Political Syncretism in Italy.* Giuseppe Di Palma. ($3.95)
8. *U.S. Foreign Policy in Sub-Saharan Africa.* Robert M. Price. ($4.50)
9. *East-West Technology Transfer in Perspective.* R.J. Carrick. ($5.50)
11. *Toward Africanized Policy for Southern Africa.* R. Libby. ($7.50)
12. *Taiwan Relations Act & Defense of ROC.* Edwin K. Snyder et al. ($7.50)
13. *Cuba's Policy in Africa, 1959-1980.* William M. LeoGrande. ($4.50)
14. *Norway, NATO, & Forgotten Soviet Challenge.* K. Amundsen. ($3.95)
15. *Japanese Industrial Policy.* Ira Magaziner and Thomas Hout. ($6.50)
16. *Containment, Soviet Behavior, & Grand Strategy.* Robert Osgood. ($5.50)
17. *U.S.-Japanese Competition-Semiconductor Industry.* M. Borrus et al. ($7.50)
18. *Contemporary Islamic Movements in Perspective.* Ira Lapidus. ($4.95)
19. *Atlantic Alliance, Nuclear Weapons, & European Attitudes.* W. Thies. ($4.50)
20. *War and Peace: Views from Moscow & Beijing.* B. Garrett & B. Glaser. ($7.95)
21. *Emerging Japanese Economic Influence in Africa.* J. Moss & J. Ravenhill. ($8.95)
22. *Nuclear Waste Disposal under the Seabed.* Edward Miles et al. ($7.50)
23. *NATO: The Tides of Discontent.* Earl Ravenal. ($7.50)
24. *Power-Sharing in South Africa.* Arend Lijphart. ($10.00)
25. *Reassessing the Soviet Challenge in Africa.* Ed. M. Clough. ($8.00)
26. *Why We Still Need the United Nations.* Ernst Haas. ($8.50)

POLITICS OF MODERNIZATION SERIES

1. *Spanish Bureaucratic-Patrimonialism in America.* M. Sarfatti. ($2.00)
2. *Civil-Military Relations in Argentina, Chile, & Peru.* L. North. ($2.00)
9. *Modernization & Bureaucratic-Authoritarianism: Studies in South American Politics.* Guillermo O'Donnell. ($8.95)